TRUE TO THE FAITH

TRUE TO THE FAITH

A FRESH APPROACH TO THE ACTS OF THE APOSTLES

David Gooding

Hodder & Stoughton

LONDON SYDNEY AUCKLAND TORONTO

FOR
MICHAEL AND ELIZABETH MIDDLETON

British Library Cataloguing in Publication Data
Gooding, D. W. (David Willoughby), 1925–
   True to the faith.
   1. Bible. N. T. Acts: Critical studies
   I. Title
   226.606

ISBN 0-340-52563-0

Published by Hodder and Stoughton,
a division of Hodder and Stoughton Ltd,
Mill Road, Dunton Green, Sevenoaks, Kent TN13 2YA
Editorial Office: 47 Bedford Square, London WC1B 3DP

Photoset by Rowland Phototypesetting Ltd,
Bury St Edmunds, Suffolk

Printed in Great Britain by Clays Ltd, St Ives plc.

Contents

Author's Preface

An expositor of the Acts of the Apostles, however far down the chain of communication, cannot escape the vibrant force of High Command's directive, given originally to the twelve apostles: 'Go . . . stand . . . speak all the words of this Life' (5:20). The risen Lord who commissioned them, lives still. His objectives are the same, his vigour undiminished. The Holy Spirit who led the apostles in their definition of the essentials of the Christian gospel in the apostolic age still expects from all followers of the living Lord the same loyalty to those same essentials. Time has not worn down the words of this imperishable Life, nor dimmed the hope they proclaim, nor reduced their relevance to our modern world, which in spite of its sophistications comes more and more in outlook and behaviour to resemble the first-century world in which Christianity was born. Under the ever-increasing flood of modern scientific and technological discoveries, people's capacity to retain a knowledge of the past grows understandably less and less. Their outlook is thus in danger of becoming historically parochial, and their grasp of historical, essential Christianity so insecure that they could, all unwittingly, come to regard as the Christian gospel forms of Christianity from which the very heart has been cut out. It is the author's hope that this fresh study of the Acts will help many a reader to capture, or if needs be to recapture, the glory, wealth, the hope and wonder of the gospel that the risen Lord still proclaims to the world through Luke's inspired work.

The book is not written for experts in New Testament scholarship, but for the general, intelligent and thoughtful public. It is based on the conviction that Acts is reliable history, though for the reasons given in Appendix 2, it has not been thought necessary constantly to discuss the question of historicity. Three works have been my constant resource: Professor I. Howard Marshall's *Acts* (Leicester: IVP, 1980); Professor F. F. Bruce's *The Book of the Acts*, revised edition (Grand Rapids: Wm B. Eerdmans, 1988); and the late Colin J. Hemer's immensely learned volume, *The Book of Acts in the Setting of Hellenistic History* (Tübingen: J. C. B. Mohr, 1989). Worthy of special mention is the delightfully fresh, accurate and vigorous translation of his own that Professor Bruce has made for the revised edition of his commentary.

Many excellent commentaries on Acts have concentrated on Luke's record of the spread of the Christian gospel and have supplied their readers with geographical, archaeological and historical information helpful for elucidating and illustrating Luke's record. They are still to be recommended as sources of that kind of information. The present exposition concentrates rather on following Luke's methods of selecting and compiling his material; and from that it concludes that while Luke is interested in describing the spread of the gospel, he is even more interested in defining for us what that gospel was that spread so rapidly throughout the world, and what it still should be today.

There is one painful element in Acts: the records of the early conflicts between Judaism and Christianity. One cannot read of such things nowadays without thinking of the appalling evil of the Holocaust; and I have therefore taken the liberty of devoting Appendix 1 to a statement of my personal attitude to these sorrowful things.

Many people deserve my thanks, and especially, once more, Mr Stewart Hamilton, Dr John Lennox, Dr Roderic Matthews, Mr Michael Middleton and Dr Arthur Williamson, who have all contributed in various ways to the production of this volume. Mrs Barbara Hamilton worked hard and long, often under considerable pressure, to produce a typescript technically accurate and aesthetically beautiful. Mr David Mackinder copy-edited the book and has contributed much to the rational organisation of the book's headings and sub-headings and to the elucidation of its otherwise obscure expressions. To one and all I offer my sincere gratitude.

David Gooding
Belfast

Introduction

WHY STUDY ACTS?

The first and obvious reason, I suppose, for studying Acts could be to get hold of some straightforward, honest-to-goodness facts about the beginnings of Christianity and about the ancient world into which it was born. And a very pressing reason that has become nowadays.

You see, it is undeniable that the modern mind finds certain features of Christianity unattractive. Not of course its teaching on the love and fatherhood of God. Nor its insistence on social concern, on care for little children and the elderly, on loving our neighbour and our enemies as ourselves, even if people grumble under their breath that this latter is a counsel of perfection and unworkable in practice.

No, the really offensive things to the modern mind are first, Christianity's supernaturalism: its claim that Jesus is God incarnate, that he rose bodily from the grave and ascended into heaven, and that he is literally coming again. And secondly, its dogmatic exclusivism: its insistence that salvation can be found in no one other than Christ, that 'there is no other name under heaven given to men by which we must be saved' (4:12). So in many modern Western countries traditional Christianity which insists on these features has gone decidedly out of favour, and membership of Christian churches has fallen into steep decline.

No Christian can view that state of affairs without concern; but not the least worrying feature of the situation is one of the recipes for recovery that is frequently advocated nowadays, not of course from those outside Christendom, but from those within. Increasingly one can hear theologians and church leaders of every kind encouraging the rest of us with the idea that the Christian gospel can once again be made effective in the modern world if only Christians are prepared to bring their gospel up-to-date and interpret it in terms that will not arouse insuperable difficulties in the modern mind.

1

And it can be done, and done safely, they assure us. The things that the modern mind finds unacceptable in the Christian gospel are not after all, they argue, an essential part of the gospel. They belonged only to the chrysalis stage of Christianity. They were part and parcel of the primitive pre-scientific thought of the ancient world, and they formed the natural, and perhaps necessary, outer husk which protected and nurtured the first, humble stirrings of truly Christian life and thought within. But they were never an essential part of that life. They could now be discarded without doing any damage to the life itself. And they must be; for to the modern mind, they point out, they bear all the marks of the infantile stage of religious development taking place in a pre-scientific environment. In those days, moreover, people's knowledge of the big world around them was very limited, and they felt that their own religion was the only valid religion, much as a child feels – and for the sake of its sense of security must be allowed to feel – that its daddy is the only daddy to be trusted in the world.

But if Christianity is to have any hope of commending itself to the modern mind, they argue, it must now burst free from the non-essential supernaturalist wrappings of its chrysalis stage, and rise up as an adult butterfly, attractively adapted to the scientific secular atmosphere of the modern world.

And in addition, they argue, it will have to come to terms with the fact that it is no longer the only butterfly in the garden. The modern expansion in our knowledge of the world has opened people's eyes to see that there are other, equally attractive religions, drawing their nectar from other sources. What we need therefore, they urge, is to cease trying to convert people of other faiths and instead, through dialogue, to profit from, and combine, the valid insights of all religions, Christianity included. One thing, they warn us, the modern mind cannot and will not tolerate any longer: the monopolistic claims of old-fashioned, fundamentalist Christianity. It was successful in the ancient world: it could not survive in ours.

But before we swallow this apparently plausible argument, we would surely be wise to re-read Luke's history of the rise of Christianity, if only to save ourselves from falling into a spectacular form of self-deception, brought on by simple ignorance, or forgetfulness, of the facts. Luke's narrative, intelligently and thoughtfully read, will show us this at least if nothing else: our modern world, for all its scientific and technological progress, is in its basic essentials no different whatever from the ancient world into which Christianity was born. To imagine otherwise is a fundamental fallacy. Indeed our Western post-Christian world, far from being different from the world of the first century, becomes every day more like it.

'Our modern scientific world does not, and cannot, believe in the possibility of dead human bodies rising out of the grave,' says someone, as though in this the modern world were somehow different from the ancient.

But the facts are that most people in the ancient world didn't believe in the possibility either. The Epicureans, whom Paul addressed in Athens (17:18), believed the world was made of atoms, and held a theory of evolution. They believed in the existence of gods; but, like the theologians who a few years ago authored the book *The Myth of God Incarnate*,* they held (for different reasons) that the gods never had and never would intervene in our world. Their scientific theory taught that the human soul as well as the human body is composed of material atoms. At death the atoms of both soul and body fly apart. The soul disintegrates at once, the body later. Nothing survives, except individual atoms. On scientific grounds, therefore, they rejected the possibility of resurrection. Paul, of course, preached them the resurrection of Christ none the less (17:31).

Most ordinary Greeks believed in the survival of the soul after death. Plato, if not Homer, had taught them that (if they needed to be taught it). But none of them believed in the resurrection of the body. Their great classical poet Aeschylus had stated that there is no such thing. When therefore Paul preached the bodily resurrection of Christ to Greeks in Athens, some of them laughed outright, none too politely (17:30–32).

But it wasn't only pagans who couldn't, or didn't, or didn't want to, believe in the possibility of bodily resurrection. Luke tells us that the earliest concerted opposition to the Christian gospel came from within the Jewish religion; came in fact from highest ranking priests and clerics in the temple of God at Jerusalem. They did not believe in the possibility of bodily resurrection either! They were all of them to a man Sadducees (4:1–7; 5:17–18; 23:6–8). They believed neither in bodily resurrection, nor in the existence of angels, nor even in the survival of the human spirit after death. And what is more, they would have cited the Bible to try and prove their case!

*John Hick (ed.), *The Myth of God Incarnate* (London: SCM Press, 1977), p. 4.

3

The phenomenon of clerics in holy orders with the Bible in their hands, so to speak, denying not only the incarnation, the bodily resurrection and ascension of Jesus, but even the theoretical possibility of such things happening, seems, I know, to be a very modern thing; and for many it has all the attractiveness of being 'with-it', 'up-to-date', 'avant-garde', and 'abreast of modern thinking'. In actual fact it is as old as the beginnings of Christianity itself. The only difference is that in those days (though not for long – see 1 Cor. 15), such people were all outside the Christian church, not in it.

We urgently need, therefore, to allow Luke's history of the rise of Christianity to remind us of the contemporary facts. When it comes to unwillingness to believe in the bodily resurrection of the Lord Jesus, on religious, philosophical, scientific or merely cultural grounds, the ancient world was not significantly different from the modern.

If, then, the apostles had listened to advice such as we get from our advanced thinkers nowadays, and had dropped their insistence on belief in the bodily resurrection of Christ, then certainly Christian churches would never have gone into decline: there never would have been any Christian churches (see 1 Cor. 15:12–20).

Or take Christianity's claim that salvation is to be found in Christ alone and in no other religion or philosophy (4:12). Admittedly it upsets many modern people; they feel it to be the result of ignorance if not of arrogance. It was natural, they say, in the ancient world where Christianity was the official religion of a monolithic culture, in which people knew very little of the world outside, and regarded everything outside as foreign and hostile anyway. But we, they claim, no longer live in a world like that. We are well on the way to a one-world culture. And anyway, we know more about other world religions nowadays than the ancients did, and as a result can no longer reasonably claim as they did, in their ignorance of the big, big world outside, that Christianity is the only way of salvation.

But once more the argument rests on a fallacy. They are thinking perhaps of the state of things in the Dark Ages or the medieval period. But in the first century the average Greek or Roman Christian knew from personal experience or by daily contact infinitely more about other religions than the average Christian (in our modern Western world) does even now. Let Luke's vivid description of Athens, with its endless altars to endless gods and goddesses, remind us that the world in which

Christianity was born was thickly populated by religions and philosophies of every kind. There was the classical religion of the Olympian gods, in its Greek and Roman versions, with their beautiful temples and official ceremonies. There were the mystery religions that offered to bring their devotees into union with the god and enrapture them with wonderful ecstatic experiences (1 Cor. 12:2). Current, at least in popular form, were the myths about the transmigration of souls, purgatory and reincarnation that came from Hinduism into Greek religion and philosophy via the Pythagoreans and Plato. There were very strict ascetic religions (Col. 2:20–23), and there were permissive religions that sanctioned fornication and homosexuality as acceptable forms of behaviour (2 Pet. 2; Jude 7–8). There were religions of the calm philosophical type (Col. 2:8); there were others where fanaticism could easily boil over into persecution, riot and murder (Acts 9:1–2; 19:21–40). There were religions that believed in the Christ as the Great World Spirit, but denied that Jesus was the Christ (1 John 2:18–22; 4:2–3). On top of all that, in many cities of the ancient world, as Acts everywhere reminds us, there were already established synagogues of the Jewish faith, often with a number of Gentile adherents. And in the midst of this welter of religions Christianity was not, of course, for the first two hundred years of its existence, the official religion of a monolithic culture, but a small, struggling and often persecuted minority within a gigantic, cosmopolitan empire.

It was not, then, because Christians did not know much about other religions that they preached Jesus Christ as the sole Saviour of the world, but because they knew all too much about them. They knew that none of them offered true cleansing of the conscience, genuine peace with God, assurance of salvation and solid hope for the future of the individual and of the world. They preached Jesus as the only Saviour, not out of narrow-mindedness or religious imperialism, but for the sheer joy of knowing and telling that God in Jesus Christ had done enough for the salvation of all mankind. No other sacrifice or salvation was valid; no comparable sacrifice was on offer elsewhere anyway; but then no other sacrifice or salvation was necessary. Peace with God was a gift, available to all, instantaneously and free.

'Yes, but,' says somebody, 'it's all right for Christians to believe these things within their own circles. But nowadays in the West we live in a pluralist society, where it would not be truly in the Christian spirit to go around trying to convert people of

5

other faiths to Christianity. It could lead to bad community relationships, if not to civil disorder.'

The danger is all too real; and the violence that is still being perpetrated in many places in the name of religion sickens every right-minded person. It is when we come to analyse the cause of it, that we need to beware of superficial diagnoses. Nowadays it is commonly put down to a 'fundamentalist' attitude in religion. But a term that can with equal propriety be applied to the small Amish and Mennonite Bible-believing churches whose members are all pacifists, and simultaneously to Islam's militant millions, is useless for analytical purposes. As far as Christendom is concerned, it has not been faithful adherence to the basic doctrines of the Bible that has caused the all too frequent intolerance, political discrimination and bloodshed in the name of religion. It has been sheer disobedience to Christ's prohibition of the use of the sword, or of violence of any kind, either to promote or to protect the cause of Christ, or to increase the church or to diminish 'heretics' and infidels. But former disobedience can scarcely now be mended by a disloyalty that soft-pedals or compromises the sovereign claims of Christ for fear that those claims will give offence.

But here again Acts comes to our aid; for in deciding what the truly Christian attitude ought to be, we can hardly ignore the practice of the apostles of the church.

It is the fact, as Acts frequently records, that the Roman magistrates and governors, for instance, were often irritated by their first encounters with Christianity. Riots would break out in areas for which they were responsible, and upon investigation all too often Christians seemed to be at the bottom of them. Sometimes, as at Philippi (16:16–40) and at Ephesus (19:23–41), it was the adherents of various Gentile religions whom the Christians had upset very badly. More often, as in Pisidian Antioch (13:50), Lystra (14:19), Thessalonica (17:5–9), Berea (17:13), Corinth (18:12–17) and Jerusalem (21:27–26:32), it was the Jews.

Now the Romans were on the whole fairly tolerant of other religions; but one thing made them very impatient, and that was if differences in religious beliefs or practices led to civil disorder. Luke himself tells us (18:2) that the Emperor Claudius at one stage commanded all Jews to depart from Rome; and from the account of this event given by the later Roman historian Suetonius (*Life of Claudius* XXV.4), it would appear that what provoked Claudius' wrath on this occasion was 'dissension and disorder in the Jewish community at Rome resulting from the introduction of Christianity into one or more of the synagogues of the city'.*

This being so, Luke obviously had some explaining to do when he wrote his 'On the Origins of Christianity' for the benefit of a certain Theophilus. Exactly who Theophilus was we do not know. From the title 'most excellent' which Luke bestows on him in the prologue to his Gospel (Luke 1:3), it would appear that he was a person of some eminence. He may have been 'a representative member of the intelligent middle-class public at Rome',† interested in Christianity, but not yet a convert. Or he may already have been a believer. In either case, it was important for Luke to show him that on no occasion was it the Christians who had started the riots. Christians did not go around insulting other people's religions or behaving objectionably in their temples (19:23–41; 21:27–29; 24:10–13). Christians, though much persecuted themselves, never persecuted anyone. Paul had indeed violently persecuted some of his fellow Jews whose religious beliefs he disliked (7:58; 8:3; 9:1–2) before he became a Christian; but after he became a Christian, he never persecuted anyone any more, and did not even retaliate against those who constantly persecuted him (28:17–22, and especially the last clause of v.19).

But if Theophilus was a thoughtful man, as he most surely was, there was a deeper question that Luke had to answer for him. Granted that the Christians did not start the riots in the sense of being the first to throw stones or physically assault their opponents; yet why did they go around constantly saying things in their sermons and public lectures which they knew would upset both Jews and Gentiles?

Why must Peter and Paul constantly push their claim that Jesus was risen from the dead and was the Messiah, even when they were preaching in Jewish synagogues, where they knew it was such a divisive issue? Why could they not concentrate on his moral teaching and his wonderful insights into the fatherhood of God, on which everyone, Christians and Jews alike, could agree?

And why must Stephen insist on saying that the temple at Jerusalem had never been more than a partial and temporary means of fellowship with God and that Jesus Christ was in

---

*F. F. Bruce, *The Book of the Acts*, New International Commentary on the New Testament (Grand Rapids, MI: Wm B. Eerdmans, ²1988), p. 347, referring to Suetonius, *Life of Claudius* XXV.4.

†See the properly cautious discussion in F. F. Bruce, *The Book of the Acts*, New International Commentary on the New Testament (Grand Rapids, MI: Wm B. Eerdmans, ²1988), pp. 28–30.

process of rendering it obsolete, when he must have realised how shockingly offensive it was to his fellow Jews' religious suscepti-bilities and to their most deeply cherished beliefs (6:8–8:3)?

And why must the apostles brand their age-long and deeply respected rite of circumcision as contributing nothing whatso-ever to anyone's salvation, be he Gentile or Jew (ch. 15)?

One of the leading spiritist-mediums in Philippi (16:16–39), whose services meant so much to so many people in that city, publicly welcomed Paul and his evangelistic team, and suggested that she and they had much in common since they were all aiming at the same goal really. Why ever did Paul turn on her, reject co-operation, denounce her particular form of religion as evil, and as a result create enormous bitterness in the city?

The leading thinkers of the time had long since suggested that all religions, whatever names they used for the Supreme Being – whether they called him Zeus, or Yahweh, or Jupiter, or Baal, or the One – all really meant the same thing. Why could not the Christians accept that all religions were simply different, but equally valid, ways of reaching the same God? Why must they offend so many people's traditions and culture, create such bitterness and provoke so much religious animosity and civil strife by continually trying to convert people from other religions to their own?

Ever since Julius Caesar, successive Roman governments had passed special legislation to protect the Jewish religion, queer though they considered that religion to be. And Luke is witness that the average Roman governor (if not corrupt like Felix, 24:26–27), would insist that the Christians had every legal right to propagate their particular ideas (26:31). But a man like Paul, who went everywhere pushing his own dogmatic views to the point where he enraged his fellow Jews and got himself rough-handled by both Jews and Gentiles – such a man seemed to them quite mad (26:24).

Why, then, did the apostles do it? Christians, at least, can hardly say that Christ's chosen apostles, baptised and filled with the Holy Spirit, and used of God to found the church, actually went about it in an un-Christian way. Then what explanation of their behaviour would Luke give to Theophilus that would justify it and convert Theophilus to Christianity if he was not already a believer, or, if he was, confirm him in his faith and inspire him to follow their example?

The answer to these questions is nothing short of the whole book of Acts. But we can cite here a few examples.

Peter's explanation to the Sanhedrin why he must continue preaching in the name of the very Jesus whom they had executed, showed that he was not motivated by revenge or religious intolerance: the salvation of all men everywhere was at stake. Jesus was God's universal Saviour for all mankind (4:12). For the sake of people's salvation he must continue proclaiming Jesus, no matter whom it embarrassed.

Peter and James took care to explain to their fellow believers why they must send out letters to the Christian churches denouncing as false the views of those 'believers' (15:5) who taught that the rite of circumcision and the keeping of the law were necessary to salvation. The letters were not sent in order to secure a narrow-minded victory for one sect of Christendom over another with regard to some minor theological point. Once more, nothing less than people's salvation was at stake. To teach that salvation is dependent on some ritual or on law-keeping was to keep people in intolerable spiritual slavery (15:10–11), said Peter, when they could be, and must be, set free. No religious tradition, however sacred, must be allowed to keep people in bondage. To do that would be to tempt God himself (15:10).

Philosophers rightly treat their own epistemological, physical, moral and political systems with due diffidence. The best of them is after all only an imperfect logical system based on arbitrarily chosen axioms. The reason why Paul asserted the resurrection of Christ before the Areopagus at Athens with such uncompromising dogmatic certainty was that the resurrection of Christ is not a philosophical theory but a historical fact, by which God has given notice to all men everywhere that Christ will be their Judge (17:30–31). Men will not have a choice of judges according to what system of philosophy they embraced on earth. All men will have to do with Christ. That is absolutely certain; and in calling on all men everywhere to repent and to prepare for facing their Judge, Paul was not deferentially presenting a motion for philosophical debate: he was delivering a command from almighty God to be obeyed.

This, at any rate, was the dynamo that motivated and empowered the apostles of our Lord Jesus Christ. Acts will gently enquire whether we are wired up to the same dynamo.

THE DIFFERENT WAY

Two things lie on the surface of Acts. The first is that Christianity sprang out of Judaism, in the sense that all the first Christians were Jews, whatever particular sect of Judaism they may have belonged to.*

The second is that Christianity was not launched on the world as a fully worked out system of doctrine and practice, accompanied by a directive that from 2 a.m. the next Sunday all believers in the Lord Jesus everywhere were to cease practising Judaism and begin practising Christianity. No, Christianity had to grow and develop. A seed contains within itself the blue-print for the fully grown plant; but the plant develops its inherent characteristics only by growing in reaction to the soil in which it is planted, under the influence of the sun, wind and rain. So Christianity grew out of Judaism as it reacted, under the instruction and direction of the Holy Spirit, to the problems and challenges it met with on its road to world-wide witness in the name of Christ.

This is what we might have expected anyway from our Lord's announcement to his apostles in the Upper Room (John 16:12–13): 'I have much more to say to you, more than you can now bear. But when he, the Spirit of truth, comes, he will guide you into all truth.' He came at Pentecost, and his coming was instantaneous (2:2). But the guiding was a process; and it is part of Luke's purpose in Acts to record for us successive stages in that process.

In the first place, Christianity had to spread geographically, as Christ indicated in his briefing of his apostles (1:8). This naturally turns Acts into a record of the geographical spread of the gospel; and serious study of the book therefore has always been very heavily concerned with the geographical questions. Rightly so; for Luke's plentiful, detailed, precise and amazingly accurate geographical notices show us that he is not writing religious myth or legend, but factual history of events that took place at such and such actual places that could have been pin-pointed on a map.†

*It is, strictly speaking, an anachronism to refer to the disciples of Christ as 'Christians' before Antioch (11:26). But since no confusion is caused, convenience outweighs accuracy.

† A helpful brief introduction to the topic is to be found in F. F. Bruce, *The New Testament Documents* (Leicester: IVP, 1960). A massively detailed and up-to-date treatment of geographical and historical matters is C. J. Hemer, *The Book of Acts in the Setting of Hellenistic History*, ed. Conrad H. Gempf (Tubingen: J. C. B. Mohr, 1989).

The gospel also spread numerically, in the ever-growing number of people who came to believe it; and qualitatively, in the spiritual growth and stability of the resultant churches. Luke himself triumphantly emphasises the fact in the formal summaries with which he concludes each of the six major sections of his work:

6:7	'And the word of God increased; and the number of the disciples multiplied in Jerusalem exceedingly; and a large number of priests yielded obedience to the faith.'
9:31	'So the church throughout the whole of Judea and Galilee and Samaria had peace, being built up; and walking in the fear of the Lord and in the encouragement of the Holy Spirit was multiplied.'
12:24	'But the word of God grew and multiplied.'
16:5	'So the churches were strengthened in the faith and increased in number daily.'
19:20	'So mightily grew the word of the Lord and prevailed.'
28:30–31	'And he [Paul] stayed there for a period of two whole years . . . preaching the kingdom of God and teaching about the Lord Jesus Christ with all boldness and without let or hindrance.'

But it soon becomes apparent that Luke is not interested solely in the spread of the gospel; for if he were, why does he tell us nothing at all about the evangelistic labours and travels of the majority of the apostles? Did none of them spread the gospel too? Time and again the concluding summaries emphasise how the word of God increased (6:7; 12:24; 19:20); but did not the word of God increase through John's preaching as well as through Paul's? Then why not a single word from any of John's sermons to put alongside the numerous examples of Paul's sermons, lectures and speeches?

We conclude, therefore, that other interests beyond the spread of the gospel controlled Luke's choice of material. How shall we decide what they were?

One of them, at least, is easy to detect, for in all six major sections of his work a recognisable pattern of events repeats itself.

Take the first section (1:1–6:7). Empowered by the Holy Spirit, newly come down from heaven, the apostles were vigorously carrying out Christ's command to be his witnesses. All was going well, thousands were being converted, when a crisis occurred: the Sanhedrin banned all preaching in the name of Jesus. Now the Sanhedrin was, for normative Judaism, the supreme

11

religious (and to some extent civil) authority; and the apostles were certainly not spiritual anarchists. To disobey and defy the Sanhedrin was a serious step to take, and one fraught with all kinds of foreseeable and unforeseeable consequences. But to obey the Sanhedrin was impossible without denying the very heart, life, soul and centre of Christianity. To deny or keep silent about the deity and Messiahship of the living Lord would have been treasonable disloyalty to Christ, in direct opposition to the Holy Spirit of God who had come to empower them to witness to Christ. Compromise was impossible. Without hesitation the apostles disobeyed and defied the Sanhedrin; and Christianity took its first step away from official Judaism. It was over the deity and Messiahship of Jesus.

Similarly in the second section (6:8–9:31). Stephen, the first Christian martyr, under the illumination of the Holy Spirit began to perceive that Christ's sacrifice at Calvary, his resurrection and entry into the immediate presence of God in heaven, carried implications that would eventually make the Jewish temple at Jerusalem obsolete, along with its whole elaborate system of priesthood, sacrifices and rituals. For advancing this view and maintaining it in public discussions and debates, he was eventually put on trial for his life before the Sanhedrin. But when he saw that the case was going against him, he made no attempt to recant or to compromise. Obviously for him the Christian understanding of man's way of approach to God inaugurated by Christ was such an essential part of the gospel that compromise here was impossible. So Stephen died, and Christianity took another major step away from official Judaism.

Likewise in Section Three (9:32–12:24). When the time came for Peter to take the gospel to the Gentile Cornelius, Peter was at first reluctant to go. Preaching the gospel to Cornelius would involve eating with him in his house; and that in turn would have contravened Judaism's code of holiness, and in particular its food laws, as Peter understood them. God therefore intervened, and taught Peter that the Old Testament food laws which he (God) had originally imposed were now cancelled. Peter was free to go and eat with Gentiles. So Peter went; but as we see Peter enter Cornelius' house, we are watching Christianity take yet another step away from Judaism, this time over the fundamental matter of the theory and practice of holiness.

The same pattern repeats itself in Section Four (12:25–16:5). Circumcision was regarded in Judaism as indispensable for membership of the holy nation and helpful, if not necessary, for salvation. All the early Christian men, therefore, had already been circumcised before they became Christians, and the question of what relationship circumcision bore to salvation through Christ had not so far surfaced in their thinking. But when Gentiles in their thousands came to faith in Christ, the question inevitably arose. Some Christians began by thinking that circumcision was still necessary for salvation and therefore Gentile believers must be circumcised. But at a meeting of the apostles and elders called in Jerusalem to consider the matter, Peter and James pronounced the official, authoritative, apostolic decision: circumcision was unnecessary for, and contributed nothing whatever to, salvation, not only in the case of Gentiles, but in the case of Jews as well. It would be impossible to exaggerate the importance of the epoch-making step which Christianity took away from Judaism at that time.

Let's pause here for a moment and reflect on what is happening. As Luke records these crises and the decisions and solutions which were reached by the apostles and the early churches, Luke is not so much reporting the spread of the gospel as describing for us what that gospel was, and how it came to be defined. He concentrates our attention on the points at which Christianity diverged from Judaism, not because he was narrow-mindedly sectarian but because he had a historian's fine sense of what was truly significant. The issues over which Christianity diverged were not peripheral matters. They constituted the very heart of the gospel. They were matters of such essential importance that compromise over them would have been disloyalty to Christ, and would have left Christianity, even supposing it survived, without a gospel.

If this is so, it carries far-reaching implications. Studying these points of divergence and the issues involved in them will define for us what apostolic Christianity was and is; will show us what are the essentials of the gospel over which we in our far distant century still must not compromise if we in our turn are to be loyal to the Lord Jesus and to maintain his gospel in our generation.

The duty to maintain the gospel has of course always been easier to assent to in theory than to define and carry out in practice; and in this particular Acts casts an instructive light on the subsequent history of Christendom. All down the centuries Christendom has shown a marked tendency to lapse into forms of Judaism and to confuse the gospel with the very things from which the apostles insisted it should be kept distinct.

The Victorian scholar Dr F. J. A. Hort described these lapses as such assimilations to Judaism on the part of Christians as arise from a recognition of the authority of the Old Testament unaccompanied by a clear perception of the true relation of the Old Testament to the New . . . This process began in the third century, and went forward with great activity after the Empire had become Christian; and we are still surrounded by its results. This was one of the elements of the mediaeval system least touched by the Reformation, the obvious reason being that the leading Reformers had themselves but an imperfect sense of the progress within Scripture and of the different kinds of instruction which are provided for us in its several parts in accordance with God's own dispensation of times and seasons as expounded by the apostles.*

A reading of Acts, then, will invite us to examine the Christianity we profess and practise today, to see whether it stands with full-blown apostolic Christianity, or whether it is still encumbered by the results of these centuries-old lapses, or is even now for the first time being tempted to compromise on essentials of the gospel for which the apostles so unyieldingly stood.

But Acts has more to teach us along this line in Section Five (16:6–19:20). At Philippi (16:16–18) Luke records how the Way of salvation was in danger of being confused in the public mind with spiritism; and how Paul insisted on the difference between the two, and got himself landed in prison because of it. Then, returning to the question of demon-possession in 19:13–19, Luke tells how at Ephesus the spirit-world itself gave powerful evidence of the difference between Jesus and Paul on the one hand, and a would-be Jewish exorcist on the other. At 17:8–9 Luke tells how certain Jews tried to make out before the city-rulers of Thessalonica that the gospel which Paul preached was really a political message, subversive of the rule of the Roman government. Luke's record of Paul's preaching at that place shows of course quite clearly the difference between Christianity and any form of politics.

Then again Paul's speech before the Areopagus at Athens (17:16–34) shows us the essential difference between the Christian gospel and both pagan religion and Greek philosophy. And finally Luke even thinks it important to relate an incident at Ephesus (19:1–7) which demonstrated the difference in spiritual experience between disciples of John the Baptist and full-blown believers in the Lord Jesus Christ.

We need not stay now to examine what all these differences were. The point is that in recording the incidents that exposed

*F. J. A. Hort, *Judaistic Christianity* (London: Macmillan, 1898), pp. 1–3.

14

these differences Luke is not only showing us the apostles preaching the gospel: he is once more inviting us to watch Christianity defining itself by these vigorous contrasts between itself and pagan spiritism, politics, religion and philosophy.

The same thing happens in the last and longest section of the book (19:21–28:31). This section is in some respects very different from the first five, since in it Paul is engaged not so much in preaching the gospel but in publicly defending it, often in the courts. He is constantly obliged to point out not what the gospel is, but what it isn't. But for our present purpose it has the same effect. Luke's record proceeds to make clear that Paul and the gospel are not what people have ignorantly imagined them to be, or what people have maliciously misrepresented them as being; Luke is thus continuing to define by contrast what Christianity really is.

Paul, then, is not a robber of pagan temples (19:37), nor a desecrator of the Jewish temple (21:28–29; 24:12), nor someone trying to make money out of religion (20:33–35), nor a crude political activist or a leader of terrorists (21:37–39). Nor is the gospel a nasty little sectarian heresy put about by a theologically uneducated demagogue (22:3–5) or by a mentally unhinged academic (26:24–26), and based on some absurd principle that no major theological school in Judaism and no educated layman could possibly credit without committing intellectual suicide (23:6–10; 24:14–25; 26:8). The Christian gospel is based on God's self-revelation through Moses and the prophets; it has a credible claim to be the fulfilment of the redemption outlined and promised in Israel's inspired scriptures; its effect is spiritually liberating and ennobling (26:18); it pleads for moral integrity and opposes corruption (24:24–27); it produces the opposite tendency to narrow nationalistic Judaism (26:17), and offers a genuine and majestic hope to all mankind (24:15; 26:6,7,23).

It goes without saying that in the ensuing ages Christendom has often allowed its gospel to become confused with pagan politics and philosophy. In some countries pagan customs and festivals have, by deliberate missionary policy, been baptised into the church. And in our own day obsession with the occult and fascination with various practices and forms of Hinduism are widespread; as are the temptations to join secret business associations which in their ceremonies worship the same old pagan deities as the ancient world did, or at the other extreme to wed the Christian gospel with Marxism to turn it into a potent political force.

In the light of all these tendencies Acts carries for us all a powerful unspoken exhortation to examine ourselves honestly to see whether the Christianity we represent and the gospel we preach are uncompromisingly the same as those established by the apostles of our Lord Jesus Christ.

Section One

Christianity and the Restoration of All Things (1:1–6:7)

Section One
Christianity and the Restoration of All Things (1:1–6:7)

PRELIMINARY OBSERVATIONS

Three towering peaks dominate the first section of Acts: the ascension of Christ on the fortieth day (1:9), the coming of the Holy Spirit on the day of Pentecost (2:1–4), and the second coming of Christ (1:11; 3:20) inaugurating the great and resplendent day of the Lord (2:20).

An intense glory plays around these lofty summits. The Man, Jesus, has been set free from the pangs of death (2:24), shown the paths of life and filled with gladness in the presence of God (2:28). Through his resurrection he has brought life and immortality to light for all mankind. He is shown to be the *Archégos*, the very Author, of life (3:15), the giver of complete salvation to all who trust him (4:12). The credibility of the Old Testament's messianic programme for the restoration of the race, of the planet, of the universe, is now established beyond doubt (1:6; 3:20–21, 24–25). The time is coming (1:6–7; 3:10–21) when cripples will no longer park themselves on the steps of the Creator's temple, looking for charity; nature will be restored to perfect health of state and function (3:16). A foretaste of it has already been given (3:1–16). Christ himself is the cornerstone of a new and fairer universal temple (4:11). Risen and ascended, he has already poured out the epoch-making gift of the Holy Spirit (1:4–5; 2:16–18, 33–36, 38–39). A substantial downpayment on the Old Testament's promises has thus been made. Human history has taken a gigantic step forward towards the full and final payment.

Impatient as we may be to survey these towering peaks in detail, it will pay us first to reconnoitre the surrounding landscape. If we are right in thinking that the first section of Acts is

19

brought to its end by the formal summary at 6:7,* then the section itself is made up of eight major passages. Classified according to their subject-matter, they fall into four pairs.

1. The period between the resurrection and Pentecost is covered by two passages (1:1–14 and 1:15–26). In the first, Christ personally prepares his apostles for world-wide witness by demonstrating to them the reality of his resurrection and then by briefing them on the programme and timetable for their witness. In the second, the apostles and a group of about one hundred and twenty believers prepare themselves for that witness by arranging the appointment of an extra apostle to take Judas Iscariot's place as a witness to Christ's resurrection (1:22).

2. Next the stupendous effect of the coming of the Holy Spirit is conveyed by the record of two miracles (2:1–47 and 3:1–4:4): the first, the miraculous speaking of foreign languages by the Christians; the second, the healing of a congenitally lame man. After each miracle Peter explains its significance to the crowd and preaches a sermon; and the number of converts is given. Both miracles, then, witness to Christ, but the first is performed on the Christians themselves, the second on one of the general public. The first calls attention to the supernatural power by which the Christians speak, and so validates their message. The second illustrates the salvation that Jesus can impart to those who receive the message.

So far, then, four stories in two pairs; but now we have reached the half-way turning-point in the section and there comes a change of mood: the priests and the captain of the temple attempt to nip nascent Christianity in the bud. In spite of that the Christians continue to make numerous converts (5:14; 6:7) and to enjoy the respect of the general populace (5:13); but now they do so at the cost of having to defy the prohibition-orders placed on them by the Sanhedrin.

3. The four stories in the second half likewise fall into two pairs. Two of them deal with the Sanhedrin's opposition (4:5–31 and 5:17–42). In both, apostles are arrested, put in prison and then brought before the Sanhedrin: on the first occasion two apostles, Peter and John; on the second, all twelve (see 5:29). On each occasion Luke naturally reports the decision of the court and then describes how the apostles and the Christian community react to its threats and punishments.

---

* 'So the word of God spread. The number of disciples in Jerusalem increased rapidly, and a large number of priests became obedient to the faith.'

4. The remaining two passages, like all the other pairs, share a common theme: they each provide an inside view of life in the early Christian community in Jerusalem. The first (4:32–5:16) tells how the propertied Christians would from time to time sell a house or a field and give the proceeds to the apostles for the relief of members in need. The second passage (6:1–7) describes the organisation which the apostles put in place for the fair distribution of the common funds and supplies thus generated.

To get a full and balanced understanding of the history Luke puts before us, we shall have to study carefully both the similarities and, more importantly, the differences between these pairs of passages that share a common theme. At the same time Luke's sense of balance is shown not only in this formal 'pairing' of passages, but also in the evenhanded emphasis which his selection of material places on the two major themes that run in almost equal proportion throughout this whole first section: the importance of spiritual things on the one hand, and of material things on the other.

This section of his work had to cover Pentecost and the spectacular explosion of spiritual energy initiated by that event. It was inevitable, therefore, that Luke should place a heavy and constant emphasis on spiritual things: on the person, power and operation of the Holy Spirit, on the profound spiritual experiences of those who received him, and on the dynamic witness they were empowered by the Spirit to maintain. What was not so necessarily to be expected is that in this section Luke should place an almost equal emphasis on material things, on food and money, on buying and selling, on houses, fields, estates and possessions. No less than three out of the eight passages in the section are largely or else totally given up to this topic.

At 2:43–45 he tells us that one of the first, and apparently spontaneous, results of the conversions that followed Peter's first sermon was that 'All the believers were together and had everything in common. Selling their possessions and goods, they gave to anyone as he had need.' Not content to record this phenomenon once, at 4:32–37 he gives another description of it, in almost the same words but in greater detail, adding for good measure the particular case of a certain Joseph who 'sold a field he owned and brought the money and put it at the apostles' feet'.

Now this so-called 'communism' disappears from view after the end of Section One, and is never met with again in the whole of the rest of Acts. We might therefore jump to the conclusion that it was a temporary, but minor, side-effect occasioned by the

21

exceptional excitement of the early days, but destined naturally to pass away when the ferment of the new wine subsided. And we might further decide that Luke has given this phenomenon the space he has, simply in order to give a faithful record of what actually happened, without necessarily wishing to imply that this phenomenon had any great importance or was any essential part of Christianity, or indeed was anything more than a temporary, peripheral detail.

But to presume so would be to overlook another highly significant feature of Luke's record. In connection with this matter of food and money, buying and selling, houses, fields and possessions, Luke has chosen to include three instances of grievous malpractice perpetrated by certain members of the early Christian circle. Consider this extraordinary catalogue:

> 'With the reward he got for his wickedness, Judas bought a field; there he fell headlong, his body burst open and all his intestines spilled out. Everyone in Jerusalem heard about this, so they called that field in their language Akeldama, that is, Field of Blood.' (1:18–19)

> '. . . a man named Ananias, together with his wife Sapphira, also sold a piece of property. With his wife's full knowledge he kept back part of the money for himself, but brought the rest and put it at the apostles' feet.
> 'Then Peter said, "Ananias, how is it that Satan has so filled your heart that you have lied to the Holy Spirit and have kept for yourself some of the money you received for the land?"' – whereupon Ananias fell down dead; and so, subsequently, did his wife. (5:1–11)

> 'In those days . . . the Grecian Jews . . . complained against the Hebraic Jews because their widows were being overlooked in the daily distribution of food.' (6:1)

At first sight it must seem strange that Luke should advertise so prominently these ugly blots on the record of the early Christian community. Of course a moment's further study reveals that Luke only records these wrong attitudes and practices in order to show how immediately and thoroughly the Christian community repudiated them. But the very fact that he records these incidents in full when he need not have recorded them at all* is surely

---

*Clearly, if he had been so led, Luke could have related the appointment of Matthias to fill the place of the traitor Judas without mentioning Judas' use of his shameful gain to purchase the field, and without going into the details of his gruesome end; could have mentioned the normal behaviour of the Christians in regard to their possessions without describing at such length the exceptional case of Ananias and Sapphira; and could have reported that seven officers were

significant. It suggests that in the eyes of the early Christians a proper realignment of one's attitude to material possessions was a necessary result of true faith in Jesus as Messiah, an inevitable result of a true response to the reception of the Holy Spirit. If that is so, we shall not get a true understanding of early essential Christianity as Luke depicts it unless we pay due regard to his sense of balance and proportion between spiritual belief and experience on the one hand and material things on the other.

Finally, one further formal feature of Luke's narrative claims attention before we proceed. As the second volume of a two-volumed work, Acts naturally begins with a résumé of the first volume. But it will pay us to notice just how Luke constructs this résumé.

'In my former book, Theophilus, I wrote about all that Jesus began to do and to teach until the day he was taken up to heaven, after giving his chosen apostles their orders through the Holy Spirit' (1:1–2).

The résumé is astonishingly brief: a verse and a half, and all that Luke has told us in the first volume about the birth, life, ministry, death and resurrection of our Lord is summarised right up to and including the ascension. Nothing is singled out for particular mention except one solitary thing, and its very solitariness indicates its importance. Before Christ was taken up, says Luke, 'he gave his chosen apostles their orders through the Holy Spirit'. The Gospel's account of those orders is given in Luke 24:46–49, and they are picked out for special mention here because the whole of Acts, in one sense, is going to be the story of the carrying out of those orders.

Since, then, verses 1–2a have summarised Christ's life and ministry right up to the ascension, we might think that the following verses would begin the new story of what began to happen after the ascension. Not so. Instead of going forwards, verse 2b takes us back to events and activities before the ascension. And when at last we arrive at the end of this first passage (v.14), we shall have got no further than the last item dealt with in the Gospel – the return of the disciples to Jerusalem immediately after the ascension (cf. Luke 24:52–53 with Acts 1:12–14). What the résumé is doing, therefore, is going back over the period between the resurrection and the ascension to pick out certain of

---

appointed to organise the fair distribution of the common funds and supplies without advertising to the world that this appointment was necessitated by initial discrimination practised by one group of Christians against another.

its features which we must be aware of and must understand if we are to follow the subsequent narrative intelligently. Some of these features will have been described in detail in the Gospel. Luke will assume we are familiar with the details: a summary reference will be enough to remind us of them. Some features will not have been mentioned before, and the fact that they are now mentioned here for the first time presumably means that they are of key importance for the understanding of Acts. We shall have to pay them special attention.

A map of Section One is given on pages 26–27.

THE MOVEMENTS

MOVEMENT 1: Christ's Programme for the Restoration of All Things (1:1–4:4)

Briefing for world-wide witness (1:1–14)

Christ the firstfruits of the coming restoration

So Jesus was alive! We cannot hope to recapture the stunned joy and awe which followed the discovery; but we can at least pay attention to the many convincing proofs that persuaded the apostles of its reality.

First there were the Lord's appearances to them, intermittent, but repeated over a period of no less than forty days. No one-off, isolated incident, but a regular succession, until these occurrences which at first shattered almost every norm they had hitherto known became virtually normal (1:3).

Then there were his demonstrations of what it means to be a resurrected human being. The apostles, like anyone else of course, had never seen such a thing before; and when for the first time Jesus suddenly appeared in their midst in the upper room, they naturally thought it was his ghost (Luke 24:36–39). And they were scared.

So Christ demonstrated that he was not a disembodied spirit. His body was not still in the grave: it was standing in front of them. No part of him was dead at all! He was totally alive as a complete human being. Death had not been survived: it had been undone. The body that before his death had been an integral part of his human personality had not been left behind, but resurrected; not superseded, but glorified.

He invited them to examine his hands and feet, for they carried the scars of Calvary (see John 20:27) and would identify him as the same physical Jesus as had been crucified. But there was more to it than that. 'Look at my hands and my feet,' he said. '*It is I myself!* Touch me and see; a ghost does not have flesh and bones, as you see I have' (Luke 24:38–40).

He thus not only identified himself to them as the same Jesus as they had known before: he taught them a basic fact about human beings. He was not denying that the human soul and spirit survive death. They do, of course. But he was implying that for human beings to be fully themselves after having died, they must regain a physical, tangible body. And not just any body; but a body related to the body they had before, now reconstructed and glorified. This, and nothing less than this, is what Luke means by 'alive', when he says (1:3) that Jesus presented himself alive to his apostles.

And the demonstrations were not by way of providing exotic, but irrelevant, information about the world beyond. The holy body that stood before them was both the firstfruits and the pattern of the great restoration of all things which they must presently go out and preach to the world as the very heart of their gospel. One day the whole of creation would be restored. One day every believer would have a glorified body like the Lord's resurrected body. But in the Man, Jesus Christ, God's mighty process for the restoration of the universe had already begun. The apostles were to go out and preach that restoration, not as a mere theory, but as a certainty, the first specimen of which they had seen with their own eyes and handled with their own hands.

And then the Lord demonstrated another thing. His resurrection body was not only physical itself: it could interact, if he chose, with our physical world, and what is more, with our physical world in its present state and not merely with the world as it will be – the world did not have to be finally and fully transformed before he could visit and interact with it. He asked for food. They gave him some broiled fish and he let them watch him eat it.* The sight of it remained permanently fixed in their memories, controlling what they meant whenever they spoke of his resurrection. Listen to Peter a year or so later, talking to

---

*Compare the reference to Christ's eating with the apostles when he briefed them, Luke 24:41–43, and the résumé in Acts 1:4, where *sunālizomenos* ('while he was eating with them') seems to be the original reading, and not *sunalizomenos*, passive of *sunālizo* ('being brought together with', i.e. 'assembling with'), nor *sunaulizomenos* ('staying with').

MOVEMENT 1: CHRIST'S PROGRAMME FOR THE RESTORATION OF ALL THINGS (1:1–4:4)

I. FROM THE RESURRECTION TO THE ASCENSION (1:1–14): Christ briefs his apostles for world-wide witness to himself

1. The forty days' demonstration by 'many convincing proofs' that Jesus is alive again after his suffering (1:3)

2. He gave them instructions (1:2); he commanded them (1:4); 'You will be my witnesses in Jerusalem . . . and to the ends of the earth' (1:8)

3. '. . . you will receive power when the Holy Spirit comes on you; and you will be my witnesses . . .' (1:8)

4. 'They all joined together constantly in prayer . . .' (1:14)

II. FROM THE ASCENSION TO PENTECOST (1:15–26): The gap in the apostolic witness caused by Judas' defection is made up

''Judas . . . shared in this ministry [apostleship].'' (With the reward he got for his wickedness, Judas bought a field; there he fell headlong, his body burst open and all his intestines spilled out. Everyone in Jerusalem heard about this, so they called that field . . . Akeldama, that is, Field of Blood) (1:16–19)

'Lord, you know everyone's heart. Show us which of these two you have chosen to take over this apostolic ministry, which Judas left to go where he belongs' (1:24–25)

'. . . one of these must become a witness with us of his resurrection' (1:22)

MOVEMENT 2: OPPOSITION TO THE PROGRAMME (4:5–6:7)

V. FIRST INVESTIGATION BY THE SANHEDRIN (4:5–31): To account for the miracle of healing, and to try to stop preaching in the name of Jesus spreading

1. The healing of a congenitally lame man, over forty years old, constitutes undeniable evidence that God has raised Jesus from the dead (4:9–10, 14, 22)

2. '"Everyone living in Jerusalem knows they have done an outstanding miracle . . ." But to stop this thing from spreading any further . . . they . . . commanded them not to speak or teach at all in the name of Jesus' (4:16–18)

3. '. . . the place where they were meeting was shaken. And they were all filled with the Holy Spirit and spoke the word of God boldly' (4:31)

4. '. . . they raised their voices together in prayer to God' (4:24)

VI. A VIEW OF THE CHRISTIAN COMMUNITY (4:32–5:16): Judgement on two dishonest members strengthens the witness of the community

'No-one claimed that any of his possessions was his own . . . those who owned lands or houses sold them, brought the money . . . and put it at the apostles' feet . . . Joseph, a Levite, . . . sold a field he owned and brought the money and put it at the apostles' feet' (4:32–37)

Ananias and Sapphira sold a piece of property, pretended to give all the money to the apostles, but kept back part for themselves. For lying to the Holy Spirit, they both fell dead. '. . . how is it that Satan has so filled your heart that you have lied to the Holy Spirit. . . ?' . . . great fear seized all who heard what had happened' (5:1–11)

'With great power the apostles continued to testify to the resurrection of the Lord Jesus' (4:33)

III. THE MIRACLE OF SPEAKING IN TONGUES (2:1–47):

Peter explains the significance of the miracle: the resultant converts number 3,000

1. The resurrection of Jesus from the grave: 'But God raised him from the dead, freeing him from the agony of death, because it was impossible for death to keep its hold on him . . . "You [God] have made known to me the paths of life . . . "' (2:24–28)

2. 'Repent and . . . you will receive the gift of the Holy Spirit' (2:38)

3. 'Exalted to the right hand of God . . . God has made this Jesus, whom you crucified, both Lord and Christ' (2:33–36)

4. 'When the people heard this, they were cut to the heart . . . Peter [said], "Repent . . . Save yourselves from this corrupt generation"' (2:37–40)

5. They devoted themselves to the apostles' teaching . . . ' (2:42)

IV. THE MIRACLE OF THE HEALING (3:1–4:4):

Peter explains the power by which the miracle has been performed: the number of converts rises to 5,000 men

1. A lame man is laid daily at the gate of the temple to beg for alms . . . (3:2–3)

2. The apostles, unable to give financial relief, give instead the superior gift of complete healing in the name of Jesus (3:4–10)

3. 'The priests . . . seized Peter and John, and . . . put them in jail . . . ' (4:1–3)

VII. SECOND INVESTIGATION BY THE COUNCIL (5:17–42):

To call the apostles to account for their defiance of the ban on preaching in the name of Jesus

1. The miraculous release of the apostles from prison: 'But . . . an angel opened the doors of the jail and brought them out. . . "Go . . . and tell the people the full message of this new life"' (5:19–20)

2. 'We are witnesses . . . and so is the Holy Spirit, whom God has given to those who obey him' (5:32)

3. 'God . . . raised Jesus from the dead – whom you had killed . . . God exalted him to his own right hand as Prince and Saviour (5:30–31)

4. 'When they heard this, they were furious and wanted to put them to death. But . . . Gamaliel [said] . . . "Leave these men alone"' (5:33–35)

5. ' . . . they never stopped teaching . . . ' (5:42)

VIII. ANOTHER VIEW OF THE CHRISTIAN COMMUNITY (6:1–7):

Another wrong is righted, without the apostles' being diverted from their ministry of the word

1. Certain widows are neglected in the daily allocation of relief (6:1)

2. The apostles point out that while the ministry of material relief is important, they must confine themselves to the ministry of the word (6:2–4). Seven officers are appointed to look after the daily allocation (6:3–6)

3. ' . . . a large number of priests became obedient to the faith' (6:7)

Cornelius and assuring him of the reality of the resurrection of Christ: 'We are the men whom God chose to be witnesses,' says Peter (10:39). And then he adds: 'We ate with him and we drank with him after he rose from the dead' (10:40–41).

Continuing demonstrations taught the apostles that Jesus' body was not in every respect the same as formerly. It had been transformed, and already belonged to the world beyond and to a new order. It could visit our world, enter it at any point instantaneously, take part in its affairs, and then leave it just as instantaneously. It was what the apostle Paul was later to describe as a 'spiritual' body (1 Cor. 15:44).*

It would be as idle to conjecture what the mechanics and physics of it could be, as it would be unscientific to claim that 'science' declares the whole thing to be impossible. True science seeks to understand and describe the normal. It is for history to tell us whether something abnormal that science cannot yet explain has in fact happened. Science is not omniscient (it cannot even explain all it can observe); it cannot rule out in advance such a possibility. If history has given overwhelming evidence that in the resurrection of Christ the great redeeming and re-creating power of God has broken into the regularities of our fallen world, true science will adjust its world-view to allow for it.

But to get back to the résumé. Christ's repeated goings and comings again established two further points basic to the Christian gospel. First, his going away did not involve some irreversible process: he could, and did, come again. And secondly, when he came again, it was still in the same physical body. When, therefore, at the ascension, they were told by the angels, 'This same Jesus, who has been taken from you into heaven, will come back in the same way as you have seen him go into heaven' (1:11), they had already been prepared for the idea that this second coming too would involve the physical, bodily return of the Lord. And when they subsequently preached the return of Christ as an essential part of the gospel (e.g. at 3:20), they were not attempting to describe the altogether indescribable, by using apocalyptic terminology that has to be demythologised before modern people can begin to understand what it means. They were announcing in

*Some have argued that in describing Christ's resurrection body as a spiritual body Paul directly contradicts the Gospels' claim that it was physical and material. But the argument is false, and rests on a misunderstanding of what Paul means by the term 'spiritual'. For a full discussion, see William Lane Craig, 'The Bodily Resurrection of Jesus', in R. T. France and David Wenham (eds), *Gospel Perspectives*, vol. 1 (Sheffield: JSOT Press, 1980), pp. 47–74.

28

straightforward terms that Christ would return to our world as literally as he had returned to them repeatedly during the forty days. With unimaginably greater splendour, no longer privately, but with world-wide awareness of his coming (Rev. 1:7), but with no less physical, bodily reality.

And then there was another convincing proof that persuaded the apostles of the reality of the resurrection of their Lord. He not only appeared to them over a period of forty days: he also spoke to them about the kingdom of God (1:3). Never to their dying day would they forget the conversations that corrected their mistaken ideas on that topic, mistaken ideas that had almost wrecked their faith when they had seen Jesus crucified.

The particular aspect of the kingdom of God that earlier interested them was not of course God's providential government of the world. They had always believed in God's kingdom in that sense, and took for granted its uninterrupted existence and ceaseless operation. Though invisible, it could, they believed, suddenly intervene and destroy an evil Pharaoh here, or chastise a proud Nebuchadnezzar there. The trouble was that the kingdom of God, in that sense, still allowed a vast amount of evil to go on in the world unchecked.

No, what had interested them was the coming of the kingdom of God in the sense of the coming of the Messiah to set up his messianic kingdom here on earth. They had heard about that from the ancient prophecies of their Old Testament; and they understood that when in that sense Messiah received his kingdom, then not just an odd Pharaoh here or a proud Belshazzar there would be destroyed. *All* evil would be put down; all governments would be destroyed or put aside; and Messiah personally would visibly establish his messianic kingdom the world through (Dan. 7). With this hope firmly in their heads, they had come to believe that Jesus of Nazareth was the Messiah, and therefore, as was natural, they were interested above all else in the timetable for the setting up of his kingdom. When would it happen?

As our Lord approached Jerusalem for the last time, they felt sure that the kingdom of God, in the messianic sense, was about to appear forthwith (Luke 19:11–27). He told them otherwise; but they would not listen. He said he must first 'go away', into the 'far country' of heaven; and only when he returned would he first reward his servants for their faithfulness in the interval and then proceed to put down all his enemies and establish his kingdom. But his words fell on uncomprehending ears, with the result that

29

when they saw him crucified, it nearly wrecked their faith (Luke 24:18–21).

They would never forget how and when and by whom their faith had been restored. It was not by coming to feel that through faith in God the human spirit can rise up again after any disaster, however devastating. It was not even by hearing a report that Jesus was alive again (Luke 24:1–11). It was by meeting the risen Lord and hearing him in person expound from every corner of the Old Testament what the divinely ordained programme was and what the order of events should be for the setting up of Messiah's kingdom: the Messiah had first to suffer, and after that, and only after that, to enter into his glory (Luke 24:26).

The suffering was now past. The Lord was risen again. Soon they would see him ascend and depart into the far country. What then would the next event be in God's programme for the restoration of all things? Their baptism in the Holy Spirit, he said (1:5). But what was that?

The firstfruits of the Spirit

With the coming of the Holy Spirit on the day of Pentecost something took place the like of which had never before happened in the whole of human history. Indeed, as Christians came later to realise (1 Cor. 12:12–13), an entity came into existence that had never before existed anywhere in the universe: the body of Christ.

Acts, for its part, helps us to grasp the all-importance of this event. First, by recording our Lord's announcement of this coming, and his strict instructions to the apostles not to leave Jerusalem until it had taken place.

Secondly, by recording Christ's description of what it was they were to expect. 'Wait', said he, 'for the promise of the Father which you heard about from me' (1:4). Had he said only 'the promise of the Father', he might have been referring simply to the Old Testament passages in which God promised to pour out his Holy Spirit (e.g. Joel 2:28–29; cf. Acts 2:16–18). But the added phrase 'which you heard about from me' points to the teaching on the topic given earlier by our Lord himself, and especially on the night before Calvary, as recorded by John.*

*Some have thought that Luke could not have intended a reference to teaching recorded by John, but only to teaching recorded in his own Gospel, as for instance at Luke 11:13. But Luke is not *inventing* our Lord's reference to his earlier teaching, only recording that he made such a reference. At that point, Luke's own Gospel

Now, in John's upper-room discourse Christ had spoken four times of the 'coming' of the Holy Spirit (John 15:26; 16:7–8, twice; 16:13), even saying on one occasion that he must go away himself, else the Holy Spirit would not come (16:7). Now, risen from the dead, and about to 'go away' himself, he was reminding his apostles of the promise that the Holy Spirit was about to 'come'.

But 'come' in what sense? The Holy Spirit had long since been active in the world, empowering the great saints and warriors of God. How could Christ say that he would not 'come' unless he himself went away? What was this obviously different and unprecedented 'coming'?

An analogy will help. When our Lord came to Bethlehem, that was not the first time the Second Person of the Trinity had visited earth. The many theophanies in Old Testament history were appearances of the pre-incarnate Son of God.* But there was an immense category difference between the many 'comings' of the pre-incarnate theophanies, and the unique coming to Bethlehem of the Word irreversibly made flesh. Similarly, there was to be a category difference between the many comings of the Holy Spirit upon people in Old Testament days and the coming of the Spirit on the day of Pentecost to take up permanent residence in the body of Christ. A new and distinctive epoch in the operations of God on earth was about to dawn.

And understandably so. The incarnation had been an event unprecedented in all the annals of creation. Calvary too was unique. Never before had earth witnessed its Creator spiked to a cross. The resurrection that followed was a first in all the history of the race since Adam. And never had heaven's eternity experienced before what it was about to experience with the ascension of the Man Jesus Christ into the very presence of God. What this at last made possible, therefore, was understandably not a simple increase in something that had been quite commonplace even before, but a happening unparalleled and hitherto impossible, the coming of the Holy Spirit to take up permanent residence in

---

was not yet written. And we cannot suppose that the risen Lord limited himself to referring to that portion of his earlier teaching that Luke was one day going to record. Moreover, with the two elements in his instruction to wait ('the promise of the Father' and 'which you have heard about from me'), cf. John 14:16, 26; 15:26; 16:7, 13–15.

*See, e.g., Genesis 32:24–30; Judges 13:15–23; Exodus 14:19 and 1 Corinthians 10:4.

the individual believer (1 Cor. 6:19) and in the church (1 Cor. 3:16–17).

In the third place, Christ further underlined the newness of the approaching epoch by emphasising the unique distinction of the operation that was to inaugurate it. 'John baptised you in water,' he reminded them, 'but you will be baptised in the Holy Spirit not many days from now' (1:5).

John, we remember, had electrified the whole nation when he first appeared in public. His voice had broken the centuries-long silence since Israel's last recognised prophet had spoken. His was the predicted 'voice-in-the-wilderness', announcing the arrival of the long-promised Messiah, whose forerunner he was (Isa. 40:3; Luke 3:1–6).

John, according to our Lord, was the greatest of all mankind (Luke 7:28). Even so, there was on John's own confession an immeasurable difference between him and Jesus. John could point to the Lamb of God: Jesus was that Lamb. John could announce the impending sacrifice for the sin of the world: Jesus offered it. John could preach about forgiveness: Jesus had the authority personally to grant it. John could demand repentance and baptise people in water in token of it. However, by his own admission (Luke 3:16) he could not baptise repentant and for-given sinners in the Holy Spirit and thus unite men with God. But the Lord Jesus could, and was now about to. And when at Pentecost he did so, he would do what no other man, how-ever holy, however exalted, had done ever since the world was formed. At Pentecost a new epoch would begin: God's redemptive work would move on to an altogether higher plane.

Finally, Christ indicated the nature of the approaching epoch by instructing them that they would be baptised in the Holy Spirit within a few days, and then making them wait for it until the day of Pentecost. That shows, at least, that the choice of the day of Pentecost for the coming of the Spirit was deliberate. But what was the point of the choice?

Maximum publicity is one possible answer. The feast of Pente-cost was one of the major religious festivals in the year. If the divine purpose was to advertise the coming of the Holy Spirit by the miracle of tongues, what better time to stage the miracle than at a festival when Jerusalem would be full of visitors from foreign countries who knew and could recognise those foreign tongues?

But publicity was not the only reason. Let's take the analogy of another famous Jewish festival, Passover. Its annual celebration was a reminder of Israel's original redemption out of Egypt, a

32

historical event that had been valid, effective and significant in its own right. Passover, then, was obviously not a prophecy, waiting to be fulfilled in the way predictions are fulfilled. But subsequent history showed it was a pattern of bigger things. Just before he suffered, the Lord Jesus indicated that through his death Passover would be 'fulfilled' (Luke 22:15–16); and spiritual minds eventually came to see that the death of Jesus at Passover time was no accident. It took place according to the pre-arrangement of God, who had ordained from before the foundation of the world that Christ should be sacrificed as our Passover (1 Cor. 5:7), to release us from a more bitter slavery than ever Pharaoh had imposed.

Pentecost was originally one of a pair of agricultural festivals, celebrating the beginning of the first harvest of the year. Before the standing corn was completely ripe and ready, a sheaf was cut and offered as firstfruits to God (Lev. 23:9–11). Fifty days later (that is, on the day of Pentecost), two loaves baked from the first flour to be milled from the newly reaped grain were also offered as firstfruits to God (Lev. 23:15–17). Harvest time in any primitive economy is always a joyous occasion. In Israel the joy was both natural and sacred. God, they believed, had given them Canaan as their inheritance; harvest was the reaping of the blessings of that God-given inheritance. Later in the year there would come other harvests, of grapes and other fruits; and they would be celebrated in other festivals. But there was nothing quite like the joy of these first two festivals, when the pinching scarcities and gloom of winter gave way to the glorious taste of the firstfruits of the year's first harvest.

Israel had been celebrating these agricultural festivals for centuries. But the year that Jesus rose from the grave there were bigger things to celebrate. His resurrection was the first break in a more terrible winter; his glorified body the firstfruits of a mightier harvest (1 Cor. 15:23). Fifty days later, on the day of Pentecost, the Holy Spirit came as the firstfruits of a greater inheritance, a foretaste and guarantee of creation's final restoration (Rom. 8:18–23; 2 Cor. 5:1–5; Eph. 1:13–14). The freshness and joy of it pervade Luke's history still.

The time of the full restoration

When next our Lord appeared to his apostles, they had a question for him (1:6): 'Lord,' they asked, 'are you at this time going to restore the kingdom to Israel?' And a very sensible question it was, one might have thought. The Old Testament promised that God would do many things through Messiah when he came; and the Lord Jesus had already done some of them. Notably, he had suffered death and risen again. He was now announcing that the promised outpouring of the Spirit was going to take place in a few days' time. But the full restoration that the Old Testament spoke of included many other things as well. The famous Joel passage, for instance, which Peter was soon to quote on the day of Pentecost, followed its promise of the outpouring of the Holy Spirit (Joel 2:28–32) by announcing the coming of the great and terrible day of the Lord, when God would 'restore the fortunes of Judah and Jerusalem', visit the Gentile nations with apocalyptic judgement, break their domination over Israel, and restore Jerusalem as the centre of the divine presence (Joel 3:1–21).

That naturally raised the question: When would these other things be fulfilled? In the Jewish understanding of the Old Testament there was to be but one coming of the Messiah. If Christians were now going to be asked to believe in two comings of one and the same Messiah, it was obviously important for the apostles to know which parts of the promised programme were going to be fulfilled when. After all, they were the men that had to go out and preach the programme. And the same thing is still true of us, of course. If we are to believe and preach two comings of the Lord, his first and his second, we need to know clearly what parts of the promised great restoration were fulfilled at his first coming, what can be fulfilled only at his second, and what we may expect to be fulfilled in between the two. Mistaken ideas on these matters would lead to confusion in our expectations and in our preaching. Indeed such confusion did occur sometimes in the minds of the early Christians, some of whom came to think that the great and resplendent day of the Lord promised by Joel had already set in before the second coming of Christ (2 Thess. 2:1–12).

We might therefore be grateful to the apostles for having asked their question. In some quarters, however, they have been severely criticised for it; and to this day the meaning of both their question and our Lord's reply are extensively debated. Let's begin, therefore, by placing before our eyes the relevant part of Luke's narrative:

> [6]So when they met together, they asked him, 'Lord, are you at this time going to restore the kingdom to Israel?'
> [7]He said to them: 'It is not for you to know the times or dates the Father has set by his own authority. [8]But you will receive power when

the Holy Spirit comes on you; and you will be my witnesses in Jerusalem, and in all Judea and Samaria, and to the ends of the earth.' (Acts 1:6–8)

The apostles' critics, of course, temper their criticisms with sympathetic excuses: the Holy Spirit, they explain, had not yet come to teach them better. Nevertheless, they say, the apostles did introduce an unfortunate anticlimax into the conversation. The Lord had recently been speaking of the coming of the Holy Spirit to give his people a true spiritual understanding of the Old Testament promises made by the Father (1:4); and the apostles' response was to come out with a question based on a grindingly literalistic interpretation of them. The Lord was about to inaugurate the new age of the Spirit when Spirit-filled witnesses would establish Christ's spiritual kingdom throughout the world and bring spiritual blessing to all nations everywhere (1:8), not just to favoured Israel. And all the apostles were concerned with was the carnal, narrow-minded, nationalistic hope that Israel would have a material, political kingdom restored to her.

Their question, it is alleged, was therefore misguided; but our Lord graciously corrected them. First he repudiated their presuppositions: there never would be a restoration of any kingdom of any kind to Israel as a nation. Then swiftly and abruptly (1:8) he redirected their thinking into better channels. The 'restoration of the kingdom' promised by God through the prophets referred to his (Christ's) own present spiritual kingdom. Inaugurated already by his death and resurrection, it was now to be established throughout the whole world by the missionary and pastoral efforts of the church in this present age (1:8). It would begin with the coming of the Holy Spirit in a few days' time.

But the apostles' critics generally end at least by praising them, or rather the coming of the Holy Spirit, which completely reorientated their outlook. 'The change', says Professor E. M. Blaiklock, 'from the spirit which dictated the question in verse (6), to that in which Peter (ii. 38,39) preached repentance and forgiveness to all whom the Lord should call, is one of the greatest evidences of the miracle of Pentecost.'*

But there are grave difficulties with this interpretation. First, at the basic level of understanding the thought-flow between the Lord and the apostles. Suppose first of all that Christ really meant

---

*E. M. Blaiklock, *The Acts of the Apostles*, Tyndale New Testament Commentaries (London: Tyndale Press, 1969), p. 50, quoting J. R. Lumby, *Cambridge Greek Testament*, 1894, p. 83.

to say that the kingdom was never going to be restored to Israel. See then what that would do to the conversation:

> *Disciples*: 'Lord, are you at this time going to restore the kingdom to Israel?'
> *Christ*: 'You cannot be told the time when that restoration will take place, because the Father has reserved all such matters to himself. And the kingdom is never going to be restored to Israel anyway.'

But that would make no sense. If the kingdom were never going to be restored, there would be no timing of it to be known by anyone, not even by the Father himself.

Let's try again. Suppose our Lord intended to say, 'Yes, I am going to restore the kingdom to Israel, but not in the narrow sense you suppose. The promised restoration of the kingdom to Israel, rightly understood, refers to the setting up of my spiritual kingdom from Pentecost onward.' See what that would do to the thought-flow of the passage:

> *Disciples*: 'Lord, are you at this time going to restore the kingdom to Israel?'
> *Christ*: 'I cannot tell you when the restoration of the kingdom to Israel will take place, because the Father has reserved all such questions of timetable to himself. Actually, the restoration of the kingdom to Israel refers to the setting up of my spiritual kingdom here and now, and of course I can tell you when it will take place. It will happen in a few days' time, at the coming of the Holy Spirit at Pentecost.'

That would make no sense either. But important as it is to get the logic of the thought-flow right, there are bigger questions to be faced. The promise of the restoration of the kingdom is nowhere more clearly enunciated than in Micah 4:8, the context of which is one of the most famous passages in the Old Testament. Let us read the promise in its context:

> [1]In the last days
> the mountain of the Lord's temple will be established
> as chief among the mountains;
> it will be raised above the hills,
> and peoples will stream to it.
>
> [2]Many nations will come and say,
> 'Come, let us go up to the mountain of the Lord,
> to the house of the God of Jacob.
> He will teach us his ways,
> so that we may walk in his paths.'
> The law will go out from Zion,
> the word of the Lord from Jerusalem.

[3]He will judge between many peoples
    and will settle disputes for strong nations far and wide.
They will beat their swords into ploughshares
    and their spears into pruning hooks.
Nation will not take up sword against nation,
    nor will they train for war any more.
[4]Every man will sit under his own vine
    and under his own fig-tree,
and no-one will make them afraid,
    for the Lord Almighty has spoken . . .

[6]'In that day,' declares the Lord,

'I will . . . assemble the exiles
    and those I have brought to grief . . .
[7]The Lord will rule over them in Mount Zion
    from that day and for ever.
[8]As for you . . . O stronghold of the Daughter of Zion,
    the former dominion will be restored to you;
    kingship will come to the Daughter of Jerusalem.' (Micah 4:1–8)

There, then, plain for all to see, is the promise of restored dominion. But for the moment, bigger and more urgent questions push it aside.

What are we to make of this glowing promise that one day armed conflict shall cease, justice shall prevail, and the world shall know universal peace? Is it only the poetic expression of an ideal, ever to be aimed at, never to be attained? Or is it a concrete promise from God? And if it is a realistic promise, with a guarantee of fulfilment, what exactly does it mean? How is it to be interpreted? And above all, when did God intend it to be fulfilled?

We seem to be back with part, at least, of the apostles' question: 'Is it at this time . . . ?' Only now we are asking it in an altered and intensely practical context. As responsible witnesses to the Lord Jesus, we must know as accurately as we can what promises from the Lord apply to this present age of the Spirit, and what not; what results we may rightly expect from our evangelism and social concern, and what not. We must not lower any God-given hope: but we must not chase mirages either. How then is the passage to be interpreted?

Let's try a 'spiritual' interpretation: the promise of the restoration of dominion to the Daughter of Zion (Micah 4:8) means the setting up of Christ's spiritual kingdom in the church at Pentecost. Micah 4:6 announces that this 'restoration' will happen 'in that day', which in the context means the day when many nations shall have renounced armed conflict. Obviously that cannot be meant literally – what significant nations disarmed before or at or after Pentecost? It is to be understood figuratively, therefore, of what began to happen, and has happened ever since, to individuals when they have believed the gospel and been reconciled to God. They have 'dropped their arms of rebellion against God', lived peaceably in the church, and never fought their fellow Christians again.

It applies to the church, then; for the nations have gone on warring against each other unabatedly since Pentecost. And what is more, it does not apply to Christians in their lives outside the church. In the last world war, for instance, thousands of true believers, being members of either the Allies or the Axis forces, fought and killed each other, as millions more have done all down the centuries in similar situations, and still do.

On this showing Micah 4:1–8, for all its grand promises, holds out little hope for our war-wracked world. And how much does it hold out even for the church? Have there been no wars over religion in Christendom?

We need go no further. If this 'spiritual' interpretation is all that Micah's promises amount to, many of us will have little stomach left for believing any other biblical promises, and certainly no heart for preaching this programme as a realistic hope for the world.

But let's try a more sophisticated, more nuanced, interpretation. Once again the promised restoration of dominion refers to the establishment of Christ's spiritual kingdom through the church at Pentecost. The establishment of the Lord's temple/house as chief among the mountains (Micah 4:1) refers again to the church and to the position of dominant world-influence she has been gradually achieving since Pentecost. The picture of verses 2–5 was meant by God as a prophecy that the nations, as nations, would gratefully come more and more to listen to the teachings of the church, and that that in turn would lead to a progressive observance of God's law among the nations and an increasing abandonment by the nations of armed struggle. This, therefore, was also the view of the future that our Lord envisaged when he briefed his apostles for their world-wide mission.

But if that is in fact what God meant through Micah, must we not still ask: How has performance matched promise? And if that is really what Christ was instructing his apostles to expect, what is to keep us now from despair? Never once in all the centuries since Pentecost has the preaching of the gospel and the establishment of Christ's spiritual kingdom led to even one major nation disarming itself, let alone to a universal disarmament. The so-called Christian nations have in fact been the world's leaders in the production of ever more lethal weapons; and even now, when mercifully there are the beginnings of an arms reduction between East and West, it is not being done as a response to the gospel of Christ, nor as a result of the nations concerned setting themselves more rigorously to learn and keep God's law. The hope that Micah's prophecy would be fulfilled by the preaching of the gospel has so far proved to be a manifest delusion. It could only be rescued by a drastic devaluation of Micah's prophetic coinage.

That does not mean that as Christians we are to become cynical. We rightly applaud the United Nations' adoption of Micah's prophecy as their ideal. We applaud, pray for and support every honest effort to make peace; and we recognise with thankfulness to God the genuine progress that has been, and even now is being made, in the direction of peace and disarmament in various quarters of the world.

But we must not deceive ourselves. History has shown that world peace has proved to be like Sisyphus' rock. Whenever it has neared the summit, it has slipped through tired fingers and careered down to the depths again. Moreover, the Bible seems to warn us that one day a kind of universal peace and safety shall at last be achieved. But it will be a false peace before the terrible storm of the day of the Lord breaks upon an unrepentant world (1 Thess. 5:1–3).

All that is very gloomy; but we have no need to despair. We do have a genuine message of hope for our war-wracked world, our terrorist-ridden cities, and our famine-tortured countries. Micah's promise was given by God, and it will certainly be fulfilled, and in such a way that its fulfilment does not have to be taken on faith against mountains of hard evidence to the contrary. Universal justice, disarmament and peace shall prevail. Everything that God has ever promised to restore will be restored (Acts 3:21) – including the kingdom to Israel in the sense that God intended. (We are not talking of the Zionist State of Israel. There will be no permanent restoration of anything to Israel or anyone else apart from the Messiah.) But if we are to save ourselves from false expectations and consequent disillusionment, we must get this matter of the timing of the restoration right. Let's go back again to the apostles' question and the Lord's answer.

First let us notice the obvious: their question was not, 'Lord, are you going to restore the kingdom to Israel?' Such a question would have invited the straight reply, 'Yes, I am' or 'No, I'm not.'

Theirs was a different question altogether. It took for granted that he was going to restore the kingdom to Israel and simply asked about its timing. The force of the Greek is 'Lord, *is it at this time* that you are going to restore the kingdom to Israel?'*

The Lord answered the precise question they asked: 'It is not for you to know times or seasons which the Father has set within his own control' (or 'set by his own authority'). He did not deny that he was going to restore the kingdom to Israel; he simply observed that they could not be told the exact timing of it, since the Father had reserved all such matters of times and dates to himself.

But the Lord's reply sets up echoes. In his famous prophetic discourse he had used similar language about the timing of the second coming: 'But of that day and hour no one knows, not even the angels of heaven, neither the Son, but the Father only' (Matt. 24:36).

Similarly in the passage which we noted earlier (1 Thess. 5: 1–3), when Paul refers to 'the times and seasons', he is talking of the coming of the day of the Lord, that is, the second coming of Christ.

The suspicion must be, therefore, that Christ's answer to the apostles' question referred the restoration of the kingdom to Israel to the unknowable time of the second coming. And that suspicion is confirmed two chapters later when Peter shows in a sermon that this is exactly how he understood the Lord's reply. His audience were Jewish, and like himself they would have understood that 'the restoration of all those things which God had promised to restore' would include, as the prophets said it would, the restoration of the kingdom to Israel. Here then is what he told his audience:

> Repent then and turn [to God] so that your sins may be wiped out, in order that times of recovery† may come to you from the Lord, and *he may send the Messiah* whom he has already appointed for you, that is Jesus. *Heaven must receive [and retain] him* UNTIL *the times of the*

*cf. H. Alford, 'The Acts of the Apostles', *The Greek New Testament*, vol. 2 (London: Rivingtons, 1871), *ad loc*: 'The stress of this question is in the words, prefixed for emphasis, *en toi chronoi toutoi*. That the Kingdom was *in some sense*, and *at some time*, to be restored to Israel, was plain; nor does the Lord deny this implication.'

†'times of recovery': 'fig., of the Messianic age', Bauer.

restoration of all things which God has spoken of through his holy prophets from ages past. (3:19–21)

Next we should observe that in 1:8 our Lord is not abruptly dismissing the disciples' interest in the restoration of the kingdom to Israel and turning deliberately to something else that had nothing to do with that restoration. As Peter pointed out to his Jewish audience (3:19–26), if they would prepare themselves for the second coming of the Messiah and for participation along with all other nations in all the blessings of the great restoration, they must repent. The world-wide, Spirit-empowered witness of the church to the Messiah is directed to that very purpose, of bringing all people everywhere, including Israel, to that necessary repentance and faith in Christ.

The frame of reference for the church's world-wide witness

Christ's terse but justly famous briefing of his disciples for their world-wide mission was now over. Its last words had not yet died away, and they were still looking at him (as people look into the face of someone whose words absorb them), when suddenly

> he was lifted up and a cloud received him out of their sight. And as they were gazing intently up into the sky as he was going, all at once there stood beside them two men dressed in white who said, 'Men of Galilee, why do you stand looking into the sky? This same Jesus who has been taken up from you into heaven will come back in the same way as you have seen him go into heaven.' (1:9–11)

In this moment they received the full answer to the question that had prompted the Lord's briefing: Are you at this time going to restore the kingdom to Israel? His ascension answered: No, not at this time. Now he must go away. Now the nobleman of the parable was going into the distant country (Luke 19:11–27).

The ascension, however, was not yet complete. The Lord was still in process of going (1:10) when two angels stood by them to assure them of the certainty of his return. The nobleman would come back. That both completed the answer to their question and gave them a vividly clear frame of reference for their mission of witness. The full restoration was not now: there would be no 'restoration of the kingdom' before the unknowable time of Jesus' second coming. But that coming was certain; the full restoration would take place then. The purpose of the interval was not the restoration of the kingdom to Israel, but world-wide witness to Christ.

41

According to Luke's own record, the goings and the comings again of the Lord during the forty days had often been instantaneous. On this occasion, however, it was different. He chose first to ascend visibly a certain distance up into the sky before the cloud of the shekinah glory of God enveloped him, and there took place (by mechanisms that are as inconceivable by us as they were invisible to the apostles) his transition into the world beyond.

That preliminary physical ascent served at least three purposes. It marked the end of the earlier appearances: there would be no more of them. It formed also a simple yet awe-inspiring and eloquent ceremony, expressing in symbolic action the infinitely higher reality that, by the invitation of the Father, Jesus of Nazareth, the Son of God, was being exalted above all heavens, to the glory which he had had with the Father before the world began. It served finally as a model for the second coming. The angels fixed no dates for that coming, for angels know no more about that than anyone else, except the Father. But they called attention to the manner of his going, and they assured the apostles that the manner of his return would be the same: 'This same Jesus . . . will come back in the same way you have seen him go into heaven' (1:11).

The Jesus who was the Word of God incarnate, in and through whom God entered our space and time, was no docetic Christ who appeared to be man when in fact he was not. He was as truly man as he was truly God. Nor was his humanity a temporary phase in God's self-revelation, to be superseded by some 'higher' form of revelation. The manner of the ascension tells us that he remains this same Jesus now, when he has returned to God's space and time, as he was in his earthly life, and as he was when in resurrection he bade his disciples handle him and see that it was he himself. And if in him God could and did enter our space and time once, we are to believe the angels that he will do so again; and that he will do so just as physically and as visibly as he was seen to leave it. In becoming genuinely human in the cause of our redemption, the Second Person of the Trinity has become what he never was before. And he will remain so eternally.

The ascension over, the apostles returned to the upper room and joined Mary the mother of Jesus, the other women, and Jesus' brothers, in waiting for the coming of the Holy Spirit to empower them to witness for the Lord. And as they waited, they prayed (1:12–14).

The case to be witnessed to (1:15–26)

It was still not seven weeks since the Lord Jesus had been executed, and within a few days the apostles must go and stand publicly in the city to begin their witness to him. The confidence of men who had seen, handled and talked with the risen Lord is not to be questioned. But they did have a problem.

The terms of their mission were clear: they were to witness to Christ (1:8). In particular they were to witness to his resurrection (1:22). But there was more to it than that. The resurrection of any man would have been an astounding event. But Jesus Christ was not just any man. The significance of his resurrection lay, in great part, in what he had done and claimed before he was crucified. An official apostolic witness therefore had to be someone who had been a constant close companion of the Lord and of his apostles right from the time of his baptism by John until the ascension (1:22). An apostle must be a direct witness of all that Christ had done and stood for, of all that was now vindicated by his resurrection.

Now, according to Luke's Gospel (Luke 19:45–48), there was one thing Jesus had done with maximum publicity during his last momentous week in Jerusalem: he had cleansed the temple. It, as much as anything else, had precipitated his death (see Mark 11:17–18).

It was the second time Jesus had cleansed the temple.* On the first occasion he had caused consternation enough – but cleansing the temple of its abuses was the kind of thing Messiah might be expected to do, and many ordinary Israelites might well have approved of his action. But on the second occasion he had virtually accused the temple authorities, in the presence of the people, of being downright thieves and robbers who had abused their sacred office for the sake of making money. It proved the last straw: they decided to destroy him before he undermined their power over the people and ruined their vested interests.

Our Lord's reaction had been to tell a parable which exposed the significance of the act they now plotted to do. Israel was God's vineyard, and the chief priests and religious leaders were the God-appointed tenants whose sacred office it was to cultivate it so that it produced fruit for the Owner's enjoyment. Over many

---

*For the first, see John 2:13–22, and especially verse 22; for the second, see Luke 19:45–48. C. Blomberg, *The Historical Reliability of the Gospels* (Leicester: IVP, 1987), pp. 171–3, lists six impressive reasons for thinking that Christ cleansed the temple on two occasions, once at the beginning and once at the end of his public ministry.

years the tenants had misappropriated the produce; but now at last the Owner's Son had come, sent by his Father to collect his due. The sin that the chief priests and religious leaders were determined to commit was to murder the Heir to the vineyard so that they might have not only the produce but the vineyard itself as well (Luke 20:9–18).

That is precisely what in fact they did; and now, less than two months later, the apostles must go up to the temple, face these same tenants, and the crowds who formed the vineyard, and claim that Jesus was risen from the dead and was thereby demonstrated to be the rightful heir to the love and loyalty of the people.

They had, then, a difficulty! And it wasn't fear. It was Judas. One of their own number had been guilty of the very same sin as the chief priests. Indeed, he had done infinitely worse than they. He had been called to the high and sacred office of being one of Messiah's companions, one of the Son and Heir's representatives. But when the Son and Heir came to claim his due, Judas had not only defected to the tenants: he had abused the knowledge he had gained in his sacred office, and had guided them to where Jesus was so that they might arrest him. He, too, had done it for money; and with his wretched gain he had bought himself a field (1:16–19).

Of course the apostles could, and did, easily arrange for another man to take over Judas' sacred ministry: there was no shortage of suitably qualified men who had remained loyal to the Lord Jesus. But that by itself would not meet the difficulty. The whole shabby story was widely known in Jerusalem, and the popular nickname people gave to Judas' field kept all the gory details of his end fresh in their memories (1:19). One can well imagine what the man in the street – or at least some men in some streets – said about it: 'That's religion for you. Doesn't matter whether it's the establishment or some fanatical little sect. When you get to the bottom of it, they're all after the same thing in the end. Money. Big houses. Fields.'

The thoughtful would raise a more serious question. 'You say Jesus is the Son of God, Israel's Messiah, Saviour and Restorer, come to right our wrongs and to expose the priests' corrupt abuse of their sacred office for money? How then did he not know any better than to choose a man like Judas to be one of his chief companions, representatives and executives – and, if you please, treasurer of his group (John 12:6)? He paid dearly for it in the end by his betrayal and death. But if he really was the Son of God, he ought to have known what Judas was like and not have chosen him. After all, if he didn't know how to choose better officials than that, what hope would he have of restoring Israel and of bringing in the kingdom of God?'

When Peter eventually rose to address what had now become a throng of some one hundred and twenty disciples, he asserted that the answer to the problem lay in the directives given by the Holy Spirit about Judas in Psalms 69 and 109. But where, we ask, did Peter get the idea from that these psalms had anything to do with Judas, or that their details could supply an authoritative directive as to what should be done about his defection?

Luke has already told us (Luke 24:27, 44–47). Peter got it, not from his prior knowledge of rabbinic principles of Old Testament interpretation, nor from the Holy Spirit given at Pentecost, but from the Lord Jesus himself. It is unthinkable that in his survey of the Law, the Prophets* and the Psalms Christ should have omitted all reference to David, the prototype king of the royal line of Judah, when, as Messiah, he was David's physical and spiritual heir. And it is equally unthinkable that he should have omitted to point out the way David came to his throne, when the whole purpose of this Old Testament survey was to establish the pattern that Messiah must suffer first before he entered his glory (Luke 24:25–26).

David, anointed by God and marked out as Israel's saviour by his victory over Goliath and in many other battles with the Philistines, was none the less – or rather because of that – rejected, persecuted and sentenced to death by the establishment, and obliged to flee to the Gentiles. There, however, he was preserved by God until eventually he returned and was acknowledged king, first by Judah and then by Israel. And then again, during Absalom's rebellion, not only did the bulk of the people turn against him, and notably the top-brass in Judah, but his close friend and adviser Ahithophel proved a traitor, joined the conspirators, and advised Absalom how David could best be tracked down and destroyed (2 Sam. 17:1–4), in the same way as Judas advised the high priest how Jesus could be found and arrested.

Our Lord would have taught his disciples that these striking analogies between the record of David's experiences and his own were not accidental: they were the watermark of God's ultimate

---

*The term 'Prophets' in the Hebrew Old Testament includes the historical books (Joshua, Judges, 1 and 2 Samuel, and 1 and 2 Kings) as well as the major and minor prophets.

design and purpose running through the inspired history of redemption. And he would have taught them how these experiences of David, though not in themselves predictions, were, so to speak, prototypes that had to be fulfilled at the higher level of Messiah's sufferings and final vindication, just as Israel's Passover, though not in itself a prediction, had to be fulfilled in his redeeming death and resurrection (Luke 22:16). In addition, he would have pointed out that some of the experiences described in David's psalms went far beyond anything that David ever experienced himself. They were not analogous to Messiah's experiences: they were direct predictions of them; for David was a prophet and spoke under the inspiration of the Holy Spirit (see Peter's remark, 2:29–31). It was our Lord's teaching, then, that led Peter to his conviction about the ultimate meaning and appropriate application of Psalms 69 and 109.

'Brethren', Peter began as he rose to address the question of Judas' defection (1:16), 'the Scripture had to be fulfilled which the Holy Spirit spoke long ago through the mouth of David concerning Judas, who served as a guide for those who arrested Jesus . . .' *Had to*. Notice the past tense. Peter is here thinking of the whole episode: that there should have been a Judas at all and that he should have held high office as an apostle and then fallen to the despicable depths of betraying the Lord for money. It had to happen. Why had to? Because Scripture had indicated that it would happen; and Scripture would inevitably be fulfilled.

This was not fatalism, of course. Peter was expressing the same thing as Christ did when he said, 'Did not the Christ *have to* suffer these things and then enter his glory?' (Luke 24:26). 'Have to' because Moses and the prophets in their various ways, through prototypes, foreshadowings, or explicit predictions, had said he would; and Scripture had to be fulfilled. Judas, for his part, did what he did out of his own free will. God did not compel him, any more than he compelled Israel's rulers to crucify Jesus when he handed him over according to his own set purpose and foreknowledge (2:23). Judas must bear the responsibility for his deed. 'The Son of Man will go as it has been decreed,' Jesus had said in Judas' hearing, 'but woe to that man who betrays him' (Luke 22:22; cf. John 13:18–20).

On the other hand, looking back from the event to the prototypical pattern, it is clear that the event fitted the pattern, hand to glove. Then see what that implies! The fact that one of the apostles whom our Lord himself had chosen had defected and betrayed the Lord was not a weakness in the apostles' case, undermining the claim that Jesus was the Messiah promised by the Old Testament prophets and foreshadowed in its histories and poetry. The very opposite! It strengthened it.

The same was true of the field which had been bought with the traitor's money. The apostles would have no need to hope that the Jerusalemites would forget all about Judas and his Field of Blood; nor would Luke have reason discreetly to omit all reference to the episode. No! Advertise it, rather! Make sure everybody remembered why Judas had to be replaced! Remind them, in fact, if they were in danger of forgetting, that the plot of land bought by the traitor's money, where Judas had met his grim, gory end, had been turned into a cemetery. The Holy Spirit's directive through David, 'May their place be deserted; let there be no-one to dwell in their tents' (Ps. 69:25), was doubtless meant (by its repeated plural 'their') to include the priests and leaders of the nation with whom Judas had collaborated to destroy Jesus; and it was destined to be fulfilled at that wider level when their temple at Jerusalem was eventually destroyed and left deserted for centuries (Matt. 23:38). But in the case of Judas and his field-turned-cemetery it had already been fulfilled – all Jerusalem could see it if they would – and fulfilled with a vivid irony and terrible eloquence.

But we should be doing the apostles, and ultimately the Lord Jesus, a grave injustice if we imagined that these verses which the apostles regarded as the directives of the Holy Spirit were in fact arbitrarily wrenched out of an original context that had little or nothing to do with the Messiah and his betrayal by Judas. The two quotations are rather open invitations to go back and explore their original context.

In Psalm 69 David is in deep and prolonged trouble, from which he has been pleading with God to deliver him – so far without success (vv. 1–3). He has incurred the hatred of innumerable powerful enemies who are out to destroy him, though they had no just cause for their hatred (v.4). The reason for their hatred, however, is in part at least because he has been consumed with zeal for the house of the Lord, with the result that he has attracted to himself the insults that people have hitherto offered to the Lord himself (v.9). His zeal has been so intense, and the backlash so severe, that even the members of his own family have lost sympathy with him, and he has become a 'stranger' to them (v.8).

But now the crushing heartbreak: God himself has wounded him (v.26). Justly enough: David freely confesses his sins and his folly (v.5). But it has brought a tidal-wave of scorn and shame upon him (vv.7, 12, 20–21). Useless to expect sympathy or comfort: gall and vinegar is all he gets (vv.20–21). They persecute the one whom God himself has smitten (v.26: not 'those' whom, as in NIV).

And so he prays: 'Let not those that wait on you be ashamed through me, O Lord God of hosts; let not those who seek you be brought to dishonour through me, O God of Israel' (v.6). It seems that there had been some whose faith in God had been coupled with their faith in David and in all he had done and stood for as God's anointed. Now that God had smitten him to the great and bitter delight of his enemies, these supporters were in danger of feeling grievously let down, and of losing faith in David and perhaps also in God. He prays therefore that God will save him (v.1), rescue and redeem him because of his enemies (v.18), and no longer hide his face from him, but vindicate him, and bring on his enemies the retribution they deserve (vv.22–24), including the desolation of their house.

Not one of the one hundred and twenty disciples in the upper room could have read this lament of David's without seeing its immediate relevance to the situation that faced them. Even as early as the first cleansing of the temple some of them had been reminded of the phrase 'The zeal of your house has consumed me' (Ps. 69:9) as they had watched Jesus' flashing eyes and corded whip earn him the undying hostility of the temple authorities (John 2:17). His friends thought he was beside himself (Mark 3:21), and his brothers had not believed on him (John 7:5), even if now, along with the 120 disciples (Acts 1:14), they thought differently and reflection on this verse and psalm strengthened the disciples' faith (John 2:22).

Just before he suffered Christ had quoted verse 4 of this psalm to prepare his apostles for what lay ahead. He had pointed out that David's experience, 'They hated me without a cause', had been fulfilled many times over in his own (John 15:25), and had warned them that they might expect the same treatment from the world when they began their witness to him after he was gone (John 15:18–25; 16:1–4). But now, as they reflected on this psalm in the upper room, they would have remembered until their cheeks burned red how they had in fact been horribly ashamed when he was sentenced and crucified. They would have relived the tempest of scorn that had swirled round his head at Calvary as the chief priests had taunted this 'temple-reformer' with his claim to be God's Son (Matt. 27:39–43). They would have shuddered at the memory of the gall and vinegar, metaphorical in David's case (Ps. 69:21), pitilessly literal in Christ's; and then at the overwhelming consternation that came within the thickness of a shadow of destroying their faith not only in Christ but in God's justice when cynical high priests could parade past the cross unscathed, while Jesus had to cry that God had smitten and forsaken him. Scorn, reproach, shame, disgrace, vitriolic persecution of One whom God had wounded – they knew all too well what Psalm 69 was describing.

They understood now of course that, unlike David, Jesus had been wounded not because of his own transgressions but for theirs; he had borne the sins of the many and given his life a ransom for them. They were no longer ashamed for his sake, they no longer felt disgraced because of him (Ps. 69:6). The flood of waters had not engulfed or swallowed him up; the pit had not closed its mouth over him for ever (Ps. 69:15).

But in a few days' time the apostles must go out and face not only the Jerusalem crowds but the very temple authorities who had had Jesus crucified. They must therefore prepare themselves for their witness. They could not appear in public with the gap caused by Judas' defection still unfilled: that would suggest they had no other witness qualified and competent to take over his office. They therefore let themselves be guided by the Holy Spirit's directive from Psalm 109:8, 'And let another take over his responsibility'. 'It must be done,' said Peter, using the verb *dein* for the second time, and this time in the present tense (1:22): 'one of these who have been with us the whole time the Lord Jesus went in and out among us . . . must become a witness with us [apostles] of his resurrection'.

So much, then, for the evidence that Psalm 69 foreshadowed Christ's rejection by the nation's leaders and the fate of his betrayer, so that Judas' defection strengthened, and not weakened, the case that Jesus was the promised Messiah. Now let's examine the other psalm.

History's cause célèbre

David's account of his sufferings in Psalm 109 is couched in the language of the law-court. Three times he speaks of those who have attacked and accused him as his legal adversaries (Heb. *satan*: vv.4, 20, 29). His opponent has 'rewarded him evil for good and hatred in return for his love' (v.5). He asks therefore that when this man's turn comes to be judged, God will set a wicked man over him, and an adversary at his right hand to act as a counsel for the prosecution (vv.6–7).*

This prototypical psalm therefore invites us to consider the dispute between Jesus of Nazareth and Judaism's religious establishment in terms of a court's proceedings. Reasonably enough: it is the greatest *cause célèbre* in the planet's history. Jesus was, of course, literally put on trial before the high priest and the council, condemned, sentenced to death, and handed over to the Romans for execution. But the resurrection reopened the case. Or rather it showed that the case had been taken up by the Supreme and Final Court of Appeal, which had delivered its indisputable verdict in favour of Jesus. In the words of Psalm 109:25, he had been an object of scorn to his accusers; and as they passed in front of his cross they had 'shaken their heads' at him (Mark 15:29–32). But God had 'stood at his right hand', like a counsel for the defence in an ancient law-court, had argued his case, had won the day and vindicated him triumphantly by raising him from the dead, thus making it clear to all that 'this was God's hand: God had done it' (Ps. 109:25–31). In a few days' time the Holy Spirit would come to promulgate the verdict of the High Court (John 16:8–11). He would convict the world of their fundamental sin of refusing to believe in the incarnate Son of God; would prove to them where the true rights of the case lay. Christ had 'gone to the Father', God had justified him, that is, had declared and demonstrated that he had been right and the priests, his judges, wrong. Jesus was, after all, the Son and Heir of the Owner of the vineyard.

Moreover, as the great Paraclete pursued his brief, the apostles too, as Christ had promised (John 15:26–27), would have the high honour of acting as his mouthpiece 'because they had been with Christ from the beginning' (cf. Acts 1:21–22). Judas, too, might have had that honour. He chose to defect; but his defection, fulfilling Scripture as it did, was one more piece of evidence in favour of the Holy Spirit's case.

The great defection

But the case cannot rest there; for as presented so far, it does but raise a more fundamental question. Granted, God foresaw that Judas would betray Christ, and he had it foreshadowed in Scripture so that when it happened everything might be seen to be working out according to God's set purpose and foreknowl-

---

* cf. the use of *satan* in the court-scene depicted in Zechariah 3:1–5.

50

edge. But why have a traitor in the scenario at all? If Christ had not chosen a traitor, there would have been no need to predict that he would. Or, to put it the other way round, if Scripture had not indicated in advance that one of the apostles would be a traitor, there would have been no need for Christ to choose, and then to lose, Judas so that the Scripture might be fulfilled (John 17:12).

The answer seems to be that as far as God is concerned, it was ordained in order to expose the essential nature of sin. It was an appalling scandal that Judaism's chief priests, to protect their corrupt financial gain, should kill the Son of the God they worshipped. It was an even worse scandal that a Christian apostle, for the same motive (but for a far less sum of money), should betray the Heir to the Universe.* But these acts were not the expression of some rare, unheard-of and altogether exceptional state of heart. God had the whole episode foreshadowed in David's history and in the inspired record of that history, so that when it happened with the Messiah it should be seen not as a mere repetition or coincidence, but as something that springs from a basic fatal flaw in mankind's attitude to the world and to God.

The Christian apostle, Judas, betrayed God's Son; the Jewish chief priests arrested him; Pilate under pressure had him crucified. And that cross, driven into the earth, revealed what since the fall had lain at earth's heart – and lies there still! Calvary was but the cone of a volcano through which at one stage in history the whole world's defection from its Creator erupted. 'He was in the world; but the world, though it owed its being to him, did not recognize him. He entered his own realm, and his own would not receive him' (John 1:10–11, NEB).

Here is the root of the world's troubles. The world, the universe, has a Personal Owner; mankind are but tenants and stewards. But people are not content to be tenants. They live as though the Landlord had no right to expect any dues of love, obedience, devotion and service from them. They live as if there were no Owner. Worse still, they aspire to being, each one of them, owners in their own right. They have no love for the Owner's Son, for whom in fact the universe was made, who was the agent in its creation, is the maintainer of its present stability, and is its redeemer and eventual restorer (Col. 1:16–20). As long

---

*The financial corruption within Christendom, all down the centuries and to this present time, has surely been worse than anything known in Judaism.

as he keeps his distance, of course, the world doesn't mind him. They can even affect a reasonable amount of religion. But let him approach, insist on his ownership and demand his dues – then the resistance starts. People have got used to living as though they owned their own lives. They denounce his demands as absolutism. They fight for their independence, if need be at the cost of rejecting the Son of God outright. This is what 'worldliness' is.

Christ is risen now. One day he will restore the universe to which he is heir. But as he waits to receive from the Father the 'uttermost parts of the earth for his possession', and the Holy Spirit argues his case with the world, he offers us the honour of being witnesses for him in the dispute. Judas too could have had that sacred honour, but he chose otherwise. He preferred money; he wanted to own a field.

He died there, in that very field, a gruesome death. His field became desolate; and the priests, his accomplices, turned it into a cemetery. His mournful Field of Blood carries its warning still. If to secure our own little fields in this world, we reject, betray or sell the world's Creator and Restorer, the very Author of life himself (3:15), how shall our little fields not be the death of us and land us in irredeemable desolation?

Some, of course, deliberately take the other side in the dispute. They deny there is an Owner. They deny that Jesus is risen from the dead. Any improvement or restoration of the earth, any hope for mankind's future on the planet, rests, they say, solely with mankind.

They too might profitably ponder the desolation of Judas' field. We are told that it was an act of pious charity on the part of the priests to allocate Judas' field as a place where foreigners might be buried (Matt. 27:7). In contemporary thought, it bestowed on those fortunate foreigners the privilege of being at the very centre of things when the messianic age should begin, the resurrection take place, and King Messiah be installed in Jerusalem. But if Jesus Christ is not God's Son risen from the dead, all hope of any other resurrection is vain (1 Cor. 15:12–19); for, so the scientists tell us, our planet is doomed to become eventually not only the graveyard, but the incinerator of the human race.

Pentecost and the day of the Lord (2:1–47)

If it is true that Jesus Christ was the Son of the Owner of the vineyard, and in addition Heir to the whole universe; and if in fact he was thrown out of his own vineyard and crucified by his own creatures, then what happened at Pentecost expresses a mercy that almost passes belief. A more easily credible story would have been that the 'tongues as of fire' that descended from heaven on that occasion were sent to lick up and consume the very stones of Jerusalem and all it contained. As it was, those tongues of fire came to announce to the murderers of Jesus that he was risen from the dead and ascended to God's right hand; to argue the case that the Jesus they killed was therefore demonstrated to be both Lord and Messiah; and that now therefore – and here comes the incredible bit – pardon and forgiveness were offered to them and to all mankind, together with a hitherto unparalleled gift of new life and of a new relationship with God.

Not but what fire of a very different kind will one day fall. Throwing out God's Son and Heir has not turned the earth into a self-contained flat, still less an impregnable fortress, inside of which mankind can effectively barricade itself against all invasion, or even interference, from outside. Men may live as if they owned the world, but they are still only tenants; and the Landlord has plans for redevelopment. He will not wait for ever before his Son and Heir takes over the property and restores the earth to what he intended it to be.

God makes no secret of his glorious designs. Nature's subjection to frustration, corruption and pain is only temporary: nature shall eventually be released, and brilliantly reconstructed (Rom. 8:20–21). But since it would be as pointless as it would be impossible to release nature from her bondage to corruption and leave her still in the control of sinful, rebellious men, there will first have to come what Scripture refers to as 'the day of the Lord'. Preceded by cosmic convulsions on a grand scale, that day will launch cataclysmic judgements on all unrepentant and recalcitrant tenants, destroying their opposition and removing them.

The Old Testament prophets were the first to speak of this day of the Lord, with its preliminary cosmic convulsions; but Christ himself used the very same language to describe the happenings that will precede his return:

There will be signs in the sun, moon and stars. On the earth, nations will be in anguish and perplexity at the roaring and tossing of the sea. Men will faint from terror, apprehensive of what is coming on the world, for the heavenly bodies will be shaken. At that time they will see the Son of Man coming in a cloud with power and great glory. (Luke 21:25–27)

And the apostle Paul similarly has written that the day of the Lord will coincide with the revelation of the Lord Jesus

> from heaven in blazing fire with his powerful angels. He will punish those who do not know God and do not obey the gospel of our Lord Jesus. They will be punished with everlasting destruction and shut out from the presence of the Lord and from the majesty of his power. (2 Thess. 1:7–9; cf. 2:1–2)

On the other hand God had already promised through the Old Testament prophet Joel that this great and resplendent day of the Lord would be preceded by not one but two events of world-wide dimension and significance; and since we are about to hear Peter cite the prophecy at length, we might as well prepare ourselves by reading it:

> In the last days, God says
> I will pour out my Spirit on all flesh.
> Your sons and daughters will prophesy,
>   your young men will see visions,
>   your old men will dream dreams.
> Even on my servants, both men and women,
>   I will pour out my Spirit in those days,
>   and they will prophesy.
> And I will show wonders in the heaven above
>   and signs on the earth below,
>   blood and fire and billows of smoke.
> The sun will be turned to darkness
>   and the moon become as blood
>   before the coming of the great and glorious
>   day of the Lord.
> And everyone who calls on the name of the Lord
>   will be saved.   (Joel 2:28–32)

Two events, then, said Joel, would precede the coming of the day of the Lord, both spectacular, both universal in their effect, but otherwise so utterly different from each other that it is impossible to imagine them happening simultaneously.

The second of these two events, he said, would take the form of terrifying cosmic and terrestrial disturbances. How long before the great day these disturbances would take place Joel did not specify; but it is obvious that they were to act as premonitory samples of the judgements that the day of the Lord would unleash.

The other event mentioned as preceding the great day would likewise be a supernatural disturbance of the earth's regularities; not physical, however, but spiritual. Not an unparalleled deluge of God's wrath, but an unprecedented outpouring of God's Spirit; not world-wide destruction, but world-wide salvation; not a prelude to the terrors of the great day of the Lord, but a foretaste and firstfruits of the eventual restoration.*

And it was this first glorious event that Peter informed the astonished crowd was taking place in the streets of Jerusalem before their very eyes. They had killed God's Son and Heir; but his death had not cancelled the promise of the Spirit: it had facilitated its fulfilment. The promise was meant for them and for their children, and indeed for as many the whole world over as the Lord would call (2:39). And the promise still stood. Already some had received the gracious gift; they too could receive it if they would, for the gift was utterly free. It was nothing less than the Holy Spirit. Not simply one of the Holy Spirit's gifts with which he equips God's people to serve him. But the Holy Spirit himself. 'Repent and be baptised, every one of you, in the name of Jesus Christ so that your sins may be forgiven. And you will receive the gift [note the singular] of the Holy Spirit' (2:38). They had murdered God's Son; he was offering them his Spirit. They had crucified the Second Person of the Trinity; he was offering them the Third. They had thrown God's Son out of the vineyard in the hope of inheriting the vineyard themselves; now he was inviting them to receive God's Spirit not just into their vineyard but into their very hearts, to be their undying life, to be the earnest and guarantee of an infinite and imperishable inheritance.

And the gift was offered universally: 'I will pour out my Spirit on all flesh.' In Old Testament times the Holy Spirit had come upon people and inspired them to deeds of power or skill, or to words of prophetic authority. But such people had never been more than a tiny select few. Now the Holy Spirit was offered to all

---

*Once more Joel does not indicate how long a time will intervene between the pouring out of God's Spirit on all flesh, and the cosmic disturbances; indeed, in his prophecy the second event follows the first without any indication of a time-lapse between the two. As far as Joel is concerned both events are mentioned together, one after the other, simply because they are both destined to happen 'after these things' (i.e. in the last days), and both are preparatory to the coming of 'the great and resplendent day of the Lord', to the ending of Israel's 'captivity', and to her final restoration (Joel 3:1, 18–21, RV). Compare how Isaiah mentioned, one after the other, 'the year of the Lord's favour' and 'the day of vengeance of our God' (Isa. 61:2) without indicating the slightest interval between the two; and yet how our Lord announced that the first had been fulfilled in his own day, but not the second, and left unspecified when the second would be fulfilled (Luke 4:19–21).

indiscriminately: men and women, young and old, without distinction.

Moreover, there was no need for any of them to fear the coming of the great and resplendent day of the Lord, with all its terrifying signs and judgements. The way of salvation was still what God had said it was through Joel, and still as universally valid: 'everyone who calls on the name of the Lord will be saved' (2:21). Only now the Lord upon whom they must call was the very Jesus whom they had crucified. He was risen and exalted. God had made him both Lord and Christ (2:36); and it was the prime purpose of the coming of the Spirit to prove to them that this was so.

The witness of the Holy Spirit to Christ

Every detail of the day of Pentecost reveals that the prime purpose for the coming of the Holy Spirit was to witness to the Lord Jesus. This appears eventually in the resounding climax of Peter's sermon: 'let all Israel be assured of this: God has made this Jesus, whom you crucified, both Lord and Christ' (2:36). But it already appears in the miracle that preceded and prepared the way for his sermon. It was a miracle of speaking.

The dominating element in the Spirit's witness would always be the spoken word. He would, of course, empower the apostles to do many signs and wonders from time to time, both to authenticate and to illustrate what was being said (2:43; 3:6–10; 4:29–30; 5:12–16). But without the word to explain their significance, no one would know what that significance was, or what it was the miracles witnessed to. Without the word no one would come to faith in Jesus as the Christ, or understand either the true terms or the true contents of the salvation that was available through him. The word, then, must be predominant; and since that word would be spoken through human lips, the first necessity would be to authenticate the channel of communication.

The first great miracle of Pentecost, therefore, did not consist in some additional external act – external that is both to the message and to the speakers of the message, like the subsequent miracle performed on the lame man (3:1–10). It consisted in the very process by which the messengers spoke. Essential to its effectiveness as a miracle was not merely that the disciples should declare the wonders of God in languages that they had never learned and still did not understand, but that what they said should be intelligible to those in the crowd whose native languages they were. The crowds themselves could then see that they were in the presence of an undeniable miracle, and that the message that they were later to listen to was meant for, and applicable to, them – whatever part of the world they came from. To have spoken in languages which neither they nor anyone else in the crowd understood, and which appeared to them as gibberish, would not have been hailed by the crowd as a miracle, but as a sign of mental derangement or worse. Naturally, the first impression that some people gained as they joined the ever-increasing crowd was of incoherent babbling which they put down to excessive drinking. But as Phrygians, for instance, edged their way round the crowd, they would presently hear someone speaking good intelligible Phrygian; and since the speaker was obviously a Galilean who did not know Phrygian (2:7), here was a self-evident miracle. And the same went for all the language groups present.*

Now the topic which the disciples were all speaking about in their different languages was the mighty works of God (2:11). Ordinarily, maybe, many in the crowd might have been inclined to regard accounts of God's mighty acts as attributable to the speakers' religious fervour and imagination rather than to the sober records of history. But now the very process by which they spoke about these mighty acts was itself a mighty act. Here in front of their very eyes the ordinary regularities of their world were being invaded by the actual supernatural power of God. What did it all mean?

Peter rose to explain what it was, and what it meant; and very soon he was reminding them of other recent mighty acts. Throughout the last three years the regularities of nature had time and again been suspended or even reversed as up and down the length of Palestine Jesus of Nazareth had done mighty acts of power, wonders and signs (2:22). Many of the locals would have known about these miracles at first hand; and those who were only visitors to the Passover festival at which he died would have heard about them from the endless conversations and discussions that had gone on in the temple and the city before the

---

*Some have pressed 2:8 ('How then is it that each of us *hears* them in his own native language?') to mean that the disciples actually spoke in their homespun Aramaic, but that God did a miracle in the hearing processes of the audience so that the original Aramaic was converted into each listener's own language as it passed through the hearer's ears and mind. But 2:4 makes it clear that the disciples *had begun to speak in other languages*, as the Holy Spirit enabled them to speak them, *before the crowd arrived*. The miracle was at the level of the speakers, not the hearers, and was designed to demonstrate that the Holy Spirit had come upon the speakers, not (as yet at any rate) upon the hearers.

crucifixion (see, e.g., John 11:56; 12:9, 17–18). Everyone had heard about the nature and quality of those miracles. None of them had been a grotesque distortion of nature; none of them simply a display of power, a mere exhibition of supernatural fireworks. Every single miracle had been a work of mercy, producing life and peace, mental and physical wholeness, release from fear and bondage, joy, confidence and satisfaction. The only apparent exception was the cursing of the fig tree; but it harmed nobody, and conveyed a healthy spiritual lesson. The power that was invading nature through Jesus of Nazareth was no alien power. His miracles expressed 'not simply a god, but God: that which is outside nature, not as a foreigner, but as her sovereign'.* The attempt by the establishment to denounce Jesus' miracles as deceptions performed by satanic powers was patently absurd (Luke 11:14–20). They had been not only miracles of power: they had been signs of the greatness, love, mercy and compassion of God, miracles of physical provision, rescue and healing that at the same time were parables of the spiritual salvation which as Saviour of the world he offered to people who could not save themselves by their merely human powers. Jesus' whole life had been the epicentre of a constant invasion of our fallen, broken, sinful world by God's supernatural power and saving grace. With what more gracious gestures could God have accredited his Son to Israel when he sent him as their rightful Messiah and Sovereign?

And yet they had had him executed. Peter's description of it is violent: 'using men outside the law as your agents you spiked him to a cross and did away with him' (2:23). Why did they do it? The chief priests did it for reasons of security. They claimed that Jesus' activity was a threat to the stability of the state. Pilate, the Roman governor, dismissed that claim as nonsense, and Herod laughed it out of court (Luke 23:1–15). The reality was that his teaching, his claims and his activity challenged their spiritual authority over the people and the security of their financial interests vested in the temple.

Some of the Pharisees did it for security reasons at another level. With tireless zeal they had built up for themselves a tremendous reputation for holiness. Jesus, however, exposed a great deal of it as merely superficial; some of it as a substitute for true holiness, a covering over of inner moral corruption; some of

---

*C. S. Lewis, 'Miracles', in *God in the Dock* (London: Collins Fount, 1979), p. 20.

it as involving heartless cruelty towards others; and much of it actual disobedience to God's word and a misrepresentation of his character (Luke 6:6–11; 11:14–12:12; 13:10–17; 14:1–6; 20:45–47). This punctured their illusion of spiritual superiority and the acceptance with God that they hoped for on the grounds of it. It threatened to destroy also their respected standing among the people.

As for the people, they had enjoyed the free meals he had put on by his miracles; and had he been willing to stand as their king and put on an endless succession of free meals, they would have supported him. But they were not interested in the spiritual significance of the miracles, or in discovering who he was in himself. The incarnate Bread of Life, come down from heaven to forge an eternal relationship between them and God, held no attraction for them (John 6). They were of the opinion that man could live by bread alone; and in the end they were persuaded that the political activist, Barabbas, would serve their interests better.

One and all they came to feel, for their various reasons, that they would be better and more secure with Jesus out of their world. So they opened the door of death, pushed him out through it, and slammed the door behind him.

But God raised him up (2:24). He did not so much bring him back through the door: in the case of Jesus he abolished the door itself. They had to learn that death was not the security barricade they had thought it was. That was why in fact God had allowed it to happen. Indeed, in a sense he planned it: 'This man, [Jesus of Nazareth,]' says Peter, 'was handed over to you by God's set purpose and foreknowledge' (2:23). Of course, that did not palliate their crime: they did what they did of their own free will, and never once imagined that what they were doing would eventually demonstrate that Jesus was God's Son.

But a question arises: If Jesus was in fact God's Son, why did not God intervene with some further spectacular miracle to save him from being put to death, and so put his accreditation beyond doubt? The answer appears from the sequel. God had purposed in Jesus to teach not only Israel but all mankind a fundamental fact about the universe: death is not a permanent, unbreakable, irreversible regularity of nature. Death, therefore, is not a final • disaster for the good, nor an impregnable barricade of protection • for the evil. The Sadducees did not believe in resurrection. They held that death ends everything. God, therefore, deliberately allowed the Sadducees to use their final weapon; but it broke in their hands. They put Jesus to death: but God raised him from the dead (2:24).

Here then, for people who had refused the message of the previous mighty acts, was the mightiest act of all; and its message was gospel indeed. 'Christ Jesus', as Paul was later to say (2 Tim. 1:10), had 'destroyed death and . . . brought life and immortality to light through the gospel'; not life and then survival after death, but life and deathlessness. God had made known to him the paths of life and filled him with joy in his presence (2:28).

The resurrection of Christ has altered the face of the universe. Not only is death not an irreversible process; it is not even a permanent institution. Moreover, if it has been reversed, destroyed, abolished in the case of one man, Jesus Christ, so it can be, on certain conditions, for all others. 'For since death came through a man, the resurrection of the dead comes also through a man. For as in Adam all die, so in Christ all will be made alive' (1 Cor. 15:21–22).

The witness of Scripture to the resurrection and exaltation of Christ

The convicting power of what Peter had been saying up to this point flowed directly of course from the Holy Spirit, who was speaking through him. But now the Holy Spirit directed Peter to appeal to that other abiding source of authority, the written word of God. Both sources of authority are necessary for effective witness. Moreover, by appealing to Scripture at this point Peter, like a good preacher, was answering in advance the objection that was rising in his hearers' minds: 'What unheard of, unlikely, incredible story is this – Jesus has been raised from the dead?'

'No, not unheard of, nor unlikely,' Peter is saying; 'for a prophecy given by God through David in Psalm 16 announced centuries ago that God would not leave Messiah's body in the grave to go to corruption; he would be raised from the dead. Everybody could have heard of it, if they wished. And since it was God who inspired that prophecy, it was impossible that death should retain its hold on the Messiah. Jesus, whom you crucified, is that Messiah, and God, as he foretold, has raised him from the dead.'

'But surely', says someone, 'in Psalm 16 David is simply talking about himself, and expressing his confidence that God will not let him die. How can you say that David is not talking about himself, but about Messiah?'

'For the obvious reason', says Peter, 'that if David was talking about himself, his confidence has been proved ultimately misplaced. He died – and that delivered his soul to Hades; he was buried – and that consigned his body to the grave. And God has left him there!

'There's his tomb; remove the entrance-stone and you will see for yourself. Whereas you will find Jesus' tomb empty. David was not speaking about himself therefore, he was speaking about Messiah.'*

'But then again, how likely is it that David would speak about Messiah?'

'Every bit likely. In the first place he was not only king: he was a prophet (2:30). And prophets normally prophesy about the future. Secondly, what subject was it likely that as a prophet he should speak about more than about his most illustrious descendant, the Messiah himself? And thirdly, he had been given a promise, sworn to on oath by God, that God would maintain his royal line upon his throne for evermore (Ps. 132:11). It is the most natural thing in the world, therefore, to find the Spirit of God inspiring David to write a prophecy to the effect that God would intervene to redeem his promise, rescue Messiah from the grave and set him upon his royal throne for ever. Much more likely this, at any rate, than that David's inspired psalm should turn out in the end to have been true only of himself, and even then only when stripped of exaggerations and applied to some minor deliverance that finally fizzled out in death.'

That, then, according to Peter, was the first reason why it was impossible for death to keep its hold on Jesus: the inevitable fulfilment of God's promise through Scripture made it impossible.

---

*The phrase 'abandon to Hades' could in itself describe two slightly different actions. A mutinous crew could be said to abandon their captain to a lonely island in the Pacific if they took him out of the ship, put him on shore, and left him there. In this case, 'not being abandoned to a lonely island' would mean 'not being put on to it'. But if a later ship called in at the island, found the captain already on it, but refused to take him off, and sailed away, then 'being abandoned to the island' would not mean being put on it, but 'not being taken off it'.

The expression 'abandon to Hades' in Psalm 16:10 could refer to David only in the first sense. But this sense will hardly fit the context in the psalm; for there the opposite of 'being abandoned to Hades' is to be shown paths of life that lead into the presence of God, to be filled with joy because there in God's right hand there are 'pleasures *for evermore*'. To fit these expressions to some experience within David's lifetime (e.g. that he survived some extreme danger and was able to return and for the time being enjoy the presence of God in the tabernacle), would be seriously to reduce their meaning.

Jesus of Nazareth and life's ultimate stability

But there was another reason, which appears when we read the whole of the passage which Peter quoted from Psalm 16. Peter himself may not have intended to make more than one point from his citation; but there is no reason why we should similarly limit ourselves and not reflect on the meaning and thought-flow of the passage as a whole.

Here it is:

> I was always beholding the Lord before me,
> Because he is at my right hand that I should not be moved.
> Therefore my heart was glad and my tongue rejoiced,
> Moreover my flesh also will dwell in hope,
> Because you will not abandon my soul to Hades,
> Nor allow your Holy One to see corruption.
> You have made known to me the paths of life,
> You will fill me full of joy with your presence.
>
> (Ps. 16:8–11; Acts 2:25–28)

The immediately striking thing about this prophecy is that it does not simply talk about Messiah, but introduces Messiah himself talking. It does not simply announce that upon his death and burial God will intervene to raise him from the dead. It presents Messiah, in confrontation with death, telling out the secret of his relationship with God that abolished death's power over him. Utterly unswerving and undeviating in the concentration of his heart's love, his soul's energies, his mind's power and his body's strength on God, he never knew a moment when his inner vision was not fixed on God in uninterrupted obedience and devotion. He was God's 'Holy One', absolutely loyal and perfectly sinless. He 'saw the Lord always before him' and was conscious that God 'was at his right hand' so that he should 'not be moved'.* It gave him a rock-like stability that opposition, persecution and even death's approach could not demolish. His was a faith in God that not even the sufferings and dereliction of Calvary could obliterate and destroy; a perfect submission to the will of God that God himself could never do anything other than vindicate by raising him from the dead. As the writer to the Hebrews was eventually to phrase it, 'he offered up prayers . . . to the one who could save him from death, and he was heard because of his reverent

---

*The Greek word for 'moved', *saleuō*, means 'shaken'. It is used of the powers in the heavens being shaken (Matt. 24:29), of the foundations of a prison being rocked (Acts 16:26), of people being shaken in mind (2 Thess. 2:2).

submission' (Heb. 5:7). God would cease to be moral if he finally disowned such faith, met such loyalty with ultimate disloyalty, or abandoned such flawless love and obedience to death, disintegration and decay. It was therefore in unshaken confidence in the character of God that Jesus bowed his head in death, with triumphant prayer on his tongue; and his flesh dwelt calmly in safety and certain hope that God would open to him the paths of life and fill him with eternal joy in his presence.

And God, of course, raised him from the dead, and so demonstrated that mankind's ultimate stability depends not merely and not finally on the regularity of the physical laws according to which the universe normally operates, but on the moral character of God its creator, which is the source and final controller of all its processes. If the sinless life of Jesus, that in its unswerving devotion to God had enjoyed unbroken fellowship with the eternal God, could in the end be abandoned by God to death and decay, then the universe would lack all ultimate stability; not only the physical earth and heavens, but all created intelligent, moral and spiritual beings would ultimately disintegrate, and all hope of any spiritual heaven would disappear. The resurrection assures us that that will never happen. God is just, loyal and true. The moral universe is stable.

It was impossible, therefore, for death to maintain its hold on Jesus. God raised him from the dead. But if the character of God demanded it, history attests it: 'God has raised this Jesus to life,' says Peter, 'and we all are witnesses of the fact' (2:32) – and at the moment of speaking, the 'all' referred to was no less than one hundred and twenty people.*

The exaltation of Jesus and the demonstration of his deity

'Then if Jesus is risen from the dead, why not produce him here and now for all of us to see him and to be convinced?'

We could easily imagine someone in the crowd interrupting Peter to voice the criticism. And if none of them did, we could perhaps be forgiven for voicing it ourselves.

The answer to the criticism, of course, is to be found in what Peter said next. The Christian witness is not simply that Jesus of Nazareth has been raised from the dead, but that in addition to being raised he has been exalted. In the first place physically and

---

*The total number of those who saw the risen Christ was of course far greater than this: cf. 1 Corinthians 15:6.

bodily exalted, by and to the right hand of God, into the immediate presence of God. And secondly, exalted in the sense that God has made him both Lord and Messiah; that is, by exalting him God has demonstrated that he is both Lord and Messiah by giving him the position in the universe that is suited to his being both Lord and Christ, the position and status that declare him to be so. This, and no less than this, is the astounding fact that the Holy Spirit has come to earth to attest! 'This Jesus, whom you crucified,' is not only Messiah, he is Lord, and Lord in the fullest sense of the term: he is Yahweh incarnate (2:36).

And the evidence of this exaltation was not that he should appear before the crowd – how would that demonstrate that he had been *exalted*? – but that he should be the One responsible for the pouring out of the Holy Spirit which they could see and hear around them.

For at this point Peter comes back to the topic with which he began. He first identified the miraculous phenomenon taking place before their very eyes: it was the promised outpouring of the Holy Spirit. But that necessarily raised the question: 'Why now? Why after so many centuries of delay was the promised Holy Spirit being poured out at this particular festival of Pentecost?' And the answer is: 'Because of Jesus.' And it is not merely that the outpouring followed the death, resurrection and exaltation of Jesus, in order to call attention to him; it is that he, upon his exaltation, did the outpouring. As the one sinless man in all of human history, it is he who has won for mankind this supreme gift, and has received it from the Father, with authority to dispense it to whomever he will. It vindicates his sinless life – but it does more. The Holy Spirit is not some created force, which any other (superior) creature could rightly control. The Holy Spirit is an uncreated, divine Person. No mere human, even if sinless, could impart him to others. If Jesus Christ has poured out the Holy Spirit – and he has – the whole house of Israel might know beyond all doubt that Jesus of Nazareth is not only Messiah: he must be God incarnate.

But if this is what the exaltation of Jesus implies, how could any Jew, brought up on the monotheism of the Old Testament, ever manage to believe in it without abandoning everything he had ever been taught?

'Easily enough' – Peter once more has his answer to their unspoken question. 'The Old Testament itself taught the exaltation of the Messiah in these terms. In Psalm 110:1 David says:

'The Lord said to my Lord:
"Sit at my right hand
until I make your enemies your footstool." '

It is at once evident that David could not be speaking of himself: David cannot be his own 'my Lord' to whom Yahweh addressed the invitation, 'Sit at my right hand'. Nor, Peter repeats, has David ascended into heaven. He must then have been referring to his Lord, Messiah.

But then, of course, the very fact that God had to invite David's Lord to come and sit at his right hand implies, as we can easily see, that there would be a time when Messiah was not seated at God's right hand and had to be elevated to that position. Yet on the other hand, what mere creature would ever be invited to such a position expressive of equality with God? Psalm 110:1, then, told in advance the whole majestic story, though necessarily in terms that remained mysterious until their fulfilment revealed their true and full import: how that Christ Jesus,

. . . being in very nature God,
did not consider equality with God something to be grasped,
but made himself nothing,
taking the very nature of a servant,
being made in human likeness.
And being found in appearance as a man,
he humbled himself
and became obedient to death – even death on a cross!
Therefore God exalted him to the highest place
and gave him the name that is above every name,
that at the name of Jesus every knee should bow,
in heaven and on earth and under the earth,
and every tongue confess that Jesus Christ is Lord,
to the glory of God the Father.   (Phil. 2:6–11)

The exaltation of Jesus and the problem of evil

Perhaps even so there were some in the crowd who still had a major objection: If Jesus really was King Messiah, where was there any evidence of his kingdom? When was he going to start putting an end to the problem of evil? And if he didn't do that, how could he be the Messiah?

The question strikes us today with even greater force than it may have struck the Jerusalem crowd. Almost two thousand years have passed since Jesus' exaltation. But where has there ever been any serious evidence that he has even attempted to

65

solve the problem of evil? Our own century has in fact witnessed in the Holocaust, in Stalin's purges, in the killing fields of Cambodia, and in a thousand atrocities besides, an out-flowering of evil greater perhaps than any previous century. Jesus has obviously not attempted to stamp out evil. How then is it credible that he is both Lord and Messiah?

Once more the psalm has the answer. It was never part of God's programme that the Messiah should proceed, immediately upon his exaltation, to stamp out evil. The invitation was: 'Sit at my right hand *until* I make your enemies your footstool.' There was to be an interval between his exaltation and the subjugation of his enemies, during which he would be seated at God's right hand, awaiting the time of his second coming. Only then would his enemies be made the footstool of his feet.

And what a mercy it was that this interval was written into the programme, for the sake of us all, of course, but particularly for the crowd who stood listening to Peter. They had crucified God incarnate, and he was now elevated to the position of supreme power in the universe. What if there had been no interval and he had proceeded at once to stamp out evil? We are, Peter pointed out, already in the last days of this present age. The cosmic convulsions will occur soon enough, to be followed by the great and resplendent day of the Lord and the dawning of the messianic age to come. But thank God for the present interval.

The final piece of evidence

By this time some three thousand people in the crowd were cut to the heart, and in alarm asked the apostles what they were to do. Peter's reply to these virtual executioners of Jesus was gospel indeed: the gift of the Holy Spirit won by the perfect obedience of the Man they had crucified could be theirs too. They need never be terrified by God's coming interventions in nature, the blood, fire and vapour of smoke, certain though their coming was. They need never be engulfed in the judgements of the day of the Lord. Instead they could now experience his present gracious intervention in mercy and salvation. Let them in true repentance acknowledge Jesus as the Lord of whom Joel spoke, and call upon him. He would give them (and any others, Jew or Gentile, that similarly called on him) the promised Holy Spirit; and in receiving the Holy Spirit, they would have the final evidence of Jesus' resurrection and ascension through their own subjective experience. And then they too, though all undeserving, could know, through the merits of Another, unshakeable stability in the midst of a changing and decaying world. Such stability comes through a personal relationship with God, formed by the undying Spirit of the living God, actually received in the here and now, and destined never to leave us in Hades either. So that we too can say, 'He is at my right hand: I shall never be moved.'

On conditions, of course. First, they would need forgiveness. The receiving of the Holy Spirit sets up the intimate, direct relationship of a shared life between the person concerned and the holy God. There can never be any such relationship set up until the question of sin and guilt is honestly faced and justly dealt with.

If, then, they were to be forgiven, they must repent; and not only of their sins in general, but of their outstanding sin: their false, rebellious attitude to Jesus Christ and to the Father who sent him. Their repentance, moreover, must be genuine, and demonstrated to be genuine. And that not as a crowd, but by each individually for himself or herself; and not by words only, but by action: 'Repent and be baptised, every one of you, in the name of Jesus Christ so that your sins may be forgiven. And you will receive the gift of the Holy Spirit' (2:38).

Two things about the conditions Peter laid down have worried certain people. First, why no mention here of the need to believe, as there normally is on other occasions (e.g. 10:43; 13:39; 16:31; 20:21)? The answer, surely, is that the people he was talking to had obviously already believed that Jesus was indeed both Lord and Christ. If they had not believed, they would not have been asking what they were to do.

Secondly, how can Peter insist that in order to obtain forgiveness and the gift of the Holy Spirit the people must first be baptised? Does not that go against the pattern recorded elsewhere (e.g. 10:44–48), according to which people first believe, receive forgiveness and the Holy Spirit, and then, and only then, get baptised? And might not the order which Peter here insists on be in danger of suggesting that forgiveness and the gift of the Holy Spirit are somehow *secured* by the ceremony of baptism, instead of solely on the ground of faith?

The answer is to be found in the particular situation that Peter was addressing. Many in the crowd before him had stood a few weeks before and shouted for the crucifixion of Jesus. Now they said they repented; but Peter was not prepared to take just their say-so for it. Nor was God. Like John the Baptist before him, Peter insisted that they 'bring forth fruits worthy of repentance' (Luke

3:8). They had publicly shouted for the murder of Jesus; if they now genuinely repented of that, let them show it by being publicly baptised in the name of Jesus. They must save themselves 'from this corrupt generation' (2:40). They could not credibly claim to have repented of the murder of Jesus and still side with and stand with his murderers. They must renounce their former position and attitude, and do so as publicly as they had once adopted it. If they were not prepared to do that, God was not prepared to recognise their repentance as genuine; and without repentance there can be no forgiveness.

The new community of the Messiah

Those then who accepted Peter's message were baptised, says Luke. And not only so. They not only distanced themselves from those who still agreed with the crucifixion of Jesus: they also joined the new community that was taking shape in Jerusalem, of those who believed in Jesus. There could be no neutral position. If you believed now that Jesus was the Messiah, you had to take your stand with his apostles, devote yourself to their teaching, join with the believers as they broke bread – symbolising the death of Jesus for their sins, and the unity of all believers in him – and take regular part in the community's prayers.

The continued performance of miracles by the apostles, moreover, not only brought them the respect of the populace, but obviously marked out the community of believers as they met day by day as a group publicly in the temple and were joined by an ever-increasing number of converts. And with a sudden crowd of over three thousand to be catered for, many of whom were, as we were informed at the beginning of the chapter, visitors to Jerusalem, expenses would run high and the resources of the local believers would be stretched to the limit. In an apparently spontaneous gesture of their new-found love and loyalty they pooled their income, and sold their possessions when necessary, in order to meet particular needs.

Thus was born on earth in Jerusalem city the community of which Christ said that the gates of Hades will not prevail against it (Matt. 16:18). Its distinguishing mark was the foundation on which it was built: the confession that Jesus, risen from the dead, is both Lord and Christ.

The Author of Life and the restoration of nature (3:1–4:4)

The miracle of the day of Pentecost was followed by many others in the ensuing weeks, but only one is described in any detail. It was chosen for lengthy treatment presumably because it completes the message given at Pentecost. The miraculous speaking in foreign languages validated the apostles' witness that Jesus of Nazareth was risen from the dead; but Peter's sermon contained no explicit promise of anybody else's resurrection (though it prompted us to think along those lines). The offer made to those who would repent was forgiveness and the gift of the Holy Spirit, both of which were spiritual benefits to be received at once and to be enjoyed in the here and now. It said nothing about any future physical benefits.

That part of our gospel, however, is now presented, first by the restoration to perfect physical soundness of a congenitally lame man, and then by Peter's exposition of the implications of the resurrection and exaltation of Christ for the hope of the restoration of all things.

The problem of congenital deformity

As Peter and John went up to the temple one day at the hour of prayer, they came upon a lame man lying at one of the gates of the temple. The man had been lame from birth, and his friends deposited him at the temple gate every day of his life to beg for money. It was a good pitch for a lame beggar. Worship of a loving and compassionate Creator has always moved people, and Jewish people in particular, to show love and compassion to their crippled fellow creatures – far more at least than religions and philosophies which have regarded suffering as the sufferer's deserved and inevitable karma.

The man appealed to Peter and John for money, but as it happened they had no money on them. Of course, if they had had money with them, they would have gladly given it; and so ought we all in similar circumstances. But all the cash and loving care given in the name of a compassionate Creator could only have alleviated, never solved, the problem presented by the lame man. The sight of a congenitally deformed human being is distressing enough in itself; but for anyone who believes in a loving Creator, to see such a cripple lying helpless on the doorstep of the Creator's temple is to be reminded of a distressingly

69

poignant question. Why, if there is a Creator who is all-loving and all-powerful, do any of his creatures suffer congenital deformity in the first place? How is it there are any mentally or physically handicapped persons to need the compassion of their mere fellow creatures?

Reverent and believing minds will accept the biblical explanation that the spiritual, mental and physical wreckage of the human race is the result of the fall – and even that, so far as it goes, is a more noble and hopeful explanation than the bleak theory that it is the only result to be expected from impersonal, purposeless forces acting undesignedly on blind matter and producing by chance personal beings doomed eventually to be mindlessly destroyed by the same blind impersonal forces. But granted we accept with the mind that the wreckage is the result of mankind's original rebellion against the Creator, the heart still has its irresistible questions. Does not the Creator himself hear the cries of his broken creation? And if he does, does he not propose to do something about it himself beyond asking us to show care and compassion? And if not, how could we who happen at the moment to be healthy continue long to worship him in his temple for his love and compassion? Would not the cries and groans of the deformed outside the temple gate choke our praises?

Though all the Christians in the world gave all their cash and worked their knuckles to the bone in the relief of suffering, it could never be the final answer to questions of this kind. And as far as the world outside is concerned, if all that the Christian gospel could say in face of the world's pain were that we ought to act the good Samaritan, and do our best to help each other, our gospel would in the end deserve not the world's gratitude, but its pity, if not its contempt. Christianity would need to have a better answer than that if it is to speak credibly in the name of an all-loving and all-powerful Creator. And of course it has such an answer.

Having no money on him to give to the cripple, Peter gave him something far better. In the name of Jesus Christ of Nazareth he performed a miracle, removed his disability and gave him perfect soundness of body. The man was naturally ecstatic with delight, and he accompanied the apostles into the temple walking, leaping and praising God. That was delightful, of course; but for us, at least, who read the story, it leaves our original question largely unanswered. Indeed, it adds to it. If the risen Christ *did* enable his apostles to perform such miracles from time to time – and I do not doubt he did – why did he not command them to drop everything else and proceed systematically to rid the whole country of every conceivable kind of sickness? Luke later records (5:12–16) that they healed all that were brought to them from the district surrounding Jerusalem. Then why did not Christ have them take the next twenty years and heal every sick person in the Roman Empire? That really would have won entry into the secular history books for Christianity! But there is no evidence that the apostles attempted any such thing.

And then, of course, the Jerusalem crowd who recognised the cripple and could see for themselves that an astounding miracle had taken place had their questions as well, and came flocking round the apostles looking for an explanation.

Perhaps the sight of a lame man now walking and leaping and praising God struck a chord deep in their minds. They would have attended their synagogues from childhood and heard the law and the prophets read every sabbath day (13:27). Some passages in the prophets were positively lyrical when they talked of the coming messianic reign. Take Isaiah 35:5–6 for example:

> Then will the eyes of the blind be opened
> and the ears of the deaf unstopped.
> Then will the lame leap like a deer,
> and the mute tongue shout for joy . . .

The cynical and unbelieving, of course, dismissed it as utopian fantasy. The faithful in Israel, on the other hand, believed the promise. The simple-hearted took it literally; the more sophisticated read it as a poetic description. Both derived immense comfort and hope from it, as thousands of believing Jews (and Christians) have done all through the painful centuries, and still do.

But now what was this? A lame man leaping!? Was this the messianic age begun? Were the prophets being fulfilled in front of their very eyes? And literally at that?

Peter's answer to this question is beyond dispute: No, this was not the messianic age begun. His exposition of Joel on the day of Pentecost had pin-pointed their position: they were in the last days of this present age (2:17). The age-to-come, the messianic age, had not yet dawned. And to put the matter beyond doubt, he would tell the crowd before he finished on this occasion that the messianic age of the restoration of all things would not begin until the return of the Messiah (3:20–21).

The miracle just performed was, like many of the miracles the Lord himself did, simply a sign, a pointer to that coming age, a sample in advance of the eventual restoration of all things, an exhibition of the powers of the age to come (Heb. 6:5). It was therefore of course a powerful assurance that the messianic age would come one day; but it raised the question all the more powerfully: Why not now? If Peter and John had the power to heal one congenitally lame man, why not all such cripples? How could it be moral, let alone Christian, to have the power and not use it for the benefit of every sufferer? Let Peter explain it himself.

Perfect wholeness and the Author of Life

First he chided the crowd for even being surprised at the miracle, 'Men of Israel, why does this surprise you?'; and then for imagining that he and John had made the man walk by their own power or godliness (3:12).

It was (and is) a widespread idea that men can by their holy lives and spiritual exercises work up a lot of merit, and in the strength of that merit perform miracles. The idea has from time to time even infected superstitious forms of Judaism and Christianity. But it has never been the true belief of either. It is in fact a completely pagan concept. Whatever miracles Christian men and women have performed, these Christians have never been more than instruments in the hand of the risen Lord who has used them, or not, when and where he has pleased. No true Christians have ever performed, or thought they have performed, a miracle through the power generated by their own merit; nor have they ever performed a miracle by some innate, quasi-independent power that enabled them to do miracles whenever they pleased, and to advertise in advance that they were going to do them. That is rather the hallmark of psychic power.

And anyway, after all the preaching that had gone on since Pentecost, and after all the other miracles, the crowd had no reason to be surprised at this further miracle or to wonder about its source. They knew in their heart of hearts what its source was, and what Peter was about to tell them. But it was important, for their own sakes and for ours, that once more he should bring home to the crowd the irrationality and perversity of what they had so recently done. By the time he has finished we shall all have learned again why this world is not yet a paradise, and why the messianic age and the restoration of all things are still delayed.

So Peter began his explanation: 'The God of Abraham, Isaac and Jacob, the God of our fathers, has glorified his servant Jesus'

(3:13). This is not the wordy rhetoric of a poor preacher. Peter is deliberately reminding the crowd of the immense historical phenomenon of the very existence of Israel among the other nations. He begins with this reference to Abraham as the founder and head of the Hebrew race, proceeds to mention the patriarchs (3:13, 35), refers to Isaiah's great prophecies of the Servant of the Lord, cites the long line of prophets (3:18, 21, 24, 25), and Samuel in particular (3:24), and above all Moses (3:22), and finally returns to the theme of Abraham, Abraham's promised seed, and the Servant of the Lord (3:25–26).

What a brilliant succession this centuries-long cavalcade has been! There has been nothing like it in any other nation in the whole of history. And its significance is beyond exaggeration. It was the first major stage in God's strategy for the ultimate reconciliation of the world to himself and for the introduction of the age of peace.

Israel was a latecomer among the nations. Her creation as a special nation through the call of Abraham and the establishment of his seed was God's response to the idolatrous interpretation of the universe into which all the nations had by that time fallen. It was God's protest movement, witnessing to the world at large that world peace and paradise cannot be built on the deification and worship of the matter, the forces and the processes of the universe, nor on the worship of man's own deified psychological and physical urges, sex, greed, self-glorification and aggression. Idolatry is false. To live as an idolater is to live a lie. Our universe is the work of the one true Creator God. Paradise can only be built on a true relationship between mankind and that Creator.

Then came Moses and a long line of prophets, protesting not only to the Gentile nations, but more particularly to Israel, that peace and paradise will never be built on religion – however chastely monotheistic – that is either amoral or immoral, unconcerned with truth, holiness and righteousness, individual, social and political. And umpteen revolutions in Gentile nations have shown us the same; for while founded on passably good principles, they have not succeeded in curing the basic sinfulness of the human heart even in their strongest supporters.

God took his time over both these 'protest movements'. The external conditions of paradise could be brought about by a flick of God's wand. But paradise without men and women to be put in it would be useless. Getting the human race to see and acknowledge that only God's recipe for paradise will work – *that* could not be achieved merely by God's inspired revelations and commands. Mankind has had – and still has – to learn it by the rigorous schooling of historical experience.

And yet from the very beginning – in fact, as Peter points out to the crowd (3:25), from the very moment that God originally made his covenant with Abraham – there was always another plank in God's programme: it was his determination to bless mankind, and to restore his fallen creation. It was the whole point of his making a covenant with Abraham that, 'In your seed all the nations of the world shall be blessed.' At first it seemed that by the phrase 'in your seed' God was referring to the nation that should arise from Abraham; and in a sense that was true. But as history proceeded, the nation time and again got itself into all sorts of moral and spiritual trouble, so severe that only the memory of the covenant made with their fathers, with Abraham and the patriarchs, kept alive the hope that one day all the nations of the earth would be blessed through Abraham's seed.

Then, as the centuries passed, God began to focus his promise more specifically. Moses, Israel's deliverer from the nation's slavery in Egypt, was inspired to promise that God would raise up in Israel a special prophet after the pattern of Moses himself (3:22; Deut. 18:15–20). Some centuries later Isaiah was commissioned to proclaim the promise that after (and in spite of) the nation's failure as God's servant, God would raise up his Servant par excellence, who would not only redeem Israel but prove to be the very Saviour of the world (3:13, 26; Isa. 49:1–6).

As Peter says (3:21, 24), one common theme, in fact, ran through all the prophets from Samuel onwards, through prototype, promise and prophecy, namely that God would send his Deliverer, King, Servant, Messiah, and that one day God would restore everything that his prophets one and all had promised he would restore. The age of peace and paradise would dawn.

But now the time had come for Peter to lance the ugly abscess that was festering in the crowd's memory. That Servant's name, he announced, is Jesus. God raised him up and sent him to you (3:26); you rejected and killed him (3:13–15); and God has glorified him by raising him to his right hand in heaven (3:13).

One can imagine the consternation, the guilt-feelings, the resentment, the objections of the crowd: 'How can you assert that so confidently? What right have you to say that?'

But the evidence was there in front of them. The cripple was standing (and walking and leaping!) in front of their very eyes. 'We did not give him this complete healing through our own power or godliness. It is the name of Jesus and the faith that

74

comes through that name, and is placed in that name, that has restored his body to perfect soundness, as you can see.' And with that Peter developed his threefold analysis of their guilt:

1. 'You handed him over . . . and you disowned him before Pilate, though he had decided to let him go' (3:13). On the day of Pentecost Peter had charged the crowd with having used men outside the (Jewish) law (i.e. Gentiles) as their agents to do away with Jesus (2:23). The point here is slightly different. Peter reminds them of the fact that when they handed God's Servant over to the Gentile Pilate, the Gentile saw no reason for crucifying him, did not want to do it, and tried his hardest to release him. But they, the very sons of the covenant, members of the privileged nation through which the promised seed and Servant was to come to bless the Gentiles, disowned him. They told the Gentiles that his claims were nonsense and worse: they insisted that the Gentiles crucify him. And without him they have never had since then a credible hope to put before the Gentiles. Indeed, they seem to have given up evangelising the Gentiles altogether.

2. 'You disowned the Holy and Righteous One and asked that a murderer be released to you' (3:14). Pilate had given them the choice between Jesus and Barabbas, thinking that, given the difference in moral character between Jesus and Barabbas (and no matter how much they disliked Jesus), they would never choose Barabbas. But faced with either a perfectly holy and righteous Man or a man who for political ends was prepared to murder, they felt more comfortable with Barabbas, and chose him. Thousands make the same choice still. Indeed, today's murderers not seldom become tomorrow's government; but the process of course does not lead to peace and paradise.

3. 'You killed the author of life' (3:15) – which showed the suicidal insanity of rebellion against God and rejection of his appointed Saviour of men. No charity from the church, no miracle of physical healing, not even the worship of God in his temple, could impart eternal life and paradise to people as long as they reject the author of life.

It goes without saying that there was no anti-Semitism about Peter, any more than there was in the classical Hebrew prophets when with tears they denounced their nation's sins. Peter was a loyal son of Israel, and ready at once to recognise that the crowd, and indeed their rulers who might even have been expected to know better, acted in a sense in ignorance (3:17).

Moreover, there was conciliation in his voice as he pointed out that God had allowed their very ignorance to bring about the suffering and death of the Messiah which the prophets had said must inevitably happen (3:18). Isaiah had explained why the Servant of the Lord must suffer. If 'the many' were to be justified, then the Servant must bear their iniquities (Isa. 53:11). He must be wounded for their transgressions, crushed for their iniquities; the punishment that brought them peace must be upon him, so that by his wounds they might be healed and reconciliation with God effected (Isa. 53:5).

God was not about to cancel his covenant with Abraham. He had, in accordance with that very covenant, sent his Servant Jesus to bless Israel first, before the blessing extended outwards to the Gentiles (3:25–26). God was adhering to his purpose: the time of universal restoration would come, the time that God had envisaged and spoken of right from the beginning of the world (3:21), the time when creation itself will be liberated from its bondage to decay and brought into the glorious freedom of the children of God (Rom. 8:21), when never again will physically deformed or mentally handicapped people be laid on the doorstep of God's temple to appeal for charity and compassion.

If the crowd would have it, their sins could be wiped out, they could be prepared for participation in Messiah's coming reign of peace and glory. The door of repentance was open, and in God's mercy, time for repentance had been built into his programme: the Messiah, now ascended, would not immediately proceed to destroy his enemies and set up his kingdom (3:19–21).

On the other hand, the Messiah was coming again (3:20). They needed to repent. Moses himself had warned them that when God raised up 'the prophet like Moses', that prophet would have to be listened to. Anybody who did not, would be completely cut off from his people (3:22–23). God would not wait for ever to set up Messiah's reign of peace.

The lesson for us

We still need to listen to Peter's exposition of the Christian gospel. The world around us is still a broken world and calls for the church's compassion and care. And we Christians must give it all we can; for 'if a man has enough to live on, and yet when he sees his brother in need shuts up his heart against him, how can it be said that the divine love dwells in him?' (1 John 3:17, NEB).

What we must not do is to make the mistake of supposing that our Christian care *is* the gospel, or of allowing our social works to get out of proportion and swamp the preaching of the gospel.

The world today no more wants to hear the diagnosis of its sin, the summons to repentance and faith in Christ, than the crowd in the temple did. It will, if we let it, lecture us on ethics, indeed on Christianity itself. 'If you would be real and true Christians,' it suggests, 'you would give up all that doctrine and dogma and preaching and trying to get people converted, and get on instead with helping the poor and the sick in the true spirit of Jesus.' The truth is that the world wants the church's charity; it does not want the church's Saviour. Faced personally with the Christ, 'the Holy and Righteous One', it prefers its sin, chooses the murderer, repudiates the need of salvation, and rejects the Saviour. It would have a paradise without repentance, God's merciful service without his Servant.

But it cannot be. Our earth is not a self-created machine which just happens to have gone a little wrong but which we with our increasing know-how and technology can put right, granted only international co-operation and a sincere effort on the part of everyone. Behind our earth and universe stands a personal Creator and a personal Saviour. Not all the technological engineering, medical treatment, social aid, economic strategy, political prudence and education of the masses that could ever be brought to bear upon earth's problems could finally solve them and produce a paradise, so long as the world remains at odds with its Creator and rejects its appointed Saviour (3:20).

So let us be sure of this: there will be no restoring of the kingdom, no 'times of refreshing', no restoration of all the things which the prophets promised would be restored, until the second coming of Christ (3:20–21). Let us listen to the explicit statement of Scripture, and not bolster ourselves up with false expectations.

And let us not quit preaching. The world's pain is immense: but its prime and pressing need is to repent and be reconciled to God (2 Cor. 5:20). Let us make sure, too, that it is the gospel we preach, and not mere morality. It is a sinful and rebellious world; but God in Christ has taken the initiative, and there is a freeway to forgiveness and reconciliation that is wide open. And let us not be ashamed of our hope, but present it positively and joyfully. The world will mock it as pie-in-the-sky; but the world itself has little enough ultimate hope for the planet – ask the cosmologists and see – and, being without God and the Messiah, no ultimate hope at all for the individual. Of what use to a young mother of thirty-three suffering from terminal cancer is the promise of a new social and political era in the future? In Christ there is hope, real hope, both for her and for the whole of nature. The God who created our world, and us upon it, anticipated mankind's rebellion, and has a programme of redemption commensurate with the need and adequate to the task. It is already far advanced. Soon the joy of restoration will fill the universe.

A clash of world-views

The crowd had been listening to Peter in one of the temple courts. Suddenly the captain of the temple arrived, arrested Peter and John, and put them in prison (4:1–3). It was a fateful moment, for here began that rift between official Judaism and early Christianity that was later to widen into an unbridgeable chasm. At this point, therefore, Luke is careful to identify for us the people who made this first attempt to suppress Christianity, and their reasons for making it.

Let it be said at once that they were not representative of the Jewish nation as a whole. The captain of the temple was accompanied by priests and Sadducees, says Luke (4:1); and the phrase 'priests *and* Sadducees' suggests that these particular Sadducees were not priests, but laymen. Such lay Sadducees, far from being typical of the bulk of the nation, belonged to a tightly closed group of aristocrats descended from the old patrician families.

The priests who accompanied the captain of the temple were probably like he was, chief priests; that is, they were high-ranking priests who filled the important priestly offices and together with the high priest controlled the temple and its services. They were not typical of the priesthood in general, who tended to be Pharisees. The high priest and the chief priests were the religious aristocracy who did all they could to keep the highest clerical offices within a narrow circle of family and friends (4:6). They too, so Luke tells us (5:17), were Sadducees.

By New Testament times the Sanhedrin contained many Pharisees. Gamaliel (5:34), who urged caution in dealing with the Christians, was one of them – and they were a considerable curb on the Sadducees. Nevertheless the Sadducean priestly aristocracy, backed by the Sadducean lay aristocracy, wielded power out of proportion to their numbers.

The high priest was president of the Sanhedrin. Moreover, he was the sole mediator between the people and God, for he alone entered the Most Holy Place on the day of atonement. The high priest acted on behalf of the nation in all negotiations with the Herodian and Roman political overlords, and under them he was to a considerable extent responsible for the behaviour of the people. Furthermore, he was the supreme spiritual authority for Jews living abroad, and the temple over which he presided was the centre of their pilgrimages and the recipient of their massive contributions of money, tithes and offerings.

The first opposition to early Christianity, then, came from the powerful Sadducean party, and it came for a mixture of reasons. First, what the apostles were preaching was the direct opposite of the Sadducees' theological beliefs. The apostles were proclaiming the resurrection of the dead (4:2), but it was a basic plank in Sadducean theology that there was no such thing as resurrection, or even survival of the human spirit after death (23:8).

Moreover, Sadducees were very much men of this world. Over recent centuries they had been deeply influenced by Hellenistic rationality and culture, and that, combined with the satisfaction of wielding religious-cum-political power in the world as it was, had induced in them worldly-mindedness and comparative laxity in matters of religion.* They had wealth (they enjoyed massive revenues from the temple), they had power, they mixed in the highest circles (both Jewish and Gentile), they were educated, polished and sophisticated. The world as it was was good enough for them. They could not see all that much wrong with it. As Paul would later say, they loved this present world. It was the only world they really believed in.

And here were these Christian apostles filling the heads of the masses with prophecy and eschatology and the hope of a coming messianic kingdom, all based on the presupposition of the reality of resurrection. It offended their Hellenistic sense of rationality, it challenged their lifestyle, their world-view, and their vested interests.

And there was worse. The Pharisees, after all, believed, like the Christians, in resurrection and the survival of the human spirit after death; and the Sadducees had learned to tolerate them. But these Christians were not only preaching resurrection, they 'were teaching the people and proclaiming *in Jesus* the resurrection of the dead' (4:2). The implications could be serious for the priestly aristocracy if the apostles' message was believed. Jesus had denounced them in front of the crowds, in their very own temple, accusing them of theft, robbery and sacrilege because of their

* E. Schurer, *The History of the Jewish People in the Age of Jesus Christ*, vol. 2, revised and edited by G. Vermes, F. Millar, M. Black (Edinburgh: T. & T. Clark, 1979), p. 412.

trading in the temple. And they had been the ring-leaders in getting him crucified. They had known how to use their political *savoir faire* to blackmail Pilate, and it was they who had cleverly swayed the crowd to choose the murderer Barabbas instead of Jesus (John 19:14–16; Mark 15:11). It would be dangerous if now the crowd were to be persuaded that the execution of Jesus was murder, that Jesus was in fact the Messiah, that God had raised him from the dead, and that one day he would return. As Sadducees they did not believe in a future personal judgement; the idea that Jesus was the Lord on whose name they must now call if they were ever to escape the judgements of the great and resplendent day of the Lord was to them nonsense. But it could spell danger if the crowd took it up. The masses must be stopped from believing it (4:17; 5:28). Already there was in Jerusalem a sizeable community of converts numbering some thousands under the control of these so-called apostles. This afternoon's preaching would produce another crop (4:4). It was time to call a halt. So they arrested Peter and John in front of the crowd, and put them in prison.

Even from this thumbnail sketch it is clear that the early Christians had much more affinity with the Pharisees' world-view than with the Sadducees' (cf. Paul's statement, 23:6, 'My brothers, I am a Pharisee, the son of a Pharisee. I stand on trial because of my hope in the resurrection of the dead'); and so has normative Christianity all down the centuries. So much so that even today many people in Christendom (and a good many outside as well) would find very strange the idea that men could make a career in priesthood, ritual and sacrifice and yet believe that death ends everything and that there is no resurrection nor final judgement. 'What would be the point of religion', they ask, 'if that were so?'

The Sadducees would have replied that the point of religion was to keep the individual and the nation in the favour of God throughout their lives on earth; and in addition to influence, if not control, the political, commercial, social and family life of the people according to God's law expressed in the first five books of the Old Testament.

During recent decades there has been more than a tendency in some quarters within Christendom to revert to a Saducean interpretation of religion. The proponents of so-called secular Christianity, prominent in the 1960s and early 1970s, theologi-cally out-Sadduceed the Sadducees. The various versions of liberation theology have, of course, sprung up to struggle against the aristocratic Sadducean attitude of some, who used the priest-hood to make themselves rich and cheated not only the people but even the lesser priests of their dues.* But when it comes to liberation theology's attitude to the second coming of Christ and to the question of how the age of justice, peace and plenty is to be brought in, its world-view is decidedly more Sadducean than Christian.

More often it is a question of emphasis rather than of adherence to a particular school of theology. In Britain, at any rate, how rarely does a broadcast sermon state the Christian hope with the same clarity and emphasis as Peter did in the sermon we have just studied. That is not because Christianity has not advanced to a fuller understanding of the resurrection, exaltation and second coming of Christ. It is more likely to be because many ostensible Christians have at heart reverted to a Sadducean world-view.

MOVEMENT 2: Opposition to the Programme (4:5–6:7)

Taking our bearings

We have reached a watershed in Luke's narrative; so let us pause and take our bearings.

Looking back on the first four major items in Section One (see pp. 20–21), we can now see how they are, so to speak, bracketed together by the theme of the restoration of all things. The question about its timing which was prominently raised in Item 1 has now been answered, equally prominently, in Item 4:

Item 1: 'Lord, is it at this time that you are going *to restore the kingdom to Israel?*' And he said, 'It is not for you to know *times and seasons . . .'* (1:6–7)

Item 4: '. . . that he may send the Christ, who has been appointed for you – even Jesus. Heaven must receive and retain him *until the times of the restoration* of all things . . .' (3:20–21)

As we proceed we shall find the next four major items brack-eted together in similar fashion:

Item 5: 'The next day the rulers, elders and teachers of the law met in Jerusalem. *Annas the high priest was there, and so were Caiaphas, John,*

---

*cf. J. Jeremias, *Jerusalem in the Time of Jesus* (London: SCM Press, 1969), pp. 106–8.

Alexander and the other men of the high priest's family. They had Peter and John brought before them . . .' (4:5–6)

Item 8: 'So the word of God spread. The number of disciples in Jerusalem increased rapidly, *and a large number of priests became obedient to the faith.*' (6:7)

The attitude of the Jewish priesthood to the early Christians, then, is going to be one of the leading themes of these last four items. In particular we shall discover that it was the high priest, the chief priests and members of the high-priestly family, as distinct from the ordinary priests, that were so strenuously opposed to the apostles. Understandably so. They, along with the lay aristocracy, were the ruling class in Judaism; and the rising influence of the apostles with the populace moved both their jealousy (5:17) and their fear (5:28).

In more recent centuries, as happens with all spiritual functions that are institutionalised, the office of high priest had been subjected to a great deal of political manipulation and intrigue, and its sanctity had been seriously tarnished. Some 'nonconformist' sects in Judaism repudiated the present holders of the office completely. But the high priest still commanded the obedience of the vast majority of the people at home and abroad, if not always their respect. The whole affair of Jesus of Nazareth, however, and now the preaching of his apostles, was in real danger of upsetting the masses.

In his Gospel Luke stressed the fact that the ordinary people were in favour of Jesus (Luke 21:37–38), and that it was only at the last minute that the ruling priestly class managed to persuade the people against him. Now in these chapters of Acts Luke emphasises the same thing: the ordinary people, even those who did not get converted, were at the beginning favourably disposed towards the apostles and the Christians. If the Christian preachers succeeded in convincing them that the crucifixion of Jesus was, after all, murder of the Messiah, it would destroy the high priest's spiritual authority with the people, and lead to who knows what political consequences. High and mighty though the chief priests and the lay aristocrats were, they could not afford to ignore what was happening to the masses (4:2, 17, 21; 5:17, 25–26). They must, so they felt, guard and maintain their authority and enforce obedience to it. Obedience to authority will therefore become the main issue at stake between the apostles and the courts: 'Peter and John replied, "Judge for yourselves whether it is right in God's sight to obey you rather than God"' (4:19); 'Peter and the other apostles replied: "We must obey God rather than men!"' (5:29).

But the same phraseology will occur in other connections, and so, like the tolling of a bell, will reinforce the idea. At 5:36 the followers of a certain upstart, Theudas, are described as 'all who obeyed him'; and at 5:37 the adherents to the cause of Judas the Galilean are similarly labelled as 'those that obeyed him'. On a happier note, Peter says at 5:32 that God has given the Holy Spirit 'to those who obey him'; and at 6:7 we read that a large number of priests 'obeyed the faith'.

Now this conflict of authority between the apostles and the spiritual leaders of official Judaism will raise an interesting question about the nature and stance of early Christianity: Was it, in its inception at least, a movement marked by disregard for duly appointed spiritual authority? And was that the cause of the eventual schism between Judaism and Christianity? Was Christianity simply a popular and basically anarchic movement?

The first thing to be observed in this connection is that the apostles, as the court recognised (4:13), were uneducated, ordinary laymen. For men like that to disobey the highest spiritual authority in the land and the whole of the Sanhedrin was in itself a bold step, requiring a great deal of nerve and courage; a step, one might think, they did not take lightly.

On top of that, the early Christians were the firmest of believers in the Old Testament, and therefore in the divine authority of Israel's religious institutions. They would normally have been the last to adopt revolutionary or anarchic attitudes in spiritual matters, or to encourage such attitudes in the crowds. And it is to be noted that nowhere in Acts do we find them working up the people's animosity against the Sanhedrin. In talking to the people they even make excuses for their rulers' crucifixion of Christ (3:17).

Christ himself, moreover, had warned them against spiritual anarchy: 'The teachers of the law and the Pharisees sit in Moses' seat. So you must obey them and do everything they tell you. But do not do what they do, for they do not practise what they preach' (Matt. 23:2–3). Whatever they might think of the failings of the individual holders of the office of expounder of Scripture, they were to respect the office itself, and the authority of the Scriptures which its occupants expounded.

And so with the priesthood. Paul on one occasion, smarting under a blatant injustice ordered by the chairman of the Jewish council before which he was being examined, denounced the chairman in the strongest of terms (23:1–5). But he immediately apologised when he discovered that the chairman was in fact the high priest, because of the scriptural injunction which he then quoted, 'Do not speak evil about the ruler of your people' (Exod. 22:28).

Warned by Christ against religious anarchy, the apostles nevertheless deliberately repudiated the commands of the high priest and defied the supreme council of their nation, as we shall now be told. So what made them take this extreme step?

Raging against God: The first investigation by the council (4:5–31)

Authority and the resurrection

The council that examined Peter and John was composed of the rulers, elders and teachers of the law. Past masters at interviewing and conducting investigations, they began proceedings by asking, as if they did not know, and as if there were a hundred and one possible answers, 'By what power or what name did you do this [miracle]?' (4:7). They already knew of course; Luke has just told us that the reason why they arrested Peter and John was because they were 'proclaiming in Jesus the resurrection of the dead' (4:2). But they were subtly preparing the apostles for their eventual demand that they drop their insistence on the necessary connection between the church's power and service in the world and her belief in the bodily resurrection of Jesus of Nazareth from the dead.

The court had no objection to the apostles giving aid to the sick and crippled, nor to their doing an occasional miracle or two. And if the apostles had been content to say vaguely that they had done this miracle in the name and by the power of God, the loving Creator of all men, the court would have been delighted and would have dropped proceedings. But for the apostles to insist that there was a necessary and indispensable connection between the miracle and the fact of the bodily resurrection of Jesus, and its implication that Jesus was the Christ, was for the court insufferable. They were, above all others, responsible for his execution. Surely these uneducated laymen would not maintain, in the face of the high priest and of the Sanhedrin, a position that implied that the high priest himself was anti-Christ and therefore anti-God?

The apostles' reply was stark and uncompromising. History

was not to be denied or forgotten, nor was the person of the living and ascended Lord Jesus to be dropped in favour of a God-whom-everybody-could-believe-in. Nor was even their social good-work to be divorced from the gospel of Jesus Christ:

> If we are being called to account today for an act of kindness shown to a cripple and are asked how he was healed,* then know this, you and all the people of Israel: It is by the name of Jesus Christ of Nazareth, whom you crucified but whom God raised from the dead, that this man stands before you healed. (4:9–10)

The apostles obviously did not believe that we should be content to do our Christian good works without pressing the claims of Christ upon anyone.

Authority and Scripture

But was not the apostles' position on the face of it absurd? Was it not ludicrous to suggest – and doubly ludicrous for a couple of laymen to suggest it – that the most eminent religious and spiritual authorities in the nation could have made such a fundamental mistake as (1) to fail to recognise God's Messiah when he came, and (2) actually to crucify him? Granted, a case could be made out that the high-priestly aristocracy were not legitimate holders of their office, that they were corrupt in handling the temple revenues, and that they tyrannised the ordinary priests. But was it even thinkable that in the area of religion and spirituality, where they were after all the chief experts, they could have made such a perverse and shocking judgement as to reject and execute the Messiah?

Yes, unfortunately, it was thinkable; the apostles' next remark forestalled the objection. They quoted a passage of Scripture from Psalm 118:22 which read: 'The stone which the builders rejected has become the head of the corner' (i.e. the massive piece of masonry that in an ancient building lay at the extreme corner, took the weight of the building and set its angle). In the context the psalmist is talking of the gate of the Lord (v.20), of sacrifice (v.27), and of the house of the Lord (v.26). The whole scene is that of the temple, and the imagery therefore has to be interpreted in this light. Who, then, could 'the builders' be, if not those in charge of the temple, the high priest, the captain of the temple

---

* 'Saved' is the word used here; and it forms the connection of thought between this verse and verse 12.

85

and the rest of the chief priests? And to whom could the figure of 'the head of the corner' apply more aptly than to the Messiah? As a prototype the psalm-passage was saying that the high priest and his colleagues would one day reject the Messiah, and find no place for him in their religious system; but that in spite of them God would intervene to make the Messiah the foundation of the nation's religious life, the cornerstone indeed of the temple of the universe.

And that was how Peter applied it: 'Jesus', he said, 'is the stone which you builders rejected; he has become the head of the corner' (4:11). It was a disconcertingly apt quotation.

Authority and salvation

By this time Peter had strictly speaking answered the question put to him. He had been asked, we remember, 'By what power, and in what name did you do the miracle?' And he had now replied that it was in the name of Jesus that the cripple was 'saved' (4:9). But Peter was not content to leave it there. The healing of the cripple was an instance of physical 'salvation' (which is why the versions translate the word, quite properly, 'made whole' or 'healed'); but the same principles applied to salvation in the highest sense of the word. Had Peter not added what he said next, the high priest might have parried the thrust of the psalm quotation by arguing to himself, if not aloud, that while Jesus was doubtless important to the apostles, it was a mistake to think that he was the only way to God and to salvation; and that if people were sincere in their rejection of Jesus, they could still find their way to God by other paths.

But not so, according to Peter, for he adds: 'Salvation is found in no-one else, for there is no other name under heaven given to men by which we must be saved' (4:12).

In a sense Peter was enunciating a principle which everyone in the Sanhedrin already believed – or professed to believe: 'I, even I, am the Lord, and apart from me there is no saviour. I have revealed and saved and proclaimed – I, and not some foreign god among you . . . Turn to me and be saved, all you ends of the earth; for I am God, and there is no other' (Isa. 43:11–12; 45:22). As strict monotheists they were not ashamed to maintain the uniqueness of God in the face of the absurdities, immoralities and cruelties of the gods that the pagan deification of nature had created. Those gods could offer no one any moral or spiritual salvation: they left people unsaved and hopeless. Judaism was –

and still is – to be admired for its long fight against, and its eventual victory over, the temptation to syncretism; for resisting the pressure to abandon monotheism on the ground that it is narrow-minded and exclusive; and for refusing the manifest untruth that all religions are really the same and that there is no difference between Yahweh and the deities of paganism. Quite apart from enormous differences in morality and ethics, and in questions of the significance of human life and the destiny of man, pagan religions save nobody.

In that the Sanhedrin would have agreed with the apostles.* The point is that Peter was not now advocating that they should deify a mere man alongside Yahweh. Rather, what God had proclaimed through Isaiah, he had asserted once more through raising Jesus Christ to his own right hand and demonstrating him to be not only Messiah but Lord: Jesus was Yahweh incarnate. By definition there was no salvation apart from Jesus. To reject Jesus was to reject God – and up to the moment the high priest, and indeed all the members of the Sanhedrin present, had rejected Jesus.

Now it was bad enough for simple uneducated laymen to tell the high-priestly aristocracy that as builders of the nation's religious life they had made an appalling error of spiritual judgement. But it was the ultimate indictment for laymen to tell the professional priesthood that they had missed the whole point of their religion: they were not saved men, and never would be unless they ate humble pie, repented, and put their faith in a man they had recently condemned to death. But that was the plain, logical implication of the gospel they preached. One can have the highest religious office, enhanced by centuries of tradition, surrounded by elevated forms of liturgy and ritual, and profess faith in the one true God – and still not be saved. That is what the apostles believed, and in the name of the risen Christ they were not afraid to say so.

The final witness

It is interesting, therefore, that Luke does not say here that the court flew into a rage and considered executing the apostles (they did that at the second trial, 5:33). Much as they disagreed with

---

*Though in the times of Antiochus Epiphanes the high priests and their narrow party, much to the outrage of the populace in general, had embraced and advocated Hellenistic culture without reserve, and, with it, religious syncretism.

their ideas on salvation, there was one thing that impressed them. They had doubtless interviewed scores of people in their professional lives, and they were shrewd judges of character. What struck them first was the bold, confident speaking of these uneducated laymen. Where did they get their confidence from in religious matters? Where their uncomfortably apt quotations of Old Testament scripture? Such knowledge in uneducated lay-men had to be accounted for; and they traced it to the fact that they had been with Jesus (4:13). The latter had once discomfited them in public by citing the same passage from the same psalm (Luke 20:17). And what was happening now was that, just as he had promised, the Holy Spirit was teaching them what to say when they stood before the rulers and authorities. Israel's rulers, having rejected the testimony of Jesus, were being testified to by the Holy Spirit. He would be their last witness (Luke 12:10–12). There was forgiveness for having rejected Jesus; but in the nature of things there could be no forgiveness for knowingly rejecting God's final witness, the Holy Spirit.

At this stage, however, they felt confident that they had enough reserves of 'spiritual' authority and status to browbeat the apostles into submission. After all, they were only laymen. The priests could not of course deny the miracle – all Jerusalem knew about it; nor could they say that such a miracle was bad in itself (4:14–16). But they felt that they only had to lean on the apostles with all their ecclesiastical and professional authority, and they could rely on the respect and fear which simple laymen have for professional priests to do its work: the apostles would crumple up. They decided to threaten them (4:17). They could not, they felt, go further and actually punish them. The pre-viously lame man was over forty years old: here was no case of hypnotic suggestion. It was a genuine miracle, and the people were glorifying God for it. To punish the apostles who had done the miracle would be to tell the people to stop glorifying God: a very difficult thing for a priest to do and still retain credibility with the people (4:21–22). So they decided to threaten the apostles (4:17) – and they were not idle threats, for they had some severe disciplines at their command.

But their tactics did not work. We leave you to judge, said Peter, whether it is right in God's sight to obey you rather than God (4:19). The apostles had had to choose. The Lord Jesus had commanded them to preach and to be his witnesses (1:2, 4, 8). They could not obey him without disobeying and defying the council; and they could not obey the council without flatly disobeying his commands. That, in turn, raised the question of who Jesus was. If Jesus had been simply a religious reformer who held, as many of his contemporaries did, that the current high priest was an illegitimate holder of the office; had he been simply a prophet who protested, as many of even the ordinary priests did, against the nepotism of the priestly aristocracy, and at the violence and tyranny they practised against ordinary priests;* had he been simply another rabbi with a radically new interpretation of the Torah, then nevertheless, in the interests of good order and religious unity, the apostles might under protest have knuckled under to the council's prohibition and have attempted gradual reform.

But Jesus was not simply a reformer, a prophet or a rabbi. God had demonstrated him to be both Lord and Christ. He was the Lord incarnate, exalted to the position of supreme power and authority in the universe. The high-priestly office (if not the current incumbent) owed its authority to the fact that its Old Testament terms of institution were inspired by God. If Jesus Christ was God incarnate, one could not in any case set aside his authority without simultaneously removing any authority the high priest might have. But to disobey the Lord Jesus out of respect for the high priest's office and for the sake of good religious order and unity was for the apostles impossible. It would have destroyed the very basis of the church (Matt. 16:13–18); and what is worse, it would have been disloyalty to him whom God has made both Lord and Christ.

Final arbitration

None the less for that, it was an extreme step for uneducated laymen to take, to defy the highest spiritual authority in the land. It is instructive, therefore, to study the detail of the prayer with which the Christian community fortified itself when they heard the apostles' report of the ban imposed by the chief priests (4:23). It reveals quite clearly their attitude to the question of where, in cases of dispute, the controlling authority lies.

First, they appealed, over the head of the chief priests and the Sanhedrin, directly to the authority of the Creator himself: 'Sovereign Lord, you made the heaven and the earth and the sea, and everything in them' (4:24).

*See J. Jeremias, *Jerusalem in the Time of Jesus* (London: SCM Press, 1969), pp. 180–1, 190, 196–8.

Secondly, they appealed to Holy Scripture, as being inspired by God, as the authority by which the high priest, the chief priests, the Sanhedrin and all their actions and attitudes must be judged: 'You spoke by the Holy Spirit through the mouth of your servant, our father David' (4:25). The Sanhedrin, they knew, would have given a very different interpretation of this scripture; but obviously they considered that they had the right and the duty themselves to judge the priests' decisions in the light of Scripture as Christ himself had given them to understand it.

Thirdly, they made their judgement on the basis not of an odd phrase or two of Scripture wrested out of their contexts, but of a detailed comparison of the Bible with their situation. They quoted Psalm 2:1–2 at length:

> Why do the nations rage
>   and the peoples plot in vain?
> The kings of the earth take their stand
>   and the rulers gather together
> against the Lord
>   and against his Anointed One,

and they proceeded to review in prayer before God the detailed way in which the concerted action of Herod and Pilate, of the Gentiles and the people of Israel, matched exactly the situation described in the psalm (4:25–28).

Fourthly, in the light of this scripture, they formulated what they felt the issue at stake was. The crucifixion of Jesus, though at one level decided beforehand by God's power and will, had been a 'raging against God', a concerted attack on God's holy and anointed servant Jesus (4:25, 27–28). This was not a matter on which they could possibly compromise. The honour of God and of his Messiah was at stake.

Finally, they asked for appropriate vindication, not for themselves, but for the name of the Lord Jesus. The vindication, they prayed, should be twofold: (1) that they might be given more than human grace, not to crumple under the Sanhedrin's threats and fluff the issue, but to speak out boldly and without compromise; and (2) that God himself would intervene by doing not just miracles, but miracles *through the name* of his holy servant Jesus (4:29–30). They had told both the crowd (3:16) and the Sanhedrin (4:10–12) that it was through the name of Jesus that the cripple had been healed; and the Sanhedrin had forbidden them, not to do miracles, but 'to speak . . . to anyone in this name' (4:17). Mere supernatural works by themselves are ambiguous: the Man of Sin will, apparently, do many of them (2 Thess. 2:9–10). What was required was that miracles be done through the name of the Lord Jesus so that his name would be vindicated, quite apart from any benefit received.

And their prayer was answered: 'the place where they were meeting was shaken. And they were all filled with the Holy Spirit and spoke the word of God boldly' (4:31).

Tempting the Spirit of the Lord: A view inside the Christian community (4:32–5:16)

The first story, then, in Movement 2 had to do with opposition to the early Christians; so will this next story. In the first story the opposition came from the outside; in this second story it will come from the inside. In the first the opposition was described as nothing less than the kings of the earth 'raging against God' (4:25–26), and it took the form of an attack on 'the Lord and his Messiah'. In the second the opposition will emanate from Satan (5:3), will use an otherwise unknown but ostensibly Christian couple, Ananias and Sapphira, and will be variously described as 'lying to God' (5:4), 'cheating, or lying to, the Holy Spirit' (5:3), and 'tempting the Spirit of the Lord' (5:9). The first story had to do throughout with the question of authority, and established the principle that where the commands of the rulers conflicted with the commands of Christ, the apostles had to repudiate the authority of the rulers and obey God rather than man. The second story will likewise have to do with authority, and will establish the reality of the government of God in the church, effected by the Holy Spirit through the apostles of the Lord Jesus.

The main story, then, in this part of Acts, will be about the malpractice of Ananias and Sapphira. Two things will help us see the significance of what they did. First, Luke has prefaced their story by an account of the normal practice of the Christian community (4:32–37), and followed it by a description of the outsiders' attitude and reaction to the Christian community (5:12–16). Secondly, in the structure of his narrative, Luke has placed the story of Ananias and Sapphira opposite that of Judas (see p. 24). The comparison will prove instructive.

The normal practice of the early Christians

Three statements are made about the normal practice of the early Christians: the first in 4:32, the second in 4:33–35, and the third in

4:36–37. All three are concerned with their attitude to material possessions; but they each add a particular nuance, and they should not be confused with one another.

The first states that they shared everything they had, and explains what led them to do this and what 'sharing' meant. 'All the believers', says Luke, 'were one in heart and mind'; and it was this overwhelming sense of spiritual unity that affected their attitude to their material possessions. They no longer claimed that their things were 'their own', that is, that they were restricted to their own private and personal use. Each wanted his fellow believers to regard and to use his possessions as though they were their own. It was perfectly spontaneous. There was no compulsion. It is nowhere said that this was a necessary and indispensable condition for being saved, or for being accepted as a genuine Christian. It was a natural voluntary reaction. And while we would not want to underestimate the devotion of these early Christians, it is a reaction that has been repeated millions of times since. Whenever believers are caught up in the reality of salvation and sense their unity with their fellow believers in Christ, they are not only willing for them to share what they have, they are eager for them to do so. It is when the church loses its sense of the reality of salvation and of the family of God, that there creeps in a selfish, possessive attitude to material things.

The second statement goes further, though we must be careful not to take it to mean more than it intends to say. What verses 33–35 are explaining is the great power of the apostles' preaching and the great grace that was with them all: 'for' says Luke (so the Greek), 'there were no needy persons among them'. What an undermining of the power of their testimony it would have been if, while they preached publicly that Jesus was the Messiah, and that all believers were his 'brothers', they had heartlessly allowed the poor 'brothers of the Messiah' to drag out their lives among them in poverty. Verses 34 and 35 tell us how the needs of the poor were met, and the NIV brings out very well the significance of the tenses (they are all imperfects) which Luke uses to describe what happened: '. . . from time to time those who owned lands or houses sold them, brought the money from the sales and put it at the apostles' feet, and it was distributed to anyone as he had need'.

Luke does not say that every believer who happened to own his or her own home, immediately upon conversion sold it and gave the proceeds away. For if they had, where would any of them have slept the night? On that principle all five thousand converts plus their wives and families would soon have been destitute of shelter; and Mary, the mother of Mark, would not have had a house for Peter to go to when he came out of prison (12:12).

No, the phrase 'those who owned lands or houses' is describing people we would call nowadays 'landlords', or 'property-owners'; and what happened is that from time to time, when special needs arose, this man or that woman – and not necessarily all at once – would realise some of their capital investment by selling a property or a piece of land, and use the proceeds to help the poor Christians.

Another detail is also important. Luke does not say that these landlords sold their properties and gave the proceeds to the poor, but that they placed the proceeds at the apostles' feet, and then it was distributed to the poor. Their action was both wise and symbolic. There was no law to forbid them, if they wanted to, from giving their money direct to individual poor Christians. But this would have been in danger of making the poor too much dependent on a few rich individuals. It was better that they were provided for by the common funds of the Jerusalem church.

But laying the money 'at the apostles' feet' surely carried an additional and deeper significance. The apostles were the official representatives and stand-ins for the Lord himself. By laying the money at their feet, the believers were not just engaging in charity: they were giving to the Lord, and expressing his sovereign rights over all they possessed. He was not simply their teacher: he was their redeemer who had bought them and all they possessed (1 Cor. 6:20). He was Israel's Messiah: the whole vineyard and its fruits were rightly his. He was exalted to the right hand of God: the universe belonged to him. With glad logic they expressed their belief by their action.

Thirdly, Luke mentions the special case of Joseph, nicknamed Barnabas, 'special' because he was a Levite (4:36–37). Seeing he came from Cyprus, it is possible that he had never exercised his sacred office as a Levite in the Jerusalem temple. But now, when he sold a field he owned, and presented the money to the Lord by laying it at the apostles' feet, he was fulfilling the spirit of the ancient law which said: 'But to the tribe of Levi, Moses had given no inheritance; the Lord, the God of Israel, is their inheritance, as he promised them' (Josh. 13:33). The later chapters of Acts will show him as a man specially devoted to the Lord, prepared to leave home and travel the world for the sake of Christ. He forms a pointed contrast to Judas, who, occupying the sacred office of apostle, abandoned it and bought a field with the proceeds of his treachery towards Christ (1:16–18).

The extraordinary case of Ananias and Sapphira

It was, then, in the context of all this spontaneously expressed devotion to Christ and his people that Ananias and his wife committed their evil deed. The severity of their punishment presupposes their deed was exceptionally serious. In order to see how serious it was, let us first clear our minds of a number of other things.

First, they were not obliged to sell their field and give the money to the church. Peter makes that abundantly clear: 'Didn't it belong to you before it was sold?' (5:4). Yes, of course it did. Conversion to Christ does not abolish the right of private property. If it were essentially wrong for a Christian to own private property, it would be wrong to give it away to someone else to own.

Secondly, 'after it was sold,' says Peter, 'wasn't the money at your disposal?' (5:4; literally, 'in your own authority'). Yes, again. If they had sold the property intending to give the money to the Lord, they still were not obliged to lay the money at the apostles' feet for them to decide what should be done with it. They themselves had the authority as stewards of the Lord's money to distribute it as they saw fit.

In this connection we need to be clear what our Lord's demands on disciples are, and what they are not. He says, 'any of you who does not give up everything he has cannot be my disciple' (Luke 14:33). Two questions arise:

1. What is included in 'everything he has'? The danger here is that we unduly restrict it to our physical possessions. But that will not do. If, as in some countries, a man will be forced to leave his wife and children and go into exile if he becomes a Christian (as once happened to a friend of mine), he must be prepared, according to Luke 14:26, to bid his wife and children farewell.

2. Granted that on becoming disciples we have to renounce all we have, in whose favour do we have to renounce them? The answer is, of course, the Lord's. A Christian woman, for instance, is told that her body is not her own, it is the Lord's (1 Cor. 6:19–20). But once she has ceded this fundamental right of ownership to him, he certainly maintains her right of private property over her body against all others. Under his lordship, she has the right to decide whom she will marry. Being a Christian

94

does not mean that she must marry any Christian man who needs a wife and asks her to marry him.

And so with our material possessions. When we cede, as we must, absolute ownership of them to the Lord, he puts them under our stewardship, and gives us, as Peter reminded Ananias, the authority to decide, under his guidance, how they shall be used: what, and how much, shall be spent on ourselves and our families, what given to the church, to evangelisation, to social relief, and so forth.

If, then, 'giving to the Lord' is understood in this narrower sense of giving to the Christian community as distinct from, say, buying oneself a new suit or car, it was still open to Ananias, when he had turned his field into money, to give some of it to the church and to keep some of it for his own use.

Where, then, lay the sin in what Ananias and Sapphira did? It lay in the first place in their 'lying to God' (5:4). When they laid the money at the apostles' feet, they made out that they were giving the whole proceeds of the sale to the Lord; and when they were explicitly asked if they were really giving all the proceeds, they affirmed it was so (5:8). But to declare that all the proceeds were being given to the Lord constituted those proceeds as belonging to the Lord in the strict and narrower sense of the term. In that case their sin was a form of embezzlement, or misappropriation, of funds that now belonged to the Lord.* It was a case, then, of literally 'robbing God', as Malachi would put it (Mal. 3:8), or of cheating the Holy Spirit by misappropriating some of his funds, as Peter described it (5:3).

Bad as this was, however, it was not the most significant element in what they did. They could, after all, have privately vowed to give the Lord the total proceeds, and then privately have gone back on their vow without going anywhere near the apostles. In that case it would have been a serious sin against the Lord, but it would have carried no implication as to the reality or otherwise of the presence of God the Holy Spirit in the church; and in those early days this was the whole point at issue, whether with the Jerusalem crowds or before the Sanhedrin. What was this power that filled the disciples at Pentecost and had them speaking intelligibly in foreign languages they had never learned? What was the power by which Peter and John had given the cripple perfect soundness of joint and limb? Their own godliness or what? (3:12). The crowd wanted to know; and the

---

*The word for 'kept back' in Greek carries this meaning.

cynical chief priests demanded to be told: 'By what power or in what name did you do this? (4:7). And what was the 'great power' by which the apostles gave their witness (4:33) and which made their preaching so effective? The apostles maintained, of course, that it was the power of God, the Holy Spirit, come to earth to witness to the resurrection and exaltation of Jesus, and using the apostles and disciples as his channels of expression. But was it so? Or was it simply a case of religious excitement and mass hysteria?

In this context what Ananias and Sapphira did was as bad as what Judas did. Satan filled Judas' heart to betray the Lord Jesus (Luke 22:3–4; John 13:2, 27). Now, once again, Satan filled Ananias' heart to cheat, and lie to, the Holy Spirit (5:3), and to do so, like Judas, for the sake of money. If Ananias could have got away with that unscathed, it would have discredited the whole reality behind Pentecost, namely that it was God the Holy Spirit who was the power in, and with, and behind the witness of the church. Like the Israelites in the wilderness (Num. 14:22), Ananias and Sapphira tempted the Spirit of the Lord in spite of all the signs and wonders that God had recently done in the name of Jesus (5:9), and they did so deliberately. If they had been poor people who felt pressurised by the devotion to Christ of others around them to make a spectacular sacrifice when they were not really able to afford it; and if in their embarrassment, and to save their faces, they had made it appear they had given more than they actually did, then surely there would have been mercy for them. But it was not so. They deliberately set about tempting the Lord and seeing how far they could go and get away with it.

They had heard the proclamation that Jesus was risen and exalted, was both Lord and Christ. They had felt the power of the preaching, seen the miraculous signs, and known the voice of the Holy Spirit within their own hearts. They had heard the warnings of the coming day of the Lord, and they wanted to escape its judgements. So they joined the church and professed devotion to Christ. But it was bogus. They were not prepared to yield complete obedience and devotion to the Lord Jesus; they only pretended they were. Imagining they could deceive the apostles, they tried to see what they could get away with. They found they were in reality tempting the Spirit of the Lord, lying to God, cheating the Holy Spirit. The Holy Spirit exposed their hypocrisy, and vindicated himself and his presence in the church. Ananias and Sapphira fell under the judgement of God.

Why did they do it? Because, it seems, like the Israelites in the wilderness, they were not true believers. But let Luke have the last word. 'All the believers', he says, 'were one in heart and mind. No-one claimed that any of his possessions was his own, but they shared everything they had' (4:32). Clearly, if that is what true believers were and did, Ananias and Sapphira were not two of them.

The effect of the judgement

The effect of God's judgement on Ananias and Sapphira was fear, both in the church and outside (5:5, 11, 13). And a very salutary and necessary fear it was. It did not inhibit true conversions, as Luke explains in 5:13–14; but it did prevent masses of people without any true faith joining the church under the excitement of the astounding miracles that were done (5:15–16), or because they were attracted by the material benefits people could receive on becoming members of the church: 'No-one else dared join them, even though they were highly regarded by the people' (5:13); but rather, there were added to the church *believers*, great numbers of men and women (5:14). The early Christians, it is true, found themselves obliged to defy the authority of the chief priests and Sanhedrin. But they were not spiritual anarchists. There was an authority in the church: it was the authority of God, the Holy Spirit, living and active among the believers.

If a clear-cut case of God's judgement happened then, someone may ask, why not now and all the time? The answer would seem to be that the judgement on Ananias and Sapphira was an exceptional case, necessary to establish and vindicate the reality of the arrival and presence of the Spirit of God in the church. But neither the coming of the Spirit nor the judgement on Ananias and Sapphira were meant to be the inauguration of the day of the Lord, any more than the healing of the cripple was meant to be the beginning of the times of the restoration of all things. That day will come, but it is programmed for later. The Lord Jesus is to judge the living and the dead at his appearing (2 Tim. 4:1). For the moment tares are not being rooted out, but they will be. And none can deceive the Lord. Remember Lot's wife, but remember also Ananias and Sapphira.

Fighting against God? The second investigation by the council (5:17–42)

The gospel was now beginning to spread rapidly not only in Jerusalem but in the surrounding countryside. The message of resurrection life it preached (5:20) was glowingly attractive, and the extraordinary miracles that accompanied it were filling Jerusalem with people from all over the place seeking healing (5:15–16). It filled the priestly aristocracy with downright jealousy (5:17), and also with apprehension (5:28). They decided they must make another attempt to suppress the movement. So they arrested the apostles, all twelve this time, and brought them before the Sanhedrin.

Guilty of the blood of Jesus?

The charge levelled at them showed the priests' annoyance at the way the apostles had completely ignored their ban on preaching in the name of Jesus. But fear mixed with their annoyance: '. . . you have filled Jerusalem with your teaching and are determined to make us guilty of this man's blood' (5:28).

What the high priest and his associates were afraid of was that the masses whom they had persuaded to shout for Jesus' crucifixion might now get so worked up by the apostles as to turn on the chief priests, perhaps even violently, for what they now regarded as the murder of Jesus. They never did, of course; nor did the Christians ever incite them to do it. But nowadays we cannot listen to the high priest expressing his fears without thinking of the Holocaust and the charge, exaggerated and to a large extent unjustified though it is, that by teaching that the Jews killed Jesus, Christians have been responsible for the evil of anti-Semitism and the attempted genocide of the Jewish people. Nothing we are about to say diminishes our confession of Christendom's real guilt in the matter of anti-Semitism (see Appendix 1, pp. 421–24). On the other hand, Peter's reply to the high priest's charge is valid and relevant still.

In the first place, of course, Peter could not be charged with anti-Semitism. He was as loyal a member of Israel as any member of the council. He was no more being anti-Semitic than were Isaiah or Jeremiah when they denounced the nation's sins. But then history was undeniable and irreversible. 'You did away with Jesus,' he said, 'hanging him on a tree' (5:30). Peter was not now addressing the whole nation, but the chief priests and the Sanhedrin. It was an unalterable fact that they had prevailed on Pilate to crucify Jesus; and in demanding crucifixion they had subjected Jesus to the most shameful and infamous death-penalty they knew. According to their law (Deut. 21:22–23), a person hanged on a tree was accursed by God.

History is, admittedly, unalterable; but why not let bygones be bygones? Why keep preaching about it to the masses? What good could it do, except play on the crowds' animosity and desire for revenge? Why not accept the ban and let the whole thing be forgotten?

'But we have to obey God rather than men,' said Peter (5:29). It is the God of our fathers (there's nothing anti-Semitic about him) who has raised up Jesus, whom you killed, and exalted him. God has reversed your verdict and wants it publicised. Will you publicly attach to Jesus the opprobrium of a death under the curse of God, and then not allow God to publicise his vindication of Jesus in case it should embarrass you? It is God who wants it publicised, and we have to carry out his orders, not yours.

But then again there need be nothing to fear in the publicity. God is not seeking revenge himself, nor trying to sow seeds of revenge in the minds of the masses, 'God has exalted Jesus by his own right hand to be a Prince and Saviour, to grant repentance to Israel and forgiveness of sins' (5:31). The whole nation of Israel, the people as well as you priests, need forgiveness. And you all without exception can have forgiveness; not only in spite of the crucifixion of Jesus, but through it.

Of course there was a necessary condition for forgiveness: repentance. Repentance for the murder of Jesus, and repentance also in the sense of acknowledging the need of salvation. But even repentance was not to be considered as a hostile, tyrannous demand, but rather as a marvellously magnanimous gift. 'God exalted [Jesus] that he might *give* repentance . . . to Israel' (5:31). It is an incalculable mercy to be allowed to repent.

'We are witnesses of these things', said Peter, that there is full forgiveness available to Israel through the death and exaltation of Jesus Christ. And more. There was no need simply to take the apostles' word for it. An even greater and more direct witness was available to them. God had already given thousands in Israel the Holy Spirit. The whole Sanhedrin could receive that same Holy Spirit and, with him, forgiveness, reconciliation and peace with God, on the same simple condition: obedient submission to God through the Lord Jesus Christ (5:32).

Gamaliel's advice

When they heard Peter's reply, they were 'cut to the heart', unfortunately not in genuine remorse and repentance, as the Jerusalem crowd had been on the day of Pentecost (2:37), but in

99

that furious anger that men feel when an argument has reached its target and deep within they know it is true, but they are determined not to repent, but to justify themselves and to silence their accusers at any cost. They flew into a rage and determined to put the apostles to death (5:33).

But then along with the apostles' testimony they received two warnings.

First, the previous day they had arrested the apostles and put them in prison overnight, ready to be brought before the Sanhedrin the next day. So when the full Sanhedrin assembled, they sent officers to fetch the prisoners from their cells. But they came back reporting that the prison was securely locked, and the guards were standing at the doors; but when the doors had been opened, there was no one inside.

The Sanhedrin scarce had time to recover from the shock, when they received another: news came that the apostles were standing in the temple courts teaching the people, as usual, their message of life and immortality through the resurrection of Christ (5:20, 25). At that the captain of the temple, who was in charge of the temple police, went personally with his officers and conducted the apostles to court.

Luke tells us that an angel opened the prison doors in the night, brought the apostles out, and told them to go and stand in the temple courts and tell the people the full message of this new life (5:19–20). But the chief priests were Sadducees (5:17); they did not believe in resurrection or angels or spirits (23:8). So doubtless they had their own rationalistic explanation of the escape. None the less for that, they were worried men, wondering what would come of this whole affair (5:24). For now there was another powerful, psychological process at work. Whether they admitted it to themselves or not, a pattern was repeating itself. Only three months ago they had set a guard over a tomb to make sure the dead body inside did not come out. And on the morning of the third day the guard reported that the body was no longer there. They had thought up their own rationalistic explanation for that as well (Matt. 28:11–15). But the parallel between that event and this present one was uncanny.

It was meant to be. It was in fact an act of mercy on God's part towards men who were determined not to repent, and who in the fury generated by the haunting memory of the crucifixion were about to be tempted to suppress the gospel by executing the apostles. It was a timely warning in advance not to add an atrocious crime to their already grievous guilt, by attempting to do the impossible. They had killed Jesus, and put a guard on his tomb. But, as Peter pointed out at Pentecost, 'it was impossible for death to keep its hold on him . . . [God had] made known to [him] the paths of life' (2:24, 28). The life that was now empowering the apostles, the life they were preaching to the crowds, was this irrepressible life of the risen Christ. They might imprison, or even kill, the apostles' bodies; they could never suppress or destroy that life. If they were determined not to repent, not to accept the Author of Life or the forgiveness and life he offered them, let them at least not add to their guilt by attempting to stop this message of life spreading to others.

The second warning was given by a member of the Sanhedrin itself, Gamaliel, a teacher of the law who was highly respected in the nation at large. Unlike the presiding high priest, the chief priests and the lay aristocrats, who were Sadducees, he was a Pharisee (5:34). He would, therefore, have believed in the doctrine and theoretical possibility of resurrection, though not (as yet, at any rate) in the particular and actual resurrection of Jesus. His advice to the Sanhedrin has been regarded by many as a cynical sitting-on-the-fence; but in so far as it went, it was good advice for men who were determined not to repent. At least it saved them from committing the atrocity of executing twelve innocent men. In that sense, therefore, Gamaliel is to be applauded. He represents what has been a majority of Jews in all the centuries, Jews who, unhappily enough, do not believe in Jesus as the Messiah, or in his resurrection, or in the salvation he offers, nor above all in his deity; but who, on the other hand, deplore his crucifixion, and oppose all persecution of people on the grounds of their faith, Christians included.

Gamaliel's advice, in brief, was this. Citing the example of two comparatively recent political rabble-rousers, who had briefly led insurrectionist movements and then had come to disaster, he argued that the Sanhedrin had no need to try to suppress this new Christian movement. If it was not of God, it would likewise come to nothing anyway. Alternatively, if this new Christian movement was of God, to attempt to suppress it would be futile. And worse: it would be a case of fighting against God (5:35–39).

The Sanhedrin were persuaded, and for the present they desisted from any idea of executing the apostles. Of course, they used their powers of discipline, flogged the apostles, and renewed their ban on preaching in the name of Jesus. But it was ineffective, indeed counter-productive. Following the instructions of the Lord Jesus (Luke 6:22–23), they rejoiced at the high honour of being counted worthy to suffer disgrace for the Name; and they went on with their preaching more vigorously and persistently than ever (5:40–42).

In the light of all this, it is a melancholy report that Paul had later to give to his Gentile converts in Thessalonica about the Jews (not in the world at large, but) of Judea – and in this context that means the leaders, particularly the Sadducean aristocracy, both priestly and lay:

> For you, brothers, became imitators of God's churches in Judaea, which are in Christ Jesus: You suffered from your own countrymen the same things those churches suffered from the Jews, who killed the Lord Jesus and the prophets and also drove us out. They displease God and are hostile to all men in their effort to keep us from speaking to the Gentiles so that they may be saved. In this way they always heap up their sins to the limit. Very shortly the wrath of God will come upon them to the uttermost. (1 Thess. 2:14–16)*

That was Paul talking within the family, so to speak, to his own converts who were suffering persecution. Two things should be set against that. First his remark to the church in Rome: 'As far as the gospel is concerned, they are enemies on your account; but as far as election is concerned, they are loved on account of the patriarchs' (Rom. 11:28). And secondly his explanation to the Jewish leaders in Rome why he was appealing to Nero Caesar: 'They [the Romans] examined me and wanted to release me, because I was not guilty of any crime deserving death. But when the Jews objected, I was compelled to appeal to Caesar – *not that I had any charge to bring against my own people*' (Acts 28:18–19).

The rest is history. The Romans destroyed the temple in AD 70. That of course did not destroy Judaism, which adapted vigorously and well to the new conditions under which it became increasingly a religion of the synagogue and the book. But with the temple gone, the Sadducean chief priests, and all the lesser priests, lost their significance and importance; and they gradually faded away.

---

*For the translation of the last sentence, which goes against that of the NIV, see C. C. Caragounis, 'Kingdom of God, Son of Man and Jesus' Self-Understanding (Part I)', *Tyndale Bulletin* 40 (1989), pp. 12–23.

Discriminating against fellow Christians: Another view of the Christian community (6:1–7)

The final item in Section One is very short, extending only from 6:1 to 6:6. Two considerations show that it is rightly to be taken as belonging to Section One. First, Luke has placed his formal division-marker at 6:7. Secondly, the topic raised in this item is germane to what has been a major topic throughout the whole of Section One; and the point it makes is necessary to complete the topic and to present it in a balanced, well-rounded way.

Item 2 was about Judas, his betrayal of Christ for money, and his field; Item 4 about the daily begging for money by the cripple; and Item 6 about Ananias and Sapphira, their lying to the Holy Spirit over money and a field. This last item also deals with the attitude of the Christian community to money and material things. It describes what they did about an abuse that arose in connection with the daily distribution of food.*

In particular the message of this item matches and complements the lesson taught by the story of the healing of the cripple. Both stories show the early Christians taking seriously their social responsibility, the one to the world around (as with the cripple) and the other to the members of the church (the daily distribution of food to the Christian widows). And both stories remind us of the all-important need to keep our social duties in their proper place and proportion, and never to allow them to usurp or eclipse the pre-eminent place and importance of the preaching of the gospel and the teaching of the Word of God.

In the story of the healing of the cripple we found the people at large quite ready to take the church's charity to relieve their poor, and the apostles ready to give not only money (if they had it) but much more besides. But when the crowd gathered to hear Peter's explanation of the miracle, he did not allow them to go away with the impression that charity to the poor and healing for the sick were the main things that Christianity was about. Quite the reverse. The main and all-important thing for Peter was the preaching of the gospel. He pointed out to the crowd that they had killed the Author of Life, and that they now needed above all other things to repent, and to believe in the Saviour, there being no other way of securing the salvation that was an absolute necessity if they were to be ready for his second coming than

---

*Some take the Greek phrase to mean not food, but money. Perhaps it implies both.

103

personal faith in Christ. To have been content to give a guilty world social relief and physical health without preaching the gospel, when its greatest and most pressing need was to be told how to get right with God and receive eternal life, would have been a very sorry distortion of true priorities. To have allowed social relief to take over to the exclusion of evangelism would have been a criminal dereliction of duty to both God and man.

The final story preaches a similar lesson; only this time in connection with the internal life of the church. It shows that the early Christians had a very vigorous and active concern for the social needs of its members. There was, in particular, a daily distribution of food to the widows. Moreover, when it was discovered that some widows were being neglected, if not positively discriminated against, the apostles advised the church to appoint efficient and spiritual men to administer the common resources in a fair and systematic way. The social needs of believers were not to be dealt with in a casual, haphazard manner. Relief work was to be properly organised.

But – and here is the major point of the story – the apostles were not prepared to administer that social relief themselves. And the reason they gave shows their urgent sense of true priorities:

> It would not be right for us to neglect the ministry of the word of God in order to wait on tables . . . Choose seven men . . . known to be full of the Spirit and wisdom. We will turn this [social] responsibility over to them and will give our attention to prayer and the ministry of the word. (6:2–4)

To press home the lesson, Luke phrases his concluding section-marker with deliberate care: 'So the word of God spread. The number of disciples in Jerusalem increased rapidly, and a large number of priests became obedient to the faith [i.e. they got converted]' (6:7).

The connection between the growth of the church and the twin activities of preaching the gospel and expounding the word was not accidental, of course; and we must let this record of the beginnings of Christianity judge us and our modern practices today. As far as the front we present to the world is concerned, many churches seem to have lost their confidence in the gospel to convert sinners and turn them into disciples of the Lord Jesus. So they concentrate solely on doing social good works, and offer the world their aid. And the world, not being aware that there is any more to Christianity than that, takes the aid, but sees no need to come to Christ for salvation; no true conversions take place, and the churches dwindle.

Similarly inside the churches. It can so easily happen that social activities become the cuckoo in the nest and virtually oust the preaching of the word and prayer. Some protest that nowadays one cannot expect congregations to put up with sermons that seriously and systematically expound the word of God; one must give them lighter and more 'relevant' fare. That may be true. But if it is, does not that suggest that they are not disciples in the Lukan and apostolic sense of the term at all? And if the churches find the word of God an intolerable bore, how can they expect the world to listen when they preach it? And if the word of God is not preached and does not spread, how will the number of the disciples increase at all, let alone rapidly?*

*The following are recommended for further reading on some of the topics raised in Section One. On miracles: C. S. Lewis, 'Miracles' and 'Religion and Science' in *God in the Dock* (London: Collins Fount, 1979), pp. 11–26, 46–50. On the ascension as both a literal, historical event and a symbolic gesture: B. M. Metzger, 'The Ascension of Jesus Christ' in *Historical and Literary Studies* (Leiden: E. J. Brill, 1968), pp. 77–87; Peter Toon, 'Historical Perspectives on the Doctrine of Christ's Ascension', *Bibliotheca Sacra* (1983), pp. 195–205, 291–301; (1984), pp. 16–27, 112–19. On the attitude of true modern science to the events of the resurrection and ascension, as distinct from the attitude of liberal scholarship and its now outmoded demythologisation: T. F. Torrance, *Space, Time and Resurrection* (Edinburgh: Handsel Press, 1976); *The Ground and Grammar of Theology* (Belfast: Christian Journals Ltd, 1980), pp. 17–20; *Theological Science* (Oxford: Oxford University Press, 1978), pp. 334–7.

Section Two

Christianity's Worship and Witness
(6:8–9:31)

Section Two
Christianity's Worship and Witness (6:8–9:31)

PRELIMINARY OBSERVATIONS

We come now to the second parting of the ways between Christianity and Judaism. The issues over which they parted this time were complex; but they may perhaps be summed up, not too inaccurately, under the heading 'Christianity's Worship and Witness'.

There are four major movements in Section Two. The first covers the long story of the prosecution, defence, and martyrdom of Stephen (6:8–8:3). The prosecution's case against him concerned his attitude to, and remarks about, the temple (6:13–14).

The second movement relates the evangelisation of Samaria (8:4–25). Now it is the fact that the Samaritans and the Jews disliked each other intensely, largely because of their differing views about worship and the temple. As the Samaritan woman at Sychar remarked to the Lord Jesus: 'Our fathers worshipped on this mountain, but you Jews claim that the place where we must worship is in Jerusalem' (John 4:20).

Questions of worship, then: in the first story, what Christianity had to say about Judaism's orthodox temple and its worship centred in Jerusalem; in the second, what Christianity had to say to the nonconformist Samaritans who, though they accepted the books of Moses as God's word, rejected the temple at Jerusalem, and worshipped on Mount Gerizim in Samaria.

The third movement presents the story of the conversion of an Ethiopian who had been to Jerusalem to worship, and on his way home was reading a copy of the prophecy of Isaiah (8:26–40). The temple at Jerusalem was not only the centre of worship for Jews; it also exercised a powerful witness to the Gentile nations around. The Ethiopian was one of many intelligent men and women in the ancient world who, dissatisfied with the crude polytheism of paganism, found themselves impressed by the imageless temple at Jerusalem, and its witness to the one true God. What Christianity would say to such people more than Judaism could, will emerge in the course of this story.

The fourth and final movement tells of the conversion of Saul of Tarsus (9:1–31). One feature catches the eye. In sending a certain Ananias to tell the now blinded Saul what to do, the Lord explained to Ananias: 'This man is my chosen instrument to carry my name before the Gentiles and their kings and before the people of Israel' (9:15). So this story too is concerned with the witness of Israel to the Gentiles.

As we have just observed, Judaism had for centuries maintained a witness for God in the world. This was particularly so in the Hellenistic and Roman periods, when thousands of expatriate Jews lived and worked in the many countries surrounding the Mediterranean, and some even rose to high office.* But the missionary movement that erupted out of Israel in the form of Christianity has proved unique in its size, vigour and effectiveness. Much of that missionary movement was spearheaded by this Saul of Tarsus; and, as we read his story, we shall want to know what it was that so radically changed him from a relentless persecutor of Christians, striving to stop Christianity spreading beyond the borders of Israel (9:2), into the biggest missionary to the world to come out of Israel.

Let us now consider the more obvious connections of thought between the four stories in this section.

In the first story, Saul of Tarsus joins in taking responsibility for Stephen's execution: 'the witnesses laid their clothes at the feet of a young man named Saul' (7:58). In the last story that same Saul is converted, never to persecute anyone again, and begins to preach the faith he previously tried to destroy.

But there is another similarity, altogether more significant. At the beginning of the first story (7:2–3), Stephen remarks: 'The God of glory appeared to our father Abraham'. At the beginning of the fourth (9:3), Luke records that 'suddenly a light from heaven flashed around him [Saul of Tarsus]'. The similarity in word and idea is obvious; but consider its significance. The appearance of the God of glory to Abraham was the fundamental spiritual experience behind the birth of the Hebrew nation. It

*Like Onias IV and Dositheus under Cleopatra II of Egypt, and Chelkias and Ananias under Cleopatra III.

would be impossible to exaggerate its importance. Its effects are with us still. But notice the direction of the movement it initiated: it brought Abraham out of the Gentiles to found a nation that would thereafter be distinct from all others, unique in its testimony to the one true God and in its protest against Gentile polytheism. ' "Leave your country and your people," God said, "and go to the land I will show you" ' (7:3).

When the light from heaven shone round about Saul, however, it began another phase in Israel's history, no less important or significant. But it took Saul, however, in exactly the opposite direction from Abraham. A Hebrew of the Hebrews (Phil. 3:5), he was sent out of the bosom of the Hebrew nation and back among the Gentiles, 'to carry [God's] name before the Gentiles and their kings' (9:15).

At first sight it might seem that the second movement contradicted the first. But that is not so. The second movement fulfilled and completed the first. When God called Abraham out of the Gentiles, it was with the purpose that in him all the families of the earth should eventually be blessed (Gen. 12:3). With the coming of the Messiah and the conversion and commissioning of Saul of Tarsus, God's original purpose in calling Abraham out of the Gentiles was going to find fulfilment in hitherto unmatched, worldwide blessing to the Gentiles. Through Saul of Tarsus, his preaching and his writings, uncountable millions of Gentiles over the course of the centuries would come to faith in the God of Abraham.

Both movements, of course, were necessary to the evangelisation of the world. God's call of Abraham out of the Gentile world did not imply that from that moment on everyone outside of Abraham and his family were abandoned by God and permanently lost. On the other hand, mankind's downward trend away from original knowledge of the one true God towards a polytheistic and idolatrous interpretation of the world, was by that time practically universal. The only way to re-establish the knowledge of the true God in the earth, and the moral behaviour demanded by that knowledge, was for God to start again with one man, to reveal himself to him, to set up a special relationship between himself and that man's descendants, and to build from that one man a whole nation that as a nation should stand conspicuously for faith in the one and only God.

It proved difficult to do; for as Israel's own prophets show, the nation was forever compromising, and departing from, its knowledge of God and lapsing into both the idolatry and the immoralities of the Gentile nations. But unless it could be done, God's further revelation through Christ could scarce have been made. What use preaching that Jesus is the Son of God to a world whose concept of God himself was everywhere false and perverse? But the battle was eventually won, and won permanently. After Israel's return from the Exile the nation as a nation never slipped back into idolatry again. Large numbers of Jews today may be agnostics or even atheists; but since the Exile the temple, while it lasted, remained, and the Jewish synagogue all over the world still remains, uncompromising in its monotheistic faith.*

Successful, then, as that first move was with Israel, it required another tactic to plant knowledge of the true God, and personal faith in him, throughout the Gentile nations of the world. So there came the time when the same God of glory had to appear to another Hebrew and to send him out, in a reverse process, from Israel to the nations. Not to convert Gentiles and bring them into the separate nation, Israel – that had, in a small way, been going on for centuries. But to establish the knowledge of the one true God among the Gentiles themselves. And God did this when the light from heaven shone round about Saul of Tarsus and he sent him out as the apostle to the Gentiles. Since then, directly or indirectly, through his preaching and writing, multi-millions of Gentiles have abandoned their idolatry. They have not become Jews, or members of the nation of Israel or of the synagogue; but they have come to believe in the God of Abraham, Isaac and Jacob, the one and only true God.

What happened at the macro-level of history ought to be true at the micro-level of our own personal experience. The God of glory appeared to Abraham and made him a pilgrim. The light from heaven shone round about Saul and made him a missionary. It is doubtful if we shall ever be true missionaries if we do not first become pilgrims. It was not a series of prohibitions and commands to abstinence that drove Abraham out of the Gentiles. It was the revelation to him of the superlative glory of the living God and the vision of the eternal city God promised him. This was the attraction that made him leave his native land and 'confess that he was a stranger and a pilgrim on the earth' (see Heb. 11:13, AV). How can we witness effectively to our modern pagan idolatrous world unless a similar sight of the glory of God

---

*Apart, that is, from the short lapse by some high priests under Antiochus Epiphanes.

112

has first broken within us that 'love of the world' which 'is not of the Father' (1 John 2:16, AV) and given us greater goals and a different lifestyle from those whose vision is earthbound?

But suppose we share Abraham's vision, and in heart have left the world as he did. That is not enough; like Paul we must become missionaries and go back into the world to make God known. We scarce can claim that the light from heaven has shone around us, unless it imbues us, in some degree at least, with the same compassion for those who sit in darkness as it did Paul.

But to return to the task in hand. We have picked out connections of thought between Movements 1 and 4: here, now, is one between Movements 2 and 3.

Luke's account of Philip's evangelisation of Samaria gives great prominence to a certain Simon who on the strength of sorcery and magic gave himself out to be someone great. An obvious religious charlatan if ever there was one! Yes, but the point is that the local Samaritans of all classes had been taken in by Simon and were making tremendous claims for him. He was, they said, the power of God called 'The Great Power'. To Jews, whether Christian or non-Christian, such claims would have seemed blasphemous. But then, of course, to the majority of Jews, then as now, the Christian claim that Jesus is the Son of God seemed, and still seems, equally blasphemous – if not more so. How can we be sure that the early Christians were not as mistaken in their claims for Jesus as the Samaritans were in their claims for Simon? How can we be sure that Jesus was not, as some Jewish scholars have maintained, simply one among several 'wonder-working' rabbis known to Judaism, whose reputation has been exaggerated by his Gentile followers to the point of blasphemy?

One answer to this question is to be found in Movement 3. There Philip preaches Jesus to the Ethiopian as the long-promised Suffering Servant of Isaiah 53 (8:32–35). Christians certainly believe that Jesus performed miracles, and highly significant miracles at that. Their faith is founded on the supreme miracle of his resurrection. But it remains true to say that it is not Jesus the miracle-worker that has won the hearts of the millions of his followers. It has been Jesus, God's Suffering Servant, the Lamb led to slaughter and silent before the shearer, the crucified Christ who was wounded for our transgressions, who was bruised for our iniquities and by whose stripes we were healed. Between him and the Simons of this world there is no comparison.

There follows a short table of selected contents which may help to keep the section as a whole before our mind's eye and to suggest how the four movements are related to each other and to the whole.

SECTION TWO: CHRISTIANITY'S WORSHIP AND WITNESS (6:8–9:31)

I. THE DEATH OF STEPHEN; SAUL'S PERSECUTION OF THE CHURCH (6:8–8:3)

1. 'The God of glory appeared to our father Abraham . . . "Leave your country and your people," God said' (7:2–3)

2. The Lord in the bush that burned but was not consumed. The Lord identifies himself to Moses as 'the God of your fathers . . . I have indeed seen the oppression of my people . . . and have come down to set them free . . .' (7:30–34)

3. '[Stephen] saw the glory of God, and Jesus standing at the right hand of God. "Look," he said, "I see . . . the Son of Man standing at the right hand of God." At this they . . . began to stone him' (7:55–58)

II. PHILIP AND THE CONVERSION OF SAMARITANS (8:4–25)

1. Samaria and the sorceries of Simon (8:9)

2. 'He [Simon] boasted that he was someone great . . . and all the people gave him their attention and exclaimed "This man is the divine power known as the Great Power"' (8:9–10)

III. PHILIP AND THE CONVERSION OF AN ETHIOPIAN (8:26–40)

1. Jerusalem and its holy scriptures (8:27–28)

2. '"He was led like a sheep to the slaughter, and as a lamb before the shearer is silent, so he did not open his mouth. In his humiliation he was deprived of justice." . . . The eunuch asked Philip, "Tell me . . . who is the prophet talking about. . . ?" Then Philip . . . told him the good news about Jesus' (8:32–35)

IV. THE CONVERSION OF SAUL THE PERSECUTOR (9:1–31)

1. Saul persecutes the disciples; the Lord identifies himself to him as 'Jesus, whom you are persecuting' (9:4–5)

2. 'A light from heaven flashed around him' (9:3); 'This man is . . . to carry my name before the Gentiles . . .' (9:15)

114

3. 'At once he began to preach . . . that Jesus is the Son of God. [And] . . . the Jews conspired to kill him' (9:20–23)

THE MOVEMENTS

MOVEMENT 1: The Gospel and Judaism's Orthodox Worship (6:8–8:3)

The tide of new life which surged through Section One sweeps on unabated in Section Two. Before its few chapters end, the gospel will have spread from Judea to Samaria; the first light of Christian dawn will have touched Ethiopia; and a special apostle will have been converted, commissioned and specially prepared to take the gospel to all levels of the Gentile world at large.

It is characteristic of life not only to spread but to mature, to progress: from childhood to manhood; from playing with dolls to being a real mother or a nurse; from school lessons to life's adult activities and responsibilities; from driving horse-drawn carriages to inventing steam-trains, motor cars, airliners and space capsules.

And so it is with spiritual life. Israel had once been a child (Hos. 1:1), historically and spiritually a new phenomenon in the world. God's love for his child in its infant days had been intense, strong and compassionate. He had broken its slavery to Egypt, given it independence and an inheritance of its own in Canaan. Year by year thereafter, Israel had gratefully remembered the Passover sacrifice that first effected its freedom. Annually it had celebrated its enjoyment of its new inheritance at the festivals of Firstfruits and Pentecost. Then, advancing from its childhood of nomadic wandering in the desert, through its teenage conquest and development of its inheritance in Canaan, it had marked its arrival at the early manhood of monarchical and imperial glory by superseding its portable desert shrine with a permanent, majestic, stone-built temple.

Now, with the coming of the Messiah, the Son of God, the time had arrived to move on into full adult maturity. The lambs of a thousand Passovers had been overtaken by the sacrifice of the Lamb of God himself; Pentecost's humble cakes of newly ground corn had been surpassed by the coming of the Spirit of God, the firstfruits of a heavenly inheritance. Now a shadow was beginning to creep up on the glorious stone-built temple at Jerusalem: it

115

was about to be eclipsed by the brighter glory of an infinitely superior dwelling-place of God.

Unhealthy change simply denies, betrays and destroys the good of the past and present; true change fulfils that good and replaces it with something better. It is right to oppose unhealthy change; but to resent and fight true change, as many Jews did, is to turn the past and present good into an evil. The boy who cannot or will not leave his toys and go to school, turns his playing with toys into an expression of human disaster.

So it was with the high priest and the chief priests, the 'builders' of the temple at Jerusalem. When God sent his Son to be the foundation-stone of a new, universal, spiritual temple, the builders tried to destroy him; and Peter had to inform them that the stone which they had rejected, God had now installed as the chief cornerstone of his new temple (4:11). Then came Stephen, and he warned those same priests that in rejecting Christ in favour of their traditional temple they were clinging to a system of worship which was fast becoming obsolete and would eventually pass away. And they murdered him for saying so, such was their antipathy to change.

Stephen thus became, after our Lord, the first Christian martyr. Now normally people do not allow themselves to be martyred except for truths or principles which they hold to be more important than life itself; and Stephen died for the difference between Judaism's approach to God and Christianity's.

Stephen, of course, was not the only one among his contemporaries to suggest that there was something unsatisfactory about Israel's worship in the temple of Jerusalem. The very strict religious community of Jews at Qumran, on the shores of the Dead Sea, had long since withdrawn from all participation in the temple services. 'For the sectaries,' says Geza Vermes, 'the temple at Jerusalem was a place of abomination; its precincts were considered polluted, its priests wicked, and the liturgical calendar prevailing there unlawful.'* They were for the time being, therefore, unable conscientiously to take part in the temple worship as currently conducted. For all that, their attitude to the temple was very different from Stephen's. They did not object to the temple and its worship in and of itself, but only to the prevailing abuses. Their hope was that one day the worship in the

---

*Geza Vermes, 'Dead Sea Scrolls', *The Interpreter's Dictionary of the Bible*, Supplementary Volume (Nashville: Abingdon, 1976), p. 215b.

temple would return to its original purity and conform once more to the Old Testament's regulations as they understood them. When that happened, as they were sure it would eventually, they would gladly take part in it again.

The early Christians, by contrast, were at first more orthodox than the people of Qumran. They happily continued going to the temple and taking part in its services (Luke 24:52–53; Acts 2:46–3:1). But then came Stephen, and he began to voice ideas which when full-grown would lead his fellow Christians to abandon the temple, its priesthood, its sacrifices and its rituals completely. He did not complain, like the men of Qumran, that the temple and its services had become unscriptural and needed to be reformed: he asserted that they had become obsolete and would soon disappear altogether. For such revolutionary and (to orthodox Jewry of the time) offensive ideas, he was presently brought before his nation's supreme council, accused, condemned and executed.

The particular charges brought against Stephen were: 'This fellow never stops speaking against this holy place and against the law. For we have heard him say that this Jesus of Nazareth will destroy this place and change the customs Moses handed down to us' (6:13–14). On the basis of these particular charges the prosecution then argued the general charge that Stephen was guilty of speaking 'words of blasphemy against Moses and against God' (6:11). Needless to say, this general charge was very serious: if proved, it carried a mandatory death sentence (Lev. 24:16). Luke advises us (6:11, 13) that the particular charges were a distortion of the facts, and that the witnesses put forward to support them were corrupt. We could almost guess as much ourselves from our reading of the four Gospels. Nowhere is Christ recorded as having said that he himself would physically destroy the temple at Jerusalem; and it is most unlikely that Stephen would ever have said he would.*

On the other hand, it is significant that nowhere in all his long speech (at least, in what Luke has recorded of that speech) did

---

*What Christ did say, of course, was that because of Israel's official rejection of their God-appointed Messiah, and their persistence in that rejection in spite of his resurrection and ascension, God would allow Israel's enemies to destroy both the city of Jerusalem and the temple (Matt. 24). There was nothing inherently blasphemous in saying that. Jeremiah in his day had told his contemporaries that God would allow the temple to be destroyed because of their sins. And it happened, under Nebuchadnezzar. Jeremiah did not of course say that he (Jeremiah) would destroy the temple; nor did Christ.

Stephen attempt to explain that he had never said, in the sense they intended, that Jesus would physically destroy the temple. The likelihood is that he did not think it worth his while: for the other part of the charge was true. He had in fact said that Jesus of Nazareth would change – indeed had changed – the customs Moses had handed down to the nation. And that would have sounded equally blasphemous to the council when they first heard it. They believed that Moses had received from God the customs which he had in turn handed down to them; and they further believed that the Old Testament scriptures in which those customs were recorded were written under direct inspiration of God. To say that Jesus Christ had changed, or would change, those customs would seem to the council self-evidently blasphemous; and it would have to be the main thrust of Stephen's speech to demonstrate from those same Old Testament scriptures that it was not blasphemous, either against God or against Moses, to say such a thing.

But questions arise. What made Stephen think in the first place that the Lord Jesus had changed, or would change, Moses' directions regarding the temple and man's approach to God? And what were the changes? And why, when he saw how bitterly his fellow Jews resented it, did he persist in talking about them? And why, when he was going to be condemned, did he think these changes so important that he preferred to die rather than recant?

The background to Stephen's thought and testimony

To understand what Stephen thought and said on these matters, it is no use our consulting his speech; for there, as we have said, he did not attempt to explain what changes Christ had made and would make; he was only concerned to show that it was not blasphemy to say that changes would and must be made. For reconstructing Stephen's own thought we must go elsewhere. Three main sources are available.

First, his own experience of Christ; secondly, what he would have learned from the apostles and the other Palestinian believers about the statements our Lord had made during his earthly ministry regarding the temple and regarding his death, resurrection and ascension; and thirdly, the much later letter to the Hebrews. Whoever the writer of that letter was, he seems, like Stephen, to have been a Hellenist, and, as Professor W. Manson has pointed out, to have developed further the ideas which Stephen first expressed.*

Stephen's experience of forgiveness

First, then, would have been Stephen's personal experience of forgiveness through Jesus Christ.

We do not know when Stephen first came to faith in Jesus as the Christ, or from whose lips he first heard the gospel. But if Acts is any guide, every sermon he is likely to have heard would have followed the same basic pattern: a statement of the facts of Christ's life (i.e., his crucifixion, resurrection and ascension), marking him out as Lord and Messiah. And then the offer of complete forgiveness and the gift of the Holy Spirit for all who truly repented and put their faith in the crucified, risen and glorified Jesus (2:38; 3:19; 10:42–43; 13:38–39). Upon believing, then, he would have received forgiveness and have known the joy and wonder of it. He would have felt a sense of acceptance with God pervade his heart as the Holy Spirit did within him what the Holy Spirit is sent to do: 'to pour out in our hearts the love of God for us' (Rom. 5:5).

This for Stephen was something completely new. Of course, as a devout Jew, he would have known about and would have experienced forgiveness before. But never before in all his days had forgiveness been offered him through believing in a man who had actually lived on this earth. Nowhere in all its pages had the Old Testament assured him that if only he believed in, say, Moses, or Elijah, he would receive forgiveness of sins. But the forgiveness he now enjoyed not only came to him *after* he believed in Jesus, or even simply *because* he believed in Jesus: it came to him *through* Jesus (Acts 4:30; 10:43; 13:39), because, as he would have been told, Jesus as the Son of Man had authority personally to dispense forgiveness of sins, and that authority had been confirmed by his resurrection (Luke 7:48–49; Acts 4:30).

And then Stephen would very soon have learned that forgiveness came through Christ in another sense. Luke tells us that from the very first the early Christians 'continued . . . in the breaking of bread' (Acts 2:42). Luke must mean more than that they ate their daily meals: what else had they done even before

---

*W. Manson, *The Epistle to the Hebrews* (London, 1951), chapter 2, 'Stephen and the World-Mission of Christianity'.

119

they became Christians? Luke means that they regularly observed the Lord's Supper; and Stephen would have joined in as soon as he was converted. There he would have heard recalled time after time the words of the Lord Jesus: 'Take and eat; this is my body . . . This is my blood of the covenant, which is poured out for many for the forgiveness of sins' (Matt. 26:26, 28).

And when Stephen asked, as he surely did, what Christ meant by saying 'This is my blood of the covenant', the apostles would have told him what they subsequently told Luke (Luke 22:20), that the covenant in question was the new covenant which God had promised through the prophet Jeremiah (Jer. 31:31–34). Stephen had a fine sense of history: that much we gather from his subsequent speech. It is impossible that he could constantly have heard this reference to the new covenant without thinking long and hard about its implications. In the ancient world in general, and in Old Testament practice in particular, covenants had to be ratified by the shedding of the blood of the covenant sacrifices. The covenant that God had made through Moses' mediation had so been ratified (Exod. 24:5–8). It was to be expected that the new covenant would have to be similarly ratified. In the Lord's Supper Christ was perpetually reminding Stephen that it was the blood of his sacrifice of himself at Calvary that ratified the new covenant.

Inevitably the question would have arisen, sooner or later: How was this new covenant related to the old one? The later writer to the Hebrews, we know, saw the relation clearly and expressed it succinctly: 'By calling this covenant "new", he has made the first one obsolete; and what is obsolete and ageing will soon disappear' (Heb. 8:13). But that same writer is at pains to point out that he drew his conclusion from the explicit statements of the Old Testament text. There God himself says that the new covenant will *not be like the old* because the old could not achieve satisfactory results (Jer. 31:32), and must be replaced by a new and different covenant. Stephen, surely, was no less perceptive than the writer to the Hebrews. He too would have seen that there would be no point in having a new covenant if the old were still satisfactory. Nor could the people of God be related to God under the terms of two different covenants simultaneously. And therefore he would have concluded, like the writer to the Hebrews, that the old covenant had been abrogated. Jesus Christ had changed the customs handed down by Moses. He was the mediator of a better covenant founded on better promises (Heb. 7:22; 8:6). And Stephen would have said so publicly, and have gone on saying so in spite of bitter opposition, and at the eventual cost of his life, because this was no minor detail of Christian thinking. Here was the very heart of the Christian gospel: the terms and conditions of forgiveness and acceptance with God under the new covenant through the sacrifice of Jesus Christ our Lord.

Christ and the new kind of temple

But Stephen would also have heard from the apostles and the Palestinian believers of Christ's actions and statements regarding the temple at Jerusalem. His cleansing of the temple was famous. Indeed, when the false witnesses at his trial accused Christ of saying (and were now accusing Stephen of repeating) 'I am able to destroy the temple of God and rebuild it in three days' (Matt. 26:61), they were presumably giving their mistaken version of something he had actually said on that occasion: 'Destroy this temple, and I will raise it again in three days' (John 2:19). John tells us that even Christ's disciples did not understand at the time that he was referring to the temple of his body; but that after his resurrection they did (John 2:22). And so of course would Stephen. He would have seen first that Christ announced a new kind of temple; and secondly that he did not merely say that as long as he lived on earth his body would form God a temple. He said that the temple of his body would be raised from the dead and 'rebuilt' as a temple. Automatically this would have reorientated Stephen's approach to God. As a devout Jew he would always have believed in God's omnipresence, as expressed for instance in the magnificent Psalm 139. But for centuries God had provided Israel with a building, a temple, a place on earth where his presence could be located in a special way, a place 'which the Lord had chosen to put his name there' (Deut. 16:2), where people could come to seek him and to find him. Millions throughout the generations had come, had sought and found. Throughout our Lord's life on earth, however, his body had formed a temple where people could find God far more directly than in the temple. And now, since his resurrection and ascension, the living, exalted Lord Jesus would continue to be the 'place' in God's universe where people might find God: Stephen would have proved it true in his own experience. When he wanted to approach God, he would naturally go direct to the living Christ. He would no longer feel that to get as near to God as possible the place to go was the temple at Jerusalem.

Truth to tell, he had never been able to get very near to God in the temple. The presence of God was located in its innermost shrine, the Most Holy Place. The laity were never allowed anywhere near it. They were not even allowed into the first division of the temple, let alone into the Most Holy Place. The priests were allowed in the first division; but even they were never allowed to enter the Most Holy Place. The only exception was that once a year, on the day of Atonement, the high priest was allowed to draw aside the great veil that normally barred access into the Most Holy Place, to enter and stand in the immediate presence of God; and there he would sprinkle the ark and the propitiatory that formed God's earthly throne with the blood of the nation's sacrifice for sin. It was, to be sure, a very solemn moment for the people who were gathered outside in the court; for the high priest was acting as their representative. If God accepted him, and he came out alive, it meant that God had accepted them, at least for the next year until the next day of Atonement. But however real and deep their sense of acceptance with God was, it never gave them freedom to come near him, or to enter the Most Holy Place. Always the door of the temple remained closed to them; always the great veil barred access into the presence of God.

Stephen, of course, would have well understood the function and significance of that veil. And therefore he would have been more than interested when the Palestinian believers told him that the moment Christ died at Calvary the veil in the temple was torn in two, from the top to the bottom (Matt. 27:51). And he would have been filled with joy and worship to hear from the apostles that after Christ had died and poured out his blood for their sins, and risen again, they had seen him bodily ascend and enter not the innermost room in the temple in Jerusalem, but into heaven itself. He had led them out as far as Bethany, and had raised his hands like a priest to bless them. It was as he stood there in that priestly attitude that he was taken up into heaven into the very presence of God. Indeed, at the end of his speech Stephen was given to see with his physical eyes what he knew by faith to be the fact: the Son of Man standing at the right hand of God (7:56) and assuring him of welcome in the Father's presence. Long since, Stephen would have been living in the enjoyment of that welcome. He would have known instinctively that the risen Christ who was blessing his people at the very moment of his ascension had not ceased to bless them thereafter. He had neither disowned nor forgotten them. He had entered the presence of God as their Saviour and representative, just as Israel's high priest had entered that Most Holy Place in the temple as Israel's representative. His acceptance with God as his people's representative was obviously complete and permanent. And so was theirs! Through Christ they now had unimpeded 'access to the Father by one Spirit', as Paul was later to express it (Eph. 2:18). Through the way that Christ had inaugurated, they were invited to enter in spirit even now into the Most Holy Place in heaven, as the writer to the Hebrews would eventually put it (Heb. 10:19–22), and were urged boldly to take up the invitation. Stephen's thought may not have been so fully worked out as that of Paul or that of the writer to the Hebrews. But he would have enjoyed as much as they did that immeasurable blessing that is the birthright of every believer in Christ: the assurance here and now of complete acceptance in the presence of God.

Knowing, as he did from Christ's prophecy, that the temple at Jerusalem would one day be destroyed would cause Stephen little grief. He was already rapidly losing interest in the temple. For centuries it had served Israel well as a God-given 'parable', as a 'copy of things in the heavens', a 'shadow of the good things to come' (Heb. 9:9; 8:5; 10:1). With the arrival through Christ of these 'good things', the mere shadow would no longer be necessary. People like Stephen who were aware that the Son of God had died for their sins, had ascended into heaven and was at that very moment standing as their representative and High Priest before God, would find it difficult to be interested much longer in watching a merely human high priest – however ornate his vestments and however impressive his ritual – draw aside a mere curtain and disappear for a few minutes each year into the back room of a building here on earth.

In one sense, then, it was not true to say that Jesus Christ would destroy the temple; and Stephen had never said he would. In another sense Christ had already destroyed the temple. The Christians did not all perceive it at once; and God did not attempt to hurry them. But as and when they came to understand more fully the redemption that Christ had obtained for them, God would eventually call on them through his inspired servants like the writer to the Hebrews to abandon the temple. To perpetuate for ever a system in which the Most Holy Place of God's presence could be entered only once a year, and that not by the ordinary people but only by a high priest, when in fact all God's believing people without distinction are welcome to enter the presence of God in heaven every day of their lives – that would be to obscure, if not to deny, the gospel. To continue offering sacrifices to obtain

123

forgiveness of sins when Christ has already obtained eternal redemption and complete forgiveness for us by his completed sacrifice at Calvary – that would be to fill people's minds with confusion over the question of their acceptance with God. To adhere to the terms and provisions of the old covenant when God has abrogated them and has introduced the new covenant – that would be to frustrate the Almighty himself.

The early Christians, filled as they were with reverence for the age-long traditions of the temple, would need, and would be given, time to grasp these things and to work out their implications. But Stephen had already grasped them. For the sake of the gospel, for the sake of people's understanding and enjoyment of salvation, he spoke out, plainly, repeatedly, uncompromisingly, and with the evident power of the Holy Spirit (6:10), until stones crushed the breath out of his body.

Stephen's speech before the Sanhedrin

It may perhaps be objected that if Stephen had really had in mind all that we have suggested in the preceding pages, he must have mentioned some of it at least in the course of his speech in order to explain to the Sanhedrin why and in what particulars he held that Jesus Christ had changed the customs handed down by Moses. And it might further be argued that the fact that he makes practically no mention of these things in his speech shows that he did not have these things in mind, and that our reconstruction of his thinking is, if not false, at least irrelevant.

But to argue so would be to misunderstand the purpose of his speech and to misconstrue its argument. The Sanhedrin would not have been interested in hearing from Stephen how and why he thought that Jesus Christ had made all the Mosaic institutions of the temple, priesthood and sacrifices obsolete. The very suggestion that Jesus would render the temple obsolete – never mind how or for what reasons – was to them a blasphemy against God and a repudiation of God's self-revelation to and through Moses. Stephen therefore had to show that it was not blasphemy; and he showed it by relating the history and character of God's self-revelation as given by that undisputed authority, the Old Testament itself. We may summarise the various elements in his argument as follows.

First, the Old Testament shows that God's self-revelation to Israel was not made all at once, but was given at different times through different people: to and through Abraham in Haran

(7:2–3), then later in Canaan (7:5–8); to and through Joseph (7:9–14); to and through Moses, first in Egypt (7:17–29), then in the land of Midian (7:30–35), then in Egypt again (7:36), then in the desert and in particular at Sinai (7:36–38, 44); through Joshua, David and Solomon (7:45–47); later through Amos (7:42–43), through Isaiah (7:48–49) and all the other prophets (7:52); and finally through the Messiah himself (7:52). The self-revelation of God, then, was not a static but a progressive thing. On the other hand, while this progressive revelation was given through many people and at different times, it was the same God who spoke and acted and so revealed himself.*

Secondly, as each epoch-making stage in the revelation of God's glory to his people produced in them a loving response of faith and obedience, it initiated new movement, new advance, new and more extensive experience of God's provision for their redemption.

The revelation of God's glory to Abraham moved him to leave the paganism of both Mesopotamia and Haran, and in faith to follow God's guidance till he arrived in Canaan, where the promised seed was given and the new nation born (7:2–8).

The later revelation of God in a vision to Jacob (Gen. 46:2–4) led him in the opposite direction, to leave Canaan and take his extended family of the patriarchs and their children down to Egypt, where they might experience in a wonderful way how God had anticipated their need. He had sent Joseph in advance to be their saviour from famine, to preserve and foster them, and to provide suitable conditions in which the extended family might develop into a tribe and then into a nation (7:9–16).

Even so, in taking Jacob and the patriarchs to Egypt, it was never God's intention that they should stay there. According to the plan he had previously announced to Abraham (7:6–7), the time came when the nation had to be on the move once more. Anticipating their need, God in his providence had Moses preserved and given the best education available in Egypt (7:19–22), and then proceeded to reveal himself to him, first at the burning bush and then at Mount Sinai, in order to equip him to deliver Israel from Egypt and bring them through the desert to Canaan (7:30–38).

---

*cf. Hebrews 1:1–2, 'In the past God spoke to our forefathers through the prophets at many times and in various ways, but in these last days he has spoken to us by his Son . . .'

Now his revelation to Israel through Moses was far more extensive than his revelation to Abraham, Isaac, Jacob and Joseph had been; and the experience of the nation had been correspondingly greater. At this point, therefore, God was able to take Israel a very significant stage further and begin to teach them for the first time what it meant to have God dwelling among them, and themselves to dwell with God. Moses was instructed to build the tabernacle (7:44). Graced with the glory of God's presence (see Exod. 40:34–38), tended by God-given ritual and enriched with costly symbolic furniture and instructive ceremonies, it was none the less only a first stage in this aspect of God's self-revelation. Later on, when the conquest of Canaan begun by Joshua was finally completed by David, God gave David plans, which his son Solomon executed, for the replacement of the portable tabernacle with a much more elaborate and glorious permanent, stone-built temple (7:45–47). One has only to read the appropriate chapters in 1 Kings and 2 Chronicles to realise the vastly enhanced concept of the glory of God and of the magnificence of his salvation that the building of this temple gave to Israel.

Even so, this was not God's final word on the subject, nor was a glorious stone-built temple the ideal temple God had in mind. It could not be. By definition, 'the Most High does not live in houses made by men' (7:48). Looking beyond the destruction of Solomon's temple, therefore, and beyond the time when those who returned from the Exile would rebuild the temple, God sought through Isaiah the prophet to stretch his people's minds by the full revelation of his greatness as the transcendent Lord Creator, and so to get them to consider the only kind of temple that would finally satisfy him: 'Heaven is my throne, and the earth is my footstool. What kind of house will you build for me?', says the Lord. 'Or where will my resting place be? Has not my hand made all these things?' (7:49–50). Even Herod's temple, for all its hitherto unparalleled (in Israel) magnificence, must become obsolete and be abandoned in favour of God's ideal tabernacle, 'the true tabernacle set up by the Lord, not by man . . . the greater and more perfect tabernacle that is not man-made, that is to say, not a part of this creation' (Heb. 8:2; 9:11).

This, then, was not anti-Jewish Christian propaganda. It could not even be rightly regarded as a sectarian view within Judaism. This was the view of the future long since advanced by the classical prophet Isaiah, and grasped by the more enlightened in Israel. Judaism, when true to the Old Testament, had always understood that God's revelation of himself was progressive, and that he could not allow his people permanently to rest and settle down short of the ideal.

But in the third place, Stephen's exposition of Old Testament history made it clear that while God's self-revelation was progressive, it was never erratic, inconsistent or arbitrary. Throughout all the apparent changes in the direction of his leading of Israel, God had always adhered to his original purpose. The self-revelation of his glory to Abraham, and through Abraham to the nation, was designed to call forth from them their response of obedience and worship. If having first led Abraham out of Mesopotamia to Canaan, God then informed him that his descendants would have to leave Canaan and go and live in Egypt for several centuries, God was not acting inconsistently, nor had he abandoned or modified his original purpose. At the end of his briefing of Abraham, God informed him that 'afterwards they will come out of that country and worship me in this place' (7:6–7; Gen. 15:13–14). The centuries in Egypt away from the promised land were not an abandonment of the purpose but a stepping-stone to its fulfilment at a higher level. The revelation of God's glory to Abraham had brought him out of Mesopotamia into Canaan, there to experience occasions of profound worship of God (Gen. 12:7, 8; 13:4, 18; 22:5, 9). As a result of the revelation of God's glory to Moses at the burning bush and at Sinai, the whole nation of Israel would leave Egypt and eventually come into Canaan, there to worship God as Abraham had done. But while Abraham never possessed any territory in Canaan, and simply erected his own family altar wherever he happened at the moment to have his tent, when Israel eventually entered Canaan they would bring with them the elaborate tabernacle, and having taken possession of the land would establish the tabernacle and its altar as a permanent centre for the whole nation's worship.*

Similarly, when after the provision of the tabernacle of Moses and the even more glorious temple of Solomon God announced through Isaiah that no earthly building could adequately serve the transcendent Creator as a dwelling-place, God was not abandoning the idea of his dwelling with men or of their dwelling with him. In the tabernacle and temple, not only did God dwell among men in some sense, but, as we have earlier remembered, once a

---

*The words 'of that country and worship me in this place' at the end of 7:7 are not found in Genesis 15:14. Stephen has added them after the model of God's word to Moses in Exodus 3:12, to make the point that even in Abraham's time God was looking forward to and beyond Moses, to the fulfilment of the purpose he had had in the call of Abraham.

127

year one man at least was allowed to enter the presence of God on earth.

In announcing that Jesus Christ had now made the temple obsolete, Stephen was saying that God had moved on to the fulfilment of that same purpose and desire, but at an infinitely higher level. 'Look,' said Stephen, 'I see heaven open and the Son of Man standing at the right hand of God' (7:56). No wonder the Sanhedrin saw his face looking like the face of an angel (6:15)! The Son of Man he saw was none other than Jesus, the real, human Jesus who had so recently walked this earth. Now that same Jesus, risen bodily from the dead, and ascended bodily into heaven, was standing at the very right hand of God. And not only for himself. As the Son of Man, the Ideal Man, he incorporated with and in himself all his people. If he could enter and be welcomed in that exalted heaven, so could they. This was new, staggeringly, gloriously new. But it was not a denial or repudiation of the idea behind the high priest's yearly entry into the most holy place on earth: it was its fulfilment, and therefore its replacement, at an infinitely higher level.

But in the fourth place, Stephen made it abundantly clear that while the successive stages in God's self-revelation were always consistent with the fulfilment, at increasingly higher levels, of his original purpose, the advent of a new stage in that revelation often required Israel to begin acting in a very different way from how they had previously acted. A child who has been taught by means of coloured bricks the basic arithmetical principles of addition, that one and one make two, will not be abandoning that basic principle when he moves on from bricks to computers. But he will abandon the bricks.

So God brought Abraham out of Mesopotamia into Canaan; and he told Isaac not to go down to Egypt, but to stay in Canaan (Gen. 26:2–3). But when the next stage in God's purpose began, God told Jacob to do the very opposite, and go down to Egypt (Gen. 46:2–4). Of course God made it clear to Jacob that he was not abandoning his original, declared purpose: the nation would eventually come back; and believing that promise, Jacob and the patriarchs had themselves buried in Canaan (7:15–16). But if Jacob had argued that since Abraham had been brought to Canaan, and Isaac had been commanded to stay there, he must himself stay in Canaan and not go down to Egypt, that would not have been faithfulness to God's word and purpose, but failure to keep pace with the living God and his ongoing revelation.

Similarly when Moses came to lead Israel out of Egypt. If

128

anyone had argued that because God had originally told Jacob to bring the patriarchs down to Egypt it was therefore wrong to leave Egypt and strike out for Canaan, that would not have been loyalty to God's revealed will, but a sadly misplaced zeal for the past. And to begin the journey from Egypt and then in their hearts to turn back to Egypt, as some of them did (7:39), was nothing short of departure from the living God.

Similarly with Stephen's contemporaries. To claim that because God himself had originally given Moses the instructions for the tabernacle, and David and Solomon the instructions for the temple, it was therefore blasphemy against God and Moses to say that Christ had now made the temple obsolete and had introduced a further and higher stage in the fulfilment of God's purpose, was both mistaken and false. It was not loyalty to God's word, but resistance to the principle of God's progressive revelation as witnessed to by that word.

Perhaps some of Stephen's contemporaries objected – as some people today may well object – that this doctrine of the progress of God's revelation is a very dangerous notion. It opens the way for any self-styled prophet to introduce new-fangled doctrines and practices that directly contradict the plain statement of God's written word, and to do so on no greater authority than the subjective judgement of the so-called prophet. Certainly Christendom has suffered much from this evil. Under the supposed guidance of the Holy Spirit, and justified by a doctrine of development, all kinds of unscriptural, and anti-scriptural, traditions, doctrines and practices have been introduced that from the start have conflicted with the Bible and in the end have supplanted it.

Some liberal theologians are particularly fond of the argument that Jesus Christ in his day discarded some of the Old Testament and reinterpreted the rest; and that in doing this, he laid down a pattern for us to follow: we are not to believe or follow the New Testament as it stands. We are to take his words and those of his apostles, follow some, discard others and reinterpret the rest in the light of whatever philosophy or world-view seems for the time being to be the most plausible.

Needless to say, Stephen's doctrine of progressive revelation bore no resemblance to this travesty. The fifth major lesson we may learn from his exposition of Old Testament history is that after God's initial appearance to Abraham every new stage in God's purpose, with its corresponding call for a change in Israel's practice, was explicitly announced and promised by God long before it happened. Jacob's vision (Gen. 46:2–4) that he claimed authorised him to take the patriarchs and their families away from Canaan to Egypt fulfilled what God had long before told Abraham would happen (7:6). And Moses' bringing of Israel out of Egypt back to the promised land had similarly been announced by God to Abraham four hundred years before (7:17).

The coming of the Messiah was not, when it happened, some previously unheard of novelty. Moses had announced it centuries before (7:37), and so had all the prophets (7:52).

The further idea that the earthly temple in Jerusalem would not prove to be God's final and permanent ideal was not invented by the Christians and suddenly announced for the first time by Stephen. God had indicated it through Isaiah centuries before (7:48–50).

And Stephen could fittingly have added, as the writer to the Hebrews did later, that the new covenant, the new priesthood after the order of Melchizedek, and the abolition of animal sacrifices in favour of something better, had all been announced in the prophets and the Psalms centuries before they were brought into being by Christ (see Heb. 7–8, 10).

In striking contrast, we find no intimation in the New Testament, either from Christ or his apostles, that in the course of the centuries elements in the Christian gospel will have to be abandoned in favour of something better. There is no indication, for instance, that the Lord's Supper will eventually become obsolete and have to be discarded in favour of another set of symbols pointing to a different and better way of forgiveness. Quite the opposite. We are told that Christians are to keep observing the Lord's Supper, thus proclaiming the Lord's death, until he comes (1 Cor. 11:26). Our subjective understanding of the revelation given us through the Son of God is, of course, meant to progress 'until we all reach unity in the faith and in the knowledge of the Son of God and become mature, attaining to the whole measure of the fulness of Christ' (Eph. 4:13). But as far as God's objective written revelation is concerned we are explicitly told that it has been 'once for all entrusted to the saints' (Jude 3). There will, of course, so the New Testament tells us, be a further stage in God's self-revelation to us: it will take place at the appearing of our great God and Saviour Jesus Christ (1 John 3:2). But until then we are neither to expect nor to accept any changes. Our task is to 'guard the good deposit that was entrusted to' us (2 Tim. 1:14). In Christ all the treasures of wisdom and knowledge are hidden (Col. 2:3). There is nothing beyond him.

But to return to Stephen's speech. The Sanhedrin were about to condemn him for blasphemy, to hustle him out of the court and to stone him to death. In so doing they would pose as the defenders of God's Word, the guardians of the orthodox faith, and the stern chastisers of heresy. Perhaps they thought that that is what they really were. But the reality was different: and Stephen had a sixth and very solemn lesson to draw for their benefit from his exposition of Old Testament history. At every fresh stage in God's self-revelation Israel had with unvarying regularity at first rejected the one whom God raised up to communicate his revelation, to be their saviour, or to lead them in the new patterns of behaviour appropriate to the new revelation.

Joseph, who proved to be God's appointed saviour for them in Egypt, came to be in Egypt because his brothers had initially hated him for the visions which God communicated to him (Gen. 37:8), and had in their jealousy sold him into Egypt (7:9).

Moses, whom God sent to deliver Israel from the bondage and injustice of Egypt, was at first rejected by his fellow nationals (7:25–29) and was obliged to flee to Midian. And even after God had revealed himself to him, first in the burning bush and then again at Sinai, and Moses had delivered the nation from Egypt, they eventually repudiated him, apostasised from the one true God, took up idolatry, and in their hearts turned back to Egypt (7:38–41).

The first generation to be given the tabernacle largely neglected it throughout the first forty years of its existence in the desert, and generally preferred to practise the crass idolatry which they picked up from the surrounding pagans. And centuries later Amos recalled this behaviour towards the tabernacle because his own contemporaries were guilty of similar heretical behaviour towards the temple, until God could no longer endure it, and banished the ten tribes to Assyria and the two tribes to Babylon (7:42–43). And prophet after prophet who promised that God would one day bring them to repentance, restore them to their land and send them the Righteous One, that is the Messiah, to lead them in paths of righteousness for his name's sake, was bitterly persecuted by his own contemporaries.

In betraying and murdering Jesus, therefore, the ruling priestly party, dominant in the nation and in the Sanhedrin, were not showing themselves to be loyal and faithful defenders of God's revelation and champions of orthodoxy. They were running all too true to type. Their rejection of Jesus the Righteous One was the obstinacy of unregenerate men antagonistic to the Holy Spirit

131

and blind and deaf to the gospel, as their forefathers had been to the law and the prophets (7:51–53).

But this was very direct and very strong language. They were furious that instead of backing down Stephen had maintained his claim that Jesus had changed and would change the customs handed down by Moses, and make the temple and its rituals obsolete. So when he finally announced that he could see heaven open and the Son of Man standing at the right hand of God, they had had enough; and within a brief hour Stephen was dead.

And within a few years, in AD 70 to be precise, the temple was no more; and the Sadducean high-priestly family and the whole order of priests gradually sank into obscurity.

But this, we may hope, was not the end of the story. Solemn though Stephen's accusation was, as he died he cried with a loud voice, so that they might all hear that he forgave them, 'Lord lay not this sin to their charge' (7:60). And even his message, when we re-read it, contains more than a glimmer of hope. Joseph's brothers, who at first rejected him, in the end came to recognise him as their saviour, repented, and were reconciled to him (7:11–14). Though Moses' fellow nationals at first repudiated him and he was obliged to flee to Midian, yet on his return they allowed him to lead them out of Egypt. And though after Sinai they once more rejected his leadership and refused to let him lead them into the promised land, yet the next generation believed him and entered their God-given inheritance. If in betraying Jesus and having him executed by the Romans his contemporaries followed the pattern of initial rejection, we may be sure that one day the nation will repeat the pattern of subsequent acceptance. They will recognise their Greater-than-Joseph, they will obey their Prophet-like-Moses, and enter through Christ into the full blessings God has irrevocably promised to Abraham and to his seed.

Some further reflections

It remains for us to consider the different ways in which Judaism and Christianity have reacted to the destruction of the temple.

It is said of the Lord Jesus that when for the last time he approached Jerusalem and saw the city, and thought of the miseries and horrors that would accompany its destruction, he wept over it (Luke 19:41–44). And every true Christian will feel the same way about it.

Israel survived the destruction of the city and temple not only as a people, but as a people with a faith in God unbroken by the catastrophe. For that all true Christians will genuinely rejoice. Israel may be enemies, as Paul says, as far as the gospel is concerned; but as far as election is concerned they are loved on account of the patriarchs, for God's gifts and his call are irrevocable (Rom. 11:28–29). They have stumbled, yes! But they have not stumbled so as to fall beyond recovery (Rom. 11:11). One day 'all Israel' (that is the nation as a whole as distinct from the present 'remnant chosen by grace', Rom. 11:5) 'will be saved' (Rom. 11:26). And even Jerusalem city, our Lord said, would be trampled on by the Gentiles only until the times of the Gentiles are fulfilled (Luke 21:24).

One secret of Israel's survival after the destruction of the temple, as Rabbi Dr Isidore Epstein points out, was the institution of the synagogue:

> They had developed the institution of the Synagogue with its elaborate liturgy, which could now take the place of the Temple for prayer and worship. Furthermore, the conception of the oral Law enabled them to reconcile development and change with loyalty to tradition, and to undertake the far-reaching adjustments in Jewish life which the new conditions demanded . . . A number of measures were adopted to meet the confusing problems that arose in the numerous observances which centred round the Temple and the priesthood. The divine services and liturgy were recast and readapted by the substitution of prayers for animal sacrifices and the insertion of supplications for the speedy restoration of the Temple and the ancient Hebrew polity.*

Now Christians would be very ready to acknowledge their debt to the institution of the synagogue, for the early churches much resembled synagogues, particularly in their form of government.† But the synagogue's 'substitution of prayers for animal sacrifices' points to an eloquent and irreconcilable difference between Judaism and Christianity. The destruction of the temple, the only place where Israel could offer sacrifices for sin, has left Judaism without atoning blood; and the inadequacy and the inconsistency of its position is seen when we consider the rationale that God gave in the Law for atoning sacrifice:

> And whatsoever man there be of the house of Israel, or of the strangers that sojourn among them, that eateth any manner of blood, I

---

*I. Epstein, *Judaism* (Harmondsworth: Penguin Books, 1959), pp. 112–13.
†And it would have been much to the good if later Christians had been content with that instead of trying to model themselves rather on the temple with its high priest, lesser priests, Levites, laity, and repeated 'bloody sacrifices'.

will set My face against that soul that eateth blood, and will cut him off from among his people. For the life of the flesh is in the blood; and I have given it to you upon the altar to make atonement for your souls; for it is the blood that maketh atonement by reason of the life. (Lev. 17:10–11)*

To this day orthodox Judaism strictly observes the prohibition on the eating of blood, regarding it as the unchanging and unchangeable law of God. But the original reason for the prohibition, so God explains, is that he appointed 'blood upon the altar' as an atonement for the soul. And yet Judaism, though it respects the prohibition, no longer gives due place to the reason. It has abandoned the idea of atonement through blood, and in its place has put prayer. But prayer is self-evidently not an equal and adequate substitute for the shedding of blood and for the sacrifice of an innocent life upon the altar, in the place of the guilty. Yet perhaps it is unfair to say that Judaism has *abandoned* the idea of atonement through blood. The cessation of animal sacrifice was forced on them by the destruction of the temple. If the temple still remained standing, orthodox Judaism, at least, would still be offering the blood of animals on the temple's altar to gain forgiveness of sins. And, as Dr Epstein reminds us, the synagogue still prays for the speedy restoration of the temple and, therefore, presumably of its sacrifices.

Christianity, by contrast, has not abandoned God's demand that sin must be atoned for by the shedding of blood. Of course Christianity will admit, indeed will insist, that the blood of animals could not, and never did, actually take away sins (Heb. 10:4). Animal sacrifices were like promissory notes. They acknowledged the debt of sin; they promised payment; they illustrated the form in which payment must ultimately be made; but in themselves they paid nothing. On the other hand, they could not simply be abandoned and forgotten. Their promises had to be fulfilled.

And that is what the Lord Jesus has done. He has honoured the myriads of promissory notes that the faithful in Israel signed by offering their animal sacrifices, and has paid their accumulated debt in full by shedding his own blood and by sacrificing himself. Of course, when the debt which has been acknowledged by a succession of promissory notes is finally paid, you may rightly

*The version quoted here is *The Holy Scriptures According to the Masoretic Text*, a translation with the aid of previous versions and with constant consultation of Jewish authorities (Philadelphia: The Jewish Publications Society of America; Cambridge: Cambridge University Press, 1917).

destroy the promissory notes. But that is a very different thing from simply abandoning them without fulfilling their promises and paying the debt. When the Lord Jesus sat down to eat his last Passover with his disciples, he said to them: 'I have eagerly desired to eat this Passover with you before I suffer. For I tell you, I will not eat it again until it finds fulfilment in the kingdom of God' (Luke 22:15–16). Judaism has simply abandoned blood sacrifice: Christ has fulfilled it.

How, then, has Christianity reacted to the destruction of the temple, its sacrifices, high priest and priesthood? If Stephen and the writer to the Hebrews are any guide, the early Christians saw them come to their end without undue dismay. They still had a High Priest, and he was infinitely superior to any one of Aaron's line. They had a tabernacle, not on earth of course: they had the greater and more perfect tabernacle in which Christ ministers and into which they had open access. And the end of the offering of animal sacrifices for the purpose of obtaining forgiveness of sins would not have struck them as a disaster either. They already had complete forgiveness of sins through the sacrifice of Christ, and they would not have seen any need to continue offering sacrifices to obtain forgiveness. One does not sacrifice anything in order to get what one has already got.

But that said, it is common knowledge that later on Christendom to an alarming extent lost its grip on the gospel and in many ways reverted to pre-Christian Judaism, reviving elements that even Judaism had abandoned.

Take the priesthood. According to the gospel of the New Testament all believers without exception are priests and there is no question of dividing the people of God into two different groups, priesthood and laity (Rev. 1:6; 5:10; 1 Pet. 2:5, 9). Similarly, according to the gospel Christians have only one high priest, like Judaism did, and that high priest is Christ.

But in later centuries Christendom could not rest content with the gospel. It went back and invented a priesthood after the model of ancient Judaism. It divided the hitherto undivided people of God into two distinct groups: priesthood and laity. Then it further divided this new 'priesthood' into the three priestly divisions of ancient Judaism: deacons (to correspond to Levites), full-blown priests, and an earthly high priest, thus ending up with an anomaly that Judaism never knew, that of having two high priests simultaneously, one in heaven and another on earth.

And then, since Judaism's priests repeatedly offered sacrifices on the altar to obtain forgiveness of sins, Christendom had altars built in its places of worship, turned the Lord's Supper into a sacrifice, and told its 'priests' that now they too had a real sacrifice which they could and must repeatedly offer on their altars in order to obtain forgiveness for themselves and for the 'laity'.

And then again, ancient Judaism's temple was divided by a great veil into two compartments: first the holy place; and then, beyond the veil, the Most Holy Place. So Christendom began building its places of worship as though they were temples after the Jewish model: first the nave, where the laity might stand or sit; and then, railed off, and sometimes screened off by an elaborate screen, or in some cases by a wall, the chancel, where during the services only the priests, their assistants and the choir might enter. No wonder the people at large got the impression that if they were not allowed to enter the most holy part of this earthly building, they certainly could not be sure that they would be allowed to enter God's heaven at last, let alone enter by faith into the holiest of all through the blood of Jesus now.

What, we may well ask, would Stephen have said about all this, if he had lived to see it? Certainly not that it was a bit of harmless, if ill-advised, antiquarianism. He believed that the differences between Judaism and Christianity in these very particulars were so essential to the heart of the gospel and to people's full enjoyment of the great salvation procured by Christ, that he was prepared to die rather than to keep silent about them. If he regarded Judaism's refusal to move forward into God's full and final revelation in Christ as a departure from the living God, what would he have said about Christendom's reversion to ancient Judaism?

The signs are that in recent decades Christendom has begun to purge itself of these centuries-old lapses into ancient Judaism. But it has still a long way to go before it stands unmistakably everywhere and at all times for the uncompromised and undiminished fullness of the truly Christian gospel.

MOVEMENT 2: The Gospel and Samaria's Unorthodox Worship (8:4–25)

The second story in Section Two is Philip's evangelisation of Samaria; and the connection of thought between this second story and the first is not far to seek. Like the Jews, the Samaritans too had a temple – or at least they had had, until the Jewish high priest John Hyrcanus destroyed it about 128 BC (some say 108 BC). Unlike the Jews' temple, theirs had been built not in Jerusalem, but on Mount Gerizim; and though by now it no longer existed, the Samaritans still worshipped at the spot where their temple had once stood. For them, this location was no accident of geography or matter of indifference. It had been chosen with deliberate care, and was maintained with vigorous ethnic and religious pride (see John 4:20).

As with the Jews, so with the Samaritans, the coming of the Holy Spirit would make possible an advance to a higher form of worship than anything that they had known before. Their temple, like that of the Jews, had been a material temple built of stone, located in its fixed position on Mount Gerizim. Now the gift of the indwelling Holy Spirit would transform every Samaritan who received him into a spiritual temple. Geographical location would no longer be significant, as our Lord had once remarked to a Samaritan woman: 'Believe me, woman, a time is coming when you will worship the Father neither on this mountain nor in Jerusalem' (John 4:21).

That time had now come; and through Philip's preaching of the gospel the Samaritans were to be offered that spring of living water (John 4:14), that gift of the Holy Spirit through faith in the Lord Jesus, which would enable them to worship God with the ideal kind of worship which alone can fully satisfy God's heart. 'A time is coming', our Lord had said to the Samaritan woman, 'and has now come when the true worshippers will worship the Father in spirit and truth, for they are the kind of worshippers the Father seeks. God is spirit, and his worshippers must worship in spirit and in truth' (John 4:23–24).

But the Samaritans had a special difficulty. The Jews for their part found it difficult enough to change from their traditional form of worship, good and God-given as it was, to that higher form of worship now made possible through Christ. Indeed many Jews never brought themselves to make the change. Many Samaritans, by contrast, proved ready and eager to make the change from their traditional way of worship to the new. But unfortunately in their traditional form of worship there was an error so basic and so serious that even when they believed on the Lord Jesus and were baptised in his name, they were not allowed or enabled for a while to make the change. The Holy Spirit without whom they would never know the Father as he really is, nor ever be able to worship him in Spirit and in truth, was temporarily withheld from them, until they were brought face to

137

face with their past error, repented of it, and knowingly forsook it (8:14–17).

Then what was that error? And why was it so serious? To find out, we must delve into their history.

The background to Philip's evangelisation of Samaria

If, as the last story showed us, respect for the temple at Jerusalem was, for the majority of Jews, an important expression of orthodoxy, the Samaritans were very unorthodox indeed. They had no respect for the temple in Jerusalem whatsoever. That was not because they were pagans. They weren't. They believed in the same one true God as the Jews did, and they accepted the five books of the Pentateuch as God's inspired word. They believed that one day God would send his Messiah into the world as the Saviour of the world.* They believed also in the day of Judgement. And they religiously offered the sacrifices required by the law of Moses.

But they repudiated Jerusalem and its temple. It was not that they thought like the people at Qumran. The latter, you remember, felt that the Jerusalem temple in and of itself was good; it was only that the prevailing abuses and irregularities in its priesthood and festivals made it impossible for them to take part in its services. The Samaritans, by contrast, did not believe in the Jerusalem temple at all.

Nor did they think like Stephen that earthly temples, levitical priesthood and animal sacrifices were obsolete and about to pass away. It is true that by the time Philip took the gospel to them they no longer had a temple of their own. But they still had a high priest, they still offered animal sacrifices at the place where their temple had been; and they had no intention of giving these things up.†

It wasn't even that they objected to the form of the Jerusalem temple or of its high priesthood.‡ No, the position of the Samar-

---

*They referred to him as *Taheb*; one possible translation of the term is 'the restorer'.

†Still to this day there is a community of Samaritans living in Shechem (modern Nablus) and another in Holon, near Tel Aviv. And at Passover time they still sacrifice a sheep at their holy place on Mount Gerizim.

‡Roger Beckwith, *The Old Testament Canon in the New Testament Church* (London: SPCK, 1985), p. 130, has recently reminded us that according to Josephus 'the

itans was this. They accepted, as the Jews did, that Moses' directive in Deuteronomy 12:4–18 laid it down that there should be only one centre at any one time in the whole of the promised land where sacrifices might legitimately be offered. They just did not believe that the temple in Jerusalem was that God-ordained centre. According to them, their Mount Gerizim was the centre. As the Samaritan woman remarked to Christ: 'Our fathers worshipped on this mountain [i.e. Gerizim], but you Jews claim that the place where we must worship is in Jerusalem' (John 4:20).

This disagreement went back to the time of the return from the Exile, when the Samaritans' worship was heavily mixed with idolatry, and the Jews had for that reason refused to allow the Samaritans to participate in the rebuilding of the temple at Jerusalem. Later the Samaritans renounced their idolatry; but the Jews still did not accept them, because of their insistence on having their own temple on Mount Gerizim.

The basic disagreement between Jews and Samaritans became a chronic, festering sore, and by the time of our Lord it had often broken out into violence of one sort or another. The Jews for their part, as we have already observed, had destroyed the Samaritans' temple; and the Samaritans had retaliated in kind.

Strack and Billerbeck instance the following story:

> R. Ishmael b. Jose was going up to Jerusalem to pray. He was walking past a plane tree (by Gerizim) where a Samaritan found him. He said to him, 'Where are you going?' He answered, 'I am going to Jerusalem to pray.' The former said, 'Would it not be better for you to pray in this blessed mountain rather than in that dunghill?'*

Somewhere between AD 6 and 9 some Samaritans went to Jerusalem at Passover time and scattered bones in the temple – an act calculated to spread the maximum ritual pollution (see Num. 19) in the Jews' most sacred place.

Again, when Christ and his disciples attempted to put up for

Samaritan temple was modelled on that at Jerusalem (*War* 1.2.6, or 1.63; *Ant.* 11.8.2, or 11.310; 13.9.1, or 13.256), that the Samaritan high priesthood was derived from the Jewish high-priestly family, through a disgraced member of it, and that many of the Samaritan priests came from Jerusalem, in similar circumstances (*Ant.* 11.8.2, 4, 7, or 11.306–12, 322–4, 346f)'.

*Strack-Billerbeck, *Kommentar zum Neuen Testament aus Talmud und Midrash*, vol. 1 (München, 1922–28), p. 549. The quotation is taken from L. Morris, *The Gospel According to John* (Grand Rapids, MI: Wm B. Eerdmans, 1973), p. 268, n. 51.

the night in a Samaritan village, the people of the village would not 'welcome him, because he was heading for Jerusalem' – which so angered James and John that they were for calling down fire from heaven on them (Luke 9:51–56). And in AD 52 the Samaritans actually killed some Jewish pilgrims at En-gannim, and of course the Jews retaliated.

The modern reaction to such religious strife is disgust and impatience, the more so since the history of Christendom contains worse examples of it than the history of the Jewish-Samaritan dispute. People weary of such rancour and violence in the name of religion. They cry a plague on both houses. They urge that true spirituality is concerned with loving one another, and that the doctrinal questions that lie at the bottom of such disputes are not worth arguing about.

But that was not Christ's attitude towards such differences. Time and again, in action and in teaching, he went out of his way to dissociate himself from the rancorous hatred and unregenerate hostility of the Jews towards the Samaritans, and positively to express the love of God towards them (Luke 10:30–37; 17:11–19; John 4). But with compassionate, firm faithfulness, he did not hesitate to bring home to the Samaritans the falsity of their position. When the Samaritan woman raised the age-long controversy, he replied: 'You Samaritans worship what you do not know; we [Jews] worship what we do know' (John 4:22).

All agree on what he meant. He was alluding to the ignorance which the Samaritans had brought on themselves by their rejection of the whole of the Old Testament beyond the Pentateuch. Westcott paraphrases our Lord's words to the woman: 'Your worship . . . is directed to One with whose character as He has revealed Himself through the prophets and in the history of His people, you are really unacquainted. You know whom to worship, but you do not know Him.'* Such ignorance was sad indeed; but it was also culpable, for it was self-induced.

In addition to that immeasurable, self-inflicted loss, there was another serious consequence. If they had accepted and read the Former and Latter Prophets and the Writings (the second and third divisions of the Old Testament), they would have found the answer to the question of where they ought to sacrifice and to worship God. They would have read in 2 Samuel 5:6–10 and 2 Samuel 7, for instance, that God entered into a covenant with

---

*B. F. Westcott, *The Gospel According to St John* (London: John Murray, 1898), p. 72.

King David of Judah and Jerusalem; that he guaranteed to maintain a special relationship between himself and David's seed; and that he ordained that David's son, Solomon, should build him a temple for his Name (2 Sam. 7:13). And they would have discovered from the remaining historical books, the Prophets and the Psalms, that Jerusalem was the place where God chose to have it built (see, for instance, Ps. 132, particularly vv.13–14; and Zech. 3–4).

It used to be said in favour of the Samaritans that when the schism between them and the Jews took place the Pentateuch was the only part of the Old Testament to be regarded even by the Jews as canonical and therefore authoritative. The Samaritans accepted the Pentateuch, therefore, because it was already canonical, but naturally after that, having repudiated Jerusalem, they ignored any further books that emanated from that source. But the modern assessment of the available evidence shows that the schism did not take place that early, in the time of Nehemiah, as used to be supposed. Even though the Samaritans built themselves a temple about 400 BC, their final break with Judaism and their final repudiation of Jerusalem did not occur until the Hasmonean period, probably after the destruction of their own temple by John Hyrcanus, say about 120 BC.* By that time the Former and Latter Prophets were certainly held by the Jews to be canonical, and in all probability the Writings as well. The Samaritans' final break with orthodox Judaism, then, and their repudiation of Jerusalem and its temple, was made – made, that is, by their leaders, priests and teachers; one could not blame the ordinary people like the woman at Sychar's well for it – in full knowledge of what those Scriptures said.†

Their repudiation of Jerusalem, therefore, and their repudiation of two thirds of the Old Testament because of their preference for Gerizim, was doubly serious. First it involved

---

*See Bruce K. Waltke, 'The Samaritan Pentateuch and the Text of the Old Testament', in J. Barton Payne (ed.), *New Perspectives on the Old Testament* (Waco, TX: Word Books, 1970), pp. 225–6, and Roger Beckwith, *The Old Testament Canon in the New Testament Church* (London: SPCK, 1985), pp. 130–1.

†The Samaritan Pentateuch contains certain notable differences from the Masoretic Text and the Septuagint, and those differences favour Gerizim as the place for God's temple. It is in the highest degree unlikely that they represent the original text of the Old Testament. See Bruce K. Waltke, 'The Samaritan Pentateuch and the Text of the Old Testament', in J. Barton Payne (ed.), *New Perspectives on the Old Testament* (Waco, TX: Word Books, 1970), pp. 225–6. The Samaritans doubtless altered the original text to make it support their preference for Gerizim.

disobedience to God's expressed will regarding worship. But in addition it obscured, if not denied, the all-important question of the source from which the Saviour of the world would come. 'You Samaritans', said the Saviour, 'worship what you do not know; we [Jews] worship what we do know, *for salvation is from the Jews*' (John 4:22). The Samaritans believed that God would one day send the Messiah, for Moses in the Pentateuch had promised that 'The Lord your God will raise up for you a prophet like me from among your own brothers' (Deut. 18:15). But as the centuries had gone by, God had added promise to promise, and prophecy to prophecy, indicating where and when and how the promised Messiah and Saviour of the world should be born; so that men might know where to look for him and from where to expect him, and be able to recognise him as authentic when he came. Among many other details, God had indicated that the Saviour would be of the line of David (Isa. 11:1), would be born in David's birthplace, Bethlehem of Judea (Mic. 5:2), and when he came officially he would come to David's city of Jerusalem as Jerusalem's King (Zech. 9:9).

Repudiation of Jerusalem and rejection of the God-given promises and prophecies of two thirds of the Old Testament had landed the Samaritans, then, in a sad and potentially dangerous ignorance. Of course it must have been hard for Samaritans, after all the hostility they had suffered from Jews, to abandon their deep-seated and long-held prejudice, and to accept that 'salvation is from the Jews'. Certainly the Lord Jesus was not justifying or excusing the wretched behaviour, pride, arrogance and rancour of Jews who should have known better. But if the Samaritans wished to find salvation and satisfaction, and to receive the gift of the Spirit to enable them to offer God the true worship he desired, they would have to recognise that the Saviour of the world was a Jew, and not a Samaritan, a king whose earthly capital was Jerusalem, not Gerizim, who called the temple at Jerusalem 'my Father's house' (Luke 2:49; cf. 19:46) – the very Jew, indeed, who had long since been indicated in the very Scriptures which for centuries they had rejected.

Philip, a Samaritan city, and the receiving of the Holy Spirit

News that their fellow countrymen of Sychar had come to faith in Jesus as the Messiah (John 4:39–41), would doubtless have spread to other towns in the province. This helps to explain the success that followed Philip's preaching of the gospel when he visited a city in Samaria.* Like his Lord before him, of course, Philip acted wisely. He did not spearhead his approach to these Samaritans by rehearsing the old controversy all over again; and he certainly did not advocate the claims of the temple at Jerusalem. He proclaimed the Christ, says Luke (8:5); and God authenticated the message by granting many miracles.

Crowds of people came to faith. But then a strange thing happened: the Holy Spirit did not come upon them (8:15–16). They did not receive the Holy Spirit when they believed, as Gentiles normally did, before they were baptised (see the case of Cornelius, 10:44–48; 11:15–17, and Peter's remarks at 15:7–9). Nor did they receive the Holy Spirit at or after their baptism, as the Jews on the day of Pentecost did (see 2:38). They were eventually given the Holy Spirit; but at first they were made to wait.

Why? Many answers have been given to this question; but the safest way to proceed is to notice what happened, and presumably what had to happen, before God was prepared to give them the Holy Spirit. Apostles from Jerusalem (notice Luke's precise language) had to come, to pray for them and to lay their hands on them; and the Samaritans for their part had to submit to having apostles from Jerusalem lay their hands on them; and then, and only then, was God prepared publicly to acknowledge the genuineness of their conversion by publicly giving them his Holy Spirit (8:14–17).

Again we ask, Why so? It was obviously not that Philip was somehow an inadequate preacher: no suggestion is made in the next story, the conversion of the Ethiopian (8:26–40), that Philip's ministry had to be supplemented by that of the Jerusalem apostles before it could be fully effective. Nor is any further case recorded in the whole of Acts of the Jerusalem apostles having to come from Jerusalem and lay their hands on converts before the converts could receive the Holy Spirit.

The answer to the question seems clear: the Samaritans were made, first by the period of waiting, then by the visual and physical gesture of the public laying on of hands, to acknowledge their dependence on Jerusalem, and their identification with the

---

*Many manuscripts read '*the* city of Samaria', as though the city in question were the main city, Sebaste, which at this time was a predominantly Gentile city. But it is unlikely that Luke intends Sebaste, otherwise he would have referred to it by name. The city in question may have been Gitta, the birthplace of Simon. It is better to follow those manuscripts which read '*a* city of Samaria'.

apostles at Jerusalem. Their long-standing repudiation of Jerusalem must be given up. True, they would not be asked to begin attending the temple at Jerusalem: both it and the holy place on Mount Gerizim were now fast becoming obsolete. Nor was God saying that for ever afterwards Jerusalem must be recognised as the ecclesiastical headquarters of the church. But they were being required to recognise what the Saviour had told the woman of Sychar: historically speaking, 'salvation is from the Jews', and it comes via Jerusalem.

There is only one Saviour of the world, and only one salvation (4:12). In a world full of a thousand and one voices, advocating the claims of innumerable religions, it is of the utmost importance that we should have clear, objective, historical evidence to establish who that one and only Saviour is. God has devoted centuries to providing that evidence: by calling Abraham; by the development of a special nation; by establishing patterns of law, of redemption and of worship through Moses; and finally and supremely through the raising up of David, King of Judah at Jerusalem, ancestor and prototype of Messiah, with numerous prophecies spread over several centuries foretelling Messiah's birth, birthplace, ministry, death, resurrection and ascension. The Christian gospel is not a philosophy that anyone, no matter who and of what country, could think up and develop – provided only that he had a touch of genius – out of universal general principles. The gospel, as Paul later put it, is 'the gospel of God – the gospel he promised beforehand through his prophets in the Holy Scriptures regarding his Son, who as to his human nature was a descendant of David . . .' (Rom. 1:1–3). The gospel is the product of a long, objective, historical and geographical process, controlled at every juncture by the God whose gospel it is.

Historically it is inseparable from Jerusalem. According to Luke, when between his resurrection and ascension Christ briefed his apostles for their world-wide mission, he did so in these words: 'This is what is written: The Christ will suffer and rise from the dead on the third day, and repentance and forgiveness of sins will be preached in his name to all nations, beginning at Jerusalem' (Luke 24:46–47). For ever and for ever the gospel is inseparably linked with certain historical events that happened at Jerusalem.

If then the Samaritans had been allowed to receive the Holy Spirit without first having given up their long-standing repudiation of Jerusalem and their rejection of all those scriptural prophecies that indicated that the Messiah would be 'of the seed

144

of David', they would have been in real danger. They could easily have imagined that they could believe in 'Jesus' and receive 'the Spirit' without repenting of their former attitude. There could have come into being two forms of Christianity: one Jewish, based on the Jesus of history, inseparably connected with Jerusalem, and the other a Samaritan version with a 'Jesus' and a 'Holy Spirit' who had nothing necessarily to do with Jerusalem at all; and they could have claimed to have a 'salvation' that was not 'from the Jews'. Such a Samaritan version would, of course, have been spurious. There are false cults even today who claim to be Christian, and talk much about Jesus and the Spirit, but who would either deny that Jesus actually and historically died at Jerusalem, or deny that he bodily rose again, and would repudiate the authority of the apostles from Jerusalem. Their Jesus and their Spirit have little or nothing to do with the historical facts.

We are not talking about imaginary dangers either. God's original directive through Moses that his people were not to offer their sacrifices just anywhere, but in one place and one place only that he himself should choose, was not motivated by narrow-minded religious exclusivism. It was meant as a protection against the real danger of being seduced by the false Canaanite cults that surrounded them in Palestine. It was so easy for people, especially in those pre-scientific days, to be taken in by the superstitions, magic and demonism of pagan religion. Deuteronomy 12 explicitly says that it was to protect Israel against such deceptions that God directed them to set up one and only one centre, where the knowledge of the true God might be perpetuated. It is true that Israel disobeyed and set up other, illegitimate, shrines – and the deportation of the ten tribes and the syncretism of the early years of Samaritan religion are a witness to what eventually came of that. It is also true that the temple at Jerusalem itself became corrupt, was destroyed at the Exile, and had to be built again. But the true tradition was never permanently obscured, and Jerusalem continued to be the centre which God had chosen and where he could be known through his written word, through the imageless temple, and through the divinely appointed system of sacrifice and worship.

But the Samaritans had repudiated God's centre, Jerusalem, and its temple, and two-thirds of God's written word. We should not be surprised, therefore, that by the time Philip reached Samaria they had paid the price of their error: they had been completely taken in by a sorcerer named Simon. He peddled a mixture of magic and spiritism, and gave himself out to be someone great. Amazed by his magic, they had been deceived into thinking that Simon was 'the divine power known as the Great Power' (8:10). Even before Philip came, proclaiming the true Messiah, the Samaritans need never have been taken in by this pagan spiritist. Annas and Caiaphas at Jerusalem may not have been the last word of true spirituality; but there was no room in their temple and its services for men like Simon. And had the Samaritans not rejected two-thirds of the Old Testament they would have found there descriptions of the true Messiah that would have saved them from being taken in by Simon, with his pagan concepts of deity, his unbiblical terminology, and his demonic powers.

Moreover, it is instructive to notice that when Simon heard about Jesus and saw the miracles done in his name, he was quite prepared to 'believe' in Jesus and get baptised in his name. But what followed showed that he had not the beginning of an idea of what the historical Jesus stood for, nor any true idea of the Spirit of God. To him 'Jesus' and 'the Spirit' were simply two demonic powers, more powerful but of the same kind as those he already used. He was prepared to pay a considerable sum of money to add 'Jesus' and 'the Spirit' to his repertoire, so as to gain greater power over people, build up his religion and increase his income.

God therefore taught the Samaritans a very needful and salutary lesson when he refused to authenticate their profession of repentance and of faith in the Lord Jesus until they submitted to, and identified themselves with, the apostles from Jerusalem.

Final reflections

We have spent a long time on the first two stories in this section of Acts, far more than we shall need to spend on the next two. Even so, we should linger briefly to consider how the lessons these two stories teach complement each other.

Stephen's story forcefully expounds the fact that God is the God of progressive revelation, the God who has been on the move through history; and it urges us to make sure that we have moved on with God into his full revelation in his Son, and not stayed in Judaism or gone back into a mixture of Christianity and pre-Christian Judaism.

Philip's story makes the opposite, but equally important, point: that true Christianity is rooted in history, and we must never cut those roots. We cannot refuse to accept the divine inspiration and authority of the Old Testament and still be true to Christ and

Christianity. And most certainly we cannot refuse the teaching and authority of the apostles from Jerusalem and still rightly lay claim to preach Christ. Those who reject the inspiration and authority of the New Testament and advocate a Christianity divorced from faith in the historicity of the events on which Christianity is founded are not in fact preaching true Christianity at all. They have cut their roots with history. What they are preaching is at best a mixture of Christian ethics with an alien, pagan, even if modern, philosophical world-view; and at worst little better than Simon's superstitions.

MOVEMENT 3: The Gospel of the Suffering Servant (8:26–40)

The third story in this section is even briefer than the second, fifteen verses as against twenty-two. Moreover, it will not be necessary to recall a large amount of historical background in order to understand the major point that the story makes and what it contributes to the message of Section Two as a whole.

Once more, as in the first two stories, we are concerned, at least at the beginning, with the temple at Jerusalem: the Ethiopian Minister of State had been up to Jerusalem to worship, and on his way back he was sitting in his chariot reading the book of Isaiah the prophet, a copy of which he had in all likelihood bought at Jerusalem (8:27–28). This leads us to think not only of Judaism's worship and approach to God, but of its witness to the Gentile nations around. There were two major elements in that witness: their temple and their Bible. Both were in their way unique. Unlike the temples of the surrounding nations, Israel's temple contained no image of the deity, and was an expression of her witness to the one, invisible, transcendent Creator. For thoughtful Gentiles, like the Ethiopian, this would have formed an impressive contrast to the intellectual absurdity and moral turpitude of the polytheism current everywhere else in the ancient world.

How many such thoughtful Gentiles there were who through the testimony of the temple had come to faith in the living God it would be difficult to estimate. Gentiles in great numbers, and sometimes Gentiles of eminent social and political standing, would offer sacrifices in the temple at Jerusalem. But this did not necessarily indicate acceptance of Judaism's monotheism or personal faith in the true God:

147

To offer sacrifice at some famous sanctuary was very often no more than an expression of a piety that had become cosmopolitan, an act of courtesy towards the nation or city concerned, by no means intended as an adherence to a particular religion. Since this happened in other celebrated sanctuaries, why not in Jerusalem also? And for their part, the Jews and their priests had no reason to reject the reverence shown to their God, even if it was only an act of politeness.*

Many Gentiles, when they discovered that Jews were not prepared to return the compliment and show respect to other nations' gods, were violently offended. They tended also to resent the uncompromising terms in which Jewish teachers, basing themselves on the standards of the Old Testament, denounced the vices and perversions common in Gentile society; for Gentile temples and priests did not normally trouble about such things. For all that, the temple at Jerusalem would have been visited by crowds of Gentiles who, though they had not fully converted to Judaism and become Jews, were nevertheless in deep sympathy with Israel's faith, and by people like the Ethiopian who were wistfully seeking something better than what Gentile polytheism could offer them.

But the fact that the Ethiopian was reading a copy of Isaiah on his return journey reminds us that there was another element in Judaism's witness to the Gentiles even more effective than the temple. That was their Bible. The institution they used for the promulgation of its message was the synagogue of the local Jewish community. In many places the Jewish community might be small, and unable to support a synagogue, as, apparently, in Philippi, where in the place where 'prayer was wont to be made' Paul encountered only women (16:13–14). But in other places, like Alexandria in Egypt, there were large, flourishing Jewish communities. Big communities or small, by New Testament times Jews had established synagogues virtually all round the ancient world.

Their impact was considerable. Acts itself is witness that there were Gentile converts to Judaism among the visitors from Rome at Pentecost (2:11), and in the synagogue at Pisidian Antioch (13:43). And even though nowadays the exact meaning of Luke's terms 'God-fearer' and 'God-worshipper' is disputed, the Roman centurion Cornelius in Caesarea (10:2), the Thyatiran purple-

*E. Schurer, *The History of the Jewish People in the Age of Jesus Christ*, vol. 2, revised and edited by G. Vermes, F. Millar, M. Black (Edinburgh: T. & T. Clark, 1979), p. 309.

seller Lydia in Philippi (16:14), and the Roman citizen Titius Justus at Corinth (18:7) had obviously all come to believe in the true God of Israel. The centurion of Luke's Gospel (Luke 7:5) had even built the Jews in his town their synagogue. From Josephus, moreover, we learn that in the first half of the first century AD Queen Helena of Adiabene and her son Izates were converted to Judaism; and it is likely that many of their subjects would have adopted the same faith. There is even some evidence that Flavius Clemens, Roman consul in AD 95 and uncle of the emperor, together with his wife Flavia Domitilla, may have been converts to Judaism.

It is, then, no part of Christianity's brief to minimise the value of the Jews' missionary witness to the Gentiles, or to deny that it was true faith in God and his word that made them the missionary force they were:

> . . . belief in the future universality of the true religion, the coming of an age when 'the Lord shall be king over all the earth,' when 'the Lord shall be one and his name One,' led to efforts to convert the Gentiles to the worship of the one true God and to faith and obedience according to the revelation he had given, and made Judaism the first great missionary religion of the Mediterranean world.*

The story of Philip and the Ethiopian, however, puts its finger on a difference between Christianity and Judaism that lies at the very heart of Christianity and forms the mainspring of Christianity's missionary movement. When Philip approached the Ethiopian's chariot, the Ethiopian was reading his copy of Isaiah and had reached the words: 'He was led like a sheep to the slaughter, and as a lamb before the shearer is silent, so he did not open his mouth. In his humiliation he was deprived of justice. Who can speak of his descendants? For his life was taken from the earth' (8:32–33 = Isa. 53:7–8).

The passage puzzled the Ethiopian, and in his innocence he asked: 'Tell me, please, who is the prophet talking about, himself or someone else?' (8:34). And Philip, of course, gave the Christian answer: 'Then Philip began with that very passage of Scripture and told him the good news about Jesus' (8:35).

Philip would have had no difficulty in showing how Jesus' sufferings and his trial and crucifixion matched those described by Isaiah. But not content with that, he would have gone on to tell

---

*G. F. Moore, *Judaism*, vol. 1 (Cambridge, MA: Harvard University Press, 1927), pp. 323–4.

the 'good news' that Jesus had risen from the dead. And he would have argued, as Peter did (3:17–18), and Paul did (13:27–37), that not only did Jesus' resurrection prove that in spite of his suffering and cross he was the Messiah; but his very sufferings themselves were proof of his Messiahship, since they fulfilled what the prophets said the Messiah must undergo.

Had Philip's explanation gone no further than that, he would already have pointed to one feature of the good news that has captured the imagination, the heart, and eventually the worshipful homage of millions of all nationalities: the proclamation of a non-retaliating Messiah who, being God's King possessed of divine power, loved his very enemies and 'when they hurled their insults at him, he did not retaliate; when he suffered, he made no threats'; the King who deliberately died not only for his fellow nationals and friends – though he died for them too – but for men and women of all nations, for the enemies of God and man, for the very people who had him crucified.

But Philip, we may be sure, would not have been content to preach to the Ethiopian the fact, however glorious, that Christ suffered without retaliating. Luke says that he began with the passage the Ethiopian was reading when he met him – which was an eminently sensible thing to do. But it passes all bounds of credibility to suggest, as many do, that he would not have gone on to explain to the Ethiopian how the earlier and later verses of Isaiah 53 applied to Jesus as well. On their basis he would have pointed out that the sufferings of Christ were not only innocent, they were substitutionary and atoning:

> But he was pierced for our transgressions, he was crushed for our iniquities; the punishment that brought us peace was upon him, and by his wounds we are healed. We all, like sheep, have gone astray, each of us has turned to his own way; and the Lord has laid on him the iniquity of us all . . . Yet it was the Lord's will to crush him and cause him to suffer, and though the Lord makes his life a guilt offering, he will see his offspring and prolong his days . . . [By] his knowledge my righteous servant will justify many, and he will bear their iniquities. (Isa. 53:5–6, 10, 11)

Here, then, is gospel indeed. The early Christians were no less insistent than Judaism on the holiness of God, on the demands of his law, and on the evil and perversity of human sin; witness the first two and a half chapters of Paul's letter to the Romans. And the early Christians were equally insistent that when anyone has been reconciled to God, redeemed, forgiven and justified through faith in the Lord Jesus, that person should apply the ethics of Christ to himself rigorously and persistently. But none of these things are the gospel by which God's enemies are reconciled to him, sinners forgiven, and transgressors justified.

> Now, brothers, I want to remind you of the gospel I preached to you . . . By this gospel you are saved . . .
> For what I received I passed on to you as of first importance: that Christ died for our sins according to the Scriptures, that he was buried, that he was raised on the third day according to the Scriptures . . . (1 Cor. 15:1–4)

Not only is this the gospel: it is the mainspring of the Christian evangelist's missionary motivation. There is an obvious reason why God's law and Christian ethics do not drive many of us to go out to the world as missionaries: we ourselves fall so terribly short of their standards and demands. Who am I to go and tell someone else to be good? But even I would go and tell that while I was still a sinner Christ died for me and by his death bought for me the gift of forgiveness and eternal redemption – with the rider that if Christ thus loved and saved me, he would obviously save anyone who repented and trusted him.

Judaism today could scarcely be said to be a missionary movement. For that there are doubtless many reasons; but one of them is this: it has no gospel to offer mankind. Its witness to the one true God and its protest against our modern forms of idolatry are still as valid and still as necessary as they were in Isaiah's day. Its stand for the value of human life, and its ethical concern in general, based as they are on God's revealed law, are beyond praise. But when it comes to mankind's fundamental problem, the real guilt of having broken God's law, it has today no satisfactory answer. In centuries past it did have an answer: the system of sacrifices that God appointed along with his law. Granted they were only symbols; yet they were something. But with the destruction of the temple they lost even those symbols – and they have no convincing reality to put in their place. The message that satisfied the Ethiopian and led him to faith, Judaism has rejected; and without it, it has no message of redemption, no atoning sacrifice, and therefore no gospel.

Christendom too is always in danger of losing its faith in the gospel, and with it its missionary zeal. People come to feel that somehow our modern world is different; that the gospel that 'Christ died for our sins . . . [and] that he was raised on the third day', the gospel that saved the Ethiopian and the Corinthians and that planted churches all round the first-century world, would

151

not save our modern sinners. So, when given the chance to address the world, they preach Christian ethics. They exhort the unregenerate to champion the poor, believe in the family, work for justice, and they forget to tell them that Christ died for our sins so that we can be – as we need to be – saved, justified and reconciled to God. And so the world remains unaware that there is a salvation to be had; converts become few, and the church ceases to be missionary. Then, to the extent that it ceases to be missionary, the church ceases to be Christian.

MOVEMENT 4: The Gospel of the Son of God (9:1–31)

The fourth and final story in Section Two is the conversion of Saul of Tarsus. It continues the topic broached earlier: Judaism's witness to the Gentile world. After all, Saul of Tarsus, the greatest missionary to the Gentiles of all time, came out of Judaism. On the other hand, Saul was not always a missionary; it was his conversion to Christ that made him one. And so, in reading his story we shall encounter yet another essential difference between Judaism and Christianity.

Acts contains three accounts of Saul's conversion. The second (22:3–21) and the third (26:9–23) are Saul's own, given in his own words. The first is Luke's, and, at its basic level, it can be analysed as three stages in a journey:

1. Saul's journey to Damascus (9:1–9)
2. Saul's stay in Damascus (9:10–22)
3. Saul's return to Jerusalem and his departure for Tarsus (9:23–30)

Even at this level it is evident that Saul's conversion was not a matter of a slight adjustment to his former beliefs, a small helpful addition to his Judaism. It involved a radical change. His original journey to Damascus was never completed. Its goal abandoned, it became an altogether different kind of journey, as the once brilliant, energetic initiator Saul (9:1–2), now blinded and led by the hand, shuffled his way into Damascus, under new management to await instructions.

And his return to Jerusalem was altogether different from what he had planned. As a young man he had left his birthplace Tarsus to come and study in the high capital of his faith, Jerusalem; and at the time of his conversion he was driving to Damascus to bring the Christian heretics back to Jerusalem. That the new heresy should exist within the confines of Jerusalem was bad enough;

and he had done his best to stamp it out there. To find it spreading through Judaea, Samaria and up to Damascus was intolerable. The heretics had to be brought back to Jerusalem and forced to submit to the discipline of the Jerusalem Sanhedrin (9:2) before they started infecting the synagogues of the Dispersion. Jerusalem in his eyes ought to be, and through his efforts would be, the enforcer of doctrinal orthodoxy in the interests of world-wide Jewry.

But when he returned to Jerusalem, he came empty-handed, a 'heretic' himself, already travelling 'the Way' he had set out to suppress (9:2). And what is more, after a brief while circumstances, under the Lord's direction, compelled him – much against his will (see 22:17–21) – to abandon Jerusalem and return to Tarsus. Never again would Jerusalem be his base. Tarsus, and then Antioch, would take over that role, as he became a missionary to Gentiles who owed no allegiance to the authority of the Jerusalem Sanhedrin, and never would; who would come to believe in the true God of Israel, but would never become Jews.

If the outward effects of Saul's conversion were dramatic, at its heart was nothing less than a revolution: a radically new concept of God. Of course, even before his conversion he was a passionate believer in the one true God. He was no pagan idolater, nor even, as some pre-Maccabean high priests had been, an advocate of syncretism. He was a loyal and stalwart heir of God's self-revelation to Abraham. That revelation had brought Abraham out from the Gentiles and from their idolatrous concepts of deity, and had made him the founder of the Hebrew race. Faith in that same one true God had made Saul too a 'Hebrew of the Hebrews' (Phil. 3:5). If Gentiles were prepared to abandon their idolatrous concepts of God, to put their faith in the God of Israel, and to convert according to the strict rules of Pharisaism, he was prepared to welcome them as true members of Israel. But he was not prepared to compromise. He would not allow that Yahweh was virtually the same as the Greek Zeus or the Syrian Baal, just a different name for the same supreme god among all the other gods. And what vexed him beyond endurance was that fellow Jews should so far abandon the glorious monotheism in which they had been brought up, as to attribute divine honours to Jesus of Nazareth. Out of sincere zeal for the sacred honour of the name of God he persecuted them with all his might and main.

And there was the tragedy. Loyal to what he knew of God, he was so convinced that his monolithic understanding of monotheism was all there was to know of God that at first he would not

153

allow God himself to teach him more; he was so confident in his own concept of God that he was prepared to fight for his concept against the actual reality of God. When the God in whom he professed to believe became incarnate, he savagely persecuted him and all who believed in him; and thus he showed himself to be not only an unbeliever, but, as he later confessed (1 Tim. 1:12–17; Rom. 5:10), an enemy, persecutor and blasphemer against God. Who shall say that his blasphemy was less serious than that of Gentile polytheism? Certainly he never forgot what he did to God incarnate and to his disciples and saints (see 1 Cor. 15:9; Eph. 3:8; 1 Tim. 1:12–17); and it for ever cured him of any feeling of superiority over his Gentile, and erstwhile polytheist, fellow Christians.

Saul's encounter with the risen Lord Jesus

When the light from heaven suddenly shone around him and a voice said 'Saul, Saul, why do you persecute me?' (9:4), Saul immediately and instinctively addressed whoever it was that was speaking to him as 'Lord'; and whatever the exact nuance he intended in that split second, he very soon came to realise that the Jesus whom he instinctively addressed as Lord was Lord in the highest sense of the term.

First there had been the build-up to his persecution of the Christians. These people were in the habit of praying to Jesus, and they talked of this praying to Jesus as 'calling on the name of the Lord'. The Ananias of this very story is a case in point. Speaking to Jesus (cf. v.17 with vv.10–16) and calling him Lord, he says 'I have heard many reports about this man [Saul] and all the harm he has done to your saints in Jerusalem. And he has come here with authority from the chief priests to arrest *all who call on your name*' (9:13–14). Moreover, it was already widely known among the Jews, even among the Jews in Damascus, as we learn from 9:21, that the Christians had this practice of calling on the name of Jesus. Indeed it was one of the reasons why they were being persecuted. 'To call on the name of the Lord' was, as we know from the Old Testament, a standard description of prayer to God. Never, therefore, in the Old Testament does any Israelite call on the name of an angel, for the simple reason that Israel was not allowed prayer to angels. When Israelites started to 'call on the name of Baal' it was regarded as downright apostasy, for it put Baal in the place of God, and Elijah executed all who fostered the practice (1 Kings 18:16–46).

We can therefore understand Saul's rage against the early Christians. In calling on the name of Jesus they were, as the Roman Pliny was later to describe it, praying to Jesus as to God. Saul knew of their practice, considered it blasphemous, and was driving up the Damascus road to suppress it when there shone around him such a light from heaven, and such a voice addressed him, that instinctively he realised it was a theophany, and addressed the speaker as Lord – only to find that the Lord was Jesus.

It is an understatement to say that in this split second his whole concept of God was revolutionised. When the God of glory appeared to Abraham, Abraham at once perceived the infinite superiority of the true God over the debased concepts of deity thought up by paganism. Now, when the light of the knowledge of God in the face of Jesus Christ shone around Saul, Saul perceived with stunned amazement that the reality of the true and living God was infinitely greater than even the true but partial revelation given of himself to the founding fathers and prophets of Israel.

When Moses discovered why the burning bush was not consumed, and stood asking the Lord within it 'What is your name?', he also discovered, to his immense encouragement, that the God of his forefathers was not simply a remote figure in past history, nor only the exalted Lord in the heavens: he had 'come down' to earth to deliver his people (Exod. 3:8), and stood identified with them in their sufferings. Not all the persecution that Pharaoh could fling against them would ever destroy them.

But with what fearful consternation did Saul now see the inextinguishable glory of the risen Lord and hear him say 'I am Jesus, whom you are persecuting' (9:5). The vision blinded him physically, as well it might, for spiritually it turned all his former boasted knowledge of God into virtual darkness. God had come down to earth as a missionary 'to seek and to save what was lost' (Luke 19:10), and Saul had not recognised him. In the person of Jesus he had lived here, and burned in the fires of Calvary – and Saul had seen nothing in this great sight. Returned now to his heaven, he still stood inseparable from his persecuted believers, disciples, saints – and here was Saul, the supposed champion of orthodoxy, playing the impossible role of a modern-day Pharaoh!

The Ethiopian's heart had been captivated by the message of the lowly Servant of the Lord who was led as a lamb to the slaughter, was dumb before his shearers, was wounded for our transgressions, and was bruised for our iniquities. But this lowly

Servant was the exalted Lord; the Nazarene was God incarnate. A sight of his glory had now brought his enemy Saul to the ground; his mercy spared him, and his divine authority ordered him to proceed to Damascus and await further instructions. Saul of Tarsus had discovered God as he really is.

Saul's reception and commissioning by the Lord Jesus

It is a striking and significant thing that in order to arrest Saul and bring him to his knees, Christ personally appeared to him direct, without any intermediary; but for the purpose of his formal reception, his filling with the Holy Spirit, the restoration of his physical sight and his commissioning, Christ did not appear to him direct, but dealt with him through a human agent, one Ananias. This is all the more noticeable in that to prepare Saul for Ananias' coming and to assure him that Ananias was the Lord's duly appointed agent, Saul had to be given another vision in addition to his experience on the road (9:11–12).

The reason for using a human agent was that, as in other cases which we have already met, Saul had to be given the opportunity to demonstrate that his repentance and faith were genuine. The Jerusalem crowd on the day of Pentecost, many of whom had publicly shouted for the crucifixion of Jesus, were required to demonstrate that their repentance was genuine by being publicly baptised in the name of Jesus and by standing clear of his murderers (2:38–40). The people of Samaria had to show that they had repented of their rejection of God's word regarding Jerusalem by submitting to the laying on of hands by the apostles from Jerusalem (8:14–17). Now Saul is made to wait for his filling with the Holy Spirit, his baptism, the restoration of his physical sight, and his commissioning until Ananias comes and lays his hands on him (9:17).

Why so? Because of the particular outrageous sin that had been the expression of Saul's enmity against the Lord Jesus. He had been breathing out murderous threats against the Lord's disciples (9:1); he had inflicted great harm on the Lord's saints in Jerusalem (9:13); he had caused havoc among those who called on the Lord's name (9:21); he was intent on imprisoning the Christians in Damascus (9:21).

But now he had addressed the exalted Jesus as Lord. Did he mean what he said? Was it the genuine expression of a repentant

156

heart? Or was it merely a superficial, temporary response extorted from him against his will by the overpowering effect of the vision? How would you tell? Very simply! If Saul had genuinely accepted Jesus as Lord, he would be prepared to acknowledge as the Lord's people the people he had despised and had been persecuting; recognise them as his brothers; and not only recognise them, but accept them, and be identified with them both in private and in public.

Ananias, whom the Lord used as his agent on this occasion, was not one of the apostles. As far as we know he held no high office in the church. He was an 'ordinary' believer, never heard of before in Scripture, and only once afterwards (22:12). There was no sacerdotal magic in his fingers. But when he laid his hands on the erstwhile persecutor of the despised Nazarene, the gesture expressed the reality of his words: 'Brother Saul!' (9:17). And what he said next indicated how this new relationship had been brought about and what was its vital force: 'the Lord – Jesus, who appeared to you on the road as you were coming here – has sent me so that you may see again and be filled with the Holy Spirit' (9:17).

Here then is a basic principle of true conversion. You can come to saving faith in Christ, as Saul did, all by yourself through personal acceptance of Jesus as Lord. But if that faith is genuine, it will lead to acceptance of the Lord's people. I can be interested in birds without going anywhere near the local bird-watchers' society. Indeed, I can refuse to have anything to do with its members, and still be a very good bird-watcher myself. But I cannot genuinely accept Christ and refuse to have anything to do with his people. They are his disciples, his saints, they call on his name; and in giving the Holy Spirit to each one of them he unites them all in one body (cf. 1 Cor. 1:2, 12:13). I cannot receive that Holy Spirit and refuse to be a member of that body. I cannot claim to love the Lord Jesus and refuse to love his saints. I cannot claim to be identified with him and refuse to be identified with his people.

Another evidence of the genuineness of Saul's conversion was his response to the Lord's commissioning. Before his conversion he 'was convinced that [he] ought to do all that was possible to oppose the name of Jesus of Nazareth' (26:9). Now as he lay blinded in a room in Damascus, Ananias brought him the Lord's commission: he was to carry the name of Jesus before the Gentiles and their kings and before the people of Israel, and he was to suffer severely for that name (9:15–16). And 'at once', says Luke, 'he began to preach in the synagogues that Jesus is the Son of God' (9:20), and to prove 'that Jesus is the Christ' (9:22).

Of course we can say that Saul's case was special. And so it was, for he was an apostle. But what applied to him at his exalted level applies in principle to us all: no true conversion has (as yet) taken place unless the person concerned is ready at once to confess the full deity of the Lord Jesus. Many people, we know, take a long while to come to full faith in Christ; like the blind man of John's famous story (John 9), they begin by believing something before they eventually believe everything.* But no one is genuinely and fully converted, no one is a true Christian, until he or she believes in and is ready to confess the full deity of Jesus. If Jesus is not God incarnate, he has no salvation for us. Morality yes, and example and exhortation – all of it very exalted. But no salvation. If he were merely God's Suffering Servant but not God's Son, his death could not atone for our sins; nor could he impart the Holy Spirit to anyone, nor incorporate all the millions of his believers into himself.†

Finally, Saul was prepared not only publicly to confess the deity of Jesus, but also to suffer for that confession. Opportunity was not long in coming; and when it came, it arose not in a wordly but in a religious and theological context. It is often so. But still today readiness to suffer for the Name is an indispensable hallmark of a genuine conversion.

Saul's escape from Damascus, return to Jerusalem and departure to Tarsus

Luke now briefly records the third element in the process that turned the 'Hebrew of the Hebrews' Saul into the apostle to the Gentiles. It was his fellow Jews' rejection of his message and persecution of himself.

On his return to Jerusalem the Christians were at first suspicious, fearing that he was not a true convert (9:26). But thanks

---

*A good example of such a gradual coming to faith would be C. S. Lewis' conversion, as recorded in his *Surprised by Joy* (London: Collins Fount, 1977).

†Note the implication of Ananias' expression 'your saints' (9:13). Anyone can have disciples: Moses did; so even did Saul soon after his conversion (9:25). But in biblical language only God has *saints*: cf. 1 Samuel 2:9, '*his* saints'; Psalm 50:5, '*my* saints'; Psalm 79:2, '*your* saints'. Ananias in conversation with the risen Jesus naturally uses the expression 'your saints'. Ananias, like all Christians from the very start, believed in the full deity of the Lord Jesus.

to Barnabas' services they eventually accepted him; and he proved his genuineness by his fearless public witness in the name of the Lord Jesus. Moreover, with the ringleader of the anti-Christian persecution now converted, the church in Judea, Galilee and Samaria had peace and began to grow spiritually and numerically (9:31). According to his own account of things (22:17–21), he would then have gladly stayed in Jerusalem; and when the Lord appeared to him in a trance in the temple and told him that the Jews at Jerusalem would not listen to him, and that therefore he was to get out of Jerusalem and take the gospel to the Gentiles, he protested. He had been more zealous for Israel's faith, more active than any or all of them in opposition to Christianity. If now he had had a personal revelation from God, would they not listen to him? Or at least respect him? But no, it was no use. Obliged to flee for his life from the Jews of Damascus (9:23–25), he was presently forced to do the same from the Hellenistic Jews of Jerusalem (9:29–30).

It was a pattern that would repeat itself over and over again; and it would cause him endless sorrow of heart (Rom. 9:1–2). But in the fact that some Jews in Damascus, in Jerusalem and all over the world came to faith in Jesus as Lord, he came to see God's pledge that God had not rejected the people whom he foreknew. One day all Israel would be saved. Meanwhile, in the wisdom of God, the very rejection of the gospel by the Jews would have the effect of speeding out its message to the Gentiles; and the conversion of Gentiles by the million to faith, not in any old god, but in the God of Abraham, Isaac and Jacob who has finally spoken in his Son, would eventually provoke Israel to a healthy jealousy and to repentance. The scales would fall from their eyes as they fell from Saul's. They too would see the Lord, and be saved (Rom. 11:1–31).

Taught by his own experience, however, he saw clearly what had to happen if ever Israel was to be saved. In one sense he himself had always been a believer in God, and a staunch one at that (23:1); but if Jesus Christ was God incarnate, then for some years he had been an unbeliever, a disobedient rejecter of God. Conversion for him had meant first of all discovering that he was not the believer in God he thought he was. The same thing would have to happen to his nation.

Explaining God's strategies for the eventual conversion of his beloved Israel, he wrote to the Gentile Christians at Rome: 'For as you once were disobedient to God but now have received mercy by their disobedience, so these now have been disobedient in

159

order that they too may now receive mercy by the mercy shown to you' (Rom 11:30–31).* The word he uses for disobedience means not so much the breaking of a commandment but rather the withholding of the obedience of faith. When he reminds the Gentiles that they were once disobedient, he is thinking of what he said earlier (Rom. 1:18–28), that God originally revealed himself to the nations but that they did not like what they saw of God and refused to accept or believe it. Now God has revealed more of himself in Jesus, and this time the Jews have not liked it, and have refused to accept or believe it. It is a disaster; and yet God is determined to turn it to their eventual good. 'God has imprisoned all men in disobedience', Paul concludes, 'in order that he may have mercy upon all men' (Rom. 11:32). The first indispensable step to true faith, and thus to salvation, is to discover that one has so far been an unbeliever. For religious people, that can be very difficult. It was so with Saul of Tarsus. For some years he fought against admitting it; but on the Damascus road he caved in, and confessed that for all his sincere faith in God, in the only sense that really mattered he had never yet believed. And in that moment he found faith, mercy and salvation. The same applies to us all, whether pagan, Jew or nominal Christian (1 Tim. 1:12–16).†

---

*This translation of Romans 11:30–31, and of verse 32 which follows, is that of C. E. B. Cranfield, *A Critical and Exegetical Commentary on The Epistle to the Romans*, vol. 2 (Edinburgh: T. & T. Clark, 1979), p. 572.

† The following article is recommended for further reading on some of the topics raised in Section Two: I. Howard Marshall, 'Church and Temple in the New Testament', *Tyndale Bulletin* 40.2 (1989), pp. 203–22.

Section Three

The Christian Theory and Practice of Holiness (9:32–12:24)

Section Three
The Christian Theory and Practice of Holiness (9:32–12:24)

PRELIMINARY OBSERVATIONS

We come now to the third major parting of the ways between Christianity and Judaism. It occurred in the general area of what we may broadly term the theory and practice of holiness. It was occasioned by the remarkable advance that was made at this time in the going out of the gospel to the Gentiles.

It was of course part of our Lord's commission to his disciples right from the very beginning that they should be his witnesses to the ends of the earth (1:8) and that they should make disciples of all the nations (Matt. 28:19). But up to this point very little had been done in this direction; and when at this stage they began to face their responsibility, they were confronted with certain ancient barriers which had to be, and were, overcome and swept away.

The story is told in two movements. Movement 1 (9:32–11:18) is concerned all through with an evangelistic and pastoral journey that Peter made from Jerusalem to Lydda, Joppa, Caesarea and back again to Jerusalem (9:32, 38; 10:1, 24; 11:2). It contains two pairs of stories. Peter's visit to Lydda and Joppa form one pair; his visit to Caesarea and its sequel in Jerusalem the other. The movement concentrates, however, on the gigantic move forward that Christianity made when Peter took the gospel to Cornelius in Caesarea.

Cornelius was a Gentile, and so were his household and friends. Left to himself Peter would never have visited Cornelius' house and eaten with him, not even for the purpose of leading him to faith in Christ. According to his traditions and beliefs it would have contravened the Old Testament's laws on holiness.

163

Holiness, if you please, was a barrier against the going out of the gospel!

Therefore, at this stage in the development of Christianity God himself intervened directly to teach Peter that the basis and practice of holiness in Christianity were going to be very different from what they had been in Judaism. As a Christian he was free to mix with Gentiles socially and to eat with them; and he must be prepared to do so for the sake of bringing them the gospel. Peter obeyed and went. As he entered Cornelius' house, Christianity took a giant step away from Judaism towards full-blown Christianity. The centuries-old barrier, the dividing wall of hostility between Jew and Gentile, already undermined by the cross, was demolished. Peace and a new oneness in Christ were put in its place (Eph. 2:14).

Movement 2, like Movement 1, contains two pairs of stories. One pair is devoted to the establishment of the church in Antioch and its affairs (11:19–26 and 27–30); the other to Herod Agrippa's imprisonment of Peter and its sequel (12:1–19 and 20–24). The unifying theme in these two pairs is persecution and its relation to the spread of the gospel.

The first pair tells how persecution all unintentionally helped to spread the gospel. It rudely put an end to any inclination the early Christians may have had to remain in Jerusalem and Judea, and flung them out towards the big Gentile world. It also effectively took the initiative for, and the administrative control of, the mission to the Gentiles out of the hands of the Jerusalem church. It thus ensured that when the gospel came to the Gentiles it was not brought by people maintained and directed by a Jewish organisation with headquarters in Jerusalem; and as a result, when the first predominantly Gentile church was set up in a Gentile country, it was not, even in its early days, under the administrative control of a church in what to them was a foreign country.

The second pair of stories in Movement 2 likewise deals with persecution. It was perpetrated by Herod Agrippa I under the old sacralist idea that the state has the duty to control people's religious beliefs and the right to suppress minority religions to support, and to curry favour with, the majority religion. In this Herod was encouraged by the Jews, whose Old Testament commanded the religious leaders in Israel to call upon the civil power to suppress heretics. The narrative tells how God intervened to show that he disapproved of these sacralist attitudes and to deliver his people from them. Such sacralism was no longer an

appropriate means for Israel to use to buttress a supposed orthodoxy and to keep religion pure. It was now, and it was eventually
shown to be, a perversion of holiness.

Seeing that the major theme of this section is the contrast
between the Jewish and the Christian theory and practice of
holiness, we ought also to notice the emphasis that is placed on a
feature that both Jewish and Christian holiness have in common:
the importance of good works. Nothing need be said to publicise
Judaism's great and compassionate tradition of almsgiving and
good works: its fame is in all the world. Something perhaps needs
to be said to remind Christians that true Christianity puts an
equal emphasis on the duty of good works.

At 9:36 we are told of a woman called Dorcas who was always
doing good and helping the poor. Her speciality was making
garments for widows.

So, too, the Gentile Cornelius, we are told (10:2, 4), gave
generously to those in need, and his gifts to the poor came up as a
remembrance before God.

Or take this description of the Lord Jesus, the supreme doer
of good, from the opening paragraph of Peter's sermon in
Cornelius' house: 'You know . . . how God anointed Jesus of
Nazareth with the Holy Spirit and power, and how he went
around doing good and healing . . .' (10:37–38).

And then again, at 11:27–30 we are told how the recently
established church at Antioch sent money for famine relief to the
Christians in Judea.

Holiness is not simply a negative thing concerned only with not
doing bad things and not touching unclean things, though of
course, as with a surgeon and germs, a very negative attitude
towards uncleanness is extremely healthy. But holiness is also
positive, in its consecration to God and to his service, and in its
devoted service towards others.

A short table of selected contents will now help us to see how
the main stories in both movements are related to each other and
to Section Three as a whole (see p. 166).

We observe that in the course of this section Peter, on his own
confession, learns not one but two important lessons, and that
when he expresses what they are, he introduces them in almost
identical language. The first is in Story 3 at 10:34: 'Of a truth [Gk.
ep' alētheias] I perceive that God is no respecter of persons' (NIV: 'I
now realise how true it is that God does not show favouritism').
The second occurs in Story 7 at 12:11: 'Now I know of a truth [Gk.
alēthōs] that the Lord has sent his angel and delivered me out of

165

SECTION THREE: THE CHRISTIAN THEORY AND PRACTICE OF HOLINESS
(9:32–12:24)

MOVEMENT 1: The Gospel Released from Jewish Social Isolationism (9:32–11:18)	MOVEMENT 2: The Gospel Freed from Jewish Administrative Centralism and Political Sacralism (11:19–12:24)
1. AENEAS (9:32–35)	**5. ANTIOCH 1 (11:19–26)**
Peter's travels through all parts (9:32)	Disciples scattered and travel (11:19)
Saints (9:32)	Disciples called Christians (11:26)
Paralysed man healed; all at Lydda and Sharon turned to the Lord	'Men from Cyprus . . . began to speak [the gospel] to Greeks also; . . . a great number . . . turned to the Lord' (11:20–21)
2. DORCAS (9:36–43)	**6. ANTIOCH 2 (11:27–30)**
Social works: clothes for widows	Social works: famine relief
3. PETER AND CORNELIUS (10:1–48)	**7. HEROD AND PETER (12:1–19)**
The end to religious and social separation between Jew and Gentile	Political discrimination on the ground of religion
Prayer: Cornelius (10:4) and Peter (10:9)	Prayer: by whole church (12:5)
Visions; angel (10:3, 16)	Vision? Angel! (12:7–9)
Peter: 'I now realise how true . . .' (10:34)	Peter: 'Now I know without a doubt . . .' (12:11)
4. PETER: THE SEQUEL (11:1–18)	**8. HEROD: THE SEQUEL (12:20–24)**
'The circumcised believers criticised him . . .' (11:2)	Herod 'had been quarrelling with the people of Tyre and Sidon' (12:20)
'They had no further objections and glorified God . . .' (11:18)	Herod 'delivered a public address . . . Because [he] did not give the glory to God, an angel . . . struck him down' (12:21–23)

the hand of Herod and from all the expectation of the people of the Jews.' The similarity of the language and the matching position of the two stories in the structure of the narrative invite us to compare the two stories very closely and carefully. The first lesson is well known and had obvious and continuing implications for the development of Christianity and for the evangelism of the world. The question that arises is: 'Was the second lesson of equal importance, and has it similarly continuing implications for us? Or is that particular story now of merely historical interest?

We should also notice the verbal similarities between Stories 4 and 8. Story 4 relates that Peter's fellow Christians at Jerusalem eventually 'had no further objections and glorified God' (11:18). Story 8 tells how Herod delivered a public address, did not give the glory to God, and was struck down by an angel for his trouble (12:21–23). The contrast is vivid. It could, of course, belong simply to the purely superficial verbal level; on the other hand, it may be worth looking to see if there is some deeper relationship between these two stories.

Not only their position but their function, each within its own movement, is the same. Story 4, the questioning of Peter about his visit to Cornelius by his Jewish fellow Christians at Jerusalem, is a natural sequel to that visit as told in Story 3. Story 8, the death of Herod, is likewise a natural sequel to Story 7, Herod's persecution of the Jerusalem church. Both sequels end on a note of triumph: Story 4 announces the final withdrawal of the Jerusalem church's opposition to the taking of the gospel to the Gentiles; and Story 8 announces the death of the persecutor of the Jerusalem church, and therefore the end of this opposition.

Both sequels, of course, provide a natural climax to their movements. Movement 1 begins with the account of Peter's travels through many parts; Story 4 brings these travels to their triumphant end with Peter's return to base at Jerusalem. Movement 2 begins with the mention of the persecution that arose in Jerusalem and Judea over the Stephen affair and the effect it had on the Jerusalem church. The movement continues with the further persecution of the Jerusalem church by Herod. Story 8 brings all persecution to an end for the time being by the ignominious and divinely inflicted death of the persecutor. The question remains, however, whether stories 4 and 8 have any thematic relationship with each other; and we must investigate it later.

All Luke's stories are of course interesting and informative. But we could be forgiven if at first sight some of them seemed more important than others, and the proportions of some of them a little strange. But Luke's careful selection and arrangement of his material in Section Three suggests that in his mind, at least, his narrative was not an uneven collection of more important, less important and unimportant details. Each item was selected and arranged in order to contribute its necessary part to the message of the whole.

THE MOVEMENTS

MOVEMENT 1: The Gospel Released from Jewish Social Isolationism (9:32–11:18)

The first major movement of Section Three concerns itself with Peter's travels. It is perhaps a point worth mentioning that according to Acts Peter did travel: Paul was not the only one to do so (cf. 1 Cor. 9:5). His travels brought him in fact to a point where he confronted the Gentile world and was used of God formally and officially to open the way for the Christian gospel to be taken to the Gentiles. His visit to Cornelius may not have been the first visit paid by a Jewish Christian to a Gentile. That is not the point. The point is that Peter's visit to Cornelius explicitly raised the theoretical and scriptural principles involved in such visits, and settled the matter at the highest level for all time.

But before Luke launches into the record of this crucial visit to Cornelius, he is led to select two incidents that occurred at an earlier stage in Peter's preaching-tour. The brevity of these two stories suggests that while important in their own right, they are in some sense preliminary to the main story. The first of them contains only four verses, the second no more than eight. If the main story is to talk about holiness, what have these two preliminary stories to say that might be relevant to that?

Aeneas (9:32–35)

'As Peter travelled about the country,' says Luke, 'he went to visit the saints in Lydda' (9:32). Notice the term 'saints', that is 'holy ones'. Luke uses various terms in Acts to denote his fellow members of the faith. 'Disciples' is his favourite one: he uses it about thirty times. 'Christian' is naturally very rare: he records the first time it was ever applied to the disciples (11:26), and he uses it only once thereafter (26:28). But 'saints' is also rare: it occurs in 9:13, here in 9:32, again in 9:41, later in 26:10, and nowhere else in Acts.* It is possible, therefore, that Luke uses the words 'disciples', 'saints' and 'Christians' as small change, without any particular emphasis on their exact connotation. But the fact that he uses 'saints' on two occasions in these preliminary stories, just before the long story on holiness, is surely no accident. Here are two preliminary stories about saints, Jewish Christian saints. Both contain a miracle, and both miracles lead to a crop of conversions among the general public: for both are exhibitions of what the Lord Jesus Christ can do in relation to this matter of sainthood.

The two stories present certain contrasts: one concerns a man, the other a woman. The woman while she lived was full of good works. The man by contrast had few good works to show: he was a paralytic and had been bedridden for eight years. It was not his fault, of course, that he could do no work. All the same, it was sad to see a full-grown man so permanently and helplessly disabled, without the strength either to make his own bed or to get his own meals. 'Aeneas, Jesus Christ heals you,' said Peter (9:34), 'Get up and tidy up your mat' (or 'get yourself a meal': the Greek can mean either). Immediately he did so, with the result that when the inhabitants of Lydda and Sharon saw the former paralytic healed and at work, able to look after himself, they 'turned to the Lord' (9:36).

The paralysis was literal and the healing a physical miracle. But we shall not be far wrong if we suppose that as with our Lord's miracles of physical healing this miracle too conveyed a deeper lesson. Our Lord's multiplication of loaves and fishes pointed to himself as the Bread of Life (John 6). His gift of physical sight to a blind man pointed beyond itself to his ability to impart spiritual sight (John 9). His healing of a paralytic and the man's subsequent ability to walk and work were explicitly offered as a demonstration of the reality of the forgiveness the man had received (Luke 5:17–26). So too with Aeneas' healing. It was in the first instance an exhibition of supernatural physical power that advertised the reality of the risen Christ. But surely it was more. It did not of course carry an implicit promise that every paralytic or quadriplegic will be instantaneously healed upon becoming a Christian. History has shown otherwise. But it did point to Christ's ability to empower all his people; in the metaphorical language of Hebrews 12:12–13, to reinvigorate their

* 'Sanctified', in 20:32 and 26:18, is of course a related term.

drooping hands and paralysed knees. Then, as the NEB puts it, 'the disabled limb will not be put out of joint, but regain its former powers'.

It is all too easy for Christians to give people an impression of holiness that repels them. It is true, of course, that all believers are 'saints' by calling. They have been sanctified by the offering of the body of Jesus Christ once for all (Heb. 10:10). In this sense one believer is no more a saint than another. The members of the church at Corinth, troubled by faults and failings and impurities and divisions though they were, are addressed as 'saints' (1 Cor. 1:2), just as the believers at Rome (Rom. 1:7) or at Philippi (Phil. 1:1) or anywhere else are.

But that is only one side of the story. True saintliness will sooner or later begin to make its presence felt; for it is not a form of weakness, encouraging people to remain in spiritually immature dependence on others, all the while obsessed with 'difficulties' and 'problems'. True saintliness is positive, vigorous, active, maturely self-supporting and able spiritually to stand on its own feet. Jesus Christ our Lord has the power to make us holy in this practical sense; to release us from unhealthy inhibitions and weaknesses; to make us strong and active in the work he gives us to do and so to make us an advertisement to the world of what true Christian saintliness is.

Dorcas (9:36–43)

Dorcas was no paralytic: she was 'always doing good and helping the poor' (9:36), Moreover, it is probably true to say that she learned her good works from Judaism even before she became a Christian. Christianity has no monopoly of good works. True Judaism has a long and sustained tradition of generous care for the poor, inculcated throughout the generations by both Moses and the prophets. Then what can Christ add to the impetus that Judaism already gave to such practical holiness?

The story is that Dorcas died, but that Peter came and raised her from the dead. Her resurrection was, presumably, only a resuscitation, like the cases reported in the Gospels. Even so, it must have been for her an amazing, unforgettable experience that remained with her for the rest of her days. Only picture her situation. She had been busy at her social relief when death intervened and brought all her work to an end. But presently she opened her eyes again, and there stood none other than the apostle Peter himself, who raised her up and took her to the next room. And there were the people for whom she had worked so hard before she died, and they were greeting her with unbounded joy and gratitude. And there, too, was the work she had done, the garments she had made, and the widows had been showing them to the great apostle himself (9:39). Such gratitude, such honour, such recognition of her labours! If ever a woman caught sight of the lasting effect and value of her work, that woman was Dorcas when she was raised from the dead. It surely gave her an added impetus to go on working with all her might and main for the rest of her life.

Now we may regard her story, if we care to, simply as a museum piece of ancient history, an extraordinary kind of miracle rare enough even in the time of our Lord and his apostles and infinitely rarer since, as again history has shown us. But if we do, we shall impoverish ourselves. Our Lord's raising of Lazarus (John 11), like Peter's raising of Dorcas, was only a resuscitation, but our Lord used it as a sign of greater things: as a pointer, first of all, to himself as the resurrection and the life, and then to the full resurrection of all his saints at his second coming. And if he so used Lazarus' resuscitation, we could scarcely be wrong to draw similar encouragement from Dorcas'. Our work for God and man is valuable in and of itself for the good it does in this life. But its significance and value do not end in the grave. The certain fact of Christ's resurrection, the glorious prospect of our own resurrection or transformation at his coming, assure us that our labour is not in vain in the Lord (1 Cor. 15:50–58). We too shall see our work again.

Here then is encouragement to persist in toil, and a warning not to indulge in shoddy workmanship. When the Lord comes and the dead are raised and the living caught up together with them to meet the Lord, all must 'appear before the judgement seat of Christ, that each one must receive what is due' to him or her 'for the things done while in the body, whether good or bad' (2 Cor. 5:10). If our works survive Christ's inspection, then ours will be a fourfold joy. First, the sheer joy of knowing we have pleased the Lord. Secondly, the joy of experiencing the eternal gratitude and friendship of those we helped on earth (Luke 16:9). Thirdly, the joy of seeing the work we did in our lifetime last eternally. And on top of that, a reward from the Saviour himself (1 Cor. 3:12–14).

But it will be possible to find our work judged as unworthy and substandard, and burned up under the Lord's investigation. A believer in that position will still be saved, since salvation is a gift,

171

and was never at any stage a reward for work done. But such a believer will sense a fourfold loss. First, the realisation of not having pleased the Lord. Secondly, the wasted opportunities to make eternal friends: no one's eternal gratitude, no one's special friendship. Thirdly, nothing to see for life's work. And fourthly, no reward (1 Cor. 3:15).

Let us, therefore, make sure that our holiness is of the practical kind, like Dorcas', and that the bright certainty of the resurrection keeps us always 'abounding in the work of the Lord' (1 Cor. 15:58, AV).

Peter and Cornelius (10:1–48)

It sounds a very strange thing indeed when you first hear it, that it was a concern for holiness that initially acted as a barrier against the spread of the gospel by the early Christians. But so it was. Left to himself Peter would never have entered the houses of uncircumcised Gentiles and eaten with them, because to his way of thinking it would have contravened the Old Testament laws on holiness. Peter and all those of his fellow Jews who kept those laws were 'saints'; people who did not keep them were 'unclean'. It was wrong for 'saints' who wanted to please God by maintaining their holiness to mix socially and to eat with 'unclean' people. And, therefore, if taking the gospel to Gentiles meant entering their homes and eating with them, it could not be done. Holiness would not allow it.

Our first reaction on hearing this might perhaps be to dismiss this whole concept of holiness as nonsense or worse, and to attribute it to appalling narrow-mindedness on the part of Peter and his particular circle of fellow Jews. But we must not do that. Perhaps they had exaggerated the requirements of the Old Testament law in their desire to prevent themselves from coming anywhere near breaking it. But it was God who gave the law. And it is to be noticed that when the Lord gave Peter his vivid object-lesson and Peter objected to the Lord's command, 'Get up, Peter. Kill and eat' (10:13), God did not say, 'Oh, Peter, do not be so narrow-minded. Forget those foolish superstitions and restrictions. Eat, man, and enjoy yourself.' No, of course not. It was God himself who had laid down those laws, and he certainly was not blaming Peter for having loyally done his best to obey them. What the Lord did say was that the laws were now repealed (10:15).

But that pushes the question one stage further back. Why ever did God lay down these laws in the first place?

The purpose of the Old Testament food laws

A widely held view has been that God did it because he was concerned for the health and hygiene of his people. In those far-off primitive days, so the argument goes, when people had no scientific understanding of germs and viruses, and no refrigeration to stop meat going bad, God forbade the eating of certain animals, birds and fish, to protect his people from the poison that those creatures could easily carry.

But this explanation is inadequate. When the Lord Jesus was on earth he cancelled these food laws – see Mark 7:19: 'In saying this, Jesus declared all foods "clean".' And that was not because science and technology had advanced so far in his day that it was now safe to eat foods that up till that time had been a danger to health! If they had been dangerous to eat in Moses' days, they were still dangerous to eat in our Lord's time. If they were now fit to eat, it was because they were consecrated by the word of God and prayer, as Paul subsequently put it (1 Tim. 4:4–5).

A better explanation of the Old Testament food laws would start from observing the reason why our Lord cancelled them:

> Nothing that enters a man from the outside can make him 'unclean'. For it doesn't go into his heart but into his stomach . . .
> . . . What comes out of a man is what makes him 'unclean'. For from within, out of men's hearts, come evil thoughts, sexual immorality, theft, murder, adultery, greed, malice, deceit, lewdness, envy, slander, arrogance and folly. All these evils come from inside and make a man 'unclean'. (Mark 7:18–23)

What our Lord was concerned about, therefore, was real *moral* uncleanness, and very forcefully he made the point that physical food entering the body cannot defile a man morally or spiritually: for it touches his stomach, not his heart.* Now the very fact that the disciples did not at first understand him (see Mark 7:15–18), and he was obliged to repeat his lesson, shows that the apostles had originally confused these two things. They originally thought that eating 'unclean food' defiled a man morally, when of

---

*To eat stolen food would of course defile a man, because the immoral act of theft would defile his heart. The food by itself would not defile him.

course it did not.* It was God's prohibition on certain kinds of food that made eating it defiling, not the food in itself.

And this is the crucial point that is made to Peter in his vision. When Peter protests against eating anything common or unclean, the voice replies: 'Do not call anything impure that God has made clean' (10:15). In what sense, we must ask, had God cleansed it? Obviously not by ridding the food of poisonous chemicals and viruses, so that from now on pork would never give anyone a tape-worm! He had cleansed it in the sense of removing the prohibition he once put on it, and allowing Peter and all others to eat it: they could now eat it with a clear conscience.

If then we have established that it was God's prohibition that had originally made the food unclean, rather than any intrinsic poison in the food itself, we are left with the question: Why did God originally forbid Israel certain foods?

The answer is: To teach them certain lessons by introducing the categories of ceremonial cleanness and uncleanness.

Leave aside for the moment these food laws. Israel as a nation were separated out from the other nations to enjoy a special relationship with God and to carry a special role among the nations. As Balaam put it, 'I see people who live apart and do not consider themselves one of the nations' (Num. 23:9). As God explained to them at Sinai: '. . . out of all nations you will be my treasured possession. Although the whole earth is mine, you will be for me a kingdom of priests and a holy nation' (Exod. 19:5–6). In accordance with this special role, therefore, they were commanded naturally enough to keep themselves pure from the moral and spiritual uncleanness that so polluted the Gentile nations. Listing and prohibiting the sexual immoralities, the religious idolatries, the commercial dishonesties, the infanticide, demonism and incest prevalent among the Canaanite nations, God explained:

> Do not defile yourselves in any of these ways, because this is how the nations that I am going to drive out before you became defiled. Even the land was defiled; so I punished it for its sin, and the land vomited

---

*Breaking a command of God would of course defile a man morally and spiritually. And that is why the Lord had to cancel the food laws. The disciples might now eat food of any kind with a clear conscience; and the food in and of itself would not defile them morally. Paul shows that this is how he understood the Lord: 'As one who is in the Lord Jesus, I am fully convinced that no food is unclean in itself. But if anyone regards something as unclean, then for him it is unclean', Romans 14:14.

out its inhabitants . . . And if you defile the land, it will vomit you out
as it vomited out the nations that were before you. (Lev. 18:24–28)

These, then, were moral and spiritual prohibitions. But
to reinforce them God added laws providing for ceremonial
cleanness:

You must therefore make a distinction between clean and unclean
animals and between unclean and clean birds. Do not defile
yourselves by any animal or bird or anything that moves along the
ground – those which I have set apart as unclean for you. You are to be
holy to me [or, to be my holy ones] because I, the Lord, am holy, and I
have set you apart from the nations to be my own. (Lev. 20:25–26)

These ceremonial and ritual laws would have both a positive
and a negative effect.

Positively, they reinforced in Israel's thinking that as a nation
they were separated *to* the Lord; specially set apart for him.
However morally and spiritually clean the members of another
nation might have been, they did not have the role that Israel as a
nation had. Israel's role, as a kingdom of priests, was special,
indeed unique. The ceremonial separation from certain kinds of
food which other nations ate reinforced and underlined the fact
that they were in a special sense separated to the Lord, specially
'holy' in a ritualistic way.

Negatively, these food laws had an immediate practical effect:
they made social mixing with Gentile nations difficult, since
Israelites could not eat Gentile food. This would not only reinforce the fact that Israel was a special nation, but also act as a
constant reminder that Israel was to avoid the moral and spiritual
uncleanness of the Gentiles.

Now of course not all Gentiles were as corrupt and filthy as the
Canaanites. But here too was a problem: many Gentiles were
guilty of corrupt habits. How could Israel therefore be protected
from their influence? The way God used was to build a wall
between Israel and *all* Gentiles. Just as a parent will do with a
child: not all men are child-molesters, but enough of them are to
make it a wise and sensible thing for parents to do, to forbid their
young children to take sweets or money or car-rides from *any* man
they don't know.

And the analogy holds good for a further point. Parents may
forbid their early-teenage daughter from going to certain sleazy
parts of a city. They do so, not because they think their daughter
is essentially better than other girls, but rather because they know
that their daughter is essentially no better than others. She has

175

the same human nature as others. She too could be corrupted as others have been. A good apple put among bad ones does not improve the bad ones: *they* corrupt *it*.

Israel under the law, says Paul, was like a child (Gal. 4:1–3); and God treated them appropriately. He put a wall of ceremonial food laws around them to remind them that they were a people separated to God, and to protect them as far as possible from Gentile pollution. And the need for and the importance of that wall can be seen from their history: when they disregarded the wall, they generally became as corrupt as the other nations.

The abrogation of the Old Testament food laws

But, of course, the wall-technique had its limitations and weaknesses. First, it led unintentionally to Israelites thinking that they were intrinsically better than Gentiles; whereas of course they were not. The Old Testament itself showed them that God's choice of them was attributable not to their superiority but to God's sovereign love. Secondly, it led to a confusion between moral and spiritual holiness on the one side and ceremonial holiness on the other. Even the disciples were amazed when our Lord pointed out that no food, in and of itself, defiles a man morally or spiritually: it does not touch his heart, but only his stomach (Mark 7:14–23). And human nature being what it is, the temptation was always there to concentrate on the externals of ceremonial holiness and to neglect real internal, moral and spiritual holiness – like those Pharisees of whom our Lord said: 'you Pharisees clean the outside of the cup and dish, but inside you are full of greed and wickedness' (Luke 11:39).

And thirdly, it led to the false idea that Israelites were God's favourites, whatever (evil) they did, whereas the Gentiles were rejected by God whatever (good) they did. Paul had to remind his fellow Jews:

> Circumcision has value if you observe the law, but if you break the law, you have become as though you had not been circumcised. If those who are not circumcised keep the law's requirements, will they not be regarded as though they were circumcised? The one who is not circumcised physically and yet obeys the law will condemn you who, even though you have the written code and circumcision, are a law-breaker. (Rom. 2:25–27)

Lack of recognition of this principle on the Jews' part led to a lot of misunderstanding, and to a great deal of hostility on the part of

Gentiles. There was anyway a natural jealousy and resentment against Israel for their claim that they stood in special relationship with God, and carried a special role. The Gentiles found what to them was Israel's stand-offishness and their holier-than-thou attitude difficult to take. But when individual Jews could be utterly unprincipled in business and yet still regard themselves as 'saints' and fit for other Jews to eat with, while Gentiles of personal integrity and business rectitude were dismissed as unfit people for these 'saints' to eat with, the potential for disgust, resentment and anger was unlimited.

With the incarnation of the Son of God, 'the time had fully come' (Gal. 4:4). The people of Israel were now to leave their childhood and learn to live and be treated as grown-up sons. One of the first things to go was the food laws. Our Lord himself cancelled them, as we have earlier seen (Mark 7:18–23). The disciples had not at once seen the implications of this, and even when they saw them, some of them would prove slow in living up to them fully. But now a crucial moment had come: the gospel must go out to the Gentiles; nothing must be allowed to stop or hinder it, or to becloud its message. Peter had to be given a direct, personal, vivid object-lesson from the Lord himself that the food laws had been cancelled and that he was therefore free to eat with the Gentile Cornelius in the course of taking him the gospel.

Imagine the anomalous situation that would have arisen if Peter had not learned the lesson. Cornelius was a man of exemplary morals and piety. Gentile though he still was, he had abandoned his ancestral idolatry and turned to the worship of the one true God of Israel, and was in fact respected by his Jewish neighbours. He gave generously to those in need, and prayed to God regularly. Moreover, he had heard of the Lord Jesus and wished to learn more about him. Yet because he was not circumcised and did not observe the food laws, he was not a 'saint'. Peter would have refused to eat with him or even to enter his house. On the other hand, take the likes of those Pharisees and Sadducees whom our Lord denounced (not all Pharisees were bad or denounced). They were inwardly rapacious, hypocrites and cruel. In heart they were so far away from God that they murdered his Son. Yet they were 'saints'! Peter, had he ever been invited, would have felt perfectly free to eat with them!

No, the time had come for change. God who had instituted the food laws had now cancelled them. He had made (that is, pronounced) all foods clean. Peter was not to go on calling common (that is, ceremonially unfit for a 'holy' people to eat) foods that God had now pronounced to be clean. He could go and eat Gentile food, in a Gentile's house, along with Gentiles. Since it would no longer be breaking a divine commandment, it would not defile his heart or conscience, and the food of itself would not of course touch his heart or defile him morally or spiritually.

Christianity, then, was making a very big break with Judaism when Peter entered Cornelius' house. But if Christianity was breaking with such an important element in Jewish holiness, what was it putting in its place? The wall was invented to serve a necessary practical purpose. It was not ideal, but it was better than nothing. The world had not changed. It was still a defiled world, no friend either to grace or to God. Was Christianity going simply to break down the wall, take a permissive attitude, and say uncleanness no longer mattered? Of course not! It will require higher standards than Judaism, more realistic, more demanding. But at the same time it will provide a power for holy living that Judaism never knew about.

The Christian way of holiness

The Christian way of holiness, then, is now to be set out in the rest of Movement 1: first in Peter's sermon in Cornelius' house; and then in the further explanation he gives to his Christian brothers in Jerusalem.

As he entered Cornelius' house, Cornelius met him and fell at his feet in reverence. Peter made him get up at once. For here was lesson number one: 'I am only a man myself' (10:26). He was a Jew. No matter: he was only a human being just like the Gentiles. There are not two classes of human being: one of higher and the other of lower rank. Just one class: human beings.

Peter was also an apostle of the Lord. Yet even so he would not allow Cornelius to bow at his feet in honour of the office he held. In spite of his office, he was a man still on the same human level as Cornelius.

Then Peter acknowledged how he himself had had to be corrected by God. 'You are well aware', he said, 'that it is against our law for a Jew to associate with a Gentile or visit him; but God has shown me that I should not call any man common or unclean' (10:28). So very often it is the man who admits that he himself has recently had to be corrected and to change his views who makes the most readily acceptable teacher of others.

But we must stay a moment with the lesson Peter says God had taught him. 'God has shown me that I should not call any man common or unclean' (10:28). The lesson the Lord taught Peter in the vision was about food: the Lord had lifted all prohibitions, he had pronounced all foods to be clean; therefore Peter was to stop regarding these foods as common, that is as unfit for saints, holy people, to eat. But now God has gone on to show Peter a further lesson. No *human being* is to be called common or unclean ('impure or unclean', NIV, would be tautologous).*

What does that mean? He cannot mean, can he, that there are no unclean people in the world? Paul says of some people that 'Having lost all sensitivity, they have given themselves over to sensuality so as to indulge in every kind of impurity . . .' (Eph. 4:19). Peter does not wish to contradict him does he? Even Peter himself, describing the way Gentiles live, says that they live 'in debauchery, lust, drunkenness, orgies, carousing and detestable idolatry' (1 Pet. 4:3).

No, to understand his meaning we must read what he says in its context. As an Israelite, he regarded himself by definition as 'holy' because he was a member of the 'holy' nation and because he kept the ceremonial food laws and washings. Gentiles, on the other hand, he held to be by definition 'common': they were not members of the holy nation; and he regarded them as unclean, because they were not circumcised, and did not keep the ceremonial food laws and ablutions. It was that situation which Peter saw was now changing. If God had cancelled the prohibitions on food and had pronounced all foods clean, Gentiles were no longer 'unclean' because they ate certain foods. More profoundly: if God were now doing away with Israel's special privilege, destroying the wall of partition between Jew and Gentile, Gentiles were no longer 'common' by definition, nor Israelites 'holy' by definition. Jew and Gentile stood alike on the same platform. There were no longer any second-class people or nations.

---

*Notice the terminology. The opposite of 'holy' in Old Testament thought can be one of two things, or both. The sabbath day, for instance, is holy in the sense that it is consecrated to the Lord. The other days, not so consecrated to the Lord, are not necessarily 'unclean'; they are common. Similarly with utensils. Pots consecrated to God's service were holy (and in addition, of course, had to be clean). Pots not consecrated were common, not necessarily unclean, though of course they could become so. So with bread. The Bread of Presence in the Tabernacle was *most* holy. Only the priests could eat it. That did not imply that ordinary bread, which any Israelite might eat, was 'unclean'. Similarly, Paul says to the Christian about food: 'For everything God created is good, and nothing is to be rejected if it is received with thanksgiving, because it is *consecrated* by the word of God and prayer' (1 Tim. 4:4–5).

Peter was presently taken indoors, and he addressed the company that had gathered. His opening words were: 'Of a truth I perceive, I grasp the fact, I realise, that God is no respecter of persons; that is, he does not show favouritism, but accepts men from every nation who fear him and do what is right' (10:34–35).

Is this yet another lesson? And if so, how has he learned it? Why, he has just heard Cornelius' explanation of what led him to ask Peter to come: four days ago an angel appeared to him as he was praying and said, 'Cornelius, God has heard your prayer and remembered your gifts to the poor' (10:31); and the explanation has taught Peter that good works are good works, and the fear of God is the fear of God, whoever it is that does the works and shows the fear. It does not matter what nation a man comes from: God does not accept one man's good works because he is a Jew and reject another's because he is a Gentile. God does not ignore one man's fear of God and prayers because he is a Gentile and accept another's because he is a Jew. There is no difference in God's sight – in this there never has been. This is not something new. God had made a distinction between Israel and the Gentiles in the area of the role and the holiness and consecration he expected from Israel; but not in the area of morality. Israel's sin was sin, just like the Gentiles'. The Gentiles' good works were good, just like Israel's.

Peter, then, has learned what Paul later says in Romans:

> God 'will give to each person according to what he has done' . . . There will be trouble and distress for every human being who does evil: first for the Jew, then for the Gentile; but glory, honour and peace for everyone who does good: first for the Jew, then for the Gentile. For God does not show favouritism. (Rom. 2:6, 9–11)

Peter is not saying (and neither is Paul) that any man, no matter of what nation, can in actual fact merit, and attain to, salvation on the ground of his good works. For this principle that God does not show favouritism applies elsewhere as well: 'There is no difference [that is, between Jew and Gentile], for all have sinned and fall short of the glory of God' (Rom. 3:22–23). What he is saying is that God values and accepts people's good works without partiality, and altogether independently of what nation they come from.

It was a very fortunate thing, therefore, that Peter learned this lesson before he began to preach to Cornelius. How unfortunate it would have been if he had walked into his house and begun his

180

sermon by declaring that Cornelius was an unclean Gentile, and that even his righteous deeds were as filthy rags. For Cornelius would have replied 'That's strange: for the other day, an angel came and told me that God had heard my prayer and remembered my gifts to the poor!'

We must not confuse two separate issues. Judged in the light of God's absolute standards of holiness, everybody's good works are little better than filthy rags. Certainly, if we attempted to depend on them for salvation, his law would have no option but to condemn both them and us. And it is to be noted that though the angel had told Cornelius that God had remembered his good works, he also told him that he still needed to be saved (11:13–14), and Cornelius made no attempt to claim his works as deserving salvation. When he eventually heard of the possibility of forgiveness and salvation through Christ, he did not retort: 'I don't need salvation: my good works are just as good as yours.' He humbly admitted his need of forgiveness and accepted salvation solely through faith in Christ.

But the fact that people's good works cannot earn them salvation does not mean that God is not interested in their doing, or attempting to do, good works. It is all too possible that we give people the wrong impression here: being so anxious to break their dependence on good works for salvation, we are in danger of giving the impression that it is no good their trying to do good works before they are saved, and that it does not in the end really matter all that much whether they do good works after they are saved either, because 'salvation is not of works'. And so we are in danger of producing a race of evangelicals who think that they are automatically better than the unsaved simply because they are believers, disciples, saints, even if their home-life, their business ethics and their works of charity are far inferior to those of people who make no profession of being saved.

The truth is that God loves good works, and he *is* interested in the good works even of people who are not yet saved. He 'remembered Cornelius' gifts to the poor' (10:31). He read them as the practical expression of Cornelius' desire to please God. Cornelius feared God, was searching for God, searching for salvation and fellowship: his works were the sign of the sincerity of his heart's search. And God in response sent an angel to tell him how to find an evangelist who could tell him how to be saved.

And though salvation is not of works, the result of salvation is to produce good works: 'our great God and Saviour, Jesus Christ, . . . gave himself for us to redeem us from all wickedness and to purify for himself a people that are his very own, eager to do what is good' (Tit. 2:13–14; cf. AV, 'zealous of good works').

Instead of beginning his sermon by emphasising Cornelius' sinfulness and need of salvation, Peter therefore began on another tack altogether. He presented the gospel as the good news of peace through Jesus Christ (10:36): it was sent to the people of Israel – there's no denying Israel's special role as the messenger – but Jesus Christ 'is Lord of all'. As Paul would put it, that same Lord over all is rich to 'all who call on him' (Rom. 10:12).

Secondly, he presented the life and activity of the Lord Jesus. The story, he reminded them, began with the baptism that John preached, calling on people to repent and prepare for the coming of the Lord. He came. God anointed him with the Holy Spirit and power; and 'he went around doing good and healing all who were under the power of the devil, because God was with him' (10:37–38).

How delightful this is! Cornelius was a man who sincerely sought to do good and help the poor. Peter presents for his admiration and faith the supreme doer of good. Even at this level Christ unites both Jew and Gentile. Serious moralists, people who genuinely love goodness and seek to do good, whatever their race, nation or background, must and do admire the goodness of Jesus Christ. 'We are witnesses of everything he did in the country of the Jews and in Jerusalem' (10:39). There spoke an apostle, chosen for this very purpose (1:8, 21–22).

But now comes the bombshell. 'They killed him by hanging him on a tree' (10:39).

Who did? Whatever for? A flood of questions bursts in on the mind. The statement is so stark! Doubtless, of course, Luke is only giving us a summary, not a verbatim report. Even so the brevity of the statement is extraordinary. What an admission! Peter does not actually say 'The Jews killed him.' Others joined with them: Herod, Pilate. But what a thing for a Jew to have to tell a Gentile: that the Jews, the saints, the people blessed with a God-given religion, zealous for righteousness, with a privileged role among the nations, killed the supreme doer of good! And not only killed him, but hanged him on a tree. That was a penalty given out to the worst of criminals. Anyone hanged on a tree was in Jewish thought 'cursed by God' (see Deut. 21:22–23). How could the human heart, how could the religious mind, be so perverse as to condemn the fairest life that ever lived as though it were the foulest? What has privilege, 'sainthood', the 'better than-the-Gentiles attitude' achieved if it has come to this? How bankrupt the religion, how woefully far short the good works. And this is not a Gentile accusing the Jews: this is a Jew confessing to a Gentile what his Jewish nation have done to Jesus!

But are Gentiles any better? Of course not! It has been an ever-increasingly loud protest by the Jews in recent decades that the fearful sin of antisemitism has been fostered by the Christians' teaching of each generation of children that it was the Jews who killed Jesus. There is some truth in the protest. Christendom has been guilty of grievous pride and cruelty. But it has been the pride and cruelty of a Christendom unregenerate and evil. Every true Gentile Christian will without hesitation confess that he is no better than the Jews who crucified Jesus. They plotted his death and used the Romans to drive in the nails, but each and every Gentile Christian will say that it was his own sin too that crucified Jesus. For this is the very heart of the gospel: he bore our sins in his body on the tree. The enmity against God exposed by the crucifixion of God incarnate is an evil that lies in every human heart, Jew and Gentile.

Here, then, at the foot of the cross of Christ, Jew and Gentile are on the same level: there is no room for boasting or pride; neither is superior to the other. They stand together in their common sinfulness.

'But God raised him from the dead' (10:40), and commissioned some of his servants to witness the reality of that resurrection: '[we] ate and drank with him after he rose from the dead' (10:41). To preach the resurrection is to preach a fact. It is not a mythical way of saying that we hope and believe that in another world somewhere beyond death this world's wrongs will be put right. It is a statement of literal fact. God has reversed men's decisions: his Son was raised from the dead – physically and bodily.

'[We] ate and drank with him after he rose from the dead,' said Peter (10:41). How significant, therefore, that Peter was now commanded to go and eat and drink with Gentiles!

Those, then, who witnessed his resurrection were now commissioned to explain its significance: 'He commanded us to preach . . . and to testify that he is the one whom God appointed as judge of the living and the dead' (10:42). We have heard this so often that perhaps it has lost its power to startle and surprise us. But see what it is saying: not 'God is going to be judge', but 'Jesus of Nazareth is going to be judge'. God's appointment of him to be judge is because of his sinless manhood. He is man: he has lived in our world. His judgement will be just, because he never sought his own will (John 5:30). He is the standard of comparison. It

183

leaves no room for the Gentile to answer back: 'I'm as good as you. What right have you to condemn me?' It leaves the Jew no room for feeling superior, for the Jews crucified him.

But the next startling – joyfully startling – thing is: all the prophets witness to this, that all who believe on him receive forgiveness through his name (10:43) – *forgiveness*, not condemnation, guilty though both Jew and Gentile are. For once more there is no difference between Jew and Gentile: the same Lord is Lord of all and richly blesses all who call upon him, for 'Everyone who calls on the name of the Lord will be saved' (Rom. 10:12–13).

Here then is the basis of true Christian holiness: it is found at the foot of the cross. Jew and Gentile both on a common level: both sinners before God, in spite of their religion and good works. Both forgiven on exactly the same terms: as a free gift through the death and resurrection of Jesus Christ. Neither left with anything to boast about over the other. Everything to rejoice in together.

That is the first element of true holiness: the realistic discovery of sin: and then of forgiveness. But there is a second element. While Peter was still speaking, the Holy Spirit came on all who heard the message. The Jewish believers who had come along with Peter were amazed. Because, of course, the gift of the Holy Spirit demonstrated that God had accepted these repentant and believing Gentiles exactly as he had accepted repentant and believing Jews. And he had done so, notice, on the ground of their faith in the Lord Jesus. He and his atoning death were not only the only basis, but the totally adequate basis. Faith in him leads to complete acceptance for everyone: nothing needs to be, nothing may be, added. And so on that ground Peter commanded them to be baptised in water. If God had accepted them, so must the Jewish Christians (10:44–48).

Peter: The sequel (11:1–18)

But Luke adds a sequel to this story; and the sequel will help us grasp further the significance of this coming of the Holy Spirit on the Gentile believers.

When Peter got back to Jerusalem, the Judaean Christians criticised him for going into a house of uncircumcised men and eating with them (11:1–3).

So Peter explained patiently and in detail the whole story: the lesson God had taught him – the vision, the invitation to visit

Cornelius, who had been commanded by an angel to send for him; and then God's decisive action in giving the Gentiles his Holy Spirit. 'As I was speaking', Peter explained, 'the Spirit came on them. God gave them the same gift as he gave us. And who was I to oppose God? God did it. I couldn't help it. I only spoke. God did the rest!' (11:15–17) Well argued, Peter!

Significant for our purpose, however, is how he described this coming of the Holy Spirit: 'I remembered what the Lord had said: "John baptised with water, but you will be baptised with the Holy Spirit"' (11:16).

Here is the second element in true holiness: first, forgiveness through the death and resurrection of Christ; but secondly, empowering through the Holy Spirit to lead a life of true holiness and witness for the Lord.

And now we see why God could afford, so to speak, to knock down the wall he once put around Israel. In those days they knew nothing of the baptism in the Holy Spirit; knew nothing of the Holy Spirit dwelling within them to empower them to live holy lives. The best that could be done, therefore, was to put a wall round them and keep them from mixing with tainted Gentile society. But of course it had its weaknesses. A wall *outside* and *around* did not make the Israelites inside it any holier in themselves. And what final answer is it anyway if holiness depends on keeping people shut away from the real world?

But with redemption and cleansing provided by the death of Christ, it became possible for the Holy Spirit to come and dwell in each believer and so to give the believer the power to live a holy life, so that the Spirit of life in Christ Jesus might set us free from the law of sin and death, and that the requirement of the law might be fulfilled in us who walk not after the flesh but after the Spirit. Now with the wall gone, but the Holy Spirit within them, the believers would be free to go anywhere in the world to take the gospel to every creature.

And there is something more. At the time, Peter and his fellow apostles may not have realised that there was a further implication in Gentiles as well as Jews being baptised in the Holy Spirit. But not many years would pass by before Paul would be inspired to write: 'we were all baptised in one Spirit into one body – whether Jews or Greeks, slave or free – and we were all given the one Spirit to drink' (1 Cor. 12:13).

Here was the end to the middle wall of partition: Jews and Gentiles, fellow members sharing the same life, incorporated in the same body of Christ.

This, then, is Christian holiness as distinct from Jewish holiness.

But to return to the Jewish believers in Jerusalem. When they heard Peter's story, they dropped all objections, and glorified God (11:18). All credit to them. To lose a privileged position, held for centuries, might have seemed to some a painful bereavement. But not to them. Those who have experienced the inexpressible and immeasurable grace of God in Christ as an inexhaustible free gift, feel themselves so rich that they can afford to share all they have equally with all others. They gave God the glory; for what a magnificent God of matchless grace it showed him to be: 'So then, God has granted even the Gentiles repentance unto life' (11:18). Does 'even the Gentiles' sound a little odd? Why not just 'Gentiles'? Well then re-phrase it, in order to see the amazing grace of it all: 'So then, God has granted even *us* repentance unto life.'

With this glorious climax, we have reached the end of Movement 1.

MOVEMENT 2: The Gospel Freed from Jewish Administrative Centralism and Political Sacralism (11:19–12:24)

Like Movement 1, Movement 2 deals with the going out of the gospel to the Gentiles. Like Movement 1, it is concerned with the barriers that were at first raised against the spread of the gospel and with how they were swept aside. Like Movement 1, it contains two pairs of stories. In Movement 1 the common factor between both pairs was Peter's travels. In this movement the common factor is persecution. The first pair tells how persecution unintentionally initiated the spread of the gospel. The second pair tells how persecution would have stopped the gospel at its source had not God intervened. Naturally enough, the reference-base in both pairs is Jerusalem.

The establishment of the church at Antioch (11:19–26)

Movement 1 has told in great detail how Peter officially opened the door of faith to the Gentiles; and how in his visit to Cornelius God deliberately raised and settled the questions about holiness that were involved.

But, as far as Acts tells us, the first great outflow of the gospel to

Gentiles and the establishment of the first predominantly Gentile church were not led by Peter, or by any of the apostles. Nor was it initiated or thereafter controlled by the church at Jerusalem.

This is truly remarkable; and the more one thinks about it, the more remarkable it becomes. What this paragraph is going to describe is something altogether new: not the planting in Antioch of a Christian Jewish synagogue to which Gentiles might be admitted on becoming Jews, but the planting of a community in which Jewish believers and Gentile believers met on equal terms – so new that a new name, 'Christians', was invented to apply to the members of this community (11:26). Whether such a church had already been planted elsewhere Luke does not tell us. As far as Acts is concerned this is the first church to be planted outside of Jerusalem and Judea (Luke does not say what happened in Samaria, or in Rome as a result of Pentecost, 2:10).

Now, the original commission given by the Lord to the apostles specified that they should be Christ's witnesses in Jerusalem, and in all Judea and Samaria, and to the ends of the earth (1:8). And one might have expected that under the pressure of that commission the apostles at Jerusalem would have at least initiated and directed the Gentile mission, even if they did not carry it out themselves. After all, it was a momentous thing!

But the opposite is true. The apostles at Jerusalem neither initiated, nor directed, nor controlled the mission. Indeed the church at Antioch was founded before the church at Jerusalem even heard of it.

What set the mission going was the persecution that arose in connection with Stephen. As 8:1 informed us, 'all except the apostles were scattered throughout Judea and Samaria'. Why the apostles stayed behind Luke does not tell us. Maybe they stopped like a captain of a ship who will be the last to leave; and maybe the effort and sacrifice required to maintain the church at Jerusalem in those circumstances preoccupied their minds and energies until, the persecution subsiding, many of those scattered through Judea and Samaria returned to Jerusalem, and further preoccupied the apostles' pastoral concern.

However that may be, even those who were scattered in the direction of Phoenicia, Cyprus and Antioch did not apparently set out with the intention of evangelising the Gentiles. At first they only spoke the message to Jews (11:19). Then, as though on the spur of the moment, some of the believers who had themselves originally come from Cyprus and Cyrene began to speak to the Greeks as well, telling them the good news about the Lord

187

Jesus (11:20). The hand of the Lord was with them, says Luke; and in that was the secret. The Lord himself was behind and with the whole operation, initiating, controlling, directing and granting good success: 'a great number . . . believed and turned to the Lord' (11:21).

The next interesting thing is what the church at Jerusalem did when it heard what had happened at Antioch. It sent Barnabas to Antioch (11:22). When he arrived, he saw, says Luke, the grace of God. That is, he recognised that what had happened was the intervention of God himself, and a display of God's grace; and he was delighted.

He then encouraged them with all their hearts to adhere to . . . Jerusalem? No! . . . to the Lord (11:23). This is exceedingly significant. Here was this immeasurably important advance of the gospel to an altogether new level: Jew and Gentile together on the same footing in a Christian church (not a Christian Jewish synagogue). The whole thing had been done without taking advice or seeking permission from the church at Jerusalem. But Barnabas does not say: 'Well, I'm glad that it has turned out as well as it has. But, of course, you ought to have consulted Jerusalem before you took such a step, and certainly before you set up a church. So in the future you will be very careful, please, to cleave to Jerusalem and always to consult Jerusalem before you take any further initiatives.'

No! If they had waited for the Jerusalem church to send them out as missionaries to the Gentiles, the church at Antioch might not have been founded yet. Indeed, though we cannot argue with certainty from silence, it is an interesting thing that in Acts we never read of the church at Jerusalem as such deliberately initiating any mission to the Gentiles.

Barnabas' advice was, then, that they should adhere to the Lord. He gave such advice, says Luke, because he was a good man and full of the Holy Spirit and of faith (11:24). His goodness is seen in the fact that he was not displeased and jealous because these unnamed believers had done such a significant work without first consulting Jerusalem. And his faith is seen in that he recognised that it was God's grace at work, and that God, who had led his servants and prospered them, could be relied upon to continue to initiate, guide, lead and protect his work, if only these new Christians and this new church would loyally adhere to the Lord. Loyalty to the Lord Jesus would require obedience in doctrine and practice to the apostles, wherever those apostles were located at any one time. But loyalty to the Lord Jesus would not require a church in Syria (or anywhere else) to submit to the administrative and organisational control of the church in Jerusalem. Jerusalem's centralist place in Judaism was not to be duplicated in Christianity. They would not need either initiatives or control from Jerusalem. And when – to anticipate a little – we discover what powerful initiatives were taken by the church in Antioch (see 13:1–3), we can see the wisdom of Barnabas' advice.

The second thing Barnabas did to encourage and help develop the church at Antioch was to fetch Saul from Tarsus; and together they met with the church for a whole year and taught great numbers of people (11:25–26). Saul had apparently left Jerusalem and gone back to Tarsus. But Barnabas had recognised in him a man specially gifted and suited and called to help the Gentiles. So he fetched him, and they systematically taught people the word of God. This is the true recipe for church growth and extension: to adhere not to some ecclesiastical headquarters but to the Lord; on the other hand not to be foolishly independent and self-sufficient, but to accept help from God's appointed teachers from outside; and again, not to make 'adhering to the Lord' an excuse for following one's own ideas and fancies, but the motivation for being vigorously and systematically taught in his word.

The third interesting thing is that the disciples were called Christians first at Antioch. It was, in a sense, most fortunate that it happened so. 'The Messiah' is a Hebrew term which Greek-speaking Jews long since translated 'Christos', that is Christ. But 'Christian', that is 'believer in, or servant of, Christ' was a brand new term which from the very first applied equally to Jew and Gentile. And with that we notice another important thing. In Movement 1 we saw how the dividing partition between Jew and Gentile was broken down. But that does not mean that now there is no distinction whatever between people. A new re-divisioning has taken place: no longer between Jew and Gentile, but between Christian Jew and Gentile on the one hand, and non-Christian Jew and Gentile on the other.

The church at Antioch and social relief (11:27–30)

In Movement 1 we saw how there was in the Jewish concept of holiness a very heavy and healthy emphasis on the practice of good works and social concern. Then we saw the inadequacies of Jewish holiness and how it had to be replaced by Christian holiness. In particular, the dividing wall that acted as a barrier between Jew and Gentile had to be removed, and the food laws that made social intercourse so difficult had to be abolished. Now at Antioch we see a church based on the principles of Christian holiness.

The question is, How will it work? What effect will it have on social conscience? Will it lead to neglect of real moral and social duty?

No! Look at what happened at Antioch. Hearing through some prophets that there was going to be a famine throughout the world, the disciples decided, apparently on their own initiative, to send help, each according to his ability, to the brothers in Judea (11:27–30). What a delightful gesture this was, and what a practical expression of the unity of Jew and Gentile in Christ. In a sense this spontaneous social concern was even more impressive than that of Dorcas (9:36–43), because it transcended all the old barriers of religious pride, prejudice and animosity, ethnic differences and geographical distance. And still today the unity in Christ that exists between believers world-wide, transcending national, ethnic, social, educational and political barriers, is a very impressive reality.

It is ironic that the original persecution that broke out over Stephen backfired on itself. At its beginning the church at Jerusalem decreased in numbers alarmingly. But not only did it lead to an expansion and not a reduction of Christianity in the world, but the newly established church at Antioch in its turn helped to support and maintain the church at Jerusalem.

Herod's persecution of the church, and Peter's escape (12:1–19)

We now meet persecution again, and once more it is aimed at the church in Jerusalem. Once more the persecution is overcome. But this time the issue and the lesson to be learned are different. It was King Herod who instigated the persecution and put James to death with the sword (12:2). Why he originally did so, we are not told; but we are told that 'when he saw that this pleased the Jews, he proceeded to seize Peter also' (12:3). So what we have here is a case of political discrimination on religious grounds.

Political discrimination on religious grounds has in this past century become more and more to be seen, in Christendom at least, for the evil thing that it is. We should never forget, however, that during the majority of the Christian centuries its practice was widespread throughout Christendom, indeed almost universal, and was the source of immense and scandalous cruelties and oppressions. So we should stop for a moment and think through the basic presuppositions that made such discrimination seem a right and wholesome thing not only to ancient Jews but to generations within Christendom, and even to some of our contemporaries.

Herod Agrippa I had some Jewish blood in his veins, for though the Herods came of Edomite ancestry and were not all that popular with the Jews, his grandmother was the Hasmonean princess Mariamne. It is perhaps understandable that when the Emperor Claudius added Judea to Agrippa's kingdom in AD 41, Agrippa should do everything he could to gain popularity with the Jews. But it is sad to see that his execution of James 'pleased the Jews', and that this encouraged him to seize Peter as well.

Professor F. F. Bruce has suggested that the reason for Herod's attack on 'some who belonged to the church' (12:1), rather than on all the members of the Jerusalem church indiscriminately, may have been because Peter and the other apostles had recently been involved in, or had approved of, the breaking down of barriers between Jews and Gentiles, and the giving of Jewish privileges (as Jews would see it) to Gentiles without requiring those Gentiles to become Jews.* If that is so, what we now witness would be a new outburst of Jewish animosity against Christianity. They had come to some *modus vivendi* with Christianity as long as Jewish Christians at least maintained all Jewish distinctive privileges against the Gentiles. But now that they began to see what the Christian gospel really involved and what Christian holiness meant – namely the abolishing of all special Jewish privileges – their animosity flared up again against the gospel.

Whether this was indeed the situation, or whether the Jewish hostility was simply the old animosity against Christianity *tout court*, fanned once more into a flame, it is important to see that what the Jews were setting themselves against was the very heart of the Christian gospel. It was not some minor feature of Christian belief and practice over which Christians in true Christian spirit might have been well advised to compromise for the sake of peaceful coexistence with Judaism.

But, of course, the Jews might well claim that they had biblical authority for using the civil power to execute people guilty of serious heresy. Deuteronomy 17:2–7 lays down the law that if

---

*F. F. Bruce, *The Book of the Acts*, New International Commentary on the New Testament (Grand Rapids, MI: Wm B. Eerdmans, [2]1988), pp. 233–4.

anyone is found to have engaged in idolatry that person, man or woman, must suffer capital punishment. And Deuteronomy 13:6–18 also contains that law, and adds that if a whole city in Israel is found to have gone over to idolatry, then the rest of the nation must get the army out and utterly destroy that city and all its inhabitants and contents. Israel, therefore, could have argued that in worshipping Jesus as God, the Christians were guilty of extreme idolatry, and of blaspheming the name of God, and therefore were rightly executed by the civil power. Certainly Christendom for centuries took the same view, that the ecclesiastical and spiritual authorities had a God-given duty to destroy heretics by handing them over to the civil power for execution; and that the civil authorities had a responsibility thus to support the ecclesiastical authorities and to keep the state religion pure.

But here comes the crux of the matter. Ancient Israel was a theocracy, set up directly by God himself. Not only its high priests, but many of its kings, were 'the anointed of the Lord'. Every member of the state had to be a member of the state religion. Every male child at eight days old had to be circumcised. Any child that wasn't, was to be 'cut off from the people'. Religion and politics were two sides of the one coin. The state was a sacral state. Under those terms, heresy was a crime against the state, and the state had a right and duty to punish it.

By the first century AD, however, Israel had long since ceased to be a sacral state. Not only the ten tribes, but Judah too had lost political power. The Assyrians had destroyed the northern monarchy, the Babylonians the southern. The house of David was at an end. Even after the return from the Exile, while the temple and the city of Jerusalem had been restored, the monarchy had not been. We can leave aside the question whether the Hasmonean kings would have been rightly regarded as 'the Lord's anointed': their dynasty had also ended. Herod the Great certainly was not the Lord's anointed. He was not even a true Israelite. He was an Idumaean, and according to Deuteronomy 17:15 was not qualified to be king over the Jews.

The Jews, then, had lost their true political head, a king of the house of David, and that not by accident. It was God who had ended David's dynasty and taken the political power out of Israel's hands and given it to the Gentiles at the Exile, because of the nation's sin and rebellion against God. And to make matters worse, Israel had recently rejected and executed their true king of David's line, the Lord's Anointed, Jesus. In light of that, Herod Agrippa I, the appointee of the Roman Emperor Claudius, was

192

certainly not recognised by God as the Lord's anointed, appointed (among other things) to execute heretics in order to keep Israel's faith and religious practice pure.

Israel, then, had long ago forfeited her right to call upon its own civil power, let alone some Gentile, or semi-Gentile, civil power to execute people whom Israel's present religious leaders regarded as heretics. And to make matters worse, it was Passover time when Herod imprisoned Peter (12:4). One has only to remember what Passover stood for, to see the sad irony of the situation. The original Passover stood for religious liberty to worship God according to one's conscience. Israel were at the time under the political authority of a Gentile monarch, the Pharaoh. In the name of God, Moses demanded of Pharaoh: 'Let my people go, so that they may worship me' (Exod. 10:3). Pharaoh proposed many compromises; but Moses insisted that only complete freedom for the nation to worship God according to their conscience and beliefs would satisfy him or God.

But now, at another Passover, Israel was encouraging its half-Gentile political authority to deny the Christian Jews their right to worship God according to their conscience, indeed their right to life itself.

We can be assured of one thing: such political discrimination on the grounds of religion was not true holiness, nor was it pleasing to God! Israelites themselves, when they were obliged to live as expatriates in foreign countries, pleaded for, and often were granted, freedom to practise their own religion. And when they were denied it, a long line of martyrs witnessed their noble protest. But the religious freedom their prophet Daniel won, though at great cost for himself, his colleagues and his people; and what Jews of every generation since had stood for and suffered for in other countries; and what courageous Jews have suffered for during many centuries of so-called Christian rule; that the Jews of Peter's day were pleased to see denied to the early Christians James and Peter.

Christendom is scarcely in a position to point an accusing finger at ancient Judaism. When eventually it formed an unholy alliance of church and state it came to regard itself every bit as much a sacral state as Judaism. Indeed it was the church that eventually used its power to instigate discrimination against, and later persecution of, the Jews;* and eventually took to persecuting

*See E. M. Smallwood, *From Pagan Protection to Christian Oppression* (The Queen's University of Belfast, 1979).

Christians who were, or were adjudged to be, heretics. And the same methods as Judaism used to maintain a sacral state were used by Christendom. In Judaism, one way of ensuring that every member of the state was also a member of the state religion was to insist that every male citizen was circumcised as a baby. In Christendom it came to be held that baptism was the equivalent of circumcision; and then eventually in different countries and in different centuries the baptism of every infant in the country was enforced by the civil law under pain of death or political disability. We need not stay here to bewail again the enormous cruelties and the unjust discrimination that were perpetrated on the ground of sacralism until comparatively recent times. They have been bewailed enough. But we should not forget the historical facts, nor allow the falsity of the presuppositions of such sacralism to be forgotten either. Such sacralism was *not* a valid form of holiness. To wed the church with the state and to use political discrimination to bolster the church's privileged position and to keep the state pure(!) was the very opposite of Christian holiness.

But to return to Peter. Having witnessed the execution of James, he now found himself in prison (12:4). It does not take much imagination to realise how he may have been thinking and feeling in those critical days. He had not only been the natural leader of the Jerusalem Christians since the day of Pentecost; he had recently led the way in breaking down the old barriers between Jews and Gentiles, in taking the gospel to Gentiles, and in accepting Gentile believers as full and genuine Christians without their becoming Jews. Now persecution had broken out. James was already dead. He himself, apart from God's intervention, would soon be dead as well. That, one suspects, did not matter all that much to Peter. But if he maintained his Christian position and the recent insights God had given him into the implications of the gospel for the evangelisation of the Gentiles, many of his fellow Jewish believers would follow his example, and they would probably soon be dead also. Humanly speaking he would be responsible for their deaths.

What should he do? Ranged on one side was what he knew was the truth, the gospel on which the salvation of multitudes of Gentiles depended. How could he compromise it?

Ranged on the other side, however, was the massive weight of Judaism's religious establishment, the vast majority of the Jewish faithful, and now all the power of the king and the state. When in the early days the Jewish religious council had forbidden him and

John to preach in the name of Jesus, Peter and John had defied them without hesitation. But now the civil power, set up by Rome, had joined in and was taking the lead in the persecution. We cannot tell how Peter felt because he has not told us. But we do know how Luther felt when he had to face not only the Pope's representative but also the Emperor of Spain. Could he be right and all those eminent authorities be wrong? Was he right to go against even the Emperor? Could he take the step of dividing Christendom?

If we do not know what Peter felt in the critical situation, we know the relief he experienced when he found himself out of prison, and what the release meant to him. That he *has* told us. His deliverance was a miracle. At its beginning he did not realise that it was really happening: he thought it was a vision (12:9). But when he stood outside the prison, and came to in the cool night air, he said: 'Now I know without a doubt that the Lord sent his angel and rescued me from Herod's clutches and from everything the Jewish people were anticipating' (12:11). Notice the issue at stake. It was not simply: 'Am I really out of prison or am I dreaming? – Ah, yes, I am really out of prison.' It was the manner of his getting out: *who* had delivered him. It was a miracle. The Lord had done it. And the implication was clear: just as God had intervened and raised Jesus from the dead, and so reversed the judgement of the Jewish Sanhedrin and their unholy arrangements with Pilate and Herod, so God had now intervened to nullify Herod Agrippa's political discrimination and religious persecution, and to repudiate and disown Judaism's sacralist attitude. God himself had set Peter free, and with him the gospel was set free. The Jewish state as a state no longer had control over matters of faith; and certainly had no power to enforce the monopoly of the state religion over God's revealed truth. The gospel was free to take the blessings of Abraham (Gal. 3:14) to the Gentiles; and the Gentiles could receive them without becoming Jews. The gospel was for the whole world, outside the control of the government of Judea, whether inside or outside the state's borders. And in setting it free from the control of the state of Judea, we may be certain that God never intended to put it under the control of any Gentile state.

The lesson that Peter learned in the cool night air outside the prison was therefore equally important as the lesson he learned through the vision that sent him to Cornelius' house and the events that took place there. God's intervention to send Peter to the Gentile Cornelius set the gospel free from the restrictive barriers of Judaism's religious food laws and isolationism. His intervention to deliver Peter from prison set the gospel free from Judaism's sacralist state-control. Both interventions were equally necessary if the gospel were to come to all the nations of the world. How could the gospel come freely to people of other nations if it were ultimately under the control of the Jewish state? Or of any state, for that matter? To this present day it is the fear of many countries (and not least in countries that still have a sacralist state – and that includes some communist states) that the gospel is really an arm of Western imperialism or Western democracy. And inside some countries the governments fear that the gospel is the arm of capitalism, or of communism, depending on the colour of the government in question. If the gospel is to win its way to the hearts of people of all nations, it must be free, and be seen to be free, from all political and state control. True, it is concerned with promoting unity between Jew and Gentile. But that unity is a unity in Christ, and not an international union of states. Certainly the gospel is concerned to promote good works and social care and responsibility. Nowhere is this illustrated more forcibly than in this very section of Acts. But those social good works spring from the gospel itself and from the salvation provided through Christ; the gospel is not the product, nor yet the servant, of any particular political theory; nor is it an arm of any government or political movement.

But to return to Peter. When he realised that his deliverance from prison was not a vision, but reality, he went to the house of John Mark's mother, Mary (12:12). There were a number of believers in the house praying for Peter's release. When they heard his knock on the door and his voice, joy and incredulity kept them some time before they admitted him. It was so difficult for the now comparatively small group of believers left in Jerusalem to believe that God would do a miracle of such a size to set Peter and the gospel free. It shows, at any rate, that the early Christians did not expect miracles every hour of the day, or every day of the week. When they reported this miracle years later to Luke, they indicated that the miracle was as much an incredible surprise to them as to anybody else.

Now the credibility of miracles depends in the first place on the character and reliability of the witness and of the record. But it depends also on a certain sense of proportion. If we were told that God intervened by sending an angel to help Peter find a button that had dropped off his shirt, the means used would appear to be so out of proportion with the importance of the situation that the story would be difficult to believe.

The credibility of the story of Peter's miraculous deliverance out of prison depends in the first place on our estimate of the reliability of the inspired historian Luke. But it will also depend on our estimate of the importance of the issue at stake. Some commentators have suggested that the story of the angel is only a heightened poetic way of saying that in God's good providence somebody in the prison-authority sympathetic to Peter let him out. But that explanation will not do. First, because Luke says it was an angel (12:7, 8, 9, 10). But in addition, only a direct, miraculous intervention of God would have been adequate to settle the issue at stake. Just as God himself had given Israel the food laws, so God himself had set up the state of Israel as a sacralist state with the civil power necessary to enforce religious belief and practice. When God cancelled the food laws, therefore, he had to be seen to do it himself. It would have been no good for Peter to suggest to his colleagues in Jerusalem that he thought the food laws could now be ignored. God had to settle the matter, by taking things out of Peter's hands and himself pouring out the Holy Spirit on the Gentiles. Similarly, if God wanted people to see that all divine authority had been removed from the sacralism of the state of Judea, the only way he could do it was by direct divine intervention. The mere opinion of Peter, or of all the apostles combined, would have been inadequate.

And as to proportions: the release of the faith, and of the preaching and practice of the gospel, from the control of the Jewish state – and from all other sacral states – was, next to the gospel message itself, a matter of fundamental importance to the evangelisation of the world.

But of course Herod Agrippa was not convinced. He persisted in the view that it was either carelessness on the part of the guards or an inside job. He had the (innocent) guards executed (12:19) – a few more victims to add to the total that unauthorised sacralism has murdered.

Herod: The sequel (12:20–24)

Herod Agrippa was not even a true Jew. Had Judaism's sacralism still been divinely approved, his appointment to the throne of the Judean state would have contravened the Old Testament scripture (Deut. 17:15). That did not stop the Jews from being pleased when he used his political power to suppress the gospel and its ministers (12:1–5). But if religious leaders, without authority from God, encourage the civil power to arbitrate in matters of faith, then the religious leaders must not be surprised if the civil power eventually begins to behave as if it were God.

At least that is what Herod Agrippa I did. In the course of certain political negotiations he arranged a great spectacle to impress the people. Wearing his royal robes he sat on his throne and delivered a public address (12:21). The crowd responded by attributing to him divine honours: 'This is the voice of a god,' they shouted, 'not of a man' (12:22). He accepted their idolatrous and absurd adulation, and 'Immediately, because Herod did not give the glory to God, an angel of the Lord struck him down, and he was eaten by worms and died' (12:23).

The structure of Luke's narrative provokes thought. We have already noticed the verbal echo between: 11:18 – '. . . they had no further objections and glorified God' and 12:21, 23 –' . . . [he] delivered a public address . . . [he] did not give the glory to God'.

But the contrast goes deeper. Acts 11:1–18 is talking about the baptism of both Jew and Gentile in the Holy Spirit. This baptism brought about an immediate unity between Jewish and Gentile believers such as had never been known before in all history. Even so, it is unlikely that at the time they would have seen its amazing implications. But they were later revealed to Paul, and Luke would have learned of them from him before he wrote Acts. As Paul explained to the Corinthians: 'we were all baptised in one Spirit into one body – whether Jews or Greeks' (1 Cor. 12:13). The body he referred to is nothing less than 'the Christ', that new and unique thing in God's universe that was brought into being at Pentecost, the body of Christ; that wonderful organism, created by placing human beings in the Spirit of God, and causing them to drink of the Spirit of God. They are thus in the Spirit of God, and the Spirit of God is in them (Rom. 8:9). The result is that there has come into being a body of which the Man Jesus is the Head, and in which every member shares the same life, and, without losing his or her individual responsibility, is no longer a mere individual, but is a member, along with the Lord Jesus and every other believer, in this bigger organism, the body of Christ. Man has been taken up into God!

And what the last paragraph of Movement 2 presents (12:20–23) is a sad and absurd counterfeit: man trying to take the place of God and apeing God, yielding to that ambition planted in the human heart at the dawn of history by the great tempter himself: 'you will be like God' (Gen. 3:5). It was a minor example of a spirit that will yet come to its full expression when *the* Antichrist, 'the man of sin', will stalk the earth and 'oppose and . . . exalt himself over everything that is called God or is worshipped, so that he sets himself up in God's temple, proclaiming himself to be God' (2 Thess. 2:4).

And there is another comparison worth considering. If it is true that there are six major sections in Acts, then this episode of Herod's deification and death comes at the end of the third section, and therefore structurally at the mid-point of the book. Now the middle point in Luke's Gospel is at 9:50, for at 9:51 the Lord Jesus, according to Luke, begins the journey that will take him via Jerusalem back to the glory from which he came. That being so, it is interesting to notice that the last major incident in the first half of Luke's Gospel is the glorification of the Man Jesus, on the mountain of transfiguration (Luke 9:28–36).

The contrast between the two episodes is vivid. In Luke's Gospel, the Man Jesus, 'the appearance of his face changed, and his clothes [become] as bright as a flash of lightning' (Luke 9:29), and the coming of the cloud of the glory of the presence of God, and the voice from the cloud: 'This is my Son, whom I have chosen . . .' (Luke 9:35). And then in Acts, the man Herod Agrippa I, dressed up in his royal robes, sitting on his throne, making a great oration, accepting divine honours – and eaten up by worms (12:20–23)!

Of course, the similarities and contrasts may not have been intended by Luke. But since both incidents were historical events which Luke was led to record, there is no reason why we should not compare and contrast them in our own minds. The progress of man through the centuries; the phenomenal increase of the power available to him in recent decades; the increasing tendency of the world to become a global village in which a few major religions and philosophies will compete for dominance; the need, therefore, for world-governments to find a way of stopping militant religions and philosophies from fanatically tearing the world to pieces; all this may yet tempt someone to try again the device which the Roman emperors adopted for unifying their empire with all its diverse religions, and for ending the strife and bloodshed that had brought down the Roman republic: namely the deification of the state in the person of the head of state, and the superimposing of this worship on all other religions. If it ever happens, it will doubtless bring a kind of peace while it lasts; but at the cost of being the biggest spiritual slavery that the world has ever known.

Section Four

The Christian Doctrine of Salvation (12:25–16:5)

Section Four
The Christian Doctrine of Salvation
(12:25–16:5)

PRELIMINARY OBSERVATIONS

We come now to the fourth major parting of the ways between Christianity and Judaism. The issue this time is salvation, its terms and conditions.

This question lies at the very heart of the gospel. The name Jesus, as we know, means 'Saviour', and it was given to our Lord, so the angel explained to Joseph, 'because he will save his people from their sins' (Matt. 1:21). Salvation, then, is what the gospel is about. As Paul would put it, 'I am not ashamed of the gospel, because it is the power of God for the salvation of everyone who believes' (Rom. 1:16).

It might, therefore, seem strange at first sight that the formal discussion by the apostles of the exact terms and conditions of salvation, and their formal doctrinal pronouncement on the topic, should come so late in Luke's narrative. Of course our Lord is proclaimed as Saviour as early as 5:31: 'God exalted him to his own right hand as Prince and Saviour that he might give repentance and forgiveness of sins to Israel'; and at 4:12 it is plainly stated that 'Salvation is found in no-one else, for there is no other name under heaven given to men by which we must be saved.' It is, moreover, made quite clear from the beginning that in order to be saved people must repent and believe. But there is no formal discussion or statement on whether in order to be saved people have to fulfil other conditions as well, such as being circumcised and keeping the law of Moses – until we arrive at this fourth section of Acts.

There is a very simple and practical reason for this. At the first, all who came to believe that Jesus was the Messiah, Son of God and Saviour were Jews. All the males among them had already

203

been circumcised. All of them from their very infancy had been rigorously impressed with their responsibility to keep the law of Moses. When they repented of their sins, therefore, and put their faith in the Saviour, many of them never stopped to think how their circumcision and law-keeping were related to their salvation; whether they were necessary pre-conditions of being saved, so that if you were not circumcised and did not keep the law you could not be saved, however truly you repented and believed in the Saviour; or whether they were things that after being saved should be done as an expression of love and loyalty to God.

But then, as the gospel spread, Gentiles in their hundreds began to repent and believe on the Lord Jesus. They were not circumcised, however, nor had they been brought up to keep the law of Moses. Yet here they were, as at Antioch for instance, meeting together as churches of Christians. Understandably, it was not long before the question surfaced with knife-edge precision and inescapable urgency: Could Gentiles be saved without being circumcised and without keeping the law of Moses? And if so, what part did circumcision play in salvation? Did it make no contribution at all? And the law of Moses neither?

Once raised, the question had to be settled unequivocally. Christianity had to define its doctrine of salvation. It did so; and thereby it took another step away from Judaism.

Section 4 extends from 12:25 to 16:5, at which point Luke places one of his narrative division-markers. The section is composed of two movements. Movement 1 begins with the return of Barnabas and Saul from Jerusalem to Antioch (12:25) and their setting out on their first missionary journey together (13:1–4). Luke's record of the journey concentrates on four major episodes: the journey through Cyprus, with special focus on the conversion of the proconsul, Sergius Paulus, in Paphos in spite of the opposition of a Jewish false prophet called Elymas (13:4–12); Paul's sermon in Pisidian Antioch and its aftermath (13:13–52); his preaching throughout Iconium, Lystra, and Derbe, but with special prominence given to a miracle performed at Lystra and its outcome (14:1–20); and finally the return via Lystra, Iconium, Pisidian Antioch, Pamphylia, Perga, and Attalia, to their base in Antioch, where they reported to the church (14:21–28).

Movement 2 describes another journey, this time from Antioch to Jerusalem and back (15:1–35); and then the beginning of yet a third journey (15:36–16:5). It too is composed of four major episodes. The first tells how false teachers came from Judea to

Antioch, and how, a fierce dispute arising, Paul, Barnabas and some others were appointed to go to the apostles and elders in Jerusalem about this problem (15:1–5). The second reports the resultant conference in Jerusalem and the decision it reached (15:6–21). The third tells how the conference wrote a letter to the Gentile believers in Antioch and elsewhere, and how it was delivered by certain chosen men along with Paul and Barnabas (15:22–35). The fourth records that after some while in Antioch, Paul and Barnabas decided to return and visit the brothers in all the places where they preached on their first missionary journey. But a very sharp difference of opinion arising, Paul and Barnabas went their separate ways, Barnabas taking Mark, and Paul taking Silas and Timothy (15:36–16:5).

What we have, then, in Section 4 is two major movements with four main episodes in each. For a simple table of contents for the section, listing some of the main details in each episode, see p. 206.

It is no accident that the material in this section forms an obvious symmetry. It results from Luke's intention to present a balanced account of this fundamental tenet of the Christian faith and of how it came to be defined.

Take the most obvious example of all: the placing of the summary division-marker at 16:5. At first sight this is strange. Luke has not placed it at the end of Paul's first missionary journey at 14:28, where it might have seemed natural; nor at the end of his journey to Jerusalem and back, at 15:35. Instead he begins his account of Paul's second missionary journey, follows it for a few verses, 15:36–16:4, then interrupts it with a narrative division-marker at 16:5, before proceeding with the rest of that same second missionary journey. Why put a division marker a twelfth of the way through this second journey?

One explanation could be that by the time Luke's narrative has reached 16:4 Paul has only managed to cover again ground that he and Barnabas had already covered on the first missionary journey. The breaking of new ground begins only at 16:6. But another more important explanation stares us in the face. At 15:1–5, Paul, along with Barnabas, fights tooth and nail against the imposition of circumcision, and eventually all the apostles state their united view that the imposition of circumcision would subvert the doctrine of salvation. Yet at 16:1–3 Paul takes Timothy and circumcises him! The apparent inconsistency over such an important matter is so glaring that time and geography sink by comparison into insignificance. It does not matter now when and where Paul circumcised Timothy, whether on his first missionary

MOVEMENT 1: The Preaching of the Good News of Salvation (12:25–14:28)	MOVEMENT 2: The Discussion of the Terms of Salvation (15:1–16:5)
1. ANTIOCH TO PAPHOS (12:25–13:12)	**5. ANTIOCH TO JERUSALEM (15:1–5)**
The false prophet Bar-Jesus (13:6) tries to turn a Gentile from the faith (13:8)	False teachers from Judea (15:1) teach that Gentiles must be circumcised in order to be saved
Paul smites the false prophet with blindness (13:9–11)	Paul and Barnabas have sharp dispute and debate with the false teachers (15:2)
2. PISIDIAN ANTIOCH (13:13–52)	**6. THE CONFERENCE (15:6–21)**
'From this man's descendants God has brought . . . the Saviour Jesus' (13:23); '. . . it is to us that this message of salvation has been sent' (13:26); '. . . a light for the Gentiles . . . salvation to the ends of the earth' (13:47)	'We believe it is through the grace of our Lord Jesus that we [Jews] are saved, just as they [Gentiles] are' (15:11)
David (13:22, 34–37) and Moses (13:39)	David (15:16) and Moses (15:21)
Old Testament quotation regarding the Gentiles (13:46–48)	Old Testament quotation regarding the Gentiles (15:14–19)
3. ICONIUM TO DERBE (14:1–20)	**7. THE LETTER (15:22–35)**
'Jews . . . stirred up the minds of the Gentiles' (14:2)	'some [men] disturbed you, troubling your minds' (15:24)
Paul and Barnabas restrain Gentiles from idolatry (14:11–18)	'. . . abstain from food sacrificed to idols . . .' (15:29)
4. THE RETURN (14:21–28)	**8. THE RETURN (15:36–16:5)**
'remain true to the faith . . . We must go through many hardships to enter the kingdom . . .' (14:22)	Paul and Barnabas have a sharp disagreement and separate. Paul circumcises Timothy! (15:36–16:3)
'they . . . reported . . . how [God] had opened the door of faith to the Gentiles' (14:27)	'So the churches were strengthened in the faith . . .' (16:5)

journey, his second or his twenty-second. The fact he did so at all must be read in the light of his stand against circumcision at Antioch and Jerusalem. And Luke has done his best to ensure that we shall so read it, by placing his division-marker at 16:5, and thus bracketing both incidents together in one and the same movement.

Of course, closer study will show that the inconsistency was only apparent, not real. At Antioch and Jerusalem false teachers were insisting that circumcision was necessary for salvation. Paul and Barnabas, therefore, implacably opposed them. But Timothy was circumcised not as a condition of his being saved – he was already saved – but out of respect for the conscience of Christian and non-Christian Jews, who would expect that anyone who claimed to be saved would be careful to carry out the requirements of the law.

Take another example of this same kind of balance. In Episode 2 Paul is heard insisting in his sermon at Pisidian Antioch that justification is by faith and not by the works of the law (13:38–39); but in Episode 3 he insists with equal vigour on obedience to the requirement of the law: 'You shall have no other gods besides me' (14:13–18).

Luke, then, is showing us the beautiful balance of the doctrine and practice of salvation by his careful selection and combination of incidents, in the same way as Paul does by his straightforward theological statement in, say, his letter to the Romans: 'we maintain that a man is justified by faith apart from observing the law' (Rom. 3:28); and then 'that the righteous requirements of the law might be fully met in us, who do not live according to the sinful nature but according to the Spirit' (Rom. 8:4).

But look again at the table of contents. Episode 1 relates that opposition to the faith and to the Lord's doctrine (13:8, 12) came, as you might expect, from outside the Christian community. Episode 5 points out, what you might not expect, that false ideas on the doctrine of salvation were being taught by people inside the Christian community (15:1–5). It is certainly honest of Luke to tell us that it was so in his day. But it is more than that. False ideas on the question of salvation did not wither away completely, simply because all the apostles, the elders and the whole church at Jerusalem denounced them. They have persisted within Christendom all down the centuries to this day. Luke's honest history, therefore, becomes an exhortation to us to check our own beliefs on the subject. It is not safe in our day, any more than it would have been in Luke's day, to suppose that the doctrine of salvation as taught in an ostensibly Christian church by ostensibly Christian teachers necessarily agrees with what the apostles taught. The only safe thing to do is to check it by the apostolic scriptures.

There are, of course, many more similarities and contrasts between the details of the two movements. But enough for the moment; their significance will appear later on.

THE MOVEMENTS

MOVEMENT 1: The Preaching of the Good News of Salvation (12:25–14:28)

Antioch to Paphos (12:25–13:12)

If Section Three of Acts was concerned with the social and political implications of the gospel's theory and practice of holiness, this present Section Four is going to concern itself with the gospel's doctrine of salvation.

Doctrine and teaching are therefore emphasised right from the very start. 'In the church at Antioch', says Luke, as he explains how Paul's first missionary journey was initiated, 'there were prophets and teachers: Barnabas, Simeon called Niger, Lucius of Cyrene, Manaen (who had been brought up with Herod the tetrarch) and Saul' (13:1). It was as these prophets and teachers were worshipping the Lord and fasting that the Holy Spirit said, 'Set apart for me Barnabas and Saul for the work to which I have called them' (13:2). Paul was later to describe this work in these words: 'I was appointed a preacher and an apostle . . . a teacher of the Gentiles in faith and truth' (1 Tim. 2:7). It was very natural, then, that the men whom God had appointed as prophets and teachers should together wait on God for him to show them how they should set about the vast task of preaching to the Gentiles and teaching them the doctrines of the Christian faith. And it was likewise very natural that men sent out by the Holy Spirit on this great task were chosen from these prophets and teachers. It is often so. It is the men who have been given the gift, rather than the church at large, who have the vision both of the need and of the way that need should be met. Happy the men who in that situation have the confidence, blessing and backing of their church in the work to which the Holy Spirit (not the church) sends them (13:4).

They went to Seleucia, and from there to Cyprus. In Cyprus

they preached the word of God in the Jewish synagogues in Salamis. Notice the plural, 'synagogues' (13:5). At the very least this implies two sermons and possibly more. Then they travelled through the whole island and came to Paphos. So far Luke has not chosen to tell us so much as one word of the sermons they preached or of the reaction they encountered. But now he stays to tell us in considerable detail what happened at Paphos, because of its special relevance to his theme: at Paphos Paul's teaching on salvation was opposed by a false prophet (13:6–12).

Paphos was the headquarters of the Roman administration of the island and had a proconsul, one Sergius Paulus, in residence. He, says Luke, was an intelligent man (13:7), and he sent for Barnabas and Saul because he wanted to hear the word of God. In the proconsul's entourage, however, there was this Jew, by the name of Bar-Jesus. Unfortunately he was no Daniel, confident in God's self-revelation in the Old Testament and bold in his witness amid the darkness of paganism. Though he claimed to be a prophet, he had gone over to paganism's own black-magic and spiritism. Like a good many more, even in Christendom, he had discovered that behind a lot of the mumbo-jumbo of spiritism, there is a real spirit world that can communicate with human beings. It was precisely because that world is real, and not because it is not real, that God strictly forbade Israel to make contact with it (Deut. 18:9–14). But the world of demons has a fascination for many people. It seems to them far more real than God and the Bible. God and the Bible talk to our conscience and moral judgement. Spiritism does not. It appeals to man's love of power. Its prophecies allow people, so they think, to foresee coming difficulty, loss and injury, and to avoid these things. It offers people power to control their circumstances and, if need be, other people. It does not speak of morality, does not demand repentance. Because people find it is real, in the sense that it actually exists and has certain powers, they do not ask if it is true, that is, if it is morally and spiritually true, if it is spiritually loyal to the Creator who is *the* Truth.

But the spirits behind spiritism, though real, are not true. They are in rebellion against the Truth. When it comes to moral and spiritual matters, demons are by definition deceiving spirits, and so are the teachings that they propagate (see 1 Tim. 4:1–2). That is why the fiercest and most outspoken protests made by demons against our Lord when he was here on earth were made in opposition to his teaching of God's word in the synagogues (see Mark 1:21–27). They will always attack God's truth, if they can,

209

and in particular they will seek to infiltrate wrong ideas about the person of Christ into the church (see 1 John 2:18–23; 4:1–6; 2 John 7). They impress people with miracles of superhuman power and with prophecies which sometimes come true, in order to deceive people over the Truth. That is why Christian doctrine, the teachings of the gospel, the exposition of God's word and truth, are so vastly important in the evangelisation of the Gentile world. It is a number one tactical error when Christian people lose their faith in the word of God as the spearhead of evangelism; for the issue at stake is ultimately not 'Where can we contact super-human power?', but 'What is Truth?'

But to return to Bar-Jesus, or Elymas (= Sorcerer) as he was also called (13:8). He was no orthodox Jew, of course. He was a downright apostate. But he was not content to have abandoned God's word himself; as we might expect from the nature of his contacts in the other world, he did his utmost to turn the proconsul from the faith. Observe again the term Luke uses: the faith (13:8), that is the body of God's revealed truth. Elymas was out not simply to stop the proconsul from developing a personal faith in it-did-not-matter-what: he was out to stop him listening to *the faith*, that is God's truth. Thereupon Paul denounced him for what he was, a tool of the devil, and announced that God would there and then strike him with temporary physical blindness. And so he did (13:11).

It was a vivid object-lesson, fitting the punishment to the crime. Here was the proconsul, born in the darkness of paganism but groping for the light of God's truth and asking Paul and Barnabas to lead him; and Elymas deliberately perverts 'the right ways of the Lord' (13:10) and tries to keep the proconsul in darkness. So Elymas is struck with physical blindness and has to go around trying to find someone to lead him physically by the hand; so that the horror of the experience of physical blindness might bring home to him, before it was too late, the seriousness of his spiritual condition and activity.

Whether it did or not, Luke concentrates our attention on the effect of all this on the proconsul. And again it is instructive to observe the terms he uses. 'When the proconsul saw what had happened', he says, 'he believed, for he was amazed at' – the power of God, we say; what else? But no! '. . . at the *teaching* about the Lord' (13:12).

Luke does not stay to tell us how deep the proconsul's faith was, and whether there were any other converts. He has made the point he wanted to make: the tactical importance, as a weapon in evangelism, of *the faith* (13:8); that is, the *word* of God (13:5, 7); that is, the *teaching* about the Lord (13:12); that is, Christian doctrine. We do well to take note. Elymas was an apostate Jew. But Christendom does not lack apostates either. Be warned, says Paul: 'The Spirit clearly says that in later times some will abandon the faith and follow deceiving spirits and things taught by demons . . . Preach the Word . . . for the time will come when men will not put up with sound doctrine . . .' (1 Tim. 4:1; 2 Tim. 4:2–3).

Pisidian Antioch (13:13–52)

The atmosphere in the synagogue at Pisidian Antioch was very different. Here was Judaism at its best, studying and preaching the word of God, and attracting to the synagogue Gentiles who were impressed by the message of the Old Testament; so impressed that they had been led to worship the one true God along with the Jews, even if they had not become Jews themselves (see 13:16). Courteously the rulers of the synagogue invited Paul and Barnabas as visiting Jews to address the congregation. Paul rose to preach, and his theme was the theme that must be central to all Christian preaching: salvation through our Lord Jesus Christ.

Justification by faith apart from the works of the law

After a careful introduction he came to his major point: 'God has brought to Israel the Saviour Jesus' (13:23); and he pressed home on his congregation that this salvation was actually being offered to them: 'it is to us that this message of salvation has been sent' (13:26). Moreover, as he reached the climax of his sermon he indicated that by 'salvation' he meant something not possible through the law of Moses, yet offered by God to all simply on the grounds of faith in Christ, namely, 'forgiveness of sins' and complete 'justification' (13:38).

Paul must have known even before he started to speak what the result would be of such direct, aggressive, unambiguous presentation of the superiority of Christ over Moses, of justification by faith over justification by attempting to keep the law; and what might be the reaction when he told these religious people that in spite of their religious endeavours they still needed to be saved. It might well stir up a hornet's nest. If he had vigorously denounced their sins and urged everybody to a renewed effort to keep the law of Moses more strictly, there might well have been little or no opposition. That, after all, is what most religious congregations expect the preachers and the prophets to say, and Jewish preachers in general could be very direct and express themselves very strongly. But to preach that people can never expect to be justified by the law of Moses, however hard and honestly they try to keep it, seems to many people to make a mock of sincere human effort to be good. And they resent it. To preach that people can be justified without works, simply by faith in Jesus, strikes them as liable to undermine moral effort altogether, and they reject it as morally irresponsible antinomianism.

Paul therefore spent the whole introduction to his sermon pointing out that the doctrine of justification and salvation by faith is not some strange novelty invented by the Christians: it is a doctrine testified to by the Law and the Prophets of the Old Testament (cf. Rom. 3:21).

Salvation by faith testified to by the Law and the Prophets

To prove his point Paul cited three instances of salvation from Israel's past history. Granted that they were at a lower level, so to speak, of salvation than the spiritual salvation offered to us in Christ. Yet they were real experiences of God as Saviour, and therefore could act as precedents that established the basic conditions on which God grants his salvation at any and every level.

First he cited the whole long story of God's choice of the nation and his establishment of them in the land of Canaan. That was a long process: it took about 450 years (13:20).* But at every turn along the road, it was God who saved the people, not they themselves. To start with, it was God who chose the patriarchs; and that, as the Old Testament itself declares, had nothing to do with their merit (see Deut. 9:6–8). Then, faithful to the promise which he had made to Abraham before Abraham even had a son, God increased the small tribe of Abraham's descendants into a numerous nation in Egypt, preserving them in spite of persecution and eventually delivering them by acts of supernatural power from the slavery of the forced-labour camps (13:17). Then he 'endured their conduct for about forty years in the desert' (13:18). Every Jew in the congregation would know exactly what Paul was referring to. In spite of God's magnificent deliverance of

---

*The NIV rightly translates 'All this took about 450 years', where 'all this' refers to the whole process thus far described from verse 17 onwards.

them from Egypt, the generation that came out of Egypt proved to be utter apostates (except two or three of them). Only the grace and undeserved mercy of God saved the nation from complete extinction (see Exod. 32:10-14; 34:5-10) and eventually brought the next generation into Canaan. And there, too, it was God who destroyed the seven nations in Canaan and gave the land to Israel as their national inheritance. The conquest of Canaan would never have even begun if God had not miraculously parted the water of the river Jordan, and brought the walls of Jericho down. All that Israel later won through their fighting depended on these initial acts of divine 'salvation'.

So far then, the first analogy. The very creation of the nation from Abraham and Sarah (when they were as good as dead), their deliverance from slavery, the gift of political freedom, the forgiveness of their national rebellion in the desert, and finally the gift of a national inheritance and their establishment in it – all these were acts of God's undeserved salvation. Not one of them was merited by Israel's keeping of the law. Deuteronomy 9:4-6 sums it up well:

> do not say to yourself, 'The Lord has brought me here to take possession of the land because of my righteousness' . . . It is not because of your righteousness or your integrity that you are going in to take possession . . . Understand, then, that it is not because of your righteousness that the Lord your God is giving you this good land . . .

A second example of salvation by grace

With that Paul passed to his second example from the Old Testament. 'After this,' he said, 'God gave them judges until the time of Samuel the prophet' (13:20). Now judges with us are people who preside in law courts, and sentence the guilty to appropriate terms of punishment. But the judges in Israel to whom Paul was referring were saviours and deliverers of the people. 'Whenever the Lord raised up a judge for them,' says Judges 2:18, 'he was with the judge and saved them out of the hands of their enemies as long as the judge lived.'

The recurring situation was, according to the book of Judges, that in spite of being given the land of Canaan, Israel never consistently kept the law of God. Far from it. Every generation or so they broke their covenant with God and went off after the crudities and absurdities of the idolatry of the surrounding nations (Judg. 2:10-23; 3:5-7). In consequence, time and time again they fell under the power of those nations and became their serfs and slaves. If their national salvation had depended in those days on their keeping of the law, they would have remained serfs for ever. But when in their misery they cried to God, he raised up for them deliverers, saviours (e.g. Judg. 3:9,15). Of course these saviours judged the people in the sense of denouncing their sin and calling for repentance. But they did more than that. Empowered by the Holy Spirit (e.g. Judg. 6:34), they delivered the people out of their subservience to their oppressors. The whole book of Judges is in fact not a record of God's blessing on the nation's meritorious law-keeping, but an account of Israel's constant sin, of God's judgement on their sin, and then of God's merciful forgiveness and salvation of his people by his grace.

A third example of God-given salvation through a God-given saviour

Eventually, however, Israel grew discontent with God's way of saving them, and impertinently demanded that God give them a king to rule over them and save them from their enemies (1 Sam. 12:8–12). To teach them that neither they nor their chosen king had the wisdom or power to save them, God gave them Saul as king (13:21). He was a disaster. Twice he led the nation in deliberate disobedience to God in critical situations. Then he proved unequal to facing the Philistines' champion Goliath in single-hero combat. Worse still, when David defeated Goliath and saved both the nation and Saul, Saul rejected and persecuted his God-given saviour and drove him out of the country. He then himself went over to witchcraft and finally led the nation into a crushing defeat at the hands of the Philistines, bringing himself to a suicide's death. The congregation would remember the story well. God's answer was to remove Saul, the people's idea of a saviour, and to give them a saviour of his own appointment: 'he made David their king. He testified concerning him: "I have found David son of Jesse a man after my own heart; he will do everything I want him to do"' (13:21–22).

David was not guiltlessly perfect. But he never became an apostate like Saul; and he did what God appointed him to do: he saved Israel from the Philistines and from all their enemies, and so laid the foundation for Solomon's reign of peace. What is more, in doing this he became a prototype of the promised Messiah. Many many times in the centuries that followed, when God promised through prophets great and small that he would send the Messiah as the nation's ultimate and supreme Saviour, he indicated that the Messiah would be a descendant of David's. Again, every Jew in the synagogue would be familiar with those messianic prophecies.

Jesus the supreme Saviour

Now Paul came to the heart of his message: that promised Saviour has come! From among David's descendants God has brought to Israel the Saviour Jesus, as he promised he would. John the Baptist was sent to prepare the people for his coming by calling on them to repent, and then, as the official forerunner of the Messiah, to present him to the nation. 'Brothers, children of Abraham, and you God-fearing Gentiles, it is to us that this message of salvation has been sent' (13:23–26).

So far so good. But now Paul had to tell the Antiochians (who in their distant country may not have heard much, if anything at all, of the goings-on at Jerusalem) what when they heard it would sound very strange: this Saviour, Jesus, whom he was recommending, had been executed at the united request of all the inhabitants and the rulers of their religious capital city, Jerusalem. What credentials were these? How would Paul put it across?

He did not hide the fact as though it were a weak point in his case. The death and resurrection of Jesus are in the first place strong evidence that Jesus is the Messiah. But more importantly they are the very means by which God has provided salvation in its fullest sense at the highest possible level. The prophets had said that the Messiah would be rejected by the nation. Isaiah had said it explicitly (Isa. 53). And not only that. The story of Saul and David in the first book of Samuel provided a clear prophetic analogy: David the saviour appointed by God, he too, as we have just seen, was rejected and driven out of the nation by Saul. Not recognising Jesus as the Messiah, then, and strangely deaf to the voices of these prophets, the people of Jerusalem and their rulers, in their very attempt to put an end to the claims of Jesus, established them (13:27–29). They did to him the very things that the prophets said Israel would do to the Messiah. And they could not be accused of conniving with him: they were out to prove he was *not* the Messiah!

David, having been rejected and thrown out of the nation by Saul, came back again and became king. And so did Jesus! God raised him from the dead, and people who had previously travelled with him from Galilee, and therefore knew him well, saw him over a period of many days after his resurrection, and witnessed so to the nation (13:31).

In all this, moreover, Paul was not blaming or denouncing Israel for crucifying Jesus: the death and resurrection of Jesus were in his opinion good news. They *were* the gospel. 'We tell you the good news,' he said: 'What God promised our fathers, he has fulfilled for us, their children, by raising up Jesus' (13:32–33). Israel had now committed the greatest of all their follies ever: they had had their God-sent Messiah and Saviour executed! In spite of that, God, consistent as ever, had raised him from the dead and through him was sending to Israel in general, and to the congregation in Antioch in particular, a message of salvation. And what is more, Jesus, having been raised from the dead, was never going to die again. Here was a Saviour who had conquered death itself. In him God had undone the results of Israel's folly to Israel's unexpected and unending advantage. How was it not the most glorious instance of salvation that Israel in their long history of salvation by God had ever encountered (13:32–34)?

The witness of the Old Testament to the resurrection of the Messiah

But Paul was not being carried away by a preacher's flights of fancy. If Scripture had prophesied that the Messiah would die, so it had also that he would be raised from the dead. And Paul cited three scriptures to prove it.

First he appealed to Psalm 2:7. The psalm begins with an attack by the nations against the Lord and against the Messiah (Ps. 2:1–3). In answer to their folly, God replies by declaring: 'I have installed my King on Zion, my holy hill' (Ps. 2:4–6). Then the Messiah, now installed, speaks: 'I will proclaim the decree of the Lord: He said to me, "You are my Son; today I have begotten you"' (Ps. 2:7).

The situation depicted in this psalm, Paul claimed, actually took place in the life and death of Jesus. The Jewish religious leaders joined with the Gentile rulers, Herod and Pilate, to have Jesus done to death. 'Though they found no proper ground for a death sentence, they asked Pilate to have him executed' (13:28). The execution was performed by hanging him on a tree (13:29), which in Jewish law was the worst and most shameful sentence that could be inflicted on a man (see Deut. 21:22–23). And when he was dead they took him down from the tree, as the law required, and laid him in a tomb (13:29). What an attack it was not only on the Messiah but on God himself: God's own law used to execute and bury God's Anointed! How evident it becomes that the law cannot change the heart's basic hostility to God and make a saint out of a sinner.

God gave his answer. In the words of the psalm, 'he installed his King on Zion, his holy hill'. And the Messiah, vindicated by the resurrection, proclaimed the decree of the Lord for the whole universe to hear what his resurrection and ascension have demonstrated: 'He said to me, "You are my Son; today I have begotten you."' The first great step in salvation, therefore, was to save Messiah himself from death (Heb. 5:7) and to exalt him to the right hand of God as the world's Prince and Saviour.*

Paul's next two quotations took the point one stage further. The Old Testament itself records cases of resurrection (see 1 Kings 17:19–23 and 2 Kings 4:20–37). But they were really only resuscitations: the people concerned eventually died again. The resurrection of Messiah, Paul pointed out, was of an altogether higher order: he is never going to die again, never going to know decay (13:34; quoting Isa. 55:3).

It is no good philosophising about death and decay and trying to comfort ourselves with the idea that they are natural. With some people the processes of disease and death start even before they are born. It is highly unnatural. Try telling a beautiful young woman and mother of twenty-eight years old who has just been told that she has incurable cancer that death and decay are only natural! Death is not 'natural' in the human race. It is an enemy introduced into the race because of sin. And it spreads a pall of profound dissatisfaction around life when people who have the intelligence to see what a delightful thing life could be are denied that satisfaction by serious illness and death.

So let us follow the direction in which Paul's quotation of Isaiah 55:3 points us, and listen to God speaking to ancient Israel of the satisfying salvation he had in store for them and for all the world:

> Come, all you who are thirsty,
>   come to the waters;
> and you who have no money,
>   come, buy and eat!

*Many commentators feel that the phrase 'by raising up Jesus' in 13:33 refers to our Lord's official presentation to the nation at his baptism, where the words 'You are my Son' were spoken by the Father to the Son. (Some manuscripts erroneously add at that point the words 'today I have begotten you'.) But the interpretation of Psalm 2 given in Acts 4:24–28 suggests that the early Christians understood Psalm 2:4–7 to refer to the time *after* the cross and not *before* it (i.e. to the resurrection and ascension, not to the baptism).

Come, buy wine and milk
  without money and without cost.
Why spend money on what is not bread,
  and your labour on what does not satisfy?
Listen, listen to me, and eat what is good,
  and your soul will delight in the richest of fare.
Give ear and come to me;
  hear me, that your soul may live.
I will make an everlasting covenant with you,
  the unfailing kindnesses of David.
See, I have made him a witness to the peoples,
  a leader and commander of the peoples.
Surely you will summon nations you know not,
  and nations that do not know you will hasten to you,
because of the Lord your God,
  the Holy One of Israel,
  for he has endowed you with splendour. (Isa. 55:1–5)

Here then was God's satisfying salvation; but what exactly were these 'unfailing kindnesses' promised by God through David? Paul identified them with the prophecy given through David about Messiah in Psalm 16:9–11. The connection of thought is obscure in English; but in Hebrew it rests on the occurrence of different forms of the same root word in the two passages. We may attempt to express it in English in this way. In Isaiah God describes his salvation as his 'loyal, steadfast kindnesses'. He further describes them as 'the loyal, steadfast kindnesses of David' because they were also spoken of in a psalm written by David when God was through him prophesying and pledging his loyalty as God to David's descendant, the Messiah. Psalm 16, which according to Paul is the passage in which God made these pledges, speaks of what God will do for his 'Holy One': 'nor will you let your Holy One see decay' (Ps. 16:10). But the word here translated 'Holy One' is related to the word for 'loyal, steadfast kindnesses' in Isaiah 55. It means something like 'Your loyal and devoted One'. Put the two passages together, then, and we have what we considered in an earlier passage (p. 62): the Messiah's unswerving loyalty, devotion and obedience to God (Ps. 16) answered by God's responsive loyalty and kindness to him (Isa. 55) in not allowing him to go to corruption, but raising him from the dead, showing him the paths of deathless life and filling him with joy and eternal pleasure at God's right hand (Ps. 16:10–11).

Now this promise of not seeing corruption, Paul argued, cannot have been intended to apply in the first instance to King

David: David died, was buried, and his body went to corruption; for he was a sinful man like the rest of us. But Jesus was sinless; and his sinless loyalty to God won for him immediate resurrection to deathless life. And not only for him, but eventually for us as well (13:32–33). Through Christ we too can one day be given the gift of resurrection and unfading life; for that also is included in the scope of salvation. Here then is a salvation that satisfies life's deepest instincts: life need not be forever frustrated and mocked by death and decay.

The heart of salvation

But the certainty of resurrection is not immediately welcome to everyone; for conscience, as well as Scripture, testifies that if there is a resurrection, there will also be a final judgement. And many people, uncertain as to what verdict God will then pass on them, find the prospect full of unease and dread. But – and here we come to the very heart of salvation, and to what is in one sense the most glorious thing about it – no one need live in that uncertainty.

Listen to Paul as he comes to the climax of his sermon on salvation. Here is the whole point of it: 'I want you to know that through Jesus the forgiveness of sins is proclaimed to you' (13:38). God wants us to know that there is forgiveness available. And when we have put our faith in Christ, God wants us to know we have been forgiven. There is no uncertainty about it, nor about the means and methods by which we receive that forgiveness. It can be summed up by putting together two phrases from the proclamation: 'through Jesus – to you'. It is the direct and immediate personal gift from the risen Lord to everyone who puts his or her faith in him.

That, one would think, is clear enough. But it wasn't clear enough for Paul. The offer of forgiveness by itself could, and in many cases still does, leave people still uncertain about their ultimate acceptance with God. Forgiveness strikes them as a piecemeal, often repeated, disjointed and never finally conclusive affair. Forgiven today for some particular sin, and moderately certain that they will be forgiven next week if necessary for other particular sins, yet they feel they cannot but remain uncertain as to what God's final verdict on them as people will be. Will he accept them or reject them? They don't know; and they imagine that it cannot be known this side of eternity.

Happily the very reverse is true: it can be known, and known in the here and now. God himself wants it to be known. Hence the added clause: 'Through him everyone who believes is justified from everything you could not be justified from by the law of Moses' (13:39).

Here, then, the nature of God's forgiveness is defined by the term 'justified'; and there are four things to be remembered about Scripture's use of that term. First, both in Hebrew and in Greek, 'to justify' means not 'to make someone righteous' but 'to declare someone righteous'. Secondly, it is always God who does the justifying. The moment someone puts his or her faith in Jesus, God declares that someone to be righteous; that is, to be quit of every charge that could be brought against them in God's court (Rom. 8:33), to be right-with-God, to be accepted by him. And thirdly, justification in this sense is not a long drawn out process; nor is it a verdict that is given today, but very probably quashed tomorrow and needing to be applied for again the day after. It is an instantaneous act that is never repeated, because it never needs to be repeated. The moment someone puts his or her faith in Christ, God pronounces his verdict on that person: 'Justified from everything!' And the verdict, once pronounced, remains eternally settled. Fourthly, the validity of the verdict depends solely on Christ: his death and resurrection release believers from the debt of all their sins, first and last, and secure them forever against all possibility of divine condemnation or rejection (Rom. 8:34). So that, having been thus justified by faith, as Paul puts it, we have here and now, and forever, peace-with-God (Rom. 5:1).

Reactions to the offer of salvation

Towards the end of his sermon Paul must have seen storm-clouds gathering in the faces of his congregation, for he suddenly became very grave. 'Take care', he pleaded, 'that what the prophets have said does not happen to you: Look you scoffers, wonder and perish, for I am going to do something in your days that you would never believe, even if someone told you' (13:40–41).

Some people's sense of values is strange. Religion that urges them to moral behaviour but never gives them any sense of complete acceptance with God – that they value highly. Salvation, which can give them forgiveness and complete acceptance with God now, and certain hope for the future – that they not only reject: they despise it. That seems to be a widespread phenomenon; but for the Jews of Paul's day, and for the Jews of

Pisidian Antioch, it was a specially ominous phenomenon. They were about to see God do a work among Gentiles such as they had never seen done before. The very next Saturday, practically the whole city would turn up to hear the word of God. Surely the synagogue would welcome it with open arms? They already had many Gentiles, some of them eminent people, attending their synagogue; and the synagogue's preaching of the law of Moses had done an excellent preparatory work in bringing them to renounce paganism, to believe in the true God, and to educate their consciences to the point where they realised their need of salvation, forgiveness and justification. Would not the synagogue now be delighted to see these Gentiles actually find salvation?

Moreover, if Paul was right in claiming that the 'unfailing kindnesses of David' in Isaiah 55 referred to God's raising of Jesus from the dead, then one might expect the rest of that prophecy to be fulfilled. It said (see p. 218) that the risen Messiah would prove to be a world-wide attraction to Gentiles, who would come flocking to him. Well, as a result of Paul's sermon and the conversations that ensued, Gentiles in (for Pisidian Antioch) unprecedented numbers – practically the whole city in fact – turned out the next week to hear Paul preach (13:42–44). Could this be the kind of thing Isaiah was talking about? And even if not, would not the synagogue be pleased to see Gentiles in such numbers interested in hearing the word of the Lord expounded?

But no! They not only opposed what Paul and Barnabas were preaching, they abused both them and their message (13:45). Luke says they did it out of jealousy, and certainly we can understand it. Christendom knows the same phenomenon. Religious leaders who know and understand religion but have no personal experience of salvation, whose sermons are never anything else than exhortations to honesty, love, caring, social responsibility, in a word, morality, and virtually never preach salvation, can get jealous and publicly criticise evangelists who draw crowds by preaching salvation. But for the Jews of Antioch it was more serious than just a fit of jealousy, as Luke now points out.

'Then Paul and Barnabas answered them boldly: "We had to speak the word of God to you first. Since you reject it and do not consider yourselves worthy of eternal life, we now turn to the Gentiles"' (13:46). Tough words! But fair. Paul and Barnabas do not say, 'In our opinion you men are not even saved men yourselves.' They state the objective fact: 'You judge yourselves unworthy of eternal life.' God was offering them the gift of eternal life. That is what salvation is. To reject the message of salvation and cling simply to religious morality is to reject the gift of eternal life. One can do it abusively; one can do it with a seemingly humble 'I don't think anyone can know in this life that he has the gift of eternal life'; but it amounts to the same thing: 'judging yourselves unworthy of eternal life'.

Judaism's rejection of the message of salvation was not going to stop Isaiah's prophecy from being fulfilled, nor Paul and Barnabas from joining in Messiah's mission to the Gentiles. 'We now turn to the Gentiles. For this is what the Lord has commanded us: "I have made you a light for the Gentiles, that you may bring salvation to the ends of the earth."'

When the Gentiles heard this, says Luke, they were glad. Understandably. They glorified the word of the Lord (13:48). Again understandably. Morality is necessary and wholesome, like hygiene and cleanliness; but, again like hygiene and cleanliness, not the be-all and end-all of life, which is nothing less than personal acceptance with, and daily and eternal fellowship with, God. Morality cannot gain that for us; but salvation, forgiveness and justification can and do. No wonder the message of the gospel moved the Gentiles to faith and worship in a way that the preaching of the law never had. And no wonder it went on spreading (13:49).

But the Jews, says Luke, used their influence with people of the upper classes in Antioch, stirred up persecution, and drove the apostles from their city (13:50). Perhaps they would have argued that Paul's preaching of grace (13:43; cf. 14:3), that is, of justification by faith apart from the works of the law, was pure antinomianism. It is an easy way to misrepresent the gospel, and is still often used. But if so, what happens in Luke's next episode will refute that charge.

Iconium to Derbe (14:1–20)

After a preliminary sketch of Paul's preaching of salvation by grace (14:3) in Iconium, and the mounting opposition of the Jews which eventually forced the apostles to leave for Lystra, Luke comes to the centre-piece of this third episode. At Lystra Paul miraculously healed a man who had been crippled from birth. The effect on the local population was electric. They were, after all, pagans, and in that part of the world not such sophisticated pagans as in other parts. They immediately cried out in the local language: 'The gods have come down to us in human form' (14:11). Deciding that Barnabas was Zeus and Paul Hermes, and led by the local priest of Zeus, they brought oxen and garlands to the city gates, and proposed to offer sacrifice to these 'gods in human form' (14:8–13).

One can easily imagine what someone like Simon Magus would have done with the opportunity if he had been Paul or Barnabas. There would have been a temple to Simon Magus in Lystra in next to no time, put up by public subscription; and Simon would not have lacked for anything for the rest of his life.

But Paul and Barnabas were not charlatans. Neither was their doctrine of 'justification by faith through grace' antinomianism. Certainly they preached that it is impossible to win acceptance with God by the keeping of the law; and that therefore salvation is, and has to be, utterly by grace. But that did not mean that they encouraged people to break the law. Here at Lystra the very first, fundamental commandment of the law was at stake: 'You shall have no other gods besides me' (Exod. 20:3). Without the slightest hesitation Paul and Barnabas rushed into the crowd, using every gesture they knew, to stop them breaking this first commandment of the law; and they proceeded to harangue these pagans, as forcefully as the most orthodox Jew would do, on the evils of polytheism and idolatry, preaching to them to drop their paganism and worship the one true God, the Creator (14:14–18).

Even so, says Luke, it was proving no easy task to stop the people offering sacrifice to them (14:18), when some Jews from Antioch and Iconium arrived on the scene. 'And when they discovered that Paul and Barnabas were strenuously pleading with the pagans to keep God's law, they did not any longer attempt to attack the apostles; for that would have given the pagans the impression that the Jews were against keeping God's law. Instead, they joined forces with Paul and Barnabas and urged the pagans to worship the true God.'

Alas, no! That is not what Luke says. With powerful brevity he remarks, 'But Jews from Antioch and Iconium came upon them, won the crowd over, stoned Paul, and bundled him out of the city, thinking he was dead' (14:19).

We can, perhaps, understand the sudden switch in the crowd's attitude from gratitude to murderous hate. Many of them would have felt rebuffed because Paul had not allowed them to sacrifice to him, and would have considered his remarks about 'turning from these worthless things to the living God' (14:15) an insult to their religion and their priest. It would thus have been

223

comparatively easy for the Jews from Antioch and Iconium to take advantage of their hurt pride and indignation to set them against Paul.

But what shall we say about the Jews who did it? What can be said, except that sometimes some religious people would prefer others to stay in their paganism, idolatry, sin and worldliness rather than 'get saved'. So antagonistic to salvation can mere religion be!

The return (14:21–28)

The happenings at Lystra have shown us this: the Christian doctrine of salvation by grace through faith was as insistent on maintaining the moral law of God as the Jews – more insistent than some of them, in fact. And now in this brief final part of this first movement we shall meet another side to the Christian doctrine. Forgiveness, justification, acceptance with God, eternal life, these all are perfectly free gifts; but those who receive them may well find that there is a heavy cost involved in receiving them.

Recovering from the near fatal assault he had suffered at Lystra, Paul went on – amazing man – to Derbe, preached the gospel there, and made many disciples (14:20–21). That for the moment was his farthermost point. From there he and Barnabas began the return journey. They visited again, in reverse order, Lystra, Iconium and Pisidian Antioch. On the way from there back to (Syrian) Antioch, their home church, they preached in Perga. But what they said, and what the results were, Luke does not tell us.

What he does concentrate on is what they said and did in the infant churches which they had recently founded in Lystra, Iconium and Pisidian Antioch. They strengthened the souls of the disciples, encouraging them to continue in the faith (14:22). We observe once more the term 'the faith' – that is, the body of Christian doctrine – which has so marked this section of Acts. But now let us notice the term 'continue in' ('remain true to', NIV). Salvation is by grace, the gift of God to every believer. But the evidence that someone is a true believer is that he or she continues in the faith. This is what our Lord said to those who professed to believe on him: 'If you continue in my word, you are truly my disciples' (John 8:31, RSV). Those who did not 'continue in his word', he pointed out, were not, and never had been, children of God. This is the message of all the epistles likewise.

'Continuing in the faith' is not a condition of being justified. But it is the natural outcome and the necessary evidence of being a genuine believer.

Secondly, Paul and Barnabas reminded their recent converts that it is through much tribulation that we must enter the kingdom (14:22). Again we should notice that suffering tribulation does not earn or merit us entry into the eternal kingdom. Entry is a gift. But if we accept that gift, the world and the devil will sooner or later combine to raise up all the tribulation they can muster against us. 'In the world you have tribulation,' said Christ (John 16:33, RSV). 'Do not be surprised . . . if the world hates you,' says John (1 John 3:13). Paul himself is a vivid example of the principle he taught his converts. Before his conversion, in the days when he was trying to earn acceptance with God by keeping the law, he suffered no tribulation. It was he who persecuted others. But when he discovered that acceptance with God is a gift, and he received it, he began a life of almost incessant tribulation (see Phil. 3).

Eventually Paul and Barnabas got back to base at Antioch. They gathered the church and reported what God had done through them for the Gentiles. The phrase they used is interesting. When Peter, after a similar journey, got back to Jerusalem and reported what God had done through him for the Gentiles, his Jewish fellow believers commented: 'So then, God has granted even the Gentiles repentance unto life' (11:18). But reporting to the church at Antioch, Paul and Barnabas told how 'God . . . had opened the door of faith to the Gentiles' (14:27). A small difference, but an apt one in the light of the major theme of Section Four: salvation and justification by grace through faith apart from the works of the law, yet leading to the keeping of the law and a willingness to pay the cost of discipleship.

MOVEMENT 2: The Discussion of the Terms of Salvation (15:1–16:5)

All the way through Movement 1 we have encountered opposition to the gospel. Now in Movement 2 we shall find the pattern repeated. Only this time there is a difference. In Movement 1 the opposition came from Judaism, both apostate and orthodox. In Movement 2 the opposition comes from within the Christian community. In Movement 1 we listened to the gospel being

225

preached in popular language, often to large congregations of non-Christians. In Movement 2 we shall hear the gospel defined in theological terms inside the Christian church.

Antioch to Jerusalem (15:1–5)

It seems a startling thing to say that opposition to the Christian doctrine of salvation came in the early years from within the Christian church itself. But so it was. 'Some men', Luke says, 'came down from Judea to Antioch and were teaching the brothers: "Unless you are circumcised, according to the custom taught by Moses, you cannot be saved"' (15:1).

Immediately Paul and Barnabas opposed them. This was no moment for toleration. The very gospel itself was at stake, the basic terms of salvation. To have kept silent here would have been disloyalty both to God's truth and to people's salvation and freedom. It would have been, as Peter later expressed it (15:10), both to tempt God and to put an intolerable yoke on the necks of the disciples. There are many secondary matters in Christianity where Christians of different persuasions must allow each other room for disagreement. But the terms and conditions of salvation are not one of those matters. Paul and Barnabas would not stand quietly by while people taught the believers 'a different gospel – which is really no gospel at all' (Gal. 1:6–7); a so-called 'gospel' which if they knowingly and deliberately received it would mean that Christ was of no value to them at all; an addition to the true gospel so contrary to its basic principle that to accept it is to wreck the gospel completely, to imply that Christ died for nothing, to leave people without salvation and to burden them with a yoke of slavery (Gal. 2:21; 5:1–4). Paul and Barnabas entered into 'sharp dispute and debate' (15:2) with the advocates of this false gospel and opposed them relentlessly.

The outcome was that Paul and Barnabas were appointed, along with some other believers, to go up to Jerusalem to see the apostles and elders about this question (15:2). That was not because Paul did not have full apostolic authority to lay down the terms and conditions of salvation himself without consulting others (see Gal. 1:1, 11–2:10). It was because the false teachers had come from Judea, and doubtless insinuated that the apostles and elders at Jerusalem agreed with them. We see that from the fact that when the apostles and elders wrote a letter to Antioch giving their view of the matter, they began by repudiating the false teachers: 'We have heard that some went out from us without our authorisation and disturbed you, troubling your minds by what they said' (15:24).

On their way to Jerusalem through Phoenicia and Samaria, Luke says, 'they told how the Gentiles had been converted. This news made all the brothers very glad' (15:3). That is the natural reaction of people who have been saved themselves to hearing about the salvation of other people; and the more 'way-out' these other people have been before their conversion – and to Jews Gentiles were very 'way-out' – the more glad they are to hear about it. The reaction in Jerusalem was the same when they heard Paul and Barnabas' report.

Except for some. 'Then some of the believers who belonged to the party of the Pharisees stood up and said, "The Gentiles must be circumcised and required to obey the law of Moses"' (15:5).

The first thing to notice about this demand is that it came from inside the church, from people whom Luke describes as believers. We shall have to ask later on in what sense they were believers, for their statement was not so innocuous as might at first sight appear. If we did not know the rest of the story, we might suppose that these 'believing' Pharisees were simply saying: 'Yes, we agree. Those Gentiles who have repented and put their faith in the Lord Jesus have been saved, have been justified and accepted by God solely on the grounds of faith. But, now of course, they must be taught how to live lives pleasing to God, and that will mean teaching them to get themselves circumcised and to keep the law of Moses.'

But they did not mean that. They were agreeing with the men who had gone down from Judea to Antioch. They were saying that you have to be circumcised and keep the law of Moses *in order to* be saved. We see that was so from what Peter said when the apostles and elders met to discuss this question, and Peter rose to pronounce on this issue. As he understood it, the question before them, raised by these Pharisees, was not 'How should saved Gentiles behave?' but 'How, and on what terms, can Gentiles – or Jews for that matter – be saved at all?' (15:10–11).

It should not surprise us, however, to find that this question was disputed among the early believers. It has been disputed in Christendom for centuries, and still is. No one in Christendom nowadays holds that you have to be circumcised to be saved. But it is widely held that the baptism of infants is Christianity's equivalent of Judaism's circumcision of infants; that this baptism actually effects the regeneration of the infant; and that baptism is

227

normally necessary for salvation, so much so that an infant dying unbaptised cannot go to heaven; and that in the case of adults too, baptism actually cleanses them from sin, and is necessary for salvation except in extreme cases like that of the dying thief, where baptism is physically impossible and God exceptionally uses other means.

And it is even more widely held that one has to keep not so much the ceremonial law, but certainly the moral law of Moses, in order to be saved. That is why both in the pulpit and in the pew the idea that people can know in this life that they have been, are, and most certainly will be saved is often rejected as self-evidently absurd. Self-evidently, because, as they say, salvation depends on keeping the moral law; and one cannot know whether one has done enough in that direction to qualify for salvation until the final judgement. For anyone to claim to be already saved, they think, is like a student claiming to have passed Finals before even having sat them.

Now it is true that some elements in salvation are spoken of in the New Testament as being future. The redemption of our physical bodies is one such element (Phil. 3:20–21; Rom. 8:23–25); and so is salvation from the wrath of God: 'we *shall be* saved from the wrath of God through him [Christ]', says Paul (Rom. 5:9). But even with these aspects of salvation futurity does not imply uncertainty. In this very passage Paul points out that (because of the consistent character of the love of God) once we have been justified by faith, salvation from the coming wrath of God is even more certain than Christ's dying for us when we were still sinners (Rom. 5:8–9). We wait for Christ as our deliverer from the coming wrath, he asserts in 1 Thessalonians 1:10; and as we wait for him to come again we are to know that God has not appointed us 'to suffer wrath, but to receive salvation through our Lord Jesus Christ' who died for us (1 Thess. 5:9–10). A believer whose life's work for Christ is substandard, and does not survive Christ's judgement, will suffer incalculable loss; but he will not lose his salvation: he himself will be saved (1 Cor. 3:15) because his salvation was never conditional upon his works, and therefore never uncertain.

Moreover, though some elements in salvation are necessarily future, others, for the believer, can rightly be spoken of as having already taken place. Justification and the receiving of eternal life are two such elements, so that Paul can inform his converts: 'by grace you *have been* saved' (Eph. 2:8–10). The formula may be old, but it is nevertheless true: the believer has been saved from the penalty of sin, is being saved from the power of sin, and one day will be saved from the very presence of sin.

The question that was raised first at Antioch and then at Jerusalem was therefore for Paul and Barnabas no matter of merely academic theology. It concerned people, their peace with God, their sense of acceptance, their freedom, their joy. All through the debate people's faces would be coming before them, the faces of the Gentiles who had been converted through their preaching. They had repented and put their faith in Christ: were they saved? They certainly had not been circumcised. If salvation depended on being circumcised, then they were not saved. And if salvation and acceptance with God depended on the final judgement's decision as to whether they had throughout their whole lives kept the moral law sufficiently well – then, of course, there could be no uncertainty about it: they never would be saved. For no one can ever be declared righteous in God's sight on that basis (Rom. 3:20).

The Jerusalem conference (15:6–21)

Peter's statement on the true doctrine of salvation

When the conference met, there was first some lengthy discussion; and then Peter got up and delivered his judgement. He had, of course, apostolic authority to do so. But he did not simply appeal to his apostolic authority and put an end to the discussion by arbitrarily announcing his decision. He pointed to certain acts of God in the recent past by which God himself had already indicated what the position was.

God's first act had been his choice of Peter as the one through whom the Gentiles should hear the gospel message and believe (15:7). Peter was referring to the Cornelius incident; and when we recall God's preparation of Peter by special immediate relevation, and then the series of providential 'coincidences' that removed any doubt about the Spirit's leading, it is indisputably clear that it was God's choice that singled out Peter from the rest as the one to take the gospel to the Gentiles. An unspoken implication lies on the surface: if these 'Pharisees who believed' were right in their doctrine that Gentiles had to be circumcised and keep the law to be saved, why had God not chosen them instead of Peter to take the message of the gospel to Cornelius? And what is more, these uncircumcised Gentiles had actually believed on the Lord Jesus as a result of Peter's preaching when multitudes of circumcised and law-keeping Jews had not.

But God did more than choose Peter to take the message of the gospel to these Gentiles. His second act was that when they believed on the Lord Jesus, God intervened directly to demonstrate that he had accepted them, by giving them his Holy Spirit. No one could question that it was God who did it, for Peter had no part in that action. Of course, no mere man, however exalted an apostle he might be, is able to give the divine Spirit of God to anybody. Only one who is God himself can do that. But on this occasion God did not even do it *through* the laying on of Peter's hands, as he had done in Samaria, for instance (8:17–18). Peter was still speaking, he had not yet reached the end of his sermon, when the Holy Spirit fell on those who heard the word (10:44). There was no ceremony. They were not circumcised. They were not (yet) baptised. They had not 'come forward', to use modern evangelical jargon. They had not been counselled, no one had laid hands on them, they had signed no decision form or made any public confession. Just where they sat, they heard the message of the gospel and believed. And immediately God gave them his Spirit, giving them to know, and then demonstrating to all present, that he had accepted them. They were justified. They were saved. They had peace with God.

But now at the conference Peter had some far-reaching lessons to draw from God's action.

First, in giving them the Spirit 'He made no distinction between us and them' (15:9). We were already circumcised when he gave us the Spirit. They were not; yet he gave them the Holy Spirit exactly as he did to us. That shows that circumcision is irrelevant to the receiving of the Holy Spirit.

Secondly, for anyone thus to be united with the living Christ, by being given, and indwelt by, the Spirit of God, is not merely a help towards salvation: it *is* salvation.

Thirdly, God obviously does not put his *Holy* Spirit into unclean hearts. If, then, he placed the Holy Spirit in these Gentiles' hearts, it wasn't because he did not know the real state of their hearts: he is the God who knows the hearts of all men (15:8). Their hearts must, then, have been purified to God's satisfaction so that he could put his Holy Spirit within them. How were they purified? Obviously not by circumcision, for they were not circumcised; and how could that operation cleanse the heart anyway? Nor by baptism: they were not yet baptised when they received the Holy Spirit. And when they were (10:46–48), it was the fact that they had already received the Holy Spirit that authorised their baptism, and not their baptism that brought about their receiving of the Spirit.

How then were their hearts purified: who purified them, by what means, and when? Peter answers all three questions.

First, it was God who did the cleansing (15:9). It was not that these Gentiles by careful spiritual discipline managed to purify their hearts at last to the point where God was able to give them his Holy Spirit. No, it was God who did the purifying. Secondly, the means God used was their faith: 'he purified their hearts by faith' (15:9); and it is in this sense that believers can be said to have purified their souls, as in 1 Peter 1:22. But to be clear what this means, we must understand it in the context of the answer to the third question: When did he purify their hearts by faith? Was it a long drawn out process according to which as their faith gradually grew stronger God was able to cleanse their hearts more and more until they reached the standard of cleanliness necessary for receiving the Holy Spirit? No! 'In this matter', said Peter, 'he made no distinction between us and them' (15:9); and to clarify the point beyond all doubt we may recall what Peter had said about it on an earlier occasion: 'God gave them the same gift as he gave us *when we believed in the Lord Jesus Christ*' (11:17).

The serious implications of the false doctrine of salvation

At this point Peter had some very strong words to say to 'the Pharisees who believed'. 'Now then, why do you try to test [AV: tempt] God by putting on the necks of the disciples a yoke that neither we nor our fathers have been able to bear?' (15:10).

To 'tempt the Lord' is a very serious thing to do. It means, to put it crudely, trying God's patience, seeing how far you can go and what you can get away with before pushing God too far and provoking him to intervene. It is forbidden in the law itself at Deuteronomy 6:16. The relevance of the prohibition to the question being discussed in the conference was this. If God had purified the hearts of the Gentiles by faith and declared himself so satisfied with that purification that he could give them his Holy Spirit, it was an appalling impertinence and insult to God for anyone – no matter how good their motives might be – to imply that the purification God himself had effected by faith was not good enough, and could not bring a person salvation and acceptance with God by itself, but must be supplemented by circumcision and keeping of the law. How far could anyone go with

231

insulting God like that and with overturning his own declared decision before bringing down on one's head his severest condemnation? Preaching ritual and law-keeping for salvation might sound as if it were morally strict, holy and commendable. It was, and still is, in fact an insult to God.

Secondly, it is both useless and cruel. Neither we nor our fathers have been able to bear that yoke, said Peter (15:10). He spoke from bitter personal experience. (This is not Christian misunderstanding; it is a Jew telling how he had found things.) It was not only that it was a grinding burden to try to keep every jot and tittle of the law, especially as it was interpreted by the stricter rabbis in the first century AD. But it never brought you peace of conscience and a sense of acceptance with God, not even when after great effort and discipline you felt you might perhaps have come somewhere near achieving the task. All it could do, perhaps, was to make you feel that you were better than others who had not tried so hard. But it could never bring peace with God. And that in turn made the task of trying to keep the law seem an endless burden.

It is still true today. No one ever achieves peace with God and a sense of acceptance on the basis of keeping the law. It is unattainable that way. God will not give his Holy Spirit on those terms. To suggest or teach that he will is to put a yoke of slavery on people's necks.

Salvation, after all, is salvation. It is a deliverance from slavery, not a demand for hard work. Think back to the analogies Paul used in Pisidian Antioch (13:16–23). Salvation for the Israelites in the slave-labour camps in Egypt did not demand additional hard work, on top of the original slavery, in order to qualify them for freedom. No, salvation and freedom were gifts, given them by God's grace and effected by his power. So it is with forgiveness, justification and the gift of God's Spirit. 'It is for freedom', says Paul, agreeing with Peter, 'that Christ has set us free. Stand firm, then, and do not let yourselves be burdened again by a yoke of slavery' (Gal. 5:1).

Peter's summing up

Historically, doctrinally, theologically and experientially, Peter's summing up is of such epoch-making importance that it calls for examination phrase by phrase.

'We believe . . .' said Peter; and by 'we' he meant all the apostles and all the elders without exception. Obviously, to

be truly Christian we must be able to identify ourselves un-
reservedly with their statement of belief.

'We believe it is through the grace of our Lord Jesus . . .'; and
by 'grace' he did *not* mean that the Lord Jesus gives us the grace to
perform the rituals, to keep the law and to do the works that will
one day, we hope, qualify us for acceptance with God and
salvation. That is what the 'Pharisees who believed' would have
said, and Peter was intending to say the very opposite. 'By grace',
therefore, means '*not* by ritual, ceremony, works or law-keeping'.

'We believe it is through the grace of our Lord Jesus that we are
saved, just as they are.' And in saying so, Peter established two
principles. First, if uncircumcised Gentiles are saved without
being circumcised, then circumcision is not necessary for salvation. And secondly, if circumcised Jews are, and have to be, saved
in the same way as uncircumcised Gentiles, then circumcision is
not only unnecessary for salvation, but, in addition, it *contributes*
nothing towards anybody's salvation, nor does law-keeping
either.

His summing-up finished, Peter sat down; and perhaps we
may be allowed to wonder how 'the Pharisees who believed'
reacted to what he had said. They had earlier been insisting that
circumcision and law-keeping were necessary for salvation. That
must have meant that their faith for salvation was, partly at least,
in these things. And that is a serious matter. Because faith partly
in Christ and partly in law-keeping is not faith at all. Add the
slightest work as a condition for salvation and you no longer have
salvation by grace (Gal. 5:2–4). If, then, before the conference
their faith for salvation was partly in their circumcision and
law-keeping, were they saved? They had believed, Luke says so
(15:5); in the sense presumably that they believed that Jesus was
the Messiah. But on the question of salvation, their views were
clean contrary to the Christian doctrine of salvation as Peter
defined it; and it matters what people believe. Let's hope they
repented, believed and accepted salvation by grace as a free gift
from the Lord Jesus.

Peter had spoken with such authority and self-evident truth
that when he sat down 'The whole assembly became silent as
they listened to Barnabas and Paul telling about the miraculous
signs and wonders God had done among the Gentiles through
them'(15:12). That must have been absorbingly interesting; but it
was not intended as light relief after the stiff theological debate. It
was part of the evidence of the truth of the doctrine of salvation by
grace through faith. Let us too make sure we grasp its relevance to

the matter under discussion. The first great pioneers in taking the gospel to the Gentiles were men who believed that the purification of the heart necessary for receiving the Holy Spirit and his testimony of acceptance by God, is through faith; and that it is through faith in the sense that a person hears the message of the gospel, believes, and on that ground receives the Holy Spirit and is there and then saved. That is what Peter believed; and what Paul and Barnabas believed; and God authenticated their evangelism by signs and wonders, not the least of which were the marvellous effects of salvation that became visible in the lives of their converts.

James' verdict

Finally James rose to deliver his verdict: he agreed with the doctrine of salvation propounded by Peter, Paul, and Barnabas one hundred per cent. There are certain difficulties in the textual details of his quotation from Amos 9:11–12, but the main lines of argument are clear enough.*

James began by observing that what Peter (as a Palestinian, James called him by his older name, Simeon) had described was God's opening move in his operation to take out a people for his

---

*The text which James cites differs from the Masoretic text in some smaller details and in one major respect. Amos 9:11 in the Masoretic text reads: 'In that day I will restore David's fallen tent. I will repair its broken places, restore its ruins, and build it as it used to be . . .' In James' quotation it runs: 'After this I will return and rebuild David's fallen tent. Its ruins I will rebuild, and I will restore it . . .' The difference in sense is minimal and does not affect James' application of the prophecy.

The larger difference comes in the next verse. The Masoretic text of Amos 9:12 reads: 'so that they may possess the remnant of Edom and all the nations that bear my name . . .' The Septuagint of this verse reads: 'so that the remnant of men and all the nations that bear my name may seek [the Lord] . . .' In James' quotation it runs: 'that the remnant of men may seek the Lord, and all the Gentiles who bear my name . . .' James is therefore nearer to the Septuagint than to the Masoretic text. The Septuagint may be based on a Hebrew text that differed from the Masoretic text (the difference in Hebrew script between the word for 'Edom' and the word for 'man', *adam*, is tiny). However, for the purpose for which James is quoting Amos, even these larger differences do not affect his argument. Finally, the Masoretic text of Amos 9:12b reads: '. . . declares the Lord who will do these things'. In James' quotation it runs: '. . . says the Lord, who does these things *that have been known for ages*'. This last (italicised) phrase seems to be an addition from Isaiah 45:21. Again, the main point of the quotation is unaffected by these differences.

name from the Gentiles. At first sight that might sound a very strange statement to Jews, almost a contradiction in terms. Israel, in their way of thinking, was 'the people for God's name'. Admittedly the patriarchal founder of the nation, Abraham, was originally a Gentile; but God had taken him, and all his descendants, out from the Gentiles in the sense that they had ceased to be Gentiles and had thereby become Israel, a special nation, a people for the Lord's possession (see Exod. 19:5–6). Now James was saying that God was making the first moves in the process of taking a people for his name from the Gentiles, in the sense that this people would not have to become Jews: they would bear the Lord's name, just like Israel did, while still remaining Gentiles. Startlingly novel though this might appear to some Jews, even to some Christian Jews, James pointed out that the idea was not really novel at all. God had announced that this was what he was going to do, centuries before (15:18), through the prophets. There ought then to be no surprise in hearing what God had recently done through Peter: the words of the prophets, James declared, agreed exactly with what God had recently done through him.

What, then, did the words of the prophets say? Two things: first, there would come a time when God would rebuild David's fallen tent. And secondly, that the rebuilding of David's tent would lead to a vast number of Gentiles seeking the Lord (if we follow the exact wording of the text as James quotes it), or to David's tent 'possessing' a large number of Gentile nations (if we follow the reading of the Masoretic text).

The imagery of 'rebuilding David's tent' has proved difficult for many people. Some have thought that 'David's tent' is the nation of Israel and that what James was saying was that large numbers of Gentiles were now going to be incorporated into (the new spiritual) Israel. Others have thought that 'the tent, or tabernacle, of David' refers to the new spiritual tabernacle or temple composed of both Jews and Gentiles, for the worship of God (see Eph. 2:14–22). Still others have felt that the rebuilding of David's tent refers to the restoration of Israel in a coming day, which restoration, they also feel, will be followed by a massive conversion of Gentiles.

But the metaphor 'David's tent' refers neither to the nation of Israel nor to the temple of God at Jerusalem, both of which were still very much in existence in James' day, and nowhere near in ruins. It is a metaphor for David's royal house and dynasty. That had been in ruins ever since Nebuchadnezzar put an end to

David's dynasty at the Exile.* And what James was saying was that now the time had come for God to rebuild David's tent, that is his royal house and dynasty, as promised in the prophets.

In what sense did James understand it? In the exact same sense as we have just heard Paul expound the parallel promises in Isaiah. In Pisidian Antioch, we remember, Paul quoted the words of Isaiah 55:3, 'I will give you the holy and sure blessings of David' (13:34; see also pp. 217–22). He then explained that these blessings promised were fulfilled when God raised the Lord Jesus from the dead, never to decay. And we further noted that, according to Isaiah's prophecy, when God fulfilled these blessings promised to David it would lead to the Messiah's being 'a witness to the peoples, a leader and commander of the peoples. Surely you will summon nations you know not, and nations that do not know you will hasten to you' (Isa. 55:3–5). James, then, was saying the same thing as Paul, namely that one day vast numbers of Gentiles would turn to the Lord and become 'his people', 'Gentiles on whom his name was called'; and that this would happen when David's royal line was restored – that is, by the birth of Jesus the Messiah in David's city, and more particularly by his resurrection from the dead (see also Acts 2:25–31; 2 Tim. 2:8).†

But notice what James did *not* understand Amos' prophecy to mean. He was not saying that this great flow of Gentiles to the Messiah, this new people for God's name from the Gentiles, would become Jews as part of national Israel.‡ He said the very opposite. He agreed with Peter that these Gentiles did not have to be circumcised and live as Jews in order to be saved and to become God's people. He also said that in his judgement they should not be asked to be circumcised and live as Jews *after* they had been saved. (He would not have said this, we fancy, about *Jewish* converts.) 'It is my judgment, therefore,' he said, 'that we

---

*This was the problem that vexed the writer of Psalm 89. He recalled God's promises to David that 'his line would continue for ever and his throne endure . . .' (Ps. 89:36); but then he noted with dismay that God had 'rejected . . . spurned . . . been very angry with your anointed one': 'You have renounced the covenant with your servant and have defiled his crown in the dust. You have broken through all his walls and reduced his strongholds to ruins' (Ps. 89:38–40).

†It is surely a strange thing to say, as some do, that David's house is still in ruins, when the greatest Son of that house has been raised from the dead, never to return to corruption.

‡Nor is James thinking in terms of the formation of a spiritual Israel composed of neither Jew nor Greek. He is in fact thinking of the *difference* between Jewish Christians and Gentile Christians.

should not make it difficult for the Gentiles who are turning to God. Instead we should write to them, telling them to abstain from food polluted by idols, from sexual immorality, from the meat of strangled animals and from blood' (15:20).

The bearing of James' judgement on the doctrine of salvation by grace

James, of course, was not, either consciously or unconsciously, contradicting by his judgement Peter's doctrine of salvation by grace with which he had just said he agreed. To undestand what he was recommending, let's look again at his list of things the Gentiles were to be asked to do. They were all negative: things to be abstained from. There is no mention of the positive duties of a believer like 'loving the Lord with all our heart, mind, soul and strength, and our neighbour as ourselves'. And even this list of things to be abstained from does not include major moral concerns like murder, lying, theft, and covetousness. James was not thinking of the great moral commandments of the law. He was not even suggesting that saved Gentiles must now be taught that the righteous requirements of the law should progressively be met in their lives through the power of the indwelling Spirit of God – true and necessary though that was, and much as everybody at the conference would have agreed with him. He was thinking, as he said, of the fact that 'Moses has been preached in every city from the earliest times and is read in the synagogues on every Sabbath' (15:21). In all these cities, therefore, Gentiles in general would know both from this constant preaching in the synagogues, and even more from their social contact with Jews, that there were certain things over which Jews had a very strong conscience: they would not eat food that had been offered to idols; their list of relationships within which marriage was forbidden was longer than that customary among Gentiles;* they would not eat the meat of animals that had been strangled, nor consume blood in any form. Gentile believers could not be expected to have a conscience about these things. But if Gentile believers did not respect the consciences of their Jewish fellow believers, it would make social fellowship impossible; and in predominantly pagan cities, to have two groups of Christians, one of which could not with a clear conscience have social

---

*And to marry within these extra forbidden relationships was to a Jew 'fornication' (so the Greek; the NIV has 'sexual immorality'). James is not thinking of sexual immorality in general here.

fellowship with the other, would, as far as non-Christians were concerned, tell seriously against the gospel. And if Jewish believers went against their consciences and behaved like Gentiles, it would do them spiritual harm. James, then, was asking Gentile believers, when necessary, to forgo their liberty in these things out of respect for the conscience of others and for the sake of the gospel's reputation and spread. Paul would subsequently write the same thing to his converts (1 Cor. 8–10; Rom. 14).

The letter (15:22–35)

So the apostles and elders and the whole church (notice it was not just the apostles, nor even the apostles plus the elders, but the whole church that acted) chose two men of their own to accompany Paul and Barnabas back to Antioch; and with them they sent a letter addressed to the Gentile believers in Antioch, Syria and Cilicia.

In it they first disowned all connection with, and authorisation of, the false teachers who had originally come to Antioch from Judea. Those men, they said, 'have troubled you with words, subverting your souls' (15:24 – NIV: 'disturbed you, troubling your minds by what they said'). That was very strong language. It resembles the expression Luke used at 14:2 to describe the tactics employed by the hostile unconverted Jews of Iconium to stop the Gentiles from listening to the gospel: 'they stirred up the souls of the Gentiles and made them evil affected against the brethren' (NIV: 'stirred up the Gentiles and poisoned their minds against the brothers'). To teach within the Christian community that salvation is by works is not a valid alternative expression of the Christian faith: it is every bit as much an assault on true Christianity as that launched by its enemies from without.

Secondly, they commended Paul and Barnabas in the highest possible terms: 'our dear friends Barnabas and Paul – men who have risked their lives for the name of our Lord Jesus Christ' (15:26).

Thirdly, they indicated that they stood unambiguously and unequivocally with Barnabas and Paul in the gospel they preached. Gentile believers did not in addition have to be circumcised and keep the law to be saved, as the false teachers had said. 'It seemed good to the Holy Spirit and to us not to burden you with anything beyond the following requirements' (15:28); and those requirements were the minor matters in which Gentile believers were asked to respect the conscience of their Jewish fellow believers (15:29).

The emissaries and the letter duly arrived in Antioch, and both its contents and the ministry of the two brothers from Jerusalem, Judas and Silas, brought great encouragement, gladness and strength to the Gentile believers (15:30–32).

In fact, more than they perhaps realised, a gigantic victory had been won. Now for all succeeding centuries the terms and conditions of salvation had been defined: salvation and justification were by grace through faith without the works of the law. There were not two gospels that were equally valid, one for Jews and one for Gentiles, one for this branch of Christianity and one for another. There was only one gospel. And all true Christians stood together on this issue. James and Peter were one with Barnabas and Paul. Any who taught differently on this matter of salvation – and there were some – stood under the explicit condemnation of all the apostles and elders without exception.

The return (15:36–16:5)

Paul's dispute with Barnabas

It is not unusual in the Christian life for great victories to be followed by minor, but painful and sad, defeats. After Paul and Barnabas had spent some time in Antioch they decided to return and visit the brothers in all the towns where they had preached the word of the Lord and see how they were doing (15:36). But there broke out such a sharp disagreement between them that they parted company. The two men who had stood so staunchly and inseparably together in the sharp dispute and debate against the false teachers now fell out and stood against each other in another sharp disagreement.

Sad as that was, we must attempt to see it in its proper context and true proportion.

First, the subject of the dispute. It was not about the doctrines of the Christian faith. On such matters, as we have seen throughout the preceding paragraphs, Paul and Barnabas, and all the other apostles, stood in unbroken agreement. It was over practical details of procedures in the Lord's work. Barnabas wanted to take the young man John Mark with them as part of their team on their second missionary journey (15:37). Paul objected. His reasons were that John Mark had deserted them early on in the course of the first missionary journey, and had not continued with them in the work (15:38). Paul apparently felt that such irresponsibility and lack of loyal persistence made him unfit to be a member of the team on the second occasion. Paul was not casting doubt on the man's salvation, nor questioning his fitness to be a member of a Christian church. But the qualifications for being a member of an apostolic evangelistic team were naturally more strict and demanding. A church must nurse and carry the weak, fearful and inconsistent. A pioneer missionary team may well think it both wise and kind not to include such people among its members. The Lord's work is not a game which people may take up when they enjoy it and abandon when its demands become rigorous.

Barnabas obviously thought that Mark's defection was not as serious as Paul thought, and that Mark should be given another chance. It has often been pointed out that in fact Mark eventually made good, even by Paul's standards, and that when Paul was imprisoned he asked for Mark to be sent to him as his assistant (2 Tim. 4:11). But even had Paul known that in advance, he still might have considered that it was better for the young man to be allowed to mature in less difficult conditions before being involved again in the rigours of pioneer evangelism.

Anyway, Paul and Barnabas could not agree, perhaps precisely because no basic principle of the faith was involved: it was a practical matter on which much could be said on both sides, and people of different temperaments would naturally give different weight to different considerations.

So they parted. But it is doubtful whether we should shed too many tears over it. The first effect of the separation was that there were now two missionary teams, both headed by capable men, instead of one. That was not necessarily a bad thing at all. The world was a big place: there was room enough for two missionary teams!

Secondly, Paul and Barnabas did not divide the church over it. Luke tells us that when Paul and his new companion Silas left they were commended by the brothers to the grace of the Lord (15:40). No mention is made of such commendation in the case of Barnabas and Mark. Perhaps the church at Antioch did not favour Barnabas' decision. But neither is there any mention of a debate in the church with the church coming to a decision and expecting Paul and Barnabas to be bound by that decision. The church at Antioch obviously did not control these missionary teams; still less did the church at Jerusalem.

Nor did Paul and Barnabas commit that grave offence against

the name and cause of Christ that has become so widespread in recent centuries. They did not set up distinct groups of churches and label them 'Pauline Churches' and 'Barnabas Churches', each with its own separate headquarters, organisation and distinct set of loyalties, thus making sure that the whole world would take notice of the dispute, and go on taking notice of the division long after the original details of the dispute had been forgotten. They simply set up Christian churches; and the world at large never knew of the dispute, and the body of Christ was not divided.

Paul's circumcision of Timothy

The final episode in Movement 2 presents yet another striking and highly significant contrast with the first. At 15:1–5, faced with the demand that the Gentile believers must be circumcised, Paul and Barnabas had implacably opposed the demand; and they had subsequently obtained a letter from the apostles, elders and church at Jerusalem stating their unanimous view that the demand was contrary to the fundamental doctrine of the faith. Yet at 16:1–5 we learn that as Paul and Silas went from town to town delivering this letter to the churches, so 'strengthening them in the faith' (16:5), they came at one point to Lystra. There they found a young disciple named Timothy, and deciding to take him along with them on their missionary journey, Paul had him circumcised!

The careful structure that Luke has given to his narrative shows that he wants us to take ample notice of this apparent inconsistency in Paul's behaviour; because in fact, when we look at it carefully, it is not an inconsistency. The reason why Paul opposed circumcision on the first occasion was that the false teachers were demanding circumcision as necessary for salvation; his circumcision of Timothy, on the other hand, had nothing whatsoever to do with Timothy's salvation. Had anyone demanded that Timothy must be circumcised in order to be saved, Paul would have resisted the demand, as he did in the case of his fellow worker, Titus. On that occasion the truth of the gospel was at stake, and also the need to act in such a way as believers everywhere should be in no doubt whatever as to what the truth of the gospel and the conditions of salvation were (Gal. 2:3–5).

With Timothy the situation was altogether different. To start with, he was a child of a mixed marriage: his father was a Greek,

241

his mother a Jewess (16:1). That was probably why he had not been circumcised as a baby. But in Jewish eyes, his mother's being a Jewess made him a Jew.

Secondly, all true Jewish Christians would have agreed with Peter that even for Jews circumcision was not necessary for salvation, neither did it contribute anything to salvation. On the other hand, many of them would have felt that since circumcision was something that God had commanded in the Old Testament that all Jews should practise, Christian Jews should practise it, simply to please the Lord.

The situation with them was as it is today with Gentile Christians in respect, say, of the sabbath (except that Jewish Christians believed that circumcision was a command given solely to Jews, and not to Gentiles, whether Christian or non-Christian). All true Christians would agree that it is not necessary to keep the sabbath in order to be saved. But after that they are divided. Some, perhaps the majority, hold that the sabbath was part of Israel's ceremonial law that has been repealed along with the food-laws, priesthood, rituals and temple, and that therefore it is not binding on Christians to keep it. Others hold that the sabbath is part of the moral law which is still in force today. They therefore hold that true believers must keep the sabbath: not to be saved, but because it is God's will for his people, and that the righteous requirements of the law should be fulfilled in those who walk not after the flesh but after the Spirit. Moreover, while they see quite clearly that sabbath-keeping is not necessary for salvation, they would regard it as such an obvious result of salvation, and so obligatory upon true believers, that if any professing believer consistently refused to keep it the genuineness of his faith might be called in question.

Imagine, then, an evangelist who is quite convinced in his own heart that he does not need to keep the sabbath; but he feels led to go and preach the gospel in a part of the world where the majority of believers feel that true Christians are under an obligation to keep the sabbath. What shall he do? If he drives his car or rides his bicycle on Sundays, he will offend the conscience of the local believers and antagonise them. If he has any practical sense, therefore, let alone Christian love, he will follow the instructions Paul gives on this very matter in Romans 14:1–18 (see especially 14:5–6). He will forgo what he regards as his rights and freedom, and keep the sabbath so as not to offend the conscience of his fellow Christians.

In addition, there might well be many local people who are not

242

saved, but are very religious and think that their sabbath observance and their law-keeping are necessary to earn them salvation. The evangelist will want to show them that salvation is not by law-keeping, it is by grace. But if they see him constantly breaking the sabbath which they regard as part of the moral law, they will dismiss his message of salvation by grace as sheer antinomianism. He might as well spend the whole week robbing the local supermarket, and then preach salvation by grace on Sundays.

For similar reasons, therefore, Paul had Timothy circumcised not as something necessary for salvation, but out of respect for the conscience of both Christian and non-Christian Jews, in order to be able the more effectively to preach the gospel among them. As he later explained to the Corinthians:

> Though I am free and belong to no man, I make myself a slave to everyone, to win as many as possible. To the Jews I became like a Jew, to win the Jews. To those under the law I became like one under the law (though I myself am not under the law), so as to win those under the law. (1 Cor. 9:19–20)

Once more, then, the carefully balanced literary structure of Luke's narrative has called our attention to a healthy balance in the beliefs and behaviour of the early Christians. May God's Holy Spirit produce a similarly balanced outlook in us.*

---

*We should be careful not to abuse this principle. If some practice either in church life or in social or private life is plainly contrary to God's word, and forbidden by it, we should not try to justify continuing it by claiming that we do not practise it in order to earn salvation, but only to fit in with local culture or tradition. If the practice is contrary to God's word, it must be discontinued whatever the effect on culture and tradition. Moreover, circumcision and the observance of the sabbath were not simply matters of culture in Israel. They were positive commandments of the Lord laid on Israel by the Old Testament. Hence the conscience of many Jewish believers against discontinuing them. It was altogether different with practices which the Pharisees had added without any scriptural authority and which actually conflicted with God's word. Deeply ingrained in Jewish culture though they had become, our Lord did not go along with them for the sake of peace, but denounced them (see Mark 7:1–23).

Section Five

Christianity and the Pagan World
(16:6–19:20)

Section Five
Christianity and the Pagan World
(16:6–19:20)

PRELIMINARY OBSERVATIONS

A noticeable change of atmosphere pervades Section Five of Acts. For this, geography is in part responsible, since at the beginning of the section Paul and his fellow missionaries enter Europe and visit a whole string of cities (some of them very famous) – Philippi, Thessalonica, Berea, Athens and Corinth – before finally returning to Asia Minor and its illustrious capital, Ephesus.

Even more responsible for the change in atmosphere is Luke's selection of material for his narrative. Up to this point he has defined Christianity's essential distinctives almost entirely in terms of its differences from various parties within Judaism or else from Judaism's step-daughter, Samaritanism. His long, detailed summaries of Peter's, Stephen's and Paul's speeches have all been taken from their addresses to various Jewish or Jewish-Christian audiences, or else to Gentiles like Cornelius who already shared, as did Christianity, Judaism's central belief in the one true God. The only exception has been Paul and Barnabas' denunciation of pagan idolatry at Lystra (14:11–18).

But now there comes a change. In Section Five no full, detailed summary is given of any of the numerous sermons that Paul did in fact preach to the Jews in their synagogues or elsewhere during this period. The topics of his discourses are sometimes given (e.g. 17:3 and 18:5), but not long summaries. His sermons and discourses would doubtless have followed the same general pattern as those which Luke has already reported. There would be no point in giving further examples. The only speech from this period that Luke summarises at any length is Paul's address to the Court of the Areopagus at Athens. Some, if not all, of the members of the court were intellectually sophisticated, but all of them, naturally enough, were pagans. In explaining to the court the essential features of Christianity, Paul inevitably does so against the background not of Judaism but of pagan religious, philosophical and political thought and practice. And Luke provides us with a comparatively full outline of this address because it is typical of the special emphasis that he wishes this section of Acts to carry.

The particular element in Paul's preaching that aroused the bemused curiosity of certain members of the Athenian court and led to his being invited to address it was his constant mention of the terms 'Jesus' and 'the resurrection'. They had the impression that he was introducing into Athens a couple of foreign gods. So they asked him to explain (17:18–19). Here, then, was Paul's opportunity to expound to pagans the heart of the distinctively Christian message; and judging from Luke's summary Paul used his opportunity to the full. His explanation of 'Jesus' and 'the resurrection' formed the great climax of his speech (17:30–31). At the same time, it was little use his proclaiming to pagan Athenians, as he did, that Jesus was God's appointed Judge of all mankind if he did not first explain what God, and what kind of God, he was referring to. Necessarily, he had to begin with and spend a great deal of his time expounding that fundamental doctrine of the gospel which Christianity inherited from Israel and holds no less tenaciously: the existence of the one, transcendent, personal, self-sufficient, omnipotent and holy Creator, Maintainer and Ruler of the universe and of all mankind (17:23–29). This, then, is the first and basic belief that distinguishes Christianity from paganism.

Paul's proclamation of Jesus as the coming Judge of all mankind put into language which pagan Gentiles could immediately understand one aspect of the second basic doctrine with which Christianity confronts paganism, namely that Jesus is the Messiah promised by God in Israel's Old Testament. Acts has long since, of course, preached Jesus as the Messiah (e.g. 2:36) and as the Judge of all (10:42). But in the first half of Acts 17 we shall find the Jews of Thessalonica vigorously maintaining before the city's Gentile magistrates that with the Christians 'Messiah' is a political term; that the Christian gospel is essentially a political manifesto, putting forward Jesus as a rival to the reigning Caesar in the political order of this present world; and that Christian evangelism is in reality an attempt to foment widespread political struggle aimed at breaking the structures of Roman imperialism and replacing them with a different form of government (17:5–8).

The charge was a specious one, for there were various parties within Judaism for whom the term 'Messiah' did carry this political meaning; and it had already given rise to insurrections at various times (see, e.g., 5:36–37; 21:37–39), and would later lead to massive rebellions against pagan Rome. Moreover, one of the Lord Jesus' own disciples, Simon, the Zealot (Luke 6:15), had before his conversion been a member of just such a messianic political group. Paul himself did not get the chance to answer the charge on that occasion: he was banished from the city. But it was imperative for the sake of the gospel, both then and now, that Luke should show from what Paul had earlier said at Thessalonica, and from what he later said at Athens, that the charge was not true; and that he should positively make clear exactly what Christianity means by proclaiming Jesus as Messiah, King and Judge, and what relation his kingship bears to Gentile politics.

The third issue at stake between Christianity and paganism in this section is what Christianity means by the Holy Spirit. As we have seen from the very beginning of Acts, the early Christians, as was natural after Pentecost, talked much about receiving the Holy Spirit, about being filled with the Spirit, and in particular about being guided by the Spirit (e.g. 8:29, 39; 10:19; 11:12; 13:2). To the average Jew this terminology would at least be intelligible, for he or she would know that the Spirit in question was the Spirit of God. But in the ancient pagan world thousands of people in all walks of life were in the habit of seeking guidance for their personal, family and business affairs from fortune-tellers, astrologers, clairvoyants, spiritists, oracles, gods and demons. Multitudes still do in the Far East, and an increasing number these days in the West. Questions would therefore naturally arise in the pagan mind, and indeed in the minds of recent Christian converts (19:18): What was the difference between the Christian experience of being led by the Spirit and the pagan practice of seeking guidance from various forms of spiritism? And was spiritism compatible with the Christian gospel? Was it acceptable for believers in the Lord Jesus to continue to worship the spirits of their ancestors, to consult fortune-tellers and to use the services of mediums and spirit-healers?

Luke's selection of material answers these questions decisively. The first quarter of Section Five opens by mentioning twice in as many verses that Paul and his fellow missionaries were guided in their travels by the Holy Spirit (16:6, 7). The last quarter of the section opens with the story of twelve men who, being disciples of John the Baptist but never having learned what it means personally to believe on the Lord Jesus, had never received the Holy Spirit. Immediately on believing, they do receive the Spirit; and Paul obviously considers this receiving of the Holy Spirit so indispensable to being a Christian that he then makes these men get baptised again, this time in the name of the Lord Jesus (19:1–7).

At the other extreme, the major story in the first quarter of Section Five takes its rise from Paul's exorcism of an evil spirit from a female fortune-teller in Philippi (16:16–19). She appeared to be favourably disposed to the gospel, and recommended both it and its preachers to the bystanders. But Paul regarded testimony from her and her spirit as unacceptable. He obviously considered spiritism incompatible with Christianity; and he demonstrated the difference between the two by casting the spirit out of the woman.

Similarly, the major story in the final quarter of Section Five is also about demonism (19:11–20); only here the difference is not between Christianity and demonism, but between true Christianity and professional exorcists who, not being Christians themselves, and with no intention of becoming such, mix Christian terminology along with the rest of their repertoire in an attempt to boost their success at exorcism. Seven Jews at Ephesus misappropriate the name of the Lord Jesus in this way. But the evil spirit in the demon-possessed man exposes their misappropriation, and its victim physically assaults and routs the would-be exorcists. This leads to a city-wide enhancement of the name and exclusive power of the Lord Jesus, and a mighty public triumph of the word of God over the occult arts for which Ephesus was internationally famous.

To sum up, then. As Luke depicts Christianity against the background of paganism, the three major areas of interest will be:

1. Christianity's proclamation of the existence and nature of the one true God, and of man's relation to him, as against both pagan religion's polytheism and the theories of (some) pagan philosophers about the origin and workings of the universe and about mankind's place and purpose within it.

2. The meaning and significance of the Christian gospel's assertion that Jesus is Messiah, King and Judge of the world, in the light both of world politics and of the systems of morality worked out by certain pagan philosophers.

3. The importance of the Christian experience of the Holy

Spirit, thrown into relief by the experience of Jews who had accepted John's baptism but had not yet believed on the Lord Jesus; and the source of that experience contrasted with the pagan world's contacts in the realm of spiritism, demonism and occult practice.

Luke's special interest in Christianity's confrontation with paganism does not mean, however, that he wishes us now to forget Judaism and the part it had played and continued to play in the pagan Gentile world. Luke points out that Paul's tactics during this period remained what they had always been. Whatever city he might be in, he invariably went first to the Jewish synagogue (if there was one) and preached the gospel to the Jews and to the synagogue's Gentile adherents (16:3; 17:2, 10, 17; 18:4, 19; 19:8). The synagogues' noble witness had everywhere brought many former pagans to faith in the one true God, and had therefore prepared them (even if unintentionally) for faith in the Lord Jesus as Messiah. Luke ungrudgingly and repeatedly records that it was from this circle of Gentile adherents in particular that many of Paul's converts in Hellenistic and Roman cities came. And of course many Jews too were converted (17:4; 18:8), as well as outright pagans (16:30–34; 17:12; 18:8).

On the other hand, of course, Luke does not hide the fact that while in most synagogues Paul was initially received with great courtesy (17:1–4, 11; 18:4, 19–20; 19:8), strong and sometimes violent opposition on the part of some members would eventually drive Paul and his converts out of the local synagogue (17:5; 18:6–7; 19:9), and from neighbouring synagogues as well (17:13). This kind of thing had happened before (13:45–46; 14:2, 5 – note here the reference to the leaders/rulers); but now in Section Five Luke reports a significant development: on two occasions Jews prosecute the Christians before the pagan authorities, charging them with treason against the state (17:7) and with fostering an illegal form of religion (18:12–17). Neither charge was true, as Luke will proceed to show. Jewish opposition of this kind was sad;* but it led to positive results for the pagan world. It precipitated the formation of independent Christian churches (as at Thessalonica, Corinth and Ephesus); it led to a massive spread and triumph of the word of the Lord in the pagan world (as in Ephesus and Asia, 19:9–10 and 20); and in places where Judaism was already known (if only vaguely to the population at large), it

---

* It was even sadder that in the post-Constantine centuries Christendom should use its political influence to suppress, slander and persecute Jews on a large scale.

helped to make the public aware that the name of the Lord Jesus had power to save and to bless them more than Judaism possessed even at its best (19:1–7), let alone at its less reputable (19:13–17).

There are, of course, subsidiary themes that reappear from time to time. One such is the relation of the gospel to business and money-making. It was taken for granted in the ancient world (as it still appears to be in some quarters of the modern) that some people should make a lot of money by turning religion into a business. The owners of the spirit-medium at Philippi are one example (16:19); and the publishers of books on the occult at Ephesus are another (19:19). It will be interesting, therefore, to see the part played by business in Paul's pioneer evangelism. Lydia at Philippi is in the fashion trade (16:14); Aquila, Priscilla and Paul at Corinth are in the business of tent-making (18:1–3). In both instances secular business provides Paul with a foothold in Europe and with the money necessary to preach the gospel free of charge to the hearers (cf. 1 Thess. 2:9; Phil. 4:15–16 with Acts 18:5; 1 Cor. 9:18 and 2 Cor. 11:7–9).

Or again. In his Areopagite speech Paul remarks that God 'determined . . . the exact places where they [the nations] should live . . . so that men would seek him and perhaps reach out for him and find him . . .' (17:26–27). In the context, Paul is referring to God's providential control of the nations throughout the course of history; but at a lower level we shall see the same principle at work in Paul's missionary journeys. As he leaves Asia and comes to Europe, home after home is opened to him: Lydia's (16:15) and then the jailer's in Philippi (16:34); Jason's, apparently, in Thessalonica (17:5–6); Priscilla and Aquila's (18:1–3) and later Titius Justus' in Corinth (18:7). All these homes play a strategic part in the planting of Christianity in Europe. It will be a matter of some interest therefore to observe, where we can, how those homes came to be where they were, how and by what circumstances and providences Paul came to them, and how they in turn were opened up to him.

Now we implied a moment ago that Section Five of Acts is composed of four quarters, or movements. The first hint that this may in fact be so is provided by the following series of four major episodes, in each of which Paul and the gospel are wrongly accused or misunderstood or misrepresented and then successfully vindicated or defended:*

* As we have already seen, a very serious accusation is brought against the gospel before the magistrates in Thessalonica at 17:5–9. But on this occasion Paul

16:16–34 (a) *A false accusation.* Paul and Silas are accused before the civil magistrates of being Jews who are 'throwing our city into an uproar by advocating customs unlawful for us Romans to accept or practice' (16:20–21). They are flogged and thrown into prison.

(b) *Vindication.* Far from stopping the power of the gospel, the imprisonment of Paul and Silas leads, through a providentially timed earthquake, to the conversion of the jailer himself and of his family. Moreover, the magistrates, discovering they are Romans, are obliged to come and deferentially escort them out of prison.

17:16–31 (a) *A misconception.* Epicureans and Stoics imagine that Paul is advocating two foreign gods, 'Jesus' and 'the resurrection'.

(b) *Clarification.* Paul explains to the Court of the Areopagus that the God he preaches is not some foreign deity: he is the Creator and Maintainer of all mankind. Nor are Jesus and the resurrection foreign deities either. The historical resurrection of the historical man, Jesus, is God's affirmation to all people everywhere that Jesus is to be the universal Judge of all mankind.

18:12–17 (a) *A false accusation.* The Jews appeal to the proconsul Gallio against Paul, on the ground that he persuades 'people to worship God in ways contrary to [presumably, the Jewish] law' (18:13).

(b) *Vindication.* Gallio dismisses the charge as being simply a matter of Jewish theology, and therefore no concern of the Roman court.

19:13–16 (a) *A misappropriation.* Certain non-Christian professional exorcists misappropriate the name Jesus and attempt to use it as a spell or charm to increase their success in exorcism.

(b) *Vindication.* The true nature and authority of Jesus are vindicated as an evil spirit retorts: 'Jesus I know . . . but who are you?' (19:15), and proceeds to rout the would-be exorcists.

The four movements are further marked out by the thought-flow that links their main episodes:

Movement 1 (16:6–40): Events on the way to, and in, Philippi
a) Paul and his team are guided by the Holy Spirit (16:6–7) and by a God-given vision, and so reach Philippi. Lydia's heart is opened by the Lord; she believes, and invites Paul and Silas to stay in her house (16:14–15).

---

has no opportunity to answer the charge. Luke himself, however, has so arranged the structure of his narrative that his readers will find the final answer to the accusation in Paul's Areopagite address at the end of that same chapter, Acts 17.

b) Paul drives out an evil spirit from a fortune-teller. As a result he and Silas are imprisoned. But God uses an earthquake to open all the doors (16:26). The jailer believes (16:34) and brings them into his house (16:32). The city magistrates deferentially escort them out of prison and request them to leave Philippi (16:39).

Movement 2 (17:1–43): Persecution drives Paul from Thessalonica to Berea and from Berea to Athens

a) At Thessalonica, and again at Berea, Paul demonstrates that according to Scripture the Messiah had to die and then to rise from the dead; and then that Jesus' death and resurrection show him to be the Messiah foretold by Scripture (17:2–3, 11).

b) At Athens, asked to explain the meaning of the terms 'Jesus' and 'the resurrection', Paul asserts that the resurrection of Jesus is God's assurance to all mankind that Jesus is to be the Judge of the world (17:18–19, 30–31).

Movement 3 (18:1–28): Events mainly at Corinth

a) Paul comes to Corinth, where he testifies to the Jews that the Messiah is Jesus (18:1, 5). The Jews are abusive; Paul leaves the synagogue and goes to the Gentiles; many are converted (18:6–11). Paul stays in Corinth for one and a half years (18:11).

b) The Jews prosecute Paul before Gallio's tribunal. Their case is dismissed (18:12–17), and after some while Paul leaves Corinth and goes to Asia (18:18–23); but Apollos comes from Asia to Corinth (18:24–28; 'Achaia' in v.27 implies Corinth, see 19:1) and 'was a great help to those who . . . had believed. For he vigorously refuted the Jews in public debate, proving from the Scriptures [what Paul had earlier preached] that the Messiah was Jesus (18:27–28).

Movement 4 (19:1–20): Events at Ephesus

a) Twelve men who had been baptised with John the Baptist's baptism learn to believe on the Lord Jesus. They are then baptised in the name of the Lord Jesus and receive the Holy Spirit. After three months in the synagogue, opposition drives Paul out. He lectures daily in Tyrannus' lecture hall for two years, 'so that all the Jews and Greeks . . . in the province of Asia heard the word of the Lord' (19:10).

b) Seven non-Christian Jews attempt to exorcise an evil spirit 'In the name of Jesus, whom Paul preaches' (19:13). The evil spirit exposes their misappropriation of the name of Jesus, and the result is that 'the name of the Lord Jesus was held in high honour' by both Jews and Greeks throughout Ephesus (19:17). This in turn leads to a great public burning of books on the occult, 'so mightily did the word of the Lord spread and prevail' (19:13–20).*

---

*The rendering 'prevail' (i.e. 'to have strength greater than someone or something else', 'to win out') is to be preferred here, as in 19:16 and Revelation 12:8; see AV and RV.

Finally, within each movement the narrative follows the same pattern. But this is best seen from a table of contents, which will also help us to perceive the relation of the component parts to each other and to the whole (see pp. 256–57).

THE MOVEMENTS

MOVEMENT 1: The Holy Spirit and the Powers of Darkness (16:6–40)

The gospel and foreign cultures

It is the fact that still to millions of people, particularly in Asia, Christianity appears to be a Western religion, foreign to their outlook and incompatible with their national ethos. They may respect it at a distance, but they resent attempts of Christian missionaries to convert them; it is, they feel, an insult to their own religions and cultures, an insensitive, not to say arrogant, form of Western imperialism.

For this reaction Christendom is itself partly to blame, in that in the past its missionaries have often linked the gospel with the national churches, or even with the governments, of their home countries, so that people of other countries have understandably gained the impression that the Christian gospel is an arm of Western colonialism. And the impression has been strengthened by the failure of missionaries sometimes to distinguish the gospel they preach from the trappings of Western culture, music, architecture, forms of service and so forth that have collected around it in the missionaries' home countries over the centuries. Other nations therefore fear Christianity as something alien which would stifle the expression of their national character.

These mistakes are of course widely recognised and freely confessed nowadays. Indeed the danger is that reaction to them takes people to the other extreme. Everywhere the suggestion is increasingly voiced that the attempt to convert people of other faiths to Christianity is false to the spirit of Christ, a regrettable form of religious fundamentalism that imagines that it, and it

MOVEMENT 1: The Holy Spirit and the Powers of Darkness (16:6-40)	MOVEMENT 2: God's Messiah and Gentile Politics, Religion and Philosophy (17:1-34)	MOVEMENT 3: God's Messiah and the New People of God (18:1-28)	MOVEMENT 4: The Holy Spirit and the Name of the Lord Jesus (19:1-20)
A. FROM PHRYGIA TO PHILIPPI	**A. THESSALONICA AND BEREA**	**A. PAUL'S STAY IN CORINTH (1)**	**A. PAUL'S STAY IN EPHESUS (1)**
1. *Phrygia to Troas and the man of Macedonia*	1. *Thessalonica and Jason's house*	1. *Corinth and Aquila and Priscilla's house*	1. *Ephesus and the twelve disciples*
The guidance of the Holy Spirit: 'kept by the Holy Spirit from preaching in the province of Asia' (16:6); 'they tried to enter Bithynia, but the *Spirit of Jesus* would not allow them to' (16:7). A man of Macedonia appears to Paul in a night-vision (16:9-10)	Paul argues in the synagogue that Jesus is the Messiah forecast in the Scriptures. The Jews accuse Paul and Silas of teaching contrary to the *decrees of Caesar* (17:1-9)	*A decree of Caesar* indirectly secures Paul a foothold in Corinth. He preaches in the synagogue every sabbath to Jews and Greeks (18:1-4)	*The reception of the Holy Spirit:* 'Did you receive *the Holy Spirit* when you believed?'; ' "We never even heard that *the Holy Spirit was given*" . . . The Holy Spirit came on them' (19:1-7)
2. *From Troas to Philippi and the house of Lydia*	2. *Berea: driven from the synagogue and city*	2. *Corinth: driven from the synagogue to the house of Titius Justus next door*	2. *Ephesus: driven from the synagogue to the lecture-hall of Tyrannus*
At the 'place of prayer', the Lord opens Lydia's heart to give heed to the things spoken by Paul. ' "If you have judged me to be a believer, come and stay in my house." She prevailed on us' (16:15)	The people in the synagogue at Berea 'were of more noble character than the Thessalonians, for they received the message with great eagerness and examined the Scriptures every day.' Many therefore believed; but Jewish persecutors from Thessalonica drove Paul and Silas away (17:10-15)	Paul gave his full time to preaching that the Messiah was Jesus. When the Jews opposed and blasphemed, Paul said 'Your blood be on your own heads!' and went next door to Titius' house. Many Corinthians believed. The Lord appeared to Paul in a night-vision; and he stayed one and a half years, preaching the word (18:5-11)	Paul preaches three months in the synagogue. When some Jews were hardened and blasphemed the Way in front of the people, he left and went to Tyrannus' lecture-hall, where he discoursed daily for two years, 'so that all . . . in the province of Asia heard the word of the Lord' (19:8-10)

B. IN PHILIPPI	B. ATHENS	B. PAUL'S STAY IN CORINTH (2)	B. PAUL'S STAY IN EPHESUS (2)
1. The false accusation	*1. The misunderstanding*	*1. The false accusation*	*1. The attempted misappropriation*
Paul drives an evil spirit out of a medium (16:16–18). Her owners accuse Paul and Silas of being 'Jews [who] are throwing our city into an uproar by advocating customs unlawful for us Romans to accept or practise' (16:19–21). Paul and Silas are flogged and imprisoned (16:22–24)	Some Stoics and Epicureans think Paul is advocating two foreign gods, 'Jesus' and 'the resurrection' (17:16–21)	The Jews prosecute Paul before Gallio's tribunal: 'This man is persuading the people to worship God in ways contrary to the law' (18:12–13)	God performs 'extraordinary miracles through Paul'. Seven Jewish exorcists attempt to exorcise an evil spirit 'in the name of Jesus, whom Paul preaches' (19:11–14)
2. The vindication	*2. The explanation*	*2. The vindication*	*2. The exposure*
Far from stopping the success of the gospel, Paul and Silas' imprisonment leads, through the intervention of a providential earthquake, to the conversion of the jailer himself, and of his family. The jailer brings Paul and Silas up into his house (16:25–34)	Paul is not advocating foreign deities. God is the Creator and Maintainer of *all* mankind. He has made *all* men out of one original man. God is near *everyone*. He now 'commands *all* people *everywhere* to repent'. He will judge *the world* in righteousness by the Man he has ordained. Assurance of this has been given by the resurrection of Jesus (17:22–31)	Gallio dismisses the case as being an internal theological dispute among Jews, and irrelevant to a Roman court of justice: 'I will not be a judge of such things' (18:14–17)	The evil spirit retorts: 'Jesus I know, and I know about Paul, but who are you?' Its victim then assaults the would-be exorcists, who rush out of the house wounded and naked (19:15–16)
3. The sequel	*3. The sequel*	*3. The sequel*	*3. The sequel*
The magistrates are obliged to come and personally conduct Paul and Silas out of prison. They then ask them to leave. Paul and Silas go to Lydia's house, encourage the brothers, then leave Philippi (16:35–40)	On hearing of the resurrection, some mock, some defer. So Paul leaves the Areopagus Court. But some adhere to Paul and become believers (17:32–34)	Paul leaves and travels to Ephesus, Caesarea, and Antioch; then begins his third missionary journey. Meanwhile Apollos comes to Ephesus preaching John's baptism (i.e. the baptism of repentance). Being further instructed by Aquila and Priscilla, he then goes to Corinth and witnesses to the Jews that the Messiah is Jesus (18:18–28)	The name of the Lord Jesus is magnified throughout Ephesus. Books on occult practice to the value of 50,000 drachmas are publicly burned, 'so mightily did the word of God prevail' (19:17–20)

alone, has the truth. The truly Christian thing to do, it is said, is to drop all exclusive claims about the uniqueness of Christ, and to engage in genuinely open-ended dialogue with people of other faiths. That means admitting the basic validity of all the major religions, confessing the limitations of all of them, Christianity included, and moving forward together in the search for ultimate truth. Only so, it is argued, can Christianity gain the respect of the people of Asia and Africa, and avoid the hitherto valid accusation that it is a Western religion imbued with the West's desire to dominate the rest of the world.

But the fact is, as Luke is about to point out, that when Paul and Silas brought the gospel to Europe, the very first batch of Europeans they met violently resented it precisely on this ground that the gospel was contrary to their national ethos. The only difference between their reaction and the modern one was that they complained that the gospel was an Eastern Asiatic religion incompatible with their Western culture. If Paul had accepted their objection as a valid reason against trying to convert people of other faiths and cultures to Christ, he would there and then have ceased his efforts to evangelise Europe, packed his bags, and gone home.

The people of Philippi, proud of their city's status as a Roman colony, and of their own status as Romans, violently objected to Paul and Silas on the ground that 'These men are Jews, and are throwing our city into an uproar by advocating customs unlawful for us Romans to accept or practise' (16:20–21). The second part of their accusation was not true, of course, as Luke will later show by recording the judgement handed down by the proconsul Gallio in Corinth (18:12–16). And the first part of the story was only half true: Paul was certainly a Jew, but he was also a Roman citizen, the equal of any man or woman in Philippi. But neither the crowd nor the magistrates gave them opportunity to state that fact, or if they did, they took no notice of it. They flogged them and bundled them off to prison.

The fact is that Romans in general disliked Jews, as we learn from the vivid expressions of the later Roman satirist Juvenal. He was appalled by their (to him) barbarous rite of circumcision, their sabbath-keeping and their esoteric law of Moses which made them stand out from the cultural norms of Roman society; he pilloried their refusal to worship any gods other than their own; and he had nothing but contempt for their little prayer-houses, tucked away down side-streets, compared with the great and aesthetically magnificent temples of the Roman state religion.* Now there was a Jewish 'prayer-house' (or at least a meeting-place for prayer) at Philippi that was frequented by women,† and as far as we know the local citizens had left it in peace, as Roman law demanded they should. But when Paul and Silas put an end to the operations of one of the local fortune-tellers, the Philippians' resentment and injured ethnic pride boiled over; and contrary to their own law they imprisoned the missionaries.

Calmer thought, however, might have shown the Philippians that ethnic pride and national culture were irrelevant to the question whether the message that Paul and Silas were proclaiming was true. Paul was not, as later the Athenians initially thought (17:18), trying to introduce foreign gods into the local culture; nor was he chauvinistically championing his own national gods against the Philippians' national gods. In the first place, he was proclaiming the one and only Creator-of-all-mankind, as much the Philippians' Creator as any other nation's. Judaism certainly believed in him, while none of the Philippians' gods claimed to be such a Creator. But the Creator was neither the product nor the national property of the Jews. 'Is God the God of Jews only?' as Paul would say. 'Is he not the God of Gentiles too? Yes, of Gentiles too, since there is only one God . . .' whose terms of salvation must be the same for all (Rom. 3:29–30). And in the second place, Paul was not advocating Judaism as a religion; he was preaching Christ as God's supreme and final self-revelation to all mankind. Israel's religion as originally given by God was pure and holy; but Paul was not even pressing that religion on the Gentiles. Contemporary Judaism, though retaining many noble features of Israel's original religion, had corrupted others, and had officially rejected and murdered God's Son. God would one day judge Judaism for it. Paul certainly was not advocating Judaism as a religion to the Philippians. And we may hasten to add that if the term 'Christianity' is taken to mean that vast religio-political system that has grown up around the name of Christ, otherwise known as Christendom, then Christians nowadays have no business trying to convert non-Christians to Christianity in that sense. That form of Christianity has often contained, and still does contain, many things that even a child could see are contrary to the Spirit of Christ and to the teaching of

---

*See Juvenal, *Satires* III, 14, 296; VI, 543; XIV, 96, 103.

†The best reading at 16:13 would appear to be 'a place where prayer was customarily made'; cf. AV. Perhaps there were not enough males to form the quorum necessary for a full-scale synagogue.

the New Testament. God will judge that too – more severely, perhaps, than anything else.

Paul, then, was not preaching Judaism, but the one true God, the Creator of all men; and not Eastern or Western Christendom – obviously not – but Christ. Moreover, in calling on people of all ethnic groups and nationalities to abandon their man-invented deities and idolatrous interpretations of the universe, Paul was only urging them to do what his own ancestors had had to do in centuries past. And, of course, we so-called Western Christians would freely acknowledge that our ancestors too were all of them worshippers of deities invented by human imagination until the gospel came from Asia to Europe and summoned them to face reality and to return to mankind's original belief in the one, self-existent Creator, and then to bow to his self-revelation in Jesus Christ.

There is no genuine cause in all this for hurt ethnic pride or cultural resentment, any more than the planet Neptune would have just cause for feeling culturally offended if the Earth tried to convert it (if it needed conversion) to the belief that it revolves round the sun, as all the other planets do. When it came to purely cultural matters, Paul (as we know from his writings) was the most adaptable of men, prepared to live as a Jew among Jews or as a Greek among Greeks (1 Cor. 9:19–22). But he never would have consented to the proposition that the choice between mono-theism and polytheism is simply a matter of preference according to one's traditional way of interpreting the universe; or that God's unique and final self-revelation in Christ may be rejected with impunity if it does not fit in with one's national, ethnic or cultural predilections.

But to return to the Philippians. Perhaps calm thought was difficult for them at this point for other reasons too. In recording Paul's action in delivering a Philippian fortune-teller from an evil spirit (16:16–18), Luke puts his finger on two very sensitive areas in paganism. The first deserves no sympathy; the other calls at least for compassionate understanding.

The fortune-teller was controlled by certain businessmen who manipulated her and her condition in order to make themselves a lot of money. When Paul set the woman free from domination by the evil spirit, he cut off the businessmen's income (16:19). Of course they did not cite this as the reason for prosecuting the missionaries; they chose rather to play on the mob's – and the magistrates' – prejudices and ethnic pride. But the threat of Christianity to their vested financial interests was the real cause of their opposition. The making of money out of religion has been a scandal all down the centuries – and still is. Nor has Christendom escaped: the recent exposure of the corruption of certain American TV evangelists provides but one more example of the long-standing misuse of Christianity in various quarters to pile up massive treasures and large sums of money in the name of Christ.

But Paul's action in putting an end to the medium's ability to tell fortunes touched a deeper nerve in paganism: it cut off one source of supernatural guidance which many people in the city craved for and felt to be an indispensable help to successful living. Of course they resented it.

There must be very few people who have never felt at some time in their lives a longing to be able to see what lies in the future. Nor is that longing necessarily mere idle curiosity, or the pure greed of people who consult the spirits, as some do, for advice on the right numbers to choose in order to win the football pools. Life presents us all from time to time with unavoidable decisions that carry far-reaching consequences for our own or other people's lives. The anguish lies in the fact that we have to decide without knowing for certain how the course we choose will turn out, whether successfully or in disaster. In these circumstances it is at least understandable that people who have never known God as a loving Father, have never had any personal experience of his salvation, forgiveness, care and guidance, who have no confidence in the wisdom of his detailed providences nor any assurance that all things work together for good for those who love God, since they know nothing of God's grand and ultimate purpose which gathers up and makes sense of all life's details – it is understandable that they should feel driven to the spirit world, to oracles, fortune-tellers, mediums and astrologers for the guidance they crave. Similarly with the bereaved. People who do not have the Christian's certainty and comfort that 'to be absent from the body is to be at home with the Lord' (2 Cor. 5:8), can understandably find the grief of their loss unbearable, and will wish to accept as true the comforting (but actually deceptive) information about the whereabouts of their departed loved-ones which impersonating, evil spirits pass on to them through spirit mediums.

Many people in the ancient world viewed these practices with a mixture of incredulity and superstitious fear. Hard-hearded philosophers like the Epicureans (whom we shall presently meet) completely rejected all claims of communication with the world beyond.* But few people in the ancient world were hard-headed philosophers, and to many of them, as still to millions today, it was all very real. When, therefore, Christianity, like true Judaism, outlawed it root and branch, denounced and fought it as partly bogus and partly all too real, evil, dangerous and degrading, it is understandable that many people should resent Christianity as an alien, hard-hearted, puritanical, interfering religion that had no feeling for, or sympathy with, the psychological needs of the individual caught up in the frightening complexities of life.

The very opposite was true, of course; but it is time we let Luke speak for himself more directly and in greater detail.

God and the individual

The proportions of the narrative in Movement 1 of Section Five of Acts are remarkable. The narrative is devoted to an event which was, by any standards, highly significant in the history of the church: Paul's first evangelistic foray into Europe and the beginnings of the first church to be established there as the result of his labours. But the founding of a church is scarcely the feature that the narrative concentrates on. True, it relates that following the conversions of Lydia and the jailer the members of both their households were also converted (16:15, 31, 33–34), though no detail is given about them. Granted, we are also told that when Paul and Silas came out of prison they went to Lydia's house, met the brothers, and encouraged them; though again we are not told how many they were. One can deduce from the narrative that Luke himself probably stayed behind in Philippi when Paul and the others left; though one has to be very sharp to pick up the clue.† All in all we can see that by the time Paul left Philippi the nucleus, at least, of a church had been formed; though Luke nowhere mentions what he surely knew when he later compiled Acts, that this nucleus eventually grew into a vigorous church that contributed significantly to Paul's evangelisation of both Europe and Asia. Instead, ninety-five per cent of his narrative in this movement concentrates on two individuals, Lydia and the

---

*The Stoics, by contrast, seem to have thought that since according to them the universe was one rational, coherent whole, deductions could possibly be made about future events from abnormalities in the appearances of the livers of sacrificial animals, or from the direction of the flights of birds.

†The first 'we' passage begins at 16:10; the last reference to 'we' for the moment is in 16:16.

jailer. The whole sweep of the first half of the movement climaxes in Lydia's conversion and the instalment of Paul and his team in her capacious house (16:6–15); and all the exciting details of the second half climax, not in the magistrates' being obliged to come and personally conduct Paul and Silas out of prison and then, if you please, asking them to leave the city! – a poor climax that would be – but in the conversion of the jailer and the intensely joyous midnight scene as he 'brought them into his house and set a meal before them', and rejoiced with all his household (16:34). Not since the story of Cornelius (ch. 10) has the narrative concentrated in such detail on the conversion of individuals.

Here, then, is our first lesson: from the proportions of Luke's narrative we learn God's sense of proportion too. God loves the whole world. He is not uninterested in the conquest of whole continents and countries by the gospel. This very section will eventually tell us that as a result of Paul's teaching in Ephesus all the Jews and Greeks who lived in the province of Asia heard the word of the Lord (19:10). But when it comes to salvation, God does not think in terms of continents and masses of people: he is interested in people as individuals. He knows each one of them, their hearts, their aspirations, their longings; he knows their work, their businesses, families and travels; he knows exactly where they are; indeed, he has 'determined . . . the exact places where they should live . . . so that men would seek him and perhaps reach out for him and find him' (17:26–27); and he knows those who do actually seek him, and he rewards their seeking.

A whole train of intricate and interlocking events lay behind Lydia's meeting with the gospel and the putting of her faith in the Lord Jesus. On the one side there was God's direct guidance of Paul and his team (16:6–10). When they first set out on this second missionary journey they had no intention, so far as we know, of visiting Philippi. Their initial plan was to 'visit the brothers in all the towns where we preached the word of the Lord [i.e. on the first missionary journey] and see how they are doing' (15:36). What they planned to do after that we are not told. But now Section Five opens with the announcement that the Holy Spirit intervened and forbade them to speak the word in Asia (16:6). The prohibition, as Section Five will itself indicate (18:18–21; 19:1–20), was only temporary. Later on God would take Paul to Ephesus to do a spectacular work that had repercussions round the whole province of Asia Minor. But for the moment God apparently had some more pressing objective in mind; though what it was, Paul and his companions were apparently not told at the time. After passing through the region of Phrygia and Galatia they tried to enter Bithynia, and God had to intervene once more: 'the Spirit of Jesus would not allow them to' (16:7). So they went down to Troas; and there God intervened yet again. At night Paul had a vision: a man of Macedonia was standing and appealing to him 'Come over to Macedonia and help us' (16:9–10). Three direct interventions by God, then, in the space of just five verses of the narrative; naturally the suspense builds up: what great objective is all this divine intervention and guidance focused on? And the answer is: the heart and home of a certain Lydia, a seller of purple cloth, at Philippi. Yes, of course there were other objectives, both in Macedonia and later in Achaia, that God had his eye on. But this was the first goal of God's guidance.

But there is another side to the story. So far we have heard of the special guidance that brought Paul and his companions to Philippi, where his normal strategy took him first to the place by the river where prayer was customarily made. But how did Lydia come to be there so that she could meet Paul, hear the gospel and put her trust in Christ? Verses 12–15 give her side of the story.

She was born in Thyatira – in what had once been the ancient kingdom of Lydia (hence her name, 'the Lydian woman') – a city famous for its production of purple dye. What brought her to Philippi? Trade, apparently. She had to earn a living like anyone else, and naturally enough she had learned the purple-trade in her home city. Philippi, being a Roman colony, would have plenty of people with sufficient money to spend on purple cloth. Inscriptions tell us that there was in fact a guild of purple-merchants in that city. So she went there and set up in the import and retail trade. Her business prospered: when she was converted, she had a house big enough to accommodate Paul and all his companions (16:15). And none of this, we may be sure, was mere accident. The God who determines the places where we should live had watched over her birth, her growth, her choice of career, her emigration to Philippi, the prosperity of her business, and the part it would eventually play in the evangelisation of Europe.

Even so, she might never have met Paul. But she had become a worshipper of the true God (16:14); where we do not know, whether in her home city of Thyatira or after she came to Philippi. We do know, however, that in Philippi she attended the place by the riverside where prayer was customarily made, a (perhaps only embryonic) Jewish synagogue. Not for her the silly ethnic and cultural prejudices of the Romans of Philippi. Through the

Jews, she had discovered the truth that there is only one God. And she had not only discovered it as a fact: she set her heart personally to seek the true and living God, as we see from her regular attendance at this humble place of prayer. And the transcendent Lord, who knows the hearts of all, read her longings, heard her prayers, and sent Paul and his companions unknowingly on their long, divinely directed journey to meet Lydia and satisfy her quest. He did more: 'he opened her heart to respond to Paul's message' (16:14). Only those who have had a similar experience will recognise what this means: that illumination of the Spirit that grips the attention and fills the mind with the intuitive awareness and certainty that what one is hearing is the very word of God, spoken directly and personally by the Lord to one's heart. And Lydia responded by believing in the Lord Jesus. She had met the God she sought.

Before we leave her story, there are one or two more things we should notice. First of all, the evidence that her faith was genuine and her spiritual experience authentic. She had no sooner believed and been baptised than she instinctively realised that all she had earned by her commerce, and in particular her home, had been given her by God, and must now be given to the Lord and used for the furtherance of the gospel. It was not that Paul had to urge and plead and eventually compel her to see that it was her duty to give a contribution to the cause of the gospel. It was she who compelled Paul and his companions to come and stay in her house. 'She would take no refusal', as Prof. F. F. Bruce puts it.[*] She insisted that if they judged her to be a genuine believer in the Lord Jesus, they must allow her to be identified with the witness to the Lord Jesus in the city; to make her home a foothold for the gospel in Philippi and a source of support for its continued spread throughout Macedonia and Achaia and the rest of the world. When later the church at Philippi time and again sent money to support Paul's pioneer evangelism (Phil. 4:15–16), Lydia's contribution, we may be sure, formed a great part of it.

From all of which, we may conclude that God's interest in the individual, his singling out of Lydia for this special visitation of his grace, was not for her sake alone. He saved her as an individual; yet not simply for her own selfish benefit, but so that she might be actively caught up in the great on-flowing tide of the love of God for the world.

[*] F. F. Bruce, *The Book of the Acts*, New International Commentary on the New Testament (Grand Rapids, MI: Wm B. Eerdmans, [2]1988), p. 310.

The second thing to reflect on is this. Luke has focused on Lydia's case in great detail, as he is about to do on the jailer's as well. But not, surely, in order to give us the impression that Lydia's case was rare or special. Rather as an example of what God was constantly doing wherever he sent Paul; and still is doing wherever he sends his messengers today. Lydia sought the true and living God; and he moved heaven and earth to make sure she found him. The Creator who determined the times set for us his creatures, and the exact places where we should live so that we should seek him and reach out for him and find him, gave us this assurance when he came and lived among us himself: 'Ask and it will be given to you; seek and you will find . . . For everyone who asks receives; [and] he who seeks finds' (Matt. 7:7–8).

The nature of divine guidance

Before moving on to consider God's interest in the second individual, the jailer, we ought to back-track a moment to reflect on the nature of God's guidance in so far, at least, as it can be seen in the experience of Paul and his companions at this time. As we have already observed, three instances of divine intervention altered the course of their journey and so brought them to Philippi.

Questions arise. What is the relation between this kind of direct guidance and people's own decision-making powers, their common sense, their moral and spiritual judgement, and their ultimate responsibility for the decisions they take? And ought all Christians to expect this kind of guidance; and if so, how often? Every day of the week? Over every, or every major, decision? Or only occasionally? Of course we must beware of generalising too much from the particular experience of Paul and his companions on this occasion. But certain principles stand out clearly.

First, then, Luke does not say that this second missionary journey was initiated by some special guidance from the Spirit. Paul's first missionary journey was (13:1–3); but this second journey had a far more prosaic origin. For that we must refer to 15:36: 'Some time later Paul said to Barnabas, "Let us go back and visit the brothers in all the towns where we preached the word of the Lord and see how they are doing."' In other words they were responding to their general pastoral duty to shepherd and feed the converts made on their previous journey. They needed no special guidance from heaven for that. They had their standing orders from the Lord for the evangelisation of the world and for the teaching and shepherding of the church. Normally, therefore, they would be expected to get on with the job of carrying out those standing orders; for unless and until they were countermanded by the Lord, they constituted his guidance without the necessity for further or constant direct interventions of special guidance. After all, I don't, or at least I shouldn't, need a personal letter from the Queen every week to guide me to pay my income tax.

The same principle applies to all believers. God has told us what his great objective for us is: we are to be conformed to the likeness of his Son. Meanwhile, and to that end, he has explicitly laid down our general duties. We are to love the Lord our God with all our heart, mind, soul and strength, and our neighbour as ourselves. We are to seek first his kingly rule in every aspect of our lives. We are to work to earn our daily bread; to love and care for our families; to bear witness in the world to the Lord Jesus and to God's way of salvation; to be involved according to our gifts and resources in world-evangelism; to love, support and encourage our fellow believers in the church; to obey the 'powers that be' in the world; to pay our rates and taxes; to do good to all people; and so forth. These are our standing orders. We need no special guidance to tell us whether we are to carry them out or not. What mother, in normal circumstances, would earnestly pray the Lord for direct special guidance whether it was his will that she give the baby its breakfast?

Secondly, it is instructive that the special guidance Paul and his companions received on the first two occasions (i.e. 16:6 and 7) was negative and preventative, aimed at stopping them from going and preaching where they would otherwise have gone and preached. First they were forbidden by the Holy Spirit to speak the word in the province of Asia. But obviously the prohibition did not carry with it detailed advance information on what their eventual goal was to be; for when they came to the border of Mysia, they tried to enter Bithynia, and the Spirit of Jesus would not allow them (16:7). They would not have tried, of course, had they known in advance where they were meant to be going.

Which shows this: special divine guidance does not necessarily lift the veil on the future for long periods in advance. It often lets us proceed from day to day doing the next obvious thing in the course of carrying out standing orders and only intervenes when we would otherwise take some course that would conflict with a particular objective the Lord has in view. Even when they were held back from going into Bithynia, they still were not told that the Lord had Macedonia and Philippi in mind. They simply went down to Troas, and not until they were there were they given the final piece of special guidance, in the form of a vision, that they were to cross over into Macedonia. How long it had taken them to get from Derbe to Troas we are not told; but quite clearly they were not in constant receipt of special guidance every day of the week. God is sparing of such direct interventions; for if he were not, he would reduce his servants to the level of children who cannot be asked simply, for example, to weed the flower bed, but have to be told in each case whether a given object is a weed or a flower. God wants his people to be adults who can be trusted to take detailed decisions on their own within the broad framework of standing orders, and of course always subject to his interventions when necessary.

And then we can profitably consider the forms their special guidance took, and the terms used to describe it. 'They were forbidden by the Holy Spirit' (16:6), says Luke, and 'the Spirit of Jesus did not allow them' (16:7). Now there are places in the New Testament where the adjective 'holy' when used with the Spirit is meant to emphasise his holy character. Such a place is 1 Thessalonians 4:8, where we are told that to reject God's instruction that we are to live holy lives is to 'reject God, who gives you his Holy Spirit'. But in other passages the adjective 'holy' seems to be used merely to indicate that the Spirit in question is the Spirit of God as distinct from any other spirit. It may be so in our present passage. But that would still leave the highly unusual phrase 'the Spirit of Jesus' to be accounted for.* We may know at once what it does not mean. It does not imply that the man Jesus has died but that his spirit lives on in the world beyond and is available to help people who seek its guidance. That would be the language of spiritism, of theosophy, and of some forms of Buddhism. No, Jesus certainly died. But he is not dead now. Acts has long since described his bodily resurrection from the dead. It is not, therefore, a question of his spirit having survived the death of his body. The 'Spirit of Jesus' is none other than the Holy Spirit, but called the Spirit of Jesus because Jesus, upon his ascension, sent the Holy Spirit of God, the other Counsellor (John 14:16–17), to instruct and guide his people.

But then the Spirit of God sent by the Lord Jesus will never guide anyone to do or say anything contrary to the moral charac-

*The AV is defective here.

268

ter of the Lord Jesus, contrary to what he did and taught when he was here on earth. The Holy Spirit is not some amoral power. All of us experience powerful ideas and urges from time to time. But we should not suppose that they all come from the Holy Spirit. We are responsible to use our moral and spiritual judgement on them; and to that end the New Testament gives us tests that we may apply to our ideas and urges, to determine whether they come from the Holy Spirit or not (e.g. Rom. 8:15; 2 Tim. 1:7; 1 Cor. 12:1–3; 1 John 4:1–3); and not least among them is the question: Is this urge or idea I have consistent with the character, behaviour, leading and commands of the Lord Jesus? True guidance by the Holy Spirit does not relieve us of our responsibility to use our moral and spiritual judgement critically to assess the guidance. It rather insists on it.

Finally for the moment there was the guidance given to Paul in the form of a vision at Troas (16:9–10). This time it was positive; not a prevention or a prohibition, but an invitation. Now in some visions Paul had, as for instance the other vision mentioned in this section (18:9–10), the Lord himself spoke to Paul direct. But that was not necessarily always so, nor in this vision at Troas. Paul saw a man of Macedonia standing and appealing – and the stance eloquently supported and enforced the appeal – 'Come over . . . and help us' (16:9). Paul would have been a strange evangelist if he had never felt, without the aid of a vision, the mute appeal of the thousands of men and women 'out there' in the big, big world who sat in darkness. The content of the vision, therefore, was hardly surprising; but the vividness of the vision carried the impression that this might now constitute special guidance from the Lord. Even so, Paul did not decide the moment he awoke that it was so. He talked it over with his companions and 'we concluded', says Luke – that is, 'we inferred' – 'that God had called us to preach the gospel to them' (16:10).

Here we must leave the topic for the moment, though we shall come back to it when we consider the nature of the guidance the Lord used to bring Paul and Silas to the exact place and circumstances where they could meet and win to faith in Christ another individual on whom God had his eye, the jailer in charge of the prison at Philippi.

But meanwhile we could sum up the lesson so far: in the affairs of daily life, and particularly in that wonderful partnership in his work that God has set up between himself and his people, God has amply briefed us on his ultimate goals and objectives, and has likewise laid down ample standing orders to guide us in achieving those goals. Within those parameters he trains us towards maturity by allowing us to take the detailed decisions of life and work, using our common sense, our moral and spiritual judgement, under his watchful eye, in the light of his ultimate goals and standing orders. If we were never allowed to decide anything, but were always controlled by constant interventions of direct guidance, we should remain moral and mental infants. But then, when his plans or our need require it, he graciously intervenes with special guidance in one form or another. But even his positive guidance never by-passes or suppresses our moral and spiritual judgement. We can never escape responsibility for sin or disobedience to God's word by claiming that the Holy Spirit led us to do it. He requires us to test everything that claims to be the Holy Spirit's guidance by this basic principle: nothing that the Holy Spirit leads us to do will ever go contrary to the character and teaching of the Lord Jesus.

The 'guidance' of the power of darkness

The slave-girl who met Paul and Silas in Philippi and followed them day after day as they went to and from the place of prayer was a fortune-teller. She professed to be able to foresee the future and so to be able by her information and advice to save people from the trouble they would encounter if they went on blindly in their ignorance of what lay ahead. Many people in the city obviously believed in her and valued her services, for her owners made a lot of money out of her predictions. Paul silenced her; and as a result got himself and Silas into a storm of trouble. Then why did he do it?

First, because her prophesyings were not mere inanities such as are produced by newspaper columnists who manage to predict in two or three sentences the exact same fortune for the thousands of their readers whose birthdays fall on the same day. Her prophecies emanated from a demon: she was possessed by a pythonic spirit, says Luke (16:16).

There was, of course, a lot of sheer charlatanry among the mediums and prophecy-mongers of the ancient world, as there still is in our modern world. But the Bible everywhere insists that as well as this mass of bogus nonsense and superstition there is a real world of spirits: there are angels that are loyal to God, and there are demons that are not. Of course many people – and not least some theologians – dismiss as primitive superstition the

270

Bible's testimony that mankind is not the highest form of life in God's created universe; but it is strange how ready they are after that to approve of scientific research based on the premise that statistically speaking it is highly likely that beings of higher intelligence than ours should exist elsewhere in the vast and mysterious universe, and that therefore it is worthwhile constantly combing outer space with radio telescopes in the hope of picking up messages from those higher intelligences. The Bible's view is neither superstition nor speculation. It includes the testimony of the Man who was and is God, the Creator incarnate himself, that there are evil spirits that can not only communicate with human beings but also in extreme cases possess them. We dismiss his testimony at our peril.

Even so, we may well ask why Paul chose to put his head into such a hornet's nest by exorcising the spirit and silencing the girl. After all, she publicly recommended them: 'These men are servants of the Most High God; who are telling you the way to be saved' (16:17). Would not the people who took her prophecies seriously be impressed by her favourable reception of the evangelists and be the more inclined to listen to the gospel? Then why antagonise everybody by publicly rejecting her co-operation when she was obviously trying to be eirenic and ecumenically minded towards Christianity?

Because, to start with, even if what she said was intended to be the truth – and there is doubt about that, as we shall presently see – spiritism is by definition incompatible with Christianity, and the spirit who spoke through her was in fact hostile to the Lord Jesus. The gospel writers all record that when our Lord was on earth evil spirits, recognising him, would publicly shout out things like 'I know who you are – the Holy One of God!' (Luke 4:34). Invariably Christ silenced them. What they said was true; but it was forced out of them by their terror at coming face to face with the incarnate Lord. It was not the expression of any repentance on their part; and it was certainly not intended to lead anyone else to repentance and faith in the Lord Jesus. Moreover, if Christ had accepted the testimony of demon-possessed people, he would have appeared in the eyes of many to authenticate spiritism. And so it was with the demon-possessed girl in Philippi. Even if what she said was true, for Paul to have accepted her testimony would have validated her form of spiritism in the eyes of the public. Paul was obliged to demonstrate that the source of the girl's testimony was demonically evil, basically and unrepentantly hostile to the Lord Jesus. In spite of all

271

appearances, the spirit-medium and the apostle Paul were not in fact 'all in the same business really': the spirit within her was an emissary of the power of darkness.

What is more, there is serious doubt whether the ostensible recommendation she gave was intended to be as true, in fact, as it might appear at first sight to be.* As used among Jews, the term 'the Most High God' referred unambiguously to the one true God. But when used, as it frequently was, by pagans it simply referred to the particular god whom the people of any locality happened to regard as the greatest god among all the other gods. That is indeed how in all probability the Philippians would have understood it; and it thus would have denied by implication the very truth which was basic to all that Paul had come to declare. Moreover, the final phrase in the slave-girl's recommendation may not have been intended as 'who are telling you *the* way to be saved', but 'who are telling you . . . *a* way to be saved'.† That is, the girl may not have been recommending the gospel as the only way of salvation, but merely as one way among others, her own included. Nor is it certain that by 'salvation' she meant what the gospel means by that term. She too by her prophecies would have offered people salvation; but she would have meant that by being able to see into the future she could inform people of what troubles lay ahead for them and advise them what steps to take to try and avoid them.

For all these reasons, then, Paul drove out the demon and demonstrated the gospel's uncompromising hostility to spiritism. But there was another reason: he did it out of compassion for the girl herself. Only consider the horrible distortion of her personality that spiritism had led to. As the exorcism eventually demonstrated, she had been invaded and taken over by an alien power. She was no longer completely free and self-controlled. When in her prophetic frenzies the demon uttered his prophecies through her, the voice that came out of her mouth would not have been her own natural voice, but a strange unnatural sound. (Which is why in later times such demon-possessed people were referred to as 'ventriloquists' in the ancient sense of that

---

*For a helpful discussion of this incident, see Paul R. Trebilco, 'Paul and Silas "Servants of the Most High God" (Acts 16.16–18)', *Journal for the Study of the New Testament* 36 (June 1989), pp. 51–73.

†When the term 'the way' is used metaphorically in Acts, the definite article is normally expressed, as, for example, 'the way of the Lord' (18:26). At 16:17 'way' is used without the definite article. The meaning is therefore ambiguous: it could be 'the way' or 'a way'.

term: 'people who speak by a spirit in the belly'.) This would have been taken by the local pagans as encouraging evidence that her prophecies came not from her but from a supernatural source, and they would have been willing to pay all the more money to her masters who exploited her condition. But to anyone imbued with the Spirit of Jesus such an alien invasion would have appeared as the absolute opposite of that noble self-control, personal freedom and enhancement of the personality that the Holy Spirit produces in those he indwells. It would have provoked intense compassion for the victim and nothing but revulsion and anger at the malevolent work of the evil spirit. 'In the name of Jesus Christ' – the words were no empty formula: 'the name' expressed all the compassion as well as the authority of the Lord Jesus – Paul commanded the spirit to come out of her (16:18); and in so doing demonstrated God's concern for the sacred inviolability of human personality.

'The spirit who is at work in those who are disobedient'

The gruesomeness of the extreme case of the spirit-medium should not overshadow the fact that there were other people in Philippi that day who were less obviously and less dramatically but no less really under the influence of what our Lord on one occasion described as 'the power of darkness' (Luke 22:53). Paul's description of the influences and pressures that condition the outlook and behaviour of unregenerate men and women employs similar terminology: 'As for you, you were dead in your transgressions and sins, in which you used to live when you followed the ways of this world and of the ruler of the kingdom of the air, the spirit who is now at work in those who are disobedient' (Eph. 2:1–2). Or again: 'The god of this age has blinded the minds of unbelievers, so that they cannot see the light of the gospel of the glory of Christ, who is the image of God' (2 Cor. 4:4). Extreme though the diagnosis may sound, the New Testament soberly affirms that Satan himself manipulates the pressures of public opinion, of vested interests, of cultural and ethnic prejudices (not to speak of every individual's own sinfulness), so as to make it appear unquestionably reasonable to reject God's gospel and to repudiate his messengers. So obviously he did that in Philippi.

Here was a young woman who from time to time lost her

self-control, lapsed into frenzy and spoke in gruesomely unnatural tones as an alien, evil spirit took over and dominated her
personality. Paul put an end to her shouting and screaming,
broke the hold of the evil power, and restored to the woman her
self-control, balance of mind, freedom of spirit and her sanity.
Who could but applaud the gospel and the power of the Lord
Jesus if that was its effect?

But then came the businessmen who owned the woman; and
they at once saw that their source of revenue was gone. Now
there is nothing wrong in making money in and of itself. But
callously to exploit the frenzies of a distraught young woman for
the sake of making money is unspeakably evil. And to object to
her return to sanity because it lost them income, and to raise up
public animosity and persecution against the gospel on that
ground, is inhumanly wicked. But then, Mammon always was
and always is a dehumanising deity.

The businessmen hauled Paul and Silas before the magistrates,
though of course they knew better than to accuse them publicly of
having cut off their source of income. The fees such men charged
for consultations could be exorbitant, and neither the magistrates
nor the mob might have found it easy to get worked up over their
loss of income. And besides, the businessmen had a credibility
problem. For days on end their spirit-medium had assured the
public that Paul and Silas were servants of the Most High God.
They could hardly now concentrate the mob's attention on what
these servants of God had done to their medium. Shrewdly
enough they chose to play on the racial and cultural prejudices of
Romans against Jews in order to rouse the blind passions of their
fellow citizens against the gospel and the evangelists. Now
cultural differences and ethnic distinctions are in themselves
beautiful things. Who could possibly wish for a world filled with
one and the same undifferentiated, monotonous culture all the
way through? But when cultural prejudice blinds people to the
gospel it ceases to be the innocent thing it normally is; and when
ethnic differences are used to provoke racism and persecution
they become self-evidently demonic, as we of the twentieth
century have cause to know.

The mob were incited to violence, as was to be expected. But
Philippi was a Roman colony; its magistrates were there to see
that Roman law and justice and the rights of the individual were
upheld; it was strictly against the law to beat a Roman citizen
without a trial; and Paul was a Roman citizen who in addition had
done nothing against the law. But the magistrates had an enraged

mob on their hands, and to stand up for Jews whose religious activities had upset leading Roman businessmen in the city was perhaps more than the magistrates either could or would want to attempt. Without giving them a chance to protest that they were Roman citizens, the magistrates had Paul and Silas flogged and thrown into jail.

Someone will say that regrettable and illegal as all this behaviour was, it was only natural in the circumstances. In a sense that is true: but it was natural only to a human nature perverted by sin, and manipulated by demonic malevolence. The dark physical prison into which they threw the messengers of Christ was in its way but a mirror image of the dominion of darkness in which they themselves were held, blinded against the light of the gospel. If ever any of them were to be rescued from the power of darkness, God would somehow have to break into their spiritual prison. His next move in that direction was to get two of his servants into the physical gaol at Philippi.

Triumph over the power of darkness

The public charge brought against Paul and Silas and the gospel was false, the verdict unjust, and the punishment cruel. God would see to it that they were vindicated, and the verdict reversed by the very magistrates who had condemned them, even if it took an earthquake to do it.

But there was more to it than that. The public slander on the gospel was the result of Paul's attack on spiritism. Compromise with spiritism would have left them free to preach. As it was, they were now imprisoned and the name of the Lord Jesus publicly discredited. Had not the power of darkness won? Moreover, if we have been following the emphasis that Movement 1 lays on God's guidance of his servants, the question naturally arises, 'What has become of God's guidance of them now?' It is a question that is particularly liable to rise in the pagan mind. To this day in the East people are apt to boast of the superior power of the gods which they worship, and of the astonishing physical feats which the spirits are able to perform through the bodies of their devotees;* and they will taunt Christians with their inability to perform anything like it.

* As for instance at the Taipusan festivals of Malaysia.

And there is a bigger question still. The whole of Acts in general, and this present movement in particular, represents the Christian missionaries as the emissaries and ambassadors of the almighty Creator, commissioned by God himself to spread the claims of Jesus to be the Son of God throughout the world, and guided in the task by the Holy Spirit of God himself. When we see Paul's tiny team setting off and trudging through Asia, coming to Europe and competing with a thousand and one other vagabond preachers, street-corner philosophers, exorcists and miracle-mongers, we could be forgiven for thinking that their claim to represent the all-powerful, majestic Ruler of the universe looks a little forlorn. But what shall we say when we see them publicly condemned, beaten and helplessly thrown into prison through the machinations of a few crooked businessmen and the racism of the mob? Where now is their God and his guidance? To the pagan mind the whole purpose of spirit-guidance is to avoid trouble, not get into it.

But there came an earthquake, we say, and it vindicated their claim that the God they preached was the God of creation. And so there did. There is no solid reason for rejecting the historicity of the miracle, unless one somehow knows in advance that miracles cannot happen, and that therefore the story of this miracle must be false.

Yet we have no sooner said this, than other critics are to be heard attacking the story on other, literary grounds. They say that the story of the imprisonment, earthquake and escape is one of a score of such escape stories current in the literature of the ancient world. In Euripides' famous play *The Bacchae*, for instance, when the god Dionysus visits Thebes in the form of a young man, King Pentheus imprisons him; but an earthquake rocks the prison and Dionysus escapes. Luke, they maintain, lifted his escape-from-prison story from some altogether different literary context, and inserted it into his account of Paul and Silas' experiences at Philippi in order to heighten the dramatic effect.* So what shall we say now?

The first thing to say is what Professor R. N. Longenecker

---

* And to support their case they point out that if verses 25–43 were removed, the reader would not notice any gap in the flow of the narrative. But the same could be said of many paragraphs in thousands of stories. It proves nothing, except that if on other grounds you want to excise the story of a miracle from a book, you can often find literary excuses for doing so. See also the discussion in C. J. Hemer, *The Book of Acts in the Setting of Hellenistic History*, ed. Conrad H. Gempf (Tübingen: J. C. B. Mohr, 1989), pp. 442–3.

acutely observes: Luke's story is *not* an escape story!* Nobody escaped, neither Paul and Silas nor the other prisoners. They could have, but they deliberately did not: 'Don't harm yourself!' Paul shouted through the dark to the jailer who was about to commit suicide because he thought that the prisoners for whom he was responsible had escaped; 'Don't harm yourself! We are all here!' (16:27–28). Whereupon 'the jailer called for lights, rushed in and fell trembling before Paul and Silas'; then bringing them out he asked, 'Sirs, what must I do to be saved?' (16:30). They replied, 'Believe in the Lord Jesus, and you will be saved – you and your household' (16:31). And so they were, as the narrative goes on to tell.

Here then is the heart and point of the story: the salvation of the jailer of Philippi and of his household, and in particular the remarkable steps God took to reach him and to save both him and his. There were, we now see, three individuals that God had specially in mind when he directed Paul and Silas by his special guidance to Philippi: Lydia, the spirit-medium, and the jailer. Of these the easiest to reach was Lydia, for she was already a seeker after God, and present at the prayer-house when they arrived. The spirit-medium was more difficult: her case involved clashing head-on with the malevolent powers of the spirit world; and as a result the god of this world fought back through his minions and had Paul and Silas imprisoned. But what seemed defeat, now turns out to have been God's strategy for seeking and saving the jailer. We know next to nothing about his past. He was probably an army veteran, put in charge of the colony's prison after retiring from active service. Whether up to this point he had ever sought God in all his life, we do not know. He may well have been one of those over whom Paul later quoted God's words: 'I was found by those who did not seek me; I revealed myself to those who did not ask for me' (Rom. 10:20). He may have heard the medium's announcement of Paul and Silas; may have heard about the exorcism; may have been present when they were flogged. But for all that we are told, the first time he met Paul and Silas may have been when fresh from their beating they were handed over to him with special orders not to allow them to escape under any circumstances, and he put them in the top-security wing of his prison.

Obviously there was no better way of making sure the jailer

*R. N. Longenecker, 'The Acts of the Apostles', in Frank E. Gaebelein (ed.), *The Expositor's Bible Commentary*, vol. 9 (Grand Rapids, MI: Zondervan, 1981), p. 464.

heard the gospel than by getting the missionaries right into his prison and under his care. And no better way of making sure he realised his need of it, than by a providential earth-tremor that would immediately make a simple pagan man feel his insecurity in this life and his need to be right with the gods or God who controlled the earth. And no better way, either, of authenticating in his mind the truth of the gospel when he heard it than by bringing him face to face with these extraordinary men who preached it. He had taken them, bruised and bleeding as they were, and fastened them in the stocks in a position that would have kept them in agony all night long. And yet here were men who when released from their chains by an earthquake made no attempt to escape, but saved his life by remaining voluntarily in prison. To the jailer the genuineness of their gospel and of the God they served needed no stronger authentication than this: he believed on the Lord Jesus and was saved.

But if these are supposed to be God's tactics for bringing the jailer to faith, must we not ask if they are credible? Almighty God could by a flick of his finger have done a miracle before the mob and the magistrates that would have had them all grovelling before Paul and Silas instead of beating them and flinging them into prison. Is it credible that he should instead deliberately lead his messengers into such shame, abuse, injustice, violence and agony simply in order to bring the jailer to faith? And that he would allow them to suffer so much for just one man and his family?

To ask this question is inevitably to ask another and a bigger, this time about the heart of the gospel itself and its credibility. It claims that the almighty Creator of the two hundred and fifty billion suns of the Andromeda galaxy, and of all other galaxies besides, handed over his incarnate Son by his set purpose and foreknowledge into the hands of sinful men to suffer an unjust trial, abuse and physical violence, and finally the agonies of crucifixion, and all this on behalf of one tiny planet – indeed did it personally for the jailer at Philippi, and as we one and all might say, did it for me. This surely is the most difficult thing in all the gospel to believe.

And yet it is altogether credible. For the issue at stake between God and the power of darkness has never been 'Who has the greatest power?' or 'Who can do the most impressive miracles?' The answer to that has always been self-evident: the Almighty. All too many human beings are fascinated by power, and suppose that sheer power is the final arbitrator in the universe. But it is not so. The issue at stake has always been – at least since Eden – the validity or otherwise of Satan's slander that put into question not God's power, but his love. That slander has penetrated and poisoned the human race ever since. It is the mainstay of the power of darkness over men's minds still. By definition it could not be settled by any exhibition of miraculous power, however stupendous. Power by itself could have everyone grovelling in terror, or open-mouthed with wonder, at the Almighty's strength; but power by itself could never convert the human heart from suspicion, disobedience, proud independence and fear, to love, trust, gratitude and obedience to God. Only almighty Love could do that. And Calvary was the place where that love was for ever demonstrated beyond all question.

There came an earthquake after Christ's sufferings on the cross, and also the mighty resurrection which proved that the One who suffered was indeed God incarnate. But it is the sufferings of Christ that reconcile our hearts to God. Luke claims that an earth tremor at Philippi providentially set the evangelists free so that they might the more effectively demonstrate and press home the truth of the gospel on the heart of the jailer and his family. A big story certainly. But if the central message of the gospel is true, a providential earth tremor is a very small item by comparison.

A question remains: What right had God to lead Paul and Silas into such suffering, even if it was for the purpose of saving the jailer? Well, Paul and Silas were not complaining. The story says that at midnight, Paul and Silas, battered and bruised, their feet in the stocks, were praying and singing hymns to God (16:25). And how credible is that? Let Paul himself answer. Some years later, in prison again, he had occasion to write a letter to some Christians in Colosse. He reminded them of their glad duty to give thanks to the Father, 'For he has rescued us from the dominion of darkness and brought us into the kingdom of the Son he loves, in whom we have redemption, the forgiveness of sins' (Col. 1:13–14). A paragraph or two later he added: 'Now I rejoice in my sufferings on your behalf and fill up what still remains to be suffered of the afflictions of Christ in my flesh for the sake of his body' (Col. 1:24). If the jailer at Philippi ever got a copy of that letter and read those words, how he would have remembered that unforgettable night when he took Paul and Silas, bathed their wounds and brought them up into his house, and the whole household 'was filled with joy because [they] had come to believe in God' through the sufferings of Paul and Silas (16:33–34).

This is the true God. This is his gospel. These are his true and loyal representatives.

The sequel

With the conversion of the jailer and his household, God's short-term aims in Paul's visit to Philippi were complete; and when next day the magistrates asked Paul and Silas to leave the city, they left.

True, they did not slip quietly out of the back door as the magistrates originally suggested. The magistrates had broken the law in having Paul and Silas beaten and imprisoned before and without a trial. It was a serious offence to treat Roman citizens in that way; and if Paul and Silas had had the resources and the mind to prosecute them in higher courts, they would have been in trouble.

But Paul and Silas did not have the resources, and they would not have done so if they had. What would have been the point of it? They did not seek revenge; and if they had, it would simply have antagonised the Romans in Philippi even more against the gospel and so against their own salvation; and it would have strengthened their prejudices against both Jews and Christians.

Nor did they stick their toes in and demand to be allowed to stay in the city. That would have renewed the opposition. The new converts could be left (along with Timothy) to stand on their own feet and quietly but vigorously evangelise their fellow citizens – which we know, from Paul's letter to them, they did to good effect.

It was better tactics, therefore, for Paul and the rest of his companions to leave; though he made the magistrates come and personally conduct him and his party out of the prison. That too was deliberate tactics. It impressed on their minds the illegality of their earlier behaviour; it forced them to admit that illegality to Paul and his companions in the presence of the jailer; and the fact that it was known to the magistrates' officers (16:35–38), as well as by the Christian converts, would doubtless have restrained the magistrates from further harassment of the Christians, at least for the time being. Paul was prepared to suffer unjustly and without revenge for the sake of other people's salvation. But he would do all in his power to save his converts from needless persecution.

MOVEMENT 2: God's Messiah and Gentile Politics, Religion and Philosophy (17:1–34)

The second movement in Section Five of Acts comprises Paul's visit to Thessalonica, Berea, and Athens. Luke has grouped them together because they happened one after another; but also because they share a common theme: God's answer to the problem that has dogged mankind ever since Eden – the problem of evil. Grappling with the problem still consumes a vast amount of human energy, ingenuity and resources. Genuine success has been achieved in some quarters and at some levels; but nowhere has it been total, and seldom permanent. Evil, whether public or private, corporate or individual, has proved to be a dragon: cut one head off, another grows. The institutions and organisations that exist for the very purpose of restraining evil are often themselves flawed by it; and sometimes they have become instances of the disease instead of its cure. Grandiose universal theories and schemes, like Plato's in the ancient world or Marx's in the modern, are justly suspect: when their advocates have been in a position to enforce them, the promised utopias have all too often turned out to be nightmares of injustice, their cost-analysis millions of lives. Indeed the Bible itself seems to warn us that world-wide peace may yet be achieved, but at the unacceptable price of a subtle but hideous enslavement of the human spirit.* Must we then conclude that evil is, and will always be, an ineradicable world-wide plague, to be more or less contained, always to be suffered, never to be eliminated from our earth at least?

No! God has an answer: the world-wide establishment of our Lord's messianic kingdom. Luke has long since described in detail the programme for the establishment of that kingdom (see especially Section One), and he has no need to repeat all that detail here. What he now reports on are certain misrepresentations and misapprehensions that arose in pagan Gentile minds over the Christians' preaching of this messianic kingdom. In Thessalonica the civil authorities were informed (by certain Jews unfortunately) that the Christian gospel was in fact a political programme aimed at subverting the Roman state. In Athens, on the other hand, some people had the impression, when they first heard Paul speak, that all he was doing was advocating that two foreign, and rather bizarre, new deities be added to the endless

---

*cf. 1 Thessalonians 5:3 with 2 Thessalonians 2:3–12; Revelation 13:4–8.

collection of religions, gods, philosophies and theories which the Athenians, with their academic approach to life, had invented to explain the universe and to help mankind cope with the problem of evil. Luke devotes the whole of Movement 2 to removing first the misrepresentation and then the misunderstanding.

In the first half of the movement (17:1–15) the misrepresentation arises from the reaction of certain Jews in Thessalonica to Paul's exposition of the Christian hope. Talking to Jews in the synagogue, Paul naturally uses the term 'Messiah' since it was a well-known part of the Jewish religious vocabulary, however much the various groups within Judaism might disagree over its interpretation. For the same reason he can appeal to the Old Testament, and does so vigorously and extensively, to show what Christianity understands to be God's programme for the introduction of our Lord's messianic kingdom.

In the second half of the movement (17:16–34) he expounds the Christian hope to Athenians. It is the same hope, of course; but now he must explain it to pagans who had never read the Old Testament in all their lives, and would not be acquainted with its technical terms. He does not speak therefore of Jesus as the Messiah, or of the establishment of his messianic kingdom. Instead he selects another Old Testament term which pagans would more easily recognise, and he announces Jesus as 'the man whom God has appointed to judge the world in righteousness' (17:31).

That is sensible on Paul's part. It would also be sensible on ours as modern Gentiles, who have only a brief summary of Paul's Areopagus speech, to remember that Paul is still a Jew and to recognise that the phrase he uses, 'to judge the world in righteousness', is taken from the Old Testament. With us the term 'judge' tends to be confined to the narrow activities of a judge in a law court, or of a judge of a competition. So when people read that Christ has been appointed to judge the world in righteousness, their thoughts tend to go at once to the final judgement, when, as the popular mind pictures it, the final whistle will be blown on earth's activities, the game will be over, the pitch deserted, the players all leave the field (and not just those who were sent off during the game for bad behaviour, or to make way for substitutes), and then prizes will be awarded for the men and women of the match, and penalties or bans imposed on others for gross misbehaviour during the match that has now ceased for ever.

But that would be altogether too restricted an interpretation of the phrase 'judge the world in righteousness'. To do justice to its intended meaning we would need to examine its background in Old Testament usage.

In the early days of Israel, for instance, the judges were men who not only judged their fellow Israelites by denouncing their sins, calling on them to repent and enforcing the law; and not only fought Israel's enemies, overcame them and delivered Israel from servitude to them; but in addition governed the people and administered the nation's justice over periods of many years. So, for instance, we read that 'Tola . . . judged Israel for twenty-three years', and 'Jephthah judged Israel for six years' (Judg. 10:1–2; 12:7), whereas 'Samuel continued as judge over Israel all the days of his life' (1 Sam. 7:15).

The very phrase 'judge the world in righteousness', which Paul will use in the Areopagus address, is taken from Old Testament contexts like the following:

> Say among the nations, 'The Lord reigns.' The world is firmly established, it cannot be moved; he will judge the people with equity. Let the heavens rejoice, let the earth be glad . . . they will sing before the Lord, for he comes, he comes to judge the earth. He will judge the world in righteousness and the peoples in his truth. (Ps. 96:10–13)

And again,

> Shout for joy to the Lord, all the earth . . . shout for joy before the Lord, the King. Let the sea resound, and everything in it, the world, and all who live in it. Let the rivers clap their hands, let the mountains sing together for joy; let them sing before the Lord, for he comes to judge the earth. He will judge the world in righteousness and the peoples with equity. (Ps. 98:4–9)

When all allowance has been made for metaphorical expressions, this language about the earth, the rivers, the seas, the mountains, the fields and the forests singing for joy and clapping their hands is scarcely meant to describe the planet's reaction to the experience of being utterly destroyed by fire, when 'The heavens will disappear with a roar; the elements . . . be destroyed by fire, and the earth and everything in it . . . be laid bare' (2 Pet. 3:10), and the earth and sky flee from the presence of the Judge at the final judgement (Rev. 20:11). In terms of our admittedly crude and doubtless inadequate analogy of a moment ago, it sounds much more like earth's welcome, when all other referees have failed, for the Perfect Referee, to control and carry on the game as it should be controlled, until it is finally wound up, and other games are instituted on other fields. It is describing in fact earth's joy at the prospect of the establishment of Christ's messianic reign, when God will judge the world in righteousness by the Man he has ordained. That reign will certainly be initiated by severe and drastic judgements, as we shall presently see; but its continuance can be described in terms taken once more from the Old Testament:

> A shoot will come up from the stump of Jesse; from his roots a Branch will bear fruit. The Spirit of the Lord will rest on him – the Spirit of wisdom and of understanding, the Spirit of counsel and of power . . . He will not judge by what he sees with his eyes, or decide by what he hears with his ears; but with righteousness he will judge the needy, with justice he will give decisions for the poor of the earth. He will strike the earth with the rod of his mouth; with the breath of his lips he will slay the wicked . . . The wolf will live with the lamb, the leopard will lie down with the goat . . . They will neither harm nor destroy on all my holy mountain . . . (Isa. 11:1–9)

This enthralling language is doubtless poetical; but like all good poetry it is intended to describe a practical reality, that of a universal reign of justice and peace when, as the final lines of the poem say, 'the earth will be full of the knowledge of the Lord as the waters cover the sea' (Isa. 11:9).

The Christian hope, therefore, is the same whether it is preached to Jews or Gentiles; it is based on the same Old Testament promises, which will be fulfilled by Christ. The question is, however, when and by what means that hope will be realised, and what relation it bears to our present largely pagan world, with its politics, religions and philosophies.

To answer it we turn first to Paul's exposition of the hope in the synagogues of Thessalonica and Berea.

God's Messiah and Gentile politics: Paul's preaching in Thessalonica

Paul's Jewish contemporaries, as the Jewish scholar Professor M. A. Fishbane has reminded us,* would have differed among themselves over the question of who and what the Messiah would be, and what he would do. In particular, they would have disagreed, as Christians still do, over whether the Messiah would introduce an age of peace and justice in this world, or only after the destruction of this world in a new heaven and earth, or in both

---

*M. A. Fishbane, *Judaism, Revelation and Traditions* (San Francisco: Harper & Row, 1987), p. 144.

successively.* But whatever their differences in interpretation, all would have agreed that the prime and ultimate authority on the matter was the Scriptures.

For Orthodox Jews that is still so, though modern Liberal Judaism, while retaining the biblical hope for the future, seems to reject the biblical means for its attainment. Following the Babylonian Amora, Rav, it holds that 'All the predicted ends have already passed; now all depends on repentance and good deeds.' That is, it considers that all specific predictions in the Old Testament about a personal Messiah have already been fulfilled in past history. For the future, Liberal Jews

> affirm the hope for a 'messianic' age in the broad sense of the redemption of mankind, but they do not believe that it will come about suddenly, dramatically, miraculously, supernaturally, through the agency of one individual (the Messiah), but slowly, gradually, progressively, through the spiritual strivings, moral exertions and social reforms of all men and nations . . . It is the universal hope expressed in such prayers as these: 'Trusting in You, O Lord our God, we hope soon to behold the glory of Your might, when false gods shall cease to take their place in the hearts of men, and the world will be perfected under Your unchallenged rule; when all mankind will call upon Your name and, forsaking evil, turn to You alone . . . Then the Lord shall be King over all the earth; on that day the Lord shall be One, and His Name One' . . . 'Violence shall rage no more, and evil shall vanish like smoke; the rule of tyranny shall pass away from the earth and You alone, O Lord, shall have dominion over all your works.'†

When, therefore, Paul went to the synagogue in Thessalonica to proclaim Jesus as the Messiah, he was obliged by the varied interpretations of the messianic promises then current to prove not simply one thing, but two. First he had to demonstrate that according to the programme laid down in the Old Testament the Messiah – whoever he turned out to be – would have to suffer and then to rise from the dead. And then – but only then – he had to take the facts of the life, death and resurrection of the Lord Jesus and, placing them alongside the Old Testament's prophesied programme, show that the Messiah it promised was in fact the Jesus whom he preached (17:1–3).

We need not here go over again the passages that Paul would

---

*For detail, see E. Schurer, *The History of the Jewish People in the Age of Jesus Christ*, vol. 2, revised and edited by G. Vermes, F. Millar, M. Black (Edinburgh: T. & T. Clark, 1979), pp. 448–554.

†J. D. Rayner and B. Hooker, *Judaism for Today* (Union of Liberal and Progressive Synagogues, 1978), pp. 37–8.

have cited from the Old Testament to prove the first part of his case; Luke has long since given us detailed examples from both Paul's and Peter's sermons. What we need to do here is to consider some of the implications that flow from this fact that the death and resurrection of the Messiah were written into the biblical programme for the establishment of the messianic kingdom.

First, the element of Messiah's sufferings. In our Lord's time it was widely held that the messianic kingdom would be established by God's raising up a political and military figure who would lead the nation of Israel in armed rebellion against the Roman imperialists, thus putting an end to their tyranny, taxes and injustices, and setting Israel politically and economically free. This idea had already spawned insurrections against Rome in the past. It was to surface again in AD 66, and yet again in AD 131/2 when Rabbi Akiba hailed a certain Bar Koziba as Messiah,* and he led the nation in a revolt against Rome. It gained a temporary independence for Judea, but soon ended in disastrous defeat.

There were many, including the apostles themselves, who at first imagined that our Lord would prove to be this kind of Messiah. They thought his announcement that 'The kingdom of God was drawn near' was a political manifesto, and that he himself would soon claim supreme political power in the nation, reform its political structures and overthrow Rome's domination. It was this unquestioned assumption that made it very difficult for the apostles to understand Christ's repeated insistence that as Messiah he must suffer, as the Scriptures said he must. This insistence eliminated at a stroke their political interpretation of his Messiahship; and much to their consternation and disappointment he further forbade them to use the sword either to establish or to protect him or his kingdom. 'My kingdom', he explained to the Roman governor, 'is not of this world. If it were, my servants would fight to prevent my arrest by the Jews. But now my kingdom is from another place' (John 18:36).

Moreover, his insistence that the Messiah must suffer did not simply mean that for the moment he would submit to his enemies, suffer, die, but then rise again and forthwith lead Israel in a political and military struggle against the Roman emperor Tiberius and his successors. He explicitly taught that his kingdom

---

*R. Akiba called him Bar-Kochba, 'Son of the Star', as an allusion to the messianic promise of Numbers 24:17, 'A star will come out of Jacob'.

would in its first phase be established by the preaching of the word in this world. As for the evil tares, he had no intention of using his powers as the executor of God's judgement to root them out and destroy them before the end of the age (Matt. 13:24–29, 37–43). And what is more, his apostle Peter, profiting from his earlier mistakes in this area, subsequently exhorted his fellow Christians likewise to

> Submit yourselves for the Lord's sake to every authority instituted among men: whether to the king, as the supreme authority, or to governors, who are sent by him to punish those who do wrong and to commend those who do right. For it is God's will that by doing good you should silence the ignorant talk of foolish men . . .
> . . . But if you suffer for doing good and you endure it, this is commendable before God. To this you were called, because Christ suffered for you, leaving you an example, that you should follow in his steps. 'He committed no sin, and no deceit was found in his mouth.' When they hurled their insults at him, he did not retaliate; when he suffered, he made no threats. Instead, he entrusted himself to him who judges justly. (1 Pet. 2:13–15, 20–23)

This then is the first thing that Paul would have made clear when he preached in the synagogue at Thessalonica. Some of the Jews in the congregation were persuaded, and they attached themselves to Paul and Silas, as did a large number of God-fearing Greeks and not a few prominent women (17:4). They later formed the nucleus of the Christian church in the city. But many of the Jews, Luke tells us, reacted very differently. They collected a mob, raised a riot, and not finding Paul and Silas in the house of a certain Jason where they expected to find him, they dragged Jason and some other brothers before the city officials, shouting: 'These men who have instigated subversion all over the world have now come here, and Jason has harboured them. They are all defying Caesar's decrees, saying that there is another king, one called Jesus' (17:5–7).

Paul never got a chance to reply to this accusation. The magistrates took recognisance from Jason that Paul would leave the city at once; and he did. We need not trouble to refute the charge either; it was so evidently a misrepresentation of the Christian gospel in general and of Paul's particular exposition of it. But obviously we have a duty ourselves towards the gospel to follow Paul's example and never interpret it in our modern world in such a way as would open it to a justified accusation of this kind. That does not mean that in an atheistic state we should stop preaching the gospel because the gospel itself would contradict the government's basic presuppositions. But it does mean that the gospel message itself would still not be an incitement to political subversion or armed insurrection against the government. It was not mere prudence that restrained the New Testament preachers and writers from exhorting the Christians to join in revolts against the outrageous and persecuting Emperor Nero, such as the Jews in Palestine raised against him in AD 66. It was consideration for both the contents and the spirit of the gospel.

But according to Paul the Scripture's programme for the establishment of the messianic kingdom involved not only Messiah's death but also his resurrection from the dead; and we may briefly remind ourselves of some of the implications of that bodily resurrection for the topic under discussion.

First, it shows that our Lord has not abandoned earth, and gone off as a disembodied spirit into some purely spiritual heaven. He has a body still, which though glorified is as literal and physical a body as it was when he was here on earth. As we saw in an earlier chapter, the resurrection of his body carries implications for the whole of the physical universe (see pp. 26–27). In him the restoration of all things has already commenced. Christians may, and do, differ over how many phases there will be in that restoration; but we can certainly affirm that God's programme for the establishment of our Lord's messianic reign involves earth. Creation herself, groaning though she is now, shall be delivered from her bondage to corruption. Her groanings will cease, her frustration and futility be ended (Rom. 8:20–22). Even in the eternal state, we are told, there will be a new earth as well as a new heaven. God will always have a material expression of his purposes: that is guaranteed by our Lord's eternal retention of his complete human nature including his human body. We do well to remember that the last view that John was given to see of the eternal city was of that city not speeding away from earth into some immaterial heaven, but descending out of heaven towards earth (Rev. 21:2).

Secondly, as Acts early reminded us, the bodily resurrection and ascension of Christ are to be followed by his bodily return. Indeed the emphasis of the New Testament is everywhere laid on the fact that the Lord Jesus will *come* again: not merely that men and women will be summoned one day to meet him in some distant heaven, but that he himself will come back again. We empty the New Testament's language of its plain significance if we reduce all its talk of his coming back to mean nothing more than his staying where he now is and our going to him. The earth where he was crucified has not seen the last of him yet (Rev. 1:7).

And thirdly, our Lord's death and bodily resurrection, so Paul subsequently told the Thessalonians in a letter he wrote them after he left, carried the guarantee that those believers who died before he returned would not miss the enjoyment of participating in his future messianic reign. 'Brothers,' Paul wrote,

> we do not want you to be ignorant about those who fall asleep, or to grieve like the rest of men, who have no hope. We believe that Jesus died and rose again and so we believe that God will bring with Jesus those who have fallen asleep in him . . . For the Lord himself will come down from heaven . . . and the dead in Christ will rise first. After that, we who are still alive and are left will be caught up together with them in the clouds to meet the Lord in the air. And so we will be with the Lord for ever. (1 Thess. 4:13–17)

And this, it seems to me, is of immense personal importance to each one of us. The ardent Marxist is urged to struggle and, if necessary, to lay down life itself for the sake of the eventual emergence of a golden age that by definition he or she will never live to see. Then what is an ardent Marxist more than an expendable means which the evolution he believes in uses for its purpose and then discards? Similarly the Liberal Jews, many of whom are unsure or even sceptical about spiritual immortality and an afterlife.* As we have seen, their vision of the eventual messianic age on earth is noble indeed, though remote enough, so history would suggest, if it all depends on the efforts of men and nations to achieve it. But if those who believe in it, who work, pray and sacrifice for it, are destined never themselves to see it, what, may we ask, *are* they? Tiny creatures that live and die to build a coral island which they will never see, for a favoured generation of ten thousand years from now to play on? Christianity has a better hope for the individual than that.

Finally, there was one item in the biblical programme for the establishment of the messianic reign that might have been misconstrued by the Jews of Thessalonica as a treasonable, if veiled, attack upon the Roman Emperor. Paul pointed out when he was with them (2 Thess. 2:5) that when the Lord Jesus returns in the brilliance of his majestic glory he will begin by judging the world in righteousness in the strict and narrow sense of the word

---

*J. D. Rayner and B. Hooker, *Judaism for Today* (Union of Liberal and Progressive Synagogues, 1978), p. 35.

'judge'. Evil shall be put down. The tares rooted out and destroyed. The 'Man of Sin', that full-flowering expression and leader of human arrogance and rebellious independence of God, will be overthrown, along with all those who do not know God and do not obey the gospel of our Lord Jesus (2 Thess. 1:7–10; 2:8–12).

Paul described the 'Man of Sin' as that lawless one whose coming 'will be in accordance with the work of Satan displayed in all kinds of counterfeit miracles, signs and wonders, and in every sort of evil that deceives those who are perishing' (2 Thess. 2:9–10). But it would have been a ludicrous misrepresentation to suggest that by this description Paul was referring to the currently reigning Roman Emperor, Claudius, or even to his successor Nero. Neither of them was ever suspected of performing counterfeit miracles to prevent people from believing the Christian gospel! The earlier emperors, Augustus and Tiberius, had issued decrees forbidding astrologers and fortune-tellers to use their arts to discover and predict the fortunes of the emperors or of the state. Understandably. If some prophecy-monger predicted that the emperor was fated to die next year, it might well have motivated political malcontents to help the prophecy towards its fulfilment. But even if what Paul was talking about had referred to the current emperor, it would not in fact have been an incitement to anyone, not even to the Christians, to rebel against him, still less to try and replace him. When the Messiah comes to put down evil and to establish his kingdom, it will not be as some kind of supernatural Bar-Kochba, or Che Guevara, or even as some heavenly Alexander the Great, in competition with the governments of the day. He shall come as the incarnate Lord, Son of the Owner of the Universe; he will do as he sees fit with every government in the world; and it is not treasonable towards any present government for Christians to say that he will.

God's Messiah and Gentile politics: Paul's experience in Berea

Paul's preaching of Jesus as the Messiah provoked a violently hostile reaction on the part of some Jews at Thessalonica; and in one sense, perhaps, it is understandable that it should. He was not preaching a slightly controversial view on a minor point of ethics. He was preaching that Jesus was the Messiah appointed by God to judge the world in righteousness; whose second coming would bring down the judgement of God on all, however religious, who having heard and known the gospel refused to accept it and obey it (2 Thess. 1:8). Which says quite starkly that religion, however sincere, which knowingly rejects the gospel of Jesus Christ is invalid and worse. Understandably, some people were going to feel deeply resentful at this radical criticism of themselves and of their religion; and when people feel like that, they sometimes erupt. Some certainly did at Thessalonica. They took to the streets, whipped up a demonstration, assaulted the house where they thought Paul was staying, staged a mass protest, denounced Paul and Silas before the magistrates, and demanded action from the law.

There are some today who would perhaps put the blame for all that on Paul himself and on what they would call his fundamentalist attitude in thinking that his interpretation of the Bible was the only correct one, and in trying to convert all other Jews to his way of thinking. This kind of fundamentalism is obviously something that vexes many religious leaders more and more these days, for they increasingly complain of it in their public pronouncements and broadcasts. Perhaps understandably; for there is enough hate-filled violence produced by religion in the world today, without gratuitously adding to it.

Even so, it is not always easy to make sense of the term fundamentalism as currently used. A political activist who, claiming to be motivated by Christian principles, takes to violence and shoots or otherwise assassinates his political opponents, and even sometimes fellow Christians, is not normally called a fundamentalist. He can in fact find himself vigorously defended and supported by church leaders, and in times past could have been supplied with money from the World Council of Churches. Modern counterparts of Paul, however, who take a firm and uncompromising stand on the essential doctrines of the Christian faith, whether among fellow Christians or in conversation with people of other faiths, but who, true to the gospel they preach, would never take to violence or shoot anybody – such people can find themselves called fundamentalists and charged with fomenting religious strife. Clearly, 'fundamentalism' is a specialised term, to be used judiciously and with a certain discrimination; but it is no use at all in coming to an understanding of what the true Christian attitude should be.

Fortunately for the task of assessing Paul's attitude and methods of evangelism, we have Luke's record of the way the Jews at Berea behaved (17:10–15). As in Thessalonica, so in Berea Paul went to the synagogue and preached the same message, doubtless appealing to the same Old Testament passages. 'Now', says Luke, 'the Bereans were of more noble character than the Thessalonians, for they received [Paul's] message with great eagerness and examined the Scriptures every day to see if what Paul said was true. Many of the Jews believed, as did also a number of prominent Greek women and many Greek men' (17:11–12). Others of course were not convinced, and did not believe. But there was no violence, only a readiness to accept that Paul sincerely believed what he preached to be God's own non-negotiable truth, an awareness on both sides that what he preached must be proved or disproved by a careful, reasoned interpretation of Scripture, and a willingness vigorously to examine whether Scripture did support what Paul claimed, and not simply to reject it out of hand. Serious as the implications were, as Paul saw and preached them, for those who rejected his message, there was no violence, neither on his part nor theirs, not until the Jews from Thessalonica turned up in Berea, stirred up the crowds, got them all agitated, and once more drove Paul out of town.

Why then did the Thessalonians do what they did? After all, they were Jews and so was Paul. They accepted the Old Testament, so did Paul. They were living in pagan cities that did not believe in the true God. Why then did they resort to violent protest marches, deliberately misrepresent Paul to the magistrates, and try to bring the civil law down on his head; and then come to Berea and break the law themselves by attempting to cause a civil disturbance? A more certain way of bringing down the wrath and contempt of the Roman government on both Christians and Jews could not be imagined.* Why then did they do it?

Luke tells us they did it out of jealousy (17:5). They saw some Jews and a large number of Gentile adherents in the synagogue at Thessalonica getting converted. The truth or otherwise of what Paul was preaching was irrelevant to them. Their religion was being attacked. They would use violence and/or the law of the land – they saw no inconsistency in using both – to defend it. Perhaps they did not realise that a religion that has to protect itself by violence and/or the law against rational argument is confessing that its faith is very insecure.

Christendom itself descended to the use of the same tactics against infidels and 'heretics' on a massive scale during certain

---

*See 18:2 and the comment on p. 6.

periods of its history; and in some countries it continued to enforce civil discrimination against such people well into the nineteenth, and in some places into the twentieth, century. Of this all Christians are now heartily ashamed. But it would surely improve the tone and cogency of many a modern denunciation of so-called fundamentalism if we all remembered what Christendom's churches have done in the past – and in the not too distant past – and publicly repented of it, before fastening that ill-defined smear-word on other people.

God's Messiah and Gentile religion and philosophy: Paul's experience in Athens

The death and resurrection of the Lord Jesus, then, were key terms in Paul's preaching to Jews at Thessalonica (17:3). So they obviously were as well when he preached the Christian hope to both Jews and Greeks in Athens and declared that the risen Lord Jesus was the Man appointed by God to judge the world in righteousness; for some of the Greeks fastened on to his constantly repeated terms 'Jesus' and 'the resurrection', were puzzled by them, and asked for elucidation. They had the impression that Paul was advocating the introduction of two foreign, and somewhat bizarre, gods, 'Jesus' and 'the resurrection', and were at a loss to know how that could help solve the great problems of life that confront all thoughtful people. Some of them were Epicureans, some of them were Stoics; and whatever the inadequacies of those philosophical systems as we now may think, they were at least serious attempts to understand the universe, to make sense of our human situation within it, and to develop intelligent principles of behaviour that would enable people to make the most of life, avoiding its evils and maximising its good.

It is the fact, of course, that by the time Paul reached Athens in the first century AD, Athens had declined from its intellectual brilliance of the classical period. Of the two philosophical systems mentioned, original Stoicism in particular had been much modified with the passage of time and it is impossible to know exactly what form of Stoicism the people who invited Paul to address the Areopagus court would have held.* But the common ground

---

*For the historicity of Paul's visit to the Areopagus and the Pauline authenticity of the speech which Luke records in summary form, see C. J. Hemer, 'The Speeches of Acts II. The Areopagus Address', *Tyndale Bulletin* 40.2 (1989), pp. 239–59.

shared by all Stoics gives us a good enough idea of what attitude they took to life, what advice they offered for coping with evil, and what hope they held out for the future. And the same goes for the Epicureans. Both systems saw clearly that a true understanding of the universe, its origin, operation, and likely end, is necessarily involved in the question of evil – where it comes from, why it is there, how to cope with it, and what hope for the future we may have in light of it. And we may say at once that, in spite of excellent features in these philosophies, when it came to hope for the future, neither of them offered much, if any at all.

Meet the Epicureans

Let's start with Epicureanism. It has been consistently misunderstood as though it was a recipe and excuse for indulgence in unrestrained pleasures of the grosser sort. But that is in fact the direct opposite of what it stood for. Admittedly, Epicureanism made pleasure the chief good to be aimed at in life; but by pleasure it meant a state of trouble-free tranquillity. And since the grosser pleasures often involve emotional turbulence, pain and hangover, Epicureanism advised avoiding such pleasures altogether. The philosophy in fact produced people who within their own fellowships were renowned for their gentle kindness, friendliness and loyalty. At the same time it bought this tranquil happiness at the cost of deliberately withdrawing from too much involvement in the rough and tumble of life. It was scarcely a philosophy that the ordinary working man, housewife or business person could follow.

Epicureans' peace of mind was further bolstered by their belief that men and women are not answerable to a Creator who cares whether people behave well or badly. They believed in the existence of gods; but according to them, these gods were as much a product of the matter of the universe as man himself is. They inhabited the inter-cosmic spaces and (being good Epicureans themselves!) they took no interest in human beings, their needs, affairs or behaviour, but lived a trouble-free life of enjoyment. Epicureans believed in copying their example.

In physics Epicureanism took over the theories of the earlier philosophers Leucippus and Democritus, who held that the universe was composed of an infinite number of indestructible atoms and of limitless space, both of them eternal. The atoms were originally free-falling through space when a slight swerve developed,* and caused a vast multiple pile-up, with atoms colliding, rebounding, and then, some of them, settling down in durable combinations. In this way the sky, air, sea, earth and all their contents eventually emerged and took shape and function. There was no Creator. Human life, so the theory ran, as well as everything else, was bound to emerge eventually (only given that initial chance swerve coming from no one knows where) because the varied basic shapes of the atoms would guarantee that, given long enough time, atoms would come up against other atoms with which they could interlock, and so more and more complicated assemblages of atoms would gradually build up; and then the principle of the survival of the fittest would ensure that the best combinations would survive to form the world as we know it today.† The theory also predicted, however, that the equilibrium of forces that happens to keep our world and human life in their present state was bound sooner or later to give way; at which point everything would disintegrate and the whole universe would go up in flames. So then, no Creator designed the human race, no intelligence gave it purpose, and no significance would survive its destruction.

Meanwhile, so Epicureans believed, man is composed of body and soul; but both of them are composed of material atoms. At death the atoms of both body and soul come adrift, disperse, and go to make up other things or people. Nothing of the man himself survives. Death for him ends everything. It was this aspect of Epicureanism that especially appealed to its famous Roman populariser, the poet Lucretius (94–55 BC), who wrote a long work in six books on Epicureanism. With an evangelist's zeal he proclaimed what to him was the chief glory and benefit of the system: it freed people from the fear of a judgement in the life to come, of punishment, and of hell.‡

But, of course, he did not preach the other side of his gospel, namely that if it is true, it not only gets rid of the fear of judgement in the life to come, it removes from millions of people all hope of ever getting justice. Hope of justice for them turns out to be a

---

*No one explained how or from what source this swerve came, or why, if space is infinite and there is no up or down, the atoms were *falling* in the first place.

†Modern theories of evolution, like those of Dr Richard Dawkins – see, for example, his *The Blind Watchmaker* (London: Longman, 1986) – which stress the effect of *gradual cumulative* development worked on by natural selection, are only more sophisticated versions of this ancient theory. Indeed the theory of evolution itself is not in fact a modern theory, but a very ancient one.

‡Lucretius, *De Rerum Natura*, i. 63–79, 102–19; iii. 1014 ff.

deceptive illusion. Take one lurid, if hackneyed, example.* Evolution produced six million Jews who believed in justice. Evolution produced Hitler. Natural selection chose the fittest, and Hitler, for the moment, survived. Pointless to argue that it was unjust. On this theory, there is no independent court of justice to which human beings may appeal against evolution, nor any independent standard of justice by which evolution's behaviour may be judged. Justice is merely a feeling or taste or preference that evolution has unthinkingly produced in some people, while at the same time it has equally unthinkingly produced the opposite feeling, taste or preference in others. Useless also to argue that evolution helped by natural selection will eventually produce a majority of those who prefer justice, who will then be able to eliminate those who prefer injustice. What about those who have unjustly perished in the meantime? Are we to write them off as evolution's throw-aways on her unthinking and unfeeling progress towards a perfectly just world? And not only a useless, but a dangerous way to argue as well. Majorities always consider their views and values to be right as against those of minorities. Suppose one day evolution and natural selection produce a majority with a preference for justice, and the majority eliminates those whose preference is different from theirs. What objective standard or independent court will guarantee that the preferred justice of the majority is indeed true justice? Perhaps the question would not matter if history had shown us that what majorities have preferred and done has always proved to be the most just thing. But history has often shown the very opposite, witness our own century perhaps more than any other.

Of course, we can always bring Epicureanism's last argument to bear upon the subject: that those who are unjustly killed, murdered, tortured or starved to death don't mind being dead, once they are dead, since nothing of them survives death to resent it. But that means that for millions of people in the present and future, as for millions in the past, death has always been and always will be, preferable to life, if only they knew it. Pessimism indeed!

---

*But we should not think only of the more lurid examples (such as Hitler's genocide, Stalin's purges, and the Khmer Rouge's massacres), but also of the myriad and one instances of corruption in business, in the legal system, in politics, and of heartless injustices in private human relationships that do not kill people, but leave them to suffer heartbreak, shame, poverty or ill-health for life.

Epicureanism, then, certainly achieved some astonishing (for its time) insights into the workings of nature;* and, in addition, produced genuine friendliness and tranquillity within its narrow and somewhat withdrawn circles. But, like its modern counterparts, faced with the problem of evil it offered no real hope for the world.

Meet the Stoics

Stoics were made of sterner stuff. They deplored setting up pleasure, of whatever kind, as the chief aim in life. They held that the only good is to be virtuous, that is to live in harmony with reason; and that not to be virtuous is the only evil. Their philosophy was extensively modified over the centuries, but in all its periods it produced people of noble character and rock-like courage. In its later form it won the allegiance of many leading Romans; and even after its decline, its influence lived on through the Middle Ages and down to the present time. The Christian Fathers were much influenced by its moral teachings; and when today people talk of 'taking things philosophically', or claim that 'there is a divine spark in everyone' or speak of 'being a citizen of the world' or of 'the brotherhood of all mankind', they show that they have been influenced by Stoicism, whether they know it or not.

But to the question that interests us at the moment, 'What hope have we that evil will one day be eliminated from our world?', Stoicism gave a very bleak answer indeed. It taught that the universe is one rational whole in which everything happens by an unbroken chain of cause and effect, which could be called 'fate', and in which everything that happens contributes to the good of the whole, which could be called 'providence'. This comes about because at the centre of the universe, and pervading all its parts, is reason, which is the active agent in the creation and in the control of all that goes on. They referred to this active agent by many names – Nature, Reason, Zeus, God – and some Stoic thinkers would refer to Zeus or God in terms that superficially taken might seem to be referring to the God of Judaism and Christianity. But in fact the Stoic God was not the transcendent, personal, loving Creator; he was as much of the substance of the

---

*Both in its basic atomist concept – though that was far removed from our modern atomic theory – and in some particulars. Its theory of smell, for instance, was remarkably near to what we nowadays know to be true.

universe as anything else: he (one would better say 'it') was simply the vital force that pervades everything.* In other words Stoics were pantheists.

Since reason thus pervaded and controlled everything, Stoics believed that the universe as it is, is 'the best of all possible worlds'. It could not be improved upon. What might appear to the individual as evil, and in some sense actually be evil, nevertheless contributed to the good of the whole. To live virtuously, therefore, was to live according to reason, and that meant accepting that everything that actually happens is part of the rational whole and makes for the good of the whole. It would therefore be rational and good, for instance, for a man to attempt to resist some individual act or national movement that seemed to him evil; but if the evil thing happened in spite of his efforts, it would be neither rational nor virtuous to grieve over it. The fact that it happened showed that it was part of the operations of universal reason and was for the good of the whole. To grieve over it would be contrary to reason. He must steel himself, control his emotions, and accept what had happened philosophically.

Moreover, the only real good in life was virtue, defined as living and acting in harmony with reason. All other apparently good things were matters of indifference. So if a wise man saw six million Jews about to be gassed, it would be good and virtuous to attempt to save them, because the action could be justified rationally. But if they were gassed in spite of his efforts, he would not grieve: his effort to save them was rational, therefore absolutely good; the six million lives of themselves were not an absolute good, but only a matter of indifference. Moreover, the fact that they died showed that the deaths were part of the operation of the world-governing reason and were for the good of the whole. His own wisdom lay in accepting what was now shown to be fate. The unwise, and therefore bad, man would try to resist fate, and allow his emotions to distress him at the loss of these lives. But in the end, the only difference it made was that the unwise man was dragged along kicking, by the irresistible processes of universal reason, Zeus, or God – call it what you will – when he could, so to speak, have come quietly.

At first sight this Stoical teaching might appear to be the same as the Christian doctrine that 'all things work together for good to those who love God', and that therefore we can and should find

---

*Faintly resembling the modern concept of energy; but in Stoicism, the vital force did not turn into matter, it pervaded matter.

comfort in submitting to the will of God. Actually it is light years removed from it. According to Christ, the 'good' to which all things work together is not the good of the whole at the cost of the individual, but the good of the individual as well as that of the whole; not the world as it is, but the world as it shall be: it is the promised 'good' that every believer will be conformed both in body and character to the likeness of God's Son, which goal will be attained in the glory of the life to come, in a world where righteousness reigns.

Not so Stoicism. It held that the present world as it is, with all its evil and suffering, is the best world that could possibly be; it could not be improved upon since it is everywhere initiated, upheld and controlled in all its parts by all-pervading reason for the good of the whole as it is. So much so, indeed, that the early Stoics taught that when the stars in their cycles eventually came round to the position from which they started, the whole universe would go up in flames, and then it would be renewed and the whole process of history in all its details would happen all over again, exactly as it did before. Later Stoics abandoned this idea of cyclical destruction and repetition; but they had no more satisfactory goal to put in its place. As to the survival of the soul after death, Stoics were vague and divided. Some held that the soul would hold together for a time: the weaker souls would break up first; the souls of the perfectly wise would manage to survive until overtaken by the next world-conflagration. Some, however, did not believe in any survival of the soul at all.

First and last, then, when it came to the question of the elimination of evil from the world, or the attainment of universal justice, neither Stoics nor Epicureans offered any hope of there ever being anything better than the world as it is. They were, as Paul would later say, without God, without the Messiah, and without hope in the world (Eph. 2:12).*

Meet the other members of the Court

Of course not all the members of the Court of the Areopagus were Stoics and Epicureans. Some may have been attached to other

---

*To revert to the question of 'guidance', which occupied the beginning of this section: since Stoics believed that all things happened by an unbroken chain of cause and effect, they held that specially gifted people like seers, astrologers and mediums could foretell future events from the flights of birds, or states of the livers of sacrificial animals, or any unusual occurrence. It led Stoics into all kinds of superstition.

forms of philosophy, or to none at all; some may still have followed the traditional state religion. Its crude and contradictory myths about the gods never did form anything like a formal creed, and it had no systematic theology. It goes without saying that the immoral and irresponsible behaviour of the gods as related by its myths gave no ground for hope that the world they supposedly controlled would ever be free of evil. How much of these myths the ordinary worshipper believed, it is difficult to know. There was no minimal requirement. Some of the more intellectual managed to hold on to some faith in the gods by demythologising them. Stoics, for instance, equated Zeus with their pantheistic world-reason and regarded the gods as names for the various processes that go on in the cosmos. But we may deduce from the way that masses of people still treat their temples in the Far East today (or even as some Westerners treat their churches too) that in the ancient world thousands of people would still have been held to the state religion by the strength of tradition, the beauty of the temples, the pageantry and mystique of the rituals, the artistic appeal of its images, and the general air of mystery; and would have been held all the more strongly when they could believe more or less what they liked about its doctrinal content and did not have to ask themselves difficult questions about its rational basis.

Paul's speech before the Court of the Areopagus

It was, then, a very mixed audience that Paul rose to address in the Areopagus Court. Given the wide differences in their presuppositions and beliefs, he had a difficult task before him to find enough common ground between all of them and himself so as to make the Christian hope relevant to their thinking; to express it in terms that would be intelligible to them; to present the basic essentials of the gospel without compromise and yet in their glorious attractiveness.

He rose to the task magnificently. Some, it is true, have felt that there was all too little of the specifically Christian gospel in what he said. But to save ourselves from falling into that mistake we should remember two things. First, what Luke has given us is only a summary, though doubtless a faithful summary, of Paul's speech. Secondly, even if Luke had supplied a full verbatim record of the speech, it still would not have given us all that Paul said to the Athenians. He had been reasoning every day with all and sundry in the market-place even before he was invited to address the court; and some court members at least would have listened in or even have taken part. In those discussions he had obviously presented the specifically Christian gospel and emphasised the person of the Lord Jesus and his resurrection just as he had done in the synagogue at Thessalonica (though doubtless using different terminology). It was in fact Paul's constant references to Jesus and the resurrection that caught the attention of the Epicureans and Stoics, and led to his invitation to explain these terms before the court.

Two things troubled them about the terms Paul used. The one was that 'Jesus' and 'the resurrection' sounded to them like two gods. Their pagan mythology was full of minor deities, some of whom had once been mythical heroes on this earth, and after death were regarded as having been elevated, like Herakles, to the company of the gods; while others of them were venerated at shrines which public piety had built for their spirits to inhabit after death. Stoics also were used to interpreting the gods of the traditional pantheon as the great and mysterious processes that keep the universe going. 'The resurrection', for all the Stoics knew, could have been one of these. Their misconception was understandable in pagans; but it was ruinously wrong, and Paul in his speech would have to concentrate on putting it right.

The other thing that troubled them about Paul's terms was that these two 'deities' which he seemed to be advocating were foreign deities; and that would have made Athenians wary of them. It was then the need to deal with these two difficulties that largely determined the shape and proportion of his speech. He had to correct the pagan concept of deity: Jesus was not a deity, one among many gods, in the pagan sense; the resurrection was not a deity at all, but a historical event; and neither of them was a *foreign* god.

Christianity not a foreign religion

So let's begin by taking in the whole sweep of Paul's address and see how he demolishes the idea that what he is preaching is foreign. The God he proclaims is 'the God who made the world and everything in it . . . [who] gives all men life and breath and everything else' (17:24–25). He cannot be held to be a foreigner in any part of his universe. Moreover, granted the multiplicity of races and cultures on the face of the earth, yet this God made all these nations without exception, and what is more, he made them all originally from one man (17:26). No nation, therefore, can stand on its national or cultural pride, and regard this God as the special property of some other nation or culture, and not suited to its own. This God also maintains all the members of every nation, for 'in him we live and move and have our being' (17:27). Asians and Europeans are not maintained by different gods according to the continent or country they inhabit. Seeing, then, that God is the Creator and Maintainer of all mankind, he has a right now 'to command all people everywhere to repent' (17:30). He is not a God who has a right to interfere in some nations and cultures because he fits in with their ethos and concepts, and no right to interfere in other nations and cultures because he is alien to their way of thinking. He made them all, he maintains all, and he commands all everywhere to repent. He is, moreover, about to judge the world in righteousness; not just part of it, but the whole of it (17:31). He has a right to judge it all, and sheer justice would demand that he should judge all equally without partiality. The time of that judgement is already fixed; and assurance that the judgement will in fact take place is now 'given to all men', and given in a form that makes it immediately relevant to all human beings everywhere, whatever their nationality or culture: a man, a human being, has been raised from the dead (17:31).

We observe that Paul does not attempt, at this point in his address at least, to explain that Jesus who died and rose again was the Son of God, true though that was, nor to expound the mysteries of the relationships within the Trinity. That might have been a very difficult thing to do at the first sitting for raw pagans whose ideas were conditioned by the myths of gods who came down to earth and had children by human women. But even if it could have been done without giving the wrong impression, it would not have been the point that Paul was wanting to make. To say that the Son of God had been raised from the dead, though true, would have made it sound as if he was different from humankind. He did not even say at this point that God had raised Jesus from the dead; for 'Jesus' would sound like a foreign name to Greeks. What Paul wanted to emphasise, and what he therefore said, was that God had raised a man from the dead. The point was not that he was a Jew, and a very special Jew at that, but that he was a human being. The bodily resurrection of that one human being carried, and still carries, implications for all human beings of all time, of every race, nation, language and culture, simply because both he and they are human.

The resurrection of Jesus: The turning-point in history

But the resurrection of one man, Jesus, is not only God's assurance that he will judge the world in righteousness: it is also the explanation why, having overlooked the past centuries of pagan ignorance of himself, God now commands all people everywhere to repent.

Here we shall have to go slowly, and carefully consider the terms Paul uses, to make sure we give Paul's statements the meaning he intended.

How is it, we may ask to start with, that the resurrection of Christ forms a reason for *now* commanding everybody, everywhere, to repent? Admittedly it gives added assurance of the fact that there will be a judgement. But was not that fact always true anyway? And did not all people everywhere in the centuries past need to repent in light of it? Why has the call to repentance become now so universal and so urgent?

Secondly, in remarking that God overlooked those past centuries of ignorance, Paul is not saying, is he, that the sins that Gentiles committed before the birth, death and resurrection of Christ will never be held against them; that they were all automatically forgiven, or indeed were overlooked and never registered against their perpetrators?

No, indeed not. Paul is not contradicting in advance, or even compromising, what he would one day write in his letter to the Romans, that the whole world, both Jew and Gentile, of all times and places, will be called to account before God's judgement bar (Rom. 1:18–2:16). Then why has the resurrection of Christ made it necessary *now* to call people of all nations everywhere to repent, in a way that was not done during the preceding centuries?

We shall find the answer if we recall from our earlier discussion the meaning of the phrase 'judge the world in righteousness' (pp. 282–84). Paul is not thinking simply of the judgement to be faced after death, such as the writer to the Hebrews describes: 'man is destined to die once, and after that to face judgment' (Heb. 9:27). There will, of course, be such a judgement, and it will be Christ who does the judging. 'I saw the dead,' says John in the Revelation, 'great and small, standing before the throne, and . . . the dead were judged according to what they had done as recorded in the books. The sea . . . and death and Hades gave up the dead that were in them, and each person was judged according to what he had done' (Rev. 20:12–13). A judgement of the dead, after death, then; the passage could not be more explicit.

303

But Christ is going to do more than judge the dead: he is going to judge the living as well, as the New Testament repeatedly affirms – 'he is the one whom God appointed as judge of the living and the dead' (10:42); [he] is ready to judge the living and the dead' (1 Pet. 4:5); 'Christ Jesus . . . will judge the living and the dead' (2 Tim. 4:1).

Then when will he judge the living? At his second coming, of course. The New Testament speaks of 'the coming wrath' in the sense not merely that it is future, but that it will come when the Lord Jesus comes. Recall again what Paul later wrote to the believers at Thessalonica not all that long after he left Athens:

> This will happen when the Lord Jesus is revealed from heaven in blazing fire with his powerful angels. He will punish those who do not know God and do not obey the gospel of our Lord Jesus. They will be punished with everlasting destruction and shut out from the presence of the Lord and from the majesty of his power on the day he comes . . . (2 Thess. 1:7–10)

It was indeed Paul's preaching of this coming of the Lord Jesus and the wrath that would accompany it that led many Thessalonians to turn 'to God from idols to serve the living and true God, and to wait for his Son from heaven, whom he raised from the dead – Jesus, who rescues us from the coming wrath' (1 Thess. 1:9–10).

Paul, then, is preaching to the elegant Court of the Areopagus the very same gospel as he preached at Thessalonica (and everywhere else): God has raised Jesus bodily from the dead; in a body which though different from what it was before, is nevertheless a physical body which can and will interact with this physical world in its present state (see p. 28). In that same body he will come again (1:11), and when he comes he will judge the living. His bodily resurrection is God's guarantee that it shall be so.

Here then is the reason why Paul calls on the Athenians *now* to repent. In centuries past Gentiles had certainly sinned, and their ignorance of the true God was culpable, as we shall presently see. When they died, if they had not repented, put their trust in God and cast themselves on his mercy, they would have been remanded in custody until the day when the dead should be judged (cf. 2 Pet. 2:4–9). But during those long centuries, in spite of the nations' sin and culpable ignorance, God did not intervene and send his Son into the world to judge the world. In his patience and forbearance he overlooked those times of ignorance. And even when at long last he did send his Son into the world, it was

304

not in order that he should judge the world, but that he might save the world. All down the pre-Christian centuries, then, the coming of Christ to judge the world was not imminent. He had to come and die first. But his death and resurrection have changed all that. Now his second coming is not only assured, it is near. We all live in the last hour. And when he comes he will judge all the living throughout the whole world. God now therefore commands all people everywhere to repent; and the command must be relayed to all the world, the Athenians included. They too urgently needed to repent.

But still he has not come: have we not then reason to doubt the whole story after all these long centuries? That objection was already being levelled at the preaching of the second coming within a comparatively short time after Paul's own death (2 Pet. 3:3–4), and the answer that was given then is valid still (2 Pet. 3:9).

The culpability of pagan ignorance of God

Now we have said that the pagans' ignorance of the true God before the first coming of Christ was culpable ignorance. We have said more: that the force of Paul's argument throughout the major part of his speech to the Areopagus court was to prove it was culpable. We now must substantiate this claim.

First take Paul's opening remark: 'Men of Athens! I see that in every way you are very religious' (17:22). We should not jump to the conclusion that Paul was necessarily intending to compliment them on this. He had earlier been distressed, so Luke tells us (17:16), as he had walked through the city and seen how the whole place was coming down with idols. He was hardly likely to be commending them now for that fact. The Greek word he used for 'religious' can mean either religious or superstitious. In some contexts it is clear which meaning the speaker intends; in others it can be left to the hearers or readers to take it in whichever sense they please. So it was here. Paul could acknowledge that they were very religious – that was the fact. His evaluation of the fact, whether their religion was valid religion or superstition, he had no need to state baldly in his opening sentence. It would become evident as he proceeded. The word, then, was a very tactful one to use: it did not of itself carry commendation. And besides, there was much about the traditional religion that the Stoics and Epicureans would rightly disapprove of. Paul was not intending to forfeit their respect in advance by siding with the traditionalists and complimenting them on their false, superstitious nonsense.

It was the inscription on one of their many altars, he explained, that had particularly impressed him with their extraordinary religiousness (17:23). The inscription could be translated either 'To an unknown god' or 'To the unknown god'; but whichever way it was meant to be read, it was not a recognition by the Athenians that there existed one supreme and true God, whom unfortunately they did not know. It was an expression of their polytheism. They believed in endless gods; and they had already erected altars to scores of them. If, as sometimes happened, they had to restore an ancient altar, and the original inscription was no longer legible, so that they did not know to which god it had originally been dedicated, they would inscribe it afresh with the words 'To the (or a) unknown god'. There was also a legend connected with a certain Epimenides, from one of whose poems Paul will later quote. During a plague he advised the Athenians to sacrifice sheep at various places to the appropriate god, and when they did not know what god was the god appropriate to a particular place, they inscribed the altar 'To the unknown god', that is, of that particular place.

Here then was the poignancy of polytheism's error. Once accept that there are many gods, you can never be sure that your worship covers them all: there is always a possibility that there are some more, as yet unknown. And yet, so long as you regard the only true God as one more, but unknown, god among hundreds of others, you cannot know him as he really is.

Paul nonetheless was merciful: 'what you worship as something unknown' (or 'in ignorance'), he declared, '[that] I am going to proclaim to you' (17:23).

We notice the neuters: *what . . . that* not 'whom . . . him'. They were not already vaguely worshipping the one true God; they were not worshipping *him* at all. At best, like almost all people instinctively do, they were worshipping 'the supernatural', the 'superhuman', the 'divine'; and what Paul was now about to do was to tell them the truth about the divine, namely that there is only one true God. He was altogether different from anything they worshipped. To worship and serve him, as Paul told the Thessalonians (1 Thess. 1:9), you had to turn from idols. You could not worship both simultaneously. And to show them this he began by pointing out the grave misconception on which their multiplicity of temples was based and which it in turn fostered.

'The God who made the world and everything in it is the Lord of heaven and earth', so he 'does not live in temples built by hands' (17:24).

The fact is so obvious that the statement of it almost amounts to a truism: if God made the whole universe, he obviously cannot be thought of as being contained by, or confined to, a building made by man. The Stoics would have approved of that; and the Epicureans, whose gods were not creators, but only part of the material universe, would nevertheless have agreed that even they could not be contained in man-made temples. Not only had philosophers seen it; the Athenian dramatic poet Euripides had centuries before expressed the same idea: 'What house built by craftsmen could enclose the form divine within enfolding walls?'* If any Athenians, then, still continued to think and behave as though it could, then such ignorant behaviour was culpable for ignoring what was self-evident and what they could have known.

Now we of course know what the Athenians may not have known, that the Jews still had a temple of God at Jerusalem, and had had one for many centuries. Indeed the Old Testament said that it was built on God's own orders (2 Sam. 7:12–13). Was Paul now saying that the Jewish temple was, and always had been, founded on a complete, and seriously wrong, conception? No, of course not.

But there are two things we should notice about Israel's experience. The one is that right from the inauguration of the first temple its builder Solomon and the nation had realised that while God might be pleased to presence himself in it, it could not, and did not, ever contain him (1 Kings 8:27); and the later prophet Isaiah saw (Isa. 66:1–2) what Stephen later proclaimed (7:48–50), that Israel's temple was not the final ideal; it was at best a symbol of reality.

But the second thing to notice about Israel's temple is this: while it lasted Israel were placed under strict prohibition not to build more than one. There was to be one 'house of God': it was never God's intention that there should be many 'houses of God'. And the point of placing this prohibition on Israel can be seen by observing what happened when Israelites, disobeying God's instructions, built temples to God all over the place. It led inevitably to an idolatrous concept of God. The one true God,

---

*Euripides, fragment 968; cited from F. F. Bruce, *The Book of the Acts*, New International Commentary on the New Testament (Grand Rapids, MI: Wm B. Eerdmans, ²1988), p. 336, n. 65.

Yahweh, inevitably became thought of as a number of 'presences': 'the Yahweh of Bethel', 'the Yahweh of Dan', 'the Yahweh of Arad', and so forth; and presently the temple of Yahweh in some town or other found itself sharing the town with 'the temple of Baal'; and before you knew where you were, Yahweh had become one of a number of localised deities.

What happened in Israel in her degenerate periods happened everywhere in paganism. The high god Zeus might have his temple in a city, but the lesser god Apollo too might have his, and all the others theirs as well. Now, had you asked the local citizens, they would have said they believed that Zeus was not confined to his temple: he roamed the whole heavens as well as the earth. But in their particular city Zeus inhabited his own temple, and Apollo his; and Athena kept to hers and did not invade the others'. In people's thinking, therefore, and indeed in their cities, their all-powerful Zeus was in fact confined absurdly enough to one temple. This, of course, was the result of starting from a false, idolatrous concept of the universe; but in turn it reinforced that false concept in the general public's minds. And the same was true – and still is true – of altars and shrines, where one is dedicated to the worship of one god, demi-god, hero or beatified human, and another to another.

The Stoics would have agreed with what Paul said next (and so would the Epicureans in their way, even though they did so for the wrong reasons). Paul asserted that 'The God who made the world . . . is not served by human hands, as if he needed anything, because he himself gives all men life and breath and everything else' (17:24–25). The truth of the proposition is self-evident: if the Creator has to, and does, give us everything we have, we have nothing of our own with which we could satisfy his needs, even if he had any. And in that sense, of course, he hasn't. Nor have we anything which he needs, which we could supply and so purchase something from him in exchange.

But the idea that people have things which the gods like and need, and which can therefore be used to purchase desired favours from the gods, was widespread in paganism. And not only in paganism; it was at certain periods to be found in ancient Israel as well.

Take the matter of sacrifice. From the earliest days, so the Old Testament indicates, God taught people to offer sacrifices for sin. They were never intended as payments to God that purchased forgiveness from him, and certainly not as bribes to encourage him to forgive. They were divinely appointed symbols that taught mankind that sin cannot be forgiven without the payment of the penalty of sin. The animal sacrifices never paid that penalty themselves: they were but symbols and foreshadowings of the great 'payment for sin' that God himself in the person of Christ would one day pay at the cross.

Similarly, God ordained that people could bring animals and other things as offerings to express their gratitude to him for his many gifts. But again those offerings were only symbolic; they were none of them payments to God for the gifts given.

This system of sacrifices, however, was very early on perverted. In ancient near-eastern literature the gods are crudely pictured as swarming like flies around the sacrifices offered by men. Much later in Israel the more subtle idea came to be prevalent that somehow the sin-offerings paid God for his forgiveness and that sacrifices could purchase God's blessings. It led to God's protest: 'I have no need of a bull from your stall or of goats from your pens, for every animal of the forest is mine . . . If I were hungry I would not tell you, for the world is mine, and all that is in it' (Ps. 50:9–12). You cannot pay God with coins that are his anyway. The idea that you can is self-evidently false.

Still more sophisticated versions of this basic fallacy have troubled not only paganism but also Judaism and Christendom. One of them is that if we are good, and especially if we are extra good, we can accumulate merit that we can then use in order to gain God's forgiveness, or a place in his heaven, or somehow release our friends from the sufferings they have deserved. And another is that the work of our hands and the offering of ourselves in service to God can somehow become part of Christ's sacrifice for sin, and so help to procure forgiveness for us.

All this is but a refined expression of the pagan idea which Paul exposed at Athens. Its sadness lies in the way it misreads and misinterprets the heart and character of the true God. He is not in business. He does not sell his love or his forgiveness to us spiritually bankrupt sinners, nor can we buy his salvation. Nor do we need to. His love gives it us free. If he uses the metaphor of buying, he does so in order to emphasise that we have no price to pay: 'Come, all you who are thirsty, come to the waters; and you who have no money, come, buy and eat! Come, buy wine and milk without money and without cost' (Isa. 55:1). God save us then from lapsing into paganism; or if we have, give us the wisdom to repent of it, just as the Athenians were called on to do.

Finally, Paul had to deal with a fallacy that was and still is very common in the pagan world: that because nations have grown up in different parts of the world and so have developed their own cultures and ways of looking at things, they have a right to conceive of God, or the gods, in a way that appeals to their particular mode of thinking. If, for instance, it appealed to the Athenian way of looking at things to think of the gods in a polytheistic way, then that was just as valid as thinking of God in the monotheistic way that appealed to Jews with their very different culture. The idea was false, though it had and still has a sufficient grain of truth in it to make it seem to many people to be true.

If you and I both look at a tulip, we shall both see a lot in common; but then you may well notice features in it that I do not, and vice versa. But if we both look at one tulip, and I claim to see a cat, a monkey and an elephant, there is either something very wrong with my eyesight or brain, or else I am not in fact looking at the tulip at all. Certainly my culture cannot be appealed to as validating my way of looking at the tulip.

Paul not only admits that God has placed mankind in different parts of the world and given them different boundaries and different climates, conditions and histories: Paul asserts it, and attributes it to God's determining sovereignty (17:26). (That would have pleased the Stoics!) The resultant true and healthy cultural differences are therefore to be seen as the will of God, who loves variety.

But beneath these cultural differences, Paul points out, there is a basic unity. It is not merely that one Creator has created all mankind, but also that he originally made us all out of one common ancestor, Adam (17:26). We can exaggerate the significance of our differences. The multiplication table is the same for all. The laws of logic cannot vary according to cultural differences. Justice, to be justice, must apply to all nations and cultures impartially. The Stoics in Paul's day had long since seen this, and they deplored narrow nationalistic and cultural differences if they hid the fact that we are all citizens of the world.

Moreover, says Paul, God's sovereignty has distributed men and women all over the world and given each their circumstances so that each might in turn use their God-given initiative to make their personal and individual quest for God, feel after him, and find him (17:27). That quest, Paul admits, might for many seem like groping.* But actually the task that God has set us is not all

---

*The word here translated by the NIV 'reach out for' means 'to reach out and feel for something' like someone in a dark room would do.

that difficult. We do not have to reach out a long way: God is not in fact far from any one of us. He wants each individual to reach out and find him, and so he has placed himself near to each one of us: 'in him we live and move and have our being' (17:28).

Nor was this simply the insight of a Jew favoured with God's special revelation of himself to Israel. The citation just quoted comes from an ancient Greek poet.* He was not referring to the true God as Christians know him, of course, but to the supreme God whoever he was. But he saw clearly enough what must be evident to all who care to open their eyes: we did not make ourselves; we do not maintain the world we live in, nor the sun that is indispensable to our life and survival. We are utterly and constantly dependent on the One who gave us life to maintain us in life. The very air we breathe is supplied by him and placed all around us and within us.

Moreover, Paul points out (17:28–29) – and he quotes another Greek poet this time, a certain Aratus, who was a fellow countryman of Paul's (they both came from Cilicia) and what is more, a Stoic – 'We are his offspring.'† Now Aratus' concept of God would have been pantheistic and therefore inadequate. But it served the point which Paul wanted to make. If as creatures we have sprung from a Creator, we can tell a great deal about our Creator from looking at ourselves. The Stoics had done that, and had got some way towards the knowledge of the true God. They found themselves possessed of reason: the Source from which they came, therefore, they reasoned, could not be less rational than they were. It must be in fact Supreme Reason, from which all rationality in the universe is derived.

That, as Paul proceeded to point out, immediately ruled out of court the pagan practice of representing God in the form of metal or stone images. Granted that educated pagans would say that those images were only visual reminders of the gods. But even as reminders they were false. They were less than human beings: as the Hebrew psalmist would say

> They have mouths, but cannot speak,
>   eyes, but they cannot see;
> they have ears, but cannot hear,
>   noses, but they cannot smell. (Ps. 115:5–6)

---

*Perhaps Epimenides of Crete (600 BC); but the authorship is disputed.

†If we translate the Greek as 'children', we should be careful to notice that Aratus was not talking about the new birth by which creatures of God become children of God (John 1:12; 3:3). In that sense not all men and women are children of God.

whereas they ought to have been not less, but more than human beings. Indeed so inconceivably greater is God than man, that God has forbidden any attempt on man's part to represent him.

But the point remains: God is doubtless infinitely greater than we humans are; but he is certainly not less. He does not have eyes like we have; but he who gave us sight is not blind himself. He does not have physical ears like ours; but as the Hebrew poet put it, 'Does he who implanted the ear not hear?' (Ps. 94:9).

It is this that gives the lie to all forms of the Epicurean theory of human origins, ancient or modern. We human beings know ourselves to be personal: the Source we come from cannot be and is not less than personal. The Stoics were right in arguing that if we are rational our Source cannot be less than rational. But they did not go far enough. We human beings are persons, not just computerised bundles of impersonal reasoning processes. Our Creator, then, is not less personal than we are, but more.

God then is indeed not far from each one of us; nor was he far from the Gentile nations of the ancient world. Creation around them told them, if only they would listen, that the Creator of heaven and earth cannot be confined to a temple. Creation around them showed them, if only they would look and see, that its Creator who had to give (and in fact had given) them all they had was self-sufficient independently of man. And they only had to look at themselves to know that their Creator was not less personal, less wise, less rational, less just than themselves. Many of them actually came to see this was so; Socrates was a notable example. Where ignorance prevailed, it was culpable.

It was denial of these truths that robbed so many in the ancient world, and perhaps still more in our modern world, of hope. If there is no personal Creator, and we human beings have arisen out of blind impersonal matter worked on by blind impersonal forces, then we who are alive today, like all our predecessors, are in a hideous prison. One day a virus will enter our body and proceed gradually to destroy us, our bodies, our brains, our aesthetic sense, our power to plan rationally and to love. We shall have the intelligence to see what it is up to; and yet intelligence enough to see that just as we did not control our coming to be, so we shall not be able to prevent this impersonal, mindless piece of matter from destroying us. The final irony will be that when it has destroyed us, it won't even know what it has done, nor that it has done it. And beyond that, for us no hope for ever.

No wonder that God in his mercy called on the Athenians to repent – to open their eyes to turn from their ignorance and to face the glorious fact: God can be found; the man Jesus is risen from the dead; there is hope for mankind and for the world.

The sequel

The sequel to Movement 2 is brief but not insignificant. Some have written off Paul's Areopagite address as if it were a failure. But there were some converts, four at the very least; and a lecture which God uses to bring even one human being to reconciliation with God, to personal fellowship with his or her Maker, and to eternal glory, is not rightly called a failure.

That more were not immediately converted is not to be wondered at – at least on Christianity's presuppositions. Man's flawed relationship with his Creator nowhere expresses itself more decidedly than in his attempt to be independent of God. The rich man will put his faith in his riches; the intelligent in his power of reason, which he then sets up as an absolute to the exclusion of faith in God. But that is to abuse reason and to require it to perform a function it was never intended to perform.*
In the physical sciences, reason does not create the evidence on which it works.† The evidence – in this case the whole of the physical universe – is given. It is there. Reason accepts it and studies it, and then comes to understand it. But it did not create it. And in all cases reason normally starts off with things it cannot yet understand, that do not fit in with its present theories. It does not dismiss these things just because they do not fit in with the tentative theories it has already arrived at.

So it is with the knowledge and understanding of God. The evidence, in this case, is God's revelation of himself as a Person perceived by faith, and leading to understanding through both faith and reason. But if a man sets up reason to the exclusion of faith, he automatically cuts off a large part of the evidence, and makes it impossible for God to reveal himself to him (Luke 10:21; 1 Cor. 1:18–31). The same attitude would make it impossible for his wife ever to prove that she loved him!

Some in the court, on hearing about the resurrection, at once

*See E. H. Andrews, *Christ and the Cosmos* (Welwyn: Evangelical Press, 1986), pp. 9–20.

†See, for example, T. F. Torrance, *Theological Science* (Oxford: Oxford University Press, 1969); Michael Polanyi, *Personal Knowledge* (London: Routledge & Kegan Paul, 1958); and Lesslie Newbigin, *Foolishness to the Greeks* (London: SPCK, 1986).

ridiculed the whole idea.* The ridicule was gratuitous. If they were traditionalists, one might have thought that there were enough downright absurdities in the myths about their gods to keep their ridicule fully occupied. If they were Stoics and Epicureans, one can only assume that they were so confident that their own presuppositions were right that they felt that there was no need to examine the evidence for the resurrection carefully: the very idea of resurrection could be dismissed out of hand. But then, of course, it was received wisdom in Athens that once a man was dead, no resurrection was possible. Aeschylus, their great tragic poet, in a play he had written about the origin of the Court of the Areopagus, had said so.† Nobody had proved it was so. But then nobody had ever felt that it needed to be proved; and it was so much part of the accepted wisdom that to suggest otherwise would at the time have seemed absurd.

The Epicureans, of course, believed that their atomist theory had actually proved that death ended everything for the individual concerned. There was no possibility of the survival of the soul, let alone of resurrection of the body. Perhaps their laughter was the loudest of all.

But then the Epicureans also believed that their atomist theory had proved that atoms were unsplittable. That was why the things were called atoms. To suggest that they could be split would have seemed to them to be contrary to all reason. They would have laughed at that as well.‡

MOVEMENT 3: God's Messiah and the New People of God (18:1–28)

There were two buildings in Corinth standing cheek by jowl. One was a synagogue, the other a private house. The Jews met for their worship and study of the Scriptures in one, the Christians in the other. Juxtaposed, yet separated; nothing, scarcely, could have expressed more eloquently or more poignantly the breach that had occurred between Jews and Christians in Corinth. How it came to be, what it signified, and what were its implications, is

---

*See F. F. Bruce's rendering in his *The Book of the Acts*, New International Commentary on the New Testament (Grand Rapids, MI: Wm B. Eerdmans; ²1988), p. 342.

† Aeschylus, *Eumenides*, 647–8.

‡ Modern Epicureans (if there were any!) would perhaps have held that sub-atomic particles are unsplittable.

to be the subject of Movement 3. And since what happened at Corinth would eventually repeat itself throughout the whole Gentile world, its stories reverberate still.

Time and time again Paul, as the apostle to the Gentiles, was at the fracture-point when such divisions took place; and the repeated and long-continued sorrow of it broke his heart (Rom. 9:1–3). It was triply sad. In the first place, for Jews and Christians, who both worshipped the same God and believed in the same Scriptures, to have to advertise their differences in this way before the eyes of a pagan city like Corinth did nothing to strengthen their common witness to the true God and against the prevailing idolatry and immorality of that city. And for the Jews to prosecute Christianity before the Roman court, and try to get it banned, as they later did, was heartbreaking.

Secondly, Judaism had done a noble job among the Gentiles, leading many of them to faith in God, teaching them God's Word, and holding out to them the glorious hope of Israel that 'The Root of Jesse will spring up, one who will arise to rule over the nations; the Gentiles will hope in him' (Isa. 11:10; Rom. 15:12). Titius Justus, the Roman, the man whose house adjoined the synagogue, had become a worshipper of God through their influence. It was sad to see the synagogue now repulsing such Gentiles who had come to believe that Jesus was that root of Jesse; and not only them but other Gentiles, who in ever-increasing numbers came to believe in the Lord Jesus, and through believing in him were brought to abandon their pagan idolatries and put their faith in the true God of Israel. When those Gentile Christians in turn tried to witness to their fellow Gentiles that their pagan deities were false, and that the only true God was the God the Jews worshipped, the synagogue's attitude to the Gentile Christians would complicate their task enormously.

Overwhelmingly saddest of all for Paul, true son of Israel that he was, were the unavoidable implications for his fellow nationals of their rejection of him whose name is the only name under heaven given among men by which we must be saved. The problem they raised called undeniably for a theological explanation. All true Christians believed – and still do – that Israel was a special nation, chosen by God to be his people, and honoured with the role of being God's witness to the pagan world, to proclaim the unique glory of the Creator and Saviour of men (Isa. 43:10–13) and to point to the coming of God's Messiah as the Light and Redeemer of the Gentiles (Isa. 42:1–9). What if Israel, God's official witness, now refused to recognise the Messiah God sent, slandered his name (18:6) and did their best to stop Gentiles believing in him? Did that invalidate the Old Testament's claim that Israel was God's chosen people and carried this God-appointed role? No, Christians could not accept that; the very gospel they preached assumed the truth of the Old Testament Scriptures (Rom. 1:2–3; 3:21) and depended on it for validation. What, then, was happening to Israel, to their position as the people of God, to their role as witnesses for God? How could the situation be explained? How should it be understood?

In between his tent-making, his preaching and his travelling Paul thought long and sorrowfully over the whole vexed question. The answer God gave him bowed his heart in profound worship at the wisdom of God's ways and strategies, designed 'so that he might have mercy on all'; and when he eventually returned to Corinth he wrote the answer at length in a letter he sent to the Christians at Rome (Rom. 9–11). The message he received from the Lord in a vision one night during his first stay at Corinth was to contribute its share to that answer.

In the meantime Luke, aware of the far-reaching significance of what happened at Corinth (and elsewhere, at Ephesus for example) records not only the story of Paul's first visit to Corinth, but the story of a certain Apollos' visit to Corinth as well. The record of both visits is heavy with a sense of God's providential guidance. It was no accident that after Paul's witness to the Jews at Corinth had been rejected by the synagogue and Paul had left the city, Apollos the learned Jewish expositor of the Old Testament from Alexandria should arrive, and, from his particular viewpoint, reinforce Paul's witness to these same Jews that the Messiah was indeed Jesus (18:5 and 27–28).

Corinth, the first period: The formation of the new people of God

At the beginning of Movement 2 we heard of Jews accusing the Christians before the magistrates of acting contrary to the decrees of Caesar and of fomenting political unrest (17:6–8). At the beginning of Movement 3 we are now to read of the Caesar at Rome and how one of his decrees, without his knowing it, led to the establishment of a large Christian church at Corinth.

The story goes as follows. Apparently (see p. 6), the arrival in Rome of Jews converted to Christianity eventually led to disturbances in one or more of the synagogues in Rome; and the Emperor Claudius reacted by issuing a decree banning all Jews from the city. How long the ban lasted we do not know; but at the outset it must have seemed a disaster to the Christians, most of whom, naturally, were Jews. In actual fact, not only were the Jews eventually allowed to return and Christianity to flourish there, but Claudius' decree led to a significant advance for the gospel elsewhere.

A Jewish couple, named Aquila and Priscilla, expelled from Rome like all other Jews, looked around (as Lydia had once done) for a suitable place where they could carry on their business, which happened to be tent-making; and it so happened that they chose Corinth. That city was a famous port, as well as being a beautiful and wealthy place; from a business point of view it was a sensible choice.

Not long after they had settled in Corinth, Paul arrived in the city. He was alone, had no funds, and to earn his keep was obliged to work at his trade, which happened to be tent-making. And so, apparently, he happened to meet Aquila and Priscilla, who, discovering their common faith and common trade, invited him to come and stay with them and join them in their business. Fortunate coincidence, we might say; but then we remember the whole story of how Paul came to Philippi and found a foothold in the house of Lydia the business-woman. Obviously the over-rulings and the providences of God are the warp which makes the woof of these stories show up a continuing pattern. For the next three months, then, it gave the penurious Paul a chance to earn his living, recoup his expenses, and gain a foothold in the city until his colleagues Silas and Timothy arrived from Macedonia with a gift from the newly established churches there (2 Cor. 11:9), which allowed Paul to leave his tent-making and mount a major evangelistic assault on the city by devoting his full time to preaching (18:5).

The burden of his message to the Jews was, as usual, that the Messiah of the Old Testament Scriptures was in fact Jesus (18:5). The synagogue's opposition eventually erupted in abuse, as it had done in other places. So Paul left the synagogue, taking with him the ruler of the synagogue and all his household, and established a Christian church next door, which was further strengthened by an influx of Gentile Corinthians who believed and were baptised (18:6–8). But we cannot help noticing the solemnity of the words Paul used on this occasion as he left the synagogue. When a similar situation arose in Pisidian Antioch some years earlier, Paul declared: 'We had to speak the word of God to you [the Jews] first. Since you reject it and do not consider yourselves worthy of eternal life, we now turn to the Gentiles' (13:46). His words to the synagogue at Corinth were graver still: 'Your blood be on your own heads! I am clear of my responsibility. From now on I will go to the Gentiles' (18:6).

Let it be said once again – for it cannot be said too many times – that Paul was not here giving vent to and licensing anti-Semitism. He was speaking with that same awesome sense of responsibility that all Israel's true prophets have always felt, Ezekiel in particular (Ezek. 3:16–21; 33:1–5), and above all the Lord Jesus himself (Luke 10:10–16; 11:49–52; 13:34–35; 19:41–44). No true man of God can believe himself charged by God to deliver a message from God that is vital for the salvation of his fellow men, and simultaneously believe that he can with impunity to himself or others compromise that message in the face of opposition, and comfort those who reject it with the thought that their rejection of God's word and salvation will not inevitably prove disastrous. Far from treacherously seeking revenge on his own Jewish flesh and blood, Paul was telling them that under God he had been made responsible for them; that he had done all he could to save them; and only now, when their continued abusive opposition made it impossible for him to do more, did he feel himself discharged from his responsibility and free, however reluctantly, to leave them to suffer the inevitable consequences of their opposition. He had a similar responsibility from God for the Gentiles. If his fellow Jews felt that they must not only reject the Messiah and Saviour themselves, but abuse both him and his message in front of the Gentiles in the synagogue, then he must remove himself next door, where he could fulfil in peace his God-given responsibility to Gentiles who wanted to hear about the Saviour.

So Paul left the synagogue, and the grief of it, and the constantly renewed sorrow of seeing the Jews meeting in one building and the Christians meeting separately in the building next door, bore upon his heart; and doubtless it began to raise ever more acutely the theological questions mentioned above.

One night the Lord spoke to Paul in a vision to encourage him to persist in his preaching; and it was not simply what he said, but it was the terms he used in saying it, that proved so fruitful in Paul's understanding of the developing situation. Only, we must be careful not to miss the overtones of the biblical language as we read the words that accompanied the vision. 'Do not be afraid,' said the Lord, 'keep on speaking, do not be silent. For I am with you, and no-one is going to attack and harm you, because I have many people in this city' (18:9–10). If we are not careful we shall read the phrase 'many people' as if it meant simply 'many persons'; as though all the Lord was saying was 'A lot of individuals in this city are going to get converted.' That would have been true, of course; but in focusing on individuals, it puts the emphasis in the wrong place. The Greek word in question, *laos*, refers to people as a group, a crowd, or a nation. Its plural does not mean 'persons', 'individuals', but 'peoples' (that is 'nations'). The older English of the Authorised Version conveys the connotation rather better: 'I have much people'. Even so, to get the full flavour of the expression in this context, we must recall that *laos* is the translation of the Hebrew word that throughout the Old Testament designates the nation Israel: 'My people', God calls them. He explained through Moses (Deut. 7:7–8) that he did not choose them because they were a numerous people; they were, in fact, few in number compared with other peoples. But he loved them and chose them, and they became his people.

And now the Lord is telling Paul that he has 'much people' in Corinth, who are now to form 'his people' in the same sense that Israel was for many centuries 'his people'. The difference is that in Old Testament times, while Israelites were 'the Lord's people', Gentiles were not. Now there had come a change: the Lord's people were to be made up of Gentiles as well as of Jews.

In the months that followed, both in Corinth and after he left, Paul naturally turned these words of the Lord over and over in his mind. He saw them, of course, as an expression of the magnificent grace of God, that Gentiles who in previous centuries were not God's people should now be given status as the people of God.* But Paul also came to see that God's conferring of this status on Gentiles who believed was not some emergency plan hastily thought up in reaction to the rejection of the Messiah by those who till now had been his people. God had long foreseen that rejection, and had formulated his plans to deal with it when it occurred.

We discover from Romans 9:23–26 a passage that Paul found especially illuminating in this connection: the opening chapters of Hosea. In the far off days when that prophet lived, the ten tribes of Israel had so departed from God that God commanded Hosea to inform them in his name that 'you are not my people, and I am not your God' (Hos. 1:9). The ten tribes, then, were disowned. But such was God's grace that in the very next breath

---

*cf. Peter's remarks in 1 Peter 2:9–10.

(1:10) he announced that the day would come when the ten tribes who were now 'Not my people' would be reinstated: 'In the place where it was said to them, "You are not my people", they will be called "sons of the living God".' A little later God repeated the same promise: 'I will say to those called "Not my people", "You are my people"; and they will say, "You are my God"' (2:23).

Paul took great comfort from those promises: even if the bulk of Israel were now about to reject the Messiah and to fall, they would certainly be restored one day; and Paul indignantly rejected the idea that God had, or ever would, finally and permanently cast off his (ancient) people Israel whom he foreknew. The nation as a whole were stumbling, that is true. But not irrevocably! One day, in fact, the nation as a whole would be saved (Rom. 11:1–2, 11, 26).

But more. In the terms in which God had centuries ago announced Israel's restoration, Paul discerned both God's well laid plans and intentions to extend to Gentiles the honour of becoming his people and also the principle on which he would do it. When Israel came to be restored, they would first have to acknowledge that they had forfeited the right to be called 'God's people'. God had pronounced them 'Not my people'. If he forgave and restored them, and conferred on them once more the honoured status of being called 'My people', it would be an action of God's pure undeserved grace. It followed then that if God's grace was prepared to, and free to, do that for Israelites who had ceased to be 'God's people', he could certainly confer the same salvation and honour on believing Gentiles who in the past had never been 'God's people'.

It was of this then that the Lord was reminding Paul in his vision during the night at Corinth. Paul had known it before, of course. As long ago as the conference in Jerusalem (15:14) James had reminded all present that God had now begun 'to take from the Gentiles a people for himself'. But the Lord's statement at Corinth was more than a reminder. It made Paul worshipfully aware that the Lord who was with him had masterminded the strategy for the evangelisation of the world. 'I have many people in this city', he told Paul; and because of that 'no-one is going to attack and harm you, for I am with you' (18:9). God had always known what he intended to do at Corinth, and what its outcome would be. That is why (unknown to Claudius) he had used Claudius' decree to bring Aquila and Priscilla to Corinth just in time to give Paul the foothold he needed in the city. Indeed from God's point of view it was no accident that much earlier still

Aquila and Priscilla and Paul (or their parents) had all of their own initiative decided that they would take up tent-making as a trade.

Now their being 'the people of God' conferred on Israel the honour of being what Paul was later to refer to as the great olive tree of God's witness to the world (Rom. 11:17–24). If the Jews in the synagogue at Corinth finally rejected the Lord Jesus as Messiah, and abused both him and his gospel in front of the Gentiles, then by their own action they disqualified themselves from their God-given role; their particular branch would be broken off from the olive tree. But God had never been at a loss what to do next. He had foreseen it. Many Gentiles (along, of course, with some of the Jews like Crispus and his family) would believe on the Lord Jesus as the Messiah and be baptised. He would confer on them the honour of being 'the people of God' every bit as much as Israel had ever been. Wild olive branches though they had been – very wild, some of them (1 Cor. 6:9–11) – they would be grafted on to the olive tree (Rom. 11:17). They would become the Lord's witnesses in Corinth.

What happened in Corinth would eventually happen all over the world. Witness to the true God would be carried on predomi-nantly, though not exclusively, by Gentile believers – until the time when, according once more to God's master strategy, the success of that witness in bringing billions of once pagan idol-atrous Gentiles to faith in the God of Abraham, Isaac and Jacob would provoke hitherto unbelieving Israel to jealousy, to repent-ance and to restoration as the people of God and as witnesses for him in the world (Rom. 11:13–14).

Corinth, the second period: The renewed appeal to the ancient people of God

When the synagogue's opposition to the claim of Jesus to be the Messiah led in fact to the founding of a vigorous and increasing Christian church next door, the Jews made another attempt to oppose if not destroy Christianity in the city: they prosecuted Paul before the newly arrived Roman governor, Gallio. They alleged that Paul was persuading people 'to worship God in ways contrary to the law' (18:13). There is some dispute over what exactly this charge implied. It is unlikely that they were accusing Paul of political treason, as the businessmen in Thessalonica did (17:6–7); for in that case Gallio could not have dismissed the case as summarily as he did.

The better understanding of the charge is that by 'contrary to the law' they meant contrary to the Jewish law. They were claiming that Paul's belief that the Messiah was Jesus was so fundamentally contrary to the beliefs of Judaism that neither he nor his one-third Jewish and two-thirds Gentile church next door with all their peculiar practices had a right to be regarded as a valid part of Judaism any more.

The point of pressing such a charge against the Christians before the Roman governor was this. The Jews in Corinth (as in other cities) were an 'authorised community', that is, they were authorised by the Roman government and therefore enjoyed all the privileges of such an authorised community and the protection of the Roman law. What they wanted to establish, therefore, was that since the Christians' beliefs put them outside the pale of Judaism, they were no longer part of its authorised community; they were not an authorised community in their own right; they could not claim the protection of the Roman law; and perhaps* they deserved punishment for operating without the necessary authorisation.

The validity of their case turned on whether the beliefs of the Christians were such fundamental heresy and as incompatible with true Judaism as the local synagogue claimed. That, of course, was a theological question; and Gallio ruled that it was no business of a Roman court of law to pronounce upon the matter. 'If you Jews were making a complaint about some misdemeanour or serious crime, it would be reasonable for me to listen to you. But since it involves questions about words and names and your own law – settle the matter yourselves. I will not be a judge of such things' (18:14–15).

So Gallio dismissed the case and had the Jews ejected from the court. Whereupon the anti-Semitism which was never far below the surface in a Gentile city boiled over: the public rounded on the Jewish ruler of the synagogue and gave him a beating in front of the court. Gallio, we are told, showed no concern whatever. But then people of other faiths or no faith at all can soon get very tired when sectarian disputes between members of what seems to them the same faith lead one party to try to get an advantage over the other party by taking it to law. Few things disgust the general public more.

---

* As F. F. Bruce suggests in his *The Book of the Acts*, New International Commentary on the New Testament (Grand Rapids, MI: Wm B. Eerdmans, [2]1988), p. 353. See also C. J. Hemer, *The Book of Acts in the Setting of Hellenistic History*, ed. Conrad H. Gempf (Tübingen: J. C. B. Mohr, 1989), pp. 119–20.

The sequel

Gallio's ruling doubtless made life more comfortable for the Christians at Corinth – and perhaps elsewhere too – but it could not settle the basic dispute between Judaism and Christianity. Of course not. That dispute, and all others like it, cannot be settled by any human court of law. Final settlement must await the day of which Paul spoke to the Athenians, when God will judge the world in righteousness by that Man whom he has appointed (17:31).

Some considerable time after Gallio delivered his judgement, Paul left Corinth for Syria; and Luke now compresses into a few verses (18:18–23) – just as he did at the beginning of Section Five when Paul was led to Europe – Paul's lengthy travels via Ephesus, Caesarea (and probably Jerusalem), and then home to base at Antioch; and after that the beginnings of his third missionary journey through the regions of Galatia and Phrygia.

Almost no other details of these extensive travels are given, except this crucial information: crucial, that is, for what God still wanted to say to the Jews at Corinth. When Paul left Corinth he took Aquila and Priscilla with him. Perhaps the Jews at Corinth heaved a sigh of relief to see these disturbers of the peace depart. But if so, their peace was not to last long.

When Paul reached Ephesus, he went as usual to the synagogue – there was as yet no Christian church there – and reasoned with the Jews (18:19). As often happened, he was initially well received and invited to stay longer. But a pressing sense of the will of God made him decline and he left with the promise 'I will come back if it is God's will' (18:21). So off he went, leaving Aquila and Priscilla behind him at Ephesus: and they of course continued to attend the synagogue.

One sabbath a man from Alexandria turned up. His name was Apollos, and some of the scholarship for which that city had earlier been famous seems to have rubbed off on him. He was a very learned man with an expert knowledge of the Old Testament scriptures, and spiritually on fire. He had been instructed in the Way of the Lord, but only to a certain point; what he taught about Jesus was accurate enough, Luke explains, as far as it went; but the only baptism he knew was the baptism of John. Nonetheless he proceeded to put what he knew to good effect in the synagogue. John's baptism and what it stood for was not all there was to know or experience about Christianity, as the first story in Movement 4 will show us when we get that far. But for Israel it was a very important prelude to, and preparation for, the coming of the Messiah. John was Messiah's official precursor, and his baptism served two functions. Objectively, it served to announce the Messiah and point him out to Israel: he was the One who when he came, as he was about to, would baptise men and women in the Holy Spirit (Luke 3:15–17). But subjectively, it was designed to prepare the people by opening their eyes to recognise the Messiah when he appeared and to 'see' his salvation in their personal experience. The absolutely indispensable preparation, according to John, was repentance. John was a Jewish prophet in the classical mode. His preaching was an exposure and denunciation of the nation's sinfulness; his baptism both a summons to repentance and a public expression of it on the part of those who received it (Luke 3:2–6). Without that repentance not even Israel herself would recognise the Messiah when he came.

Basically, all human beings are the same. Paul's message to the Athenians, whether they were religious or philosophical or both, was a divine summons to own their ignorance and sinfulness, and to repent. John's message to Israel had been the same. Now here was Apollos, taking the Jews of Ephesus back over recent history to John's baptism, as he sought to convince them that Jesus was the Messiah and to prepare them to receive salvation.

Of course there was more to the Christian gospel than the baptism of John; and when Priscilla and Aquila heard Apollos preach they invited him home and explained the way of God to him more adequately. It was very providential that they happened to be in Ephesus at the time and were able to do this for him before he went, as he later did, to Corinth; for otherwise it might have been a little embarrassing and confusing for the recent converts in the new Christian church there to have among them such a learned Old Testament scholar and Christian preacher who knew less about Christianity than they did.

As it was, he went to Corinth fully equipped and 'was a great help to those who by [God's] grace had believed. For he vigorously refuted the Jews in public debate, proving from the Scriptures that Jesus was the Christ [Messiah]' (18:27–28). In spite of the division between the Jews and the Christians there were apparently channels of communication still open. Apollos made the best use of them; and we may be sure he did not forget to remind them of John's baptism, its historical significance, and its moral and spiritual importance.

And that was kind of God to arrange this final testimony to the Jews at Corinth. One is reminded of what happened during

Christ's final week in Jerusalem. The chief priests, teachers of the law and leaders of the people had by this time made up their minds to destroy him; and they accosted him as he was preaching the gospel to the people. Imperiously they demanded that he tell them what authority he had to do the things he was doing, and who gave him that authority.

He replied by asking another question. 'Tell me,' he said, 'John's baptism – was it from heaven, or from men?' They at once saw the far-reaching implications of the question; and in front of the crowd as they were, they found the question unanswerable (Luke 19:47–20:8).

The Jews at Corinth had likewise abusively rejected the Jesus whom Paul had preached to them as their Messiah; and had publicly denounced the Christians before the Roman governor. Now Paul was gone, and the infant church might well have quaked in its shoes. But God sent them Apollos to conduct public debate with the Jews; Apollos, that mighty biblical scholar and exegete, whose strong point was the significance of John's baptism. He was a great help to the believers, says Luke. Let's hope that in God's mercy he was a help to many in the synagogue as well; for very often it is not intellectual difficulties, but failure to repent of sin that keeps people from seeing that Jesus is the Christ.

MOVEMENT 4: The Holy Spirit and the Name of the Lord Jesus (19:1–20)

Movement 4 returns to the theme that was so prominent in Movement 1: the Holy Spirit in contrast with the evil spirits of paganism. Movement 4 will bring that theme to a grand climax with the triumph of the word of the Lord over the spiritism and occult practice for which the city of Ephesus was so famous.

In this connection Movement 4 also emphasises the name of the Lord Jesus. In the first half of the movement, it is when the twelve disciples of verses 1–7 are baptised in the name of the Lord Jesus that they receive the Holy Spirit. In the second half of the movement, it is the attempted misuse of the name of the Lord Jesus by certain Jewish exorcists (19:13) that leads to their defeat by an evil spirit (19:15–16) and thus to a further enhancement of the name of the Lord Jesus throughout Ephesus (19:17).

This emphasis brings us back to that basic essential in the Christian gospel which filled the first section of Acts: the relation of the risen Lord Jesus to the Holy Spirit of God. The pouring out of the Holy Spirit by the ascended Jesus demonstrated that God had made him both Lord (in the highest possible sense of that term) and Messiah (2:33–36). The pouring out of the Holy Spirit made available to all who would believe on the Lord Jesus a spiritual status and experience higher than ever was available before. But now Movement 4 analyses for us the experience of two very different groups of Jews whose experience of the Lord Jesus and of the Holy Spirit was defective; and thereby it shows us once more, and from this special point of view, what true Christianity is.

Paul's stay in Ephesus (1): The Holy Spirit and inadequate Christian experience

The case of the twelve men at Ephesus has been and still is much disputed, and therefore our attempt to understand it must try to follow the thought-flow of the narrative as closely as possible.

The twelve men are called 'disciples'; disciples of whom is not specified, and therefore we may presume that the expression here, as elsewhere in Acts, means that they were, or claimed to be, disciples of the Lord Jesus. On meeting them Paul asked 'Did you receive the Holy Spirit when you believed?' (19:2). Probably the reason he put such a question to them was that he sensed a spiritual lack in them. But whether he did or not, their reply revealed that there was indeed a deficiency in their spiritual experience. 'We never even heard if there is a Holy Spirit' they said (19:2). Their expression seems strange, but resembles the one used in John 7:39: 'the Spirit was not yet, for Jesus had not yet been glorified'. The meaning in John 7:39 is clear: the Holy Spirit had not yet come, and would not come until the Lord Jesus rose from the dead and ascended (see John 16:7); which is why many versions render the verse 'the Spirit had not yet been given . . .' Presumably a similar meaning is to be attached to the twelve men's reply. But how could it be that disciples of the Lord Jesus should not have heard that the Holy Spirit had come? Where had they been all the time? And in what sense were they disciples if that was so?

'Then what baptism did you receive?' Paul asked. 'John's baptism,' they replied. And that explained things. John's baptism was a baptism of repentance, as we have just been considering. Those who accepted it were responding to John's call to repent in order to prepare themselves for the coming of the Messiah. These men, then, had repented, had sincerely confessed their sins, had been baptised publicly to express their repentance, and had doubtless done their best since then to live consistently with the stand they had taken.

Now repentance is certainly necessary to becoming a Christian, but by itself it is not enough. Something else is needed. And what that something is Paul proceeded to tell them by pointing out what John the Baptist himself had said was necessary in addition to repentance. 'John's baptism', said Paul, 'was a baptism of repentance. He told the people *to believe in the one coming after him*, that is, in Jesus' (19:4).

This obviously was new to them; for if it had not been, why would Paul have pointed it out to them? And why did hearing it prove to be so crucial and decisive in their experience? 'On hearing this,' Luke says, 'they were baptised in the name of the Lord Jesus. When Paul placed his hands on them, the Holy Spirit came on them' (19:6). Not only so. Their case set a precedent. It was to show for all time to come the vital difference between a disciple who has repented but not yet personally believed on the Lord Jesus, and one who has so believed. So on that occasion the Holy Spirit publicly marked the difference by a special and evident sign: 'the Holy Spirit came on them, and they spoke in tongues and prophesied'.

The classical statement of the steps necessary to becoming a Christian in the true and full sense of the term is given by Paul later in Acts, in his address to the elders of the church at Ephesus (20:21). There are two steps, not just one: repentance before God *and* faith in our Lord Jesus. That it is possible to take the first step without taking the second is shown by this very story of the twelve men; and it is to be feared that there may be many people still in virtually the same position as they were before they met Paul. These people, too, have sincerely repented; they constantly confess their sins to God; and in a general way they accept as a fact that Jesus is the Saviour of the world. But on their own admission they lack peace with God and assurance in their hearts that they will most certainly be saved through Christ from the wrath of God. Now it is the delight of the Holy Spirit to impart this peace and assurance to all who believe on the Lord Jesus (Rom. 5:1–11). Where therefore this peace and assurance are lacking, one reason could be that the person concerned has taken the first step of repentance, but has never yet taken the second, maybe through lack of understanding of what it means personally to believe on the Lord Jesus, or like the twelve men at

Ephesus through not knowing that there is this second step to be taken.

A question remains. Why, when these men believed, did Paul insist that they be baptised all over again? They had been baptised once with John's baptism. Why make them be baptised again, this time in the name of the Lord Jesus? We may be sure that it was not for narrow-minded legalistic or ritualistic reasons. It was to make the necessary and healthy point: people who have not yet personally believed on the Lord Jesus are not yet Christians in the full and true sense of the word. When for the first time they take that happy step and become believers, it is then, and only then, meaningful for them to be baptised in the name of the Lord Jesus. It would have been a sad dereliction of duty on Paul's part to allow the world to think that the deficient, Spirit-less experience of the twelve men before they believed was true, full-blooded Christianity.

The deficiency in the twelve men's experience had an obvious cause: their lack of knowledge of the word of the Lord. And it follows that the way to make good that kind of spiritual deficiency is to preach and expound the word of God. It is invigorating to read how Paul proceeded to set about the task. For three months he preached boldly in the synagogue. When, as earlier in Corinth, the synagogue rejected his message and publicly maligned the Way, Paul left them, took the disciples with him to the lecture hall of a certain Tyrannus, where he discoursed day after day for a solid two years, until all who lived in the province of Asia, whether Jews or Greeks, heard the word of the Lord (19:8–10). As a result, not only was the church in Ephesus founded and built up: churches also sprang up in places that Paul never visited himself, as converts of his preaching at Ephesus turned into preachers of the word themselves. The church at Colosse, founded by Paul's convert Epaphroditus, was but one example.

Paul's stay in Ephesus (2): Evil spirits and bogus Christian practice

The story of the spirit-medium in Philippi has already made the point that Christianity is to be distinguished from spiritism; that it is indeed uncompromisingly opposed to spiritism. Now the last major story in Movement 4, and in Section Five as a whole, returns to a similar point and underlines it: Christianity is not magic, either black or white; it is its relentless enemy.

Ephesus was famous even in the ancient world for every form of magic and occult practice; and that is saying something, when the whole of the ancient world was awash with it. Unfortunately magic was not only prevalent in the pagan world: it had invaded certain levels of Judaism, just as in later centuries it invaded Christendom, and still does to this day. 'To fail to consider magic', writes Dr P. S. Alexander, 'would be to neglect an area of immense importance in the study of early Judaism . . . Magic flourished among the Jews despite strong and persistent condemnation by the religious authority.'* We are now to see a sorry example of that; and the point of the story, as of Luke's record of it, is to expose the pretence of magic to be a legitimate form or application of Christianity.

But first, in our reaction against magic we must avoid going to the opposite, equally wrong, extreme. The New Testament everywhere shows its belief in the existence of a personal devil, and of evil spirits, and of the possibility of demon-possession and the necessity of exorcism. Liberal theology has often denied the existence of these things, and has either assigned them to the overheated imagination of Christians living in a pre-scientific age, or accounted for them as elements of magic that slipped into primitive Christianity from the surrounding pagan world. But that will not do. Such explanations impugn the authority and the practice of the Lord Jesus himself. He is often reported as having cast out evil spirits; and someone who was so mistaken over the problem of evil as to wrestle with non-existent spirits would thereby forfeit all claim to be the Saviour of the world, let alone God incarnate.

This very passage of Acts begins by listing extraordinary miracles that God did through Paul while he was in Ephesus. But they were not magic. Observe Luke's careful language in verse 11: God did the miracles, through Paul's instrumentality. On this occasion God used unusual methods. Luke not only admits it, he calls attention to it. God even used Paul's handkerchiefs and aprons. But it was God who exercised the power and did the miracles; there was no magical power in the handkerchiefs and aprons. When an officer of the Queen lays his staff of office on someone's shoulder and commands him to do this or that, the rod certainly expresses the Queen's authority delegated to the officer

---

*See E. Schurer, *The History of the Jewish People in the Age of Jesus Christ*, vol. 3.1, revised and edited by G. Vermes, F. Millar, M. Black (Edinburgh: T. & T. Clark, 1979), p. 342.

and backs the command; but there is no magical power in the rod itself. What then is the difference between what Paul did and what the seven Jews did (or attempted to do) of whom we are about to read?

The ancient world, as we have said, was full of practitioners of the occult who went around making a living by claiming to cure illnesses and cast out demons. Among them were Jews, and from among them Luke calls our attention to one particular family, a father and seven sons. The father, says Luke, was a Jewish chief priest. We have no way of knowing whether this was a bogus title that the man had assumed in order to boost his professional prestige, or whether he was in reality a son of a Jewish chief-priestly family. If the latter, it is a very sorry sight to see a man from such a background so spiritually debased. Be that as it may, his seven sons, like many of the other Jewish magicians, took to invoking the name of the Lord Jesus over those who were demon-possessed. They would say 'In the name of Jesus, whom Paul preaches, I command you to come out' (19:13). And there is the essence of superstition and magic as distinct from faith.

'But surely', someone will protest, 'they must have had faith in Jesus to invoke his name. After all, they made their living by practising exorcism and such like things, and obviously they were not going to use a name in which they had no faith.'

But that raises the question once more, What is faith? The fact that these men regarded the name of Jesus as having a certain potency does not imply that they believed in the Lord Jesus in the biblical sense of the phrase. It was part of the technique of pagan exorcists, for instance, to include among the many names which they used as spells and incantations the Old Testament name of God. C. J. Hemer cites as an example a heathen plaque from Puteoli, containing an invocation which includes the words Sabaoth, the holy name Iao (= Yahweh), and El, along with names such as Michael and Nephtho;* and the much-quoted 'Magical Papyrus' at Paris contains the phrase 'I adjure you by Jesus, the God of the Hebrews'. By New Testament times the name of God, 'Yahweh', was regarded by the Jews as being so sacred that in orthodox circles no one would pronounce it. They used, as they still do today, a substitute. It had thus become a kind of secret name, and in the eyes of practitioners of magic the

---

*C. J. Hemer, *The Book of Acts in the Setting of Hellenistic History*, ed. Conrad H. Gempf (Tübingen: J. C. B. Mohr, 1989), p. 121.

knowledge of this secret name gave them great power. It was a name to conjure with, literally.

The pagans' use of God's name in this fashion clearly did not imply genuine faith in God. Quite the reverse. Their use in one and the same breath of both the name of God and that of the archangel Michael and of Nephtho was by implication a denial of the uniqueness of God: Iao (a form of Yahweh) was to them simply one powerful name among many. That was in itself blasphemous.* In addition, it took no account of the moral character of God: Iao to them was simply a supernatural spirit-power, and all they were interested in was to bend this power to their use. They were no more interested in the moral character of God than a modern man is concerned about the moral character of the electricity he plugs into. Indeed, it was not God as a Person that they were interested in; it was simply his name, used as a spell or incantation.

The same was true of Sceva's sons. They were not interested in Christ's moral teaching, nor in his spiritual teaching. They had not believed on the Lord Jesus in the biblical sense of that phrase: they had not repented of sin, and sought forgiveness and rec-onciliation with God through faith in the Lord Jesus. They were not Christians: they never pretended to be. Jesus to them was simply the name of some great spirit-power in the world beyond, which could be harnessed by an expert magician for his own use so long as he knew the appropriate formula, spell or incantation for doing so. They had observed the miracles which Paul had done in the name of the Lord Jesus; and they thought that this name was a useful one to add to their repertoire. They enjoyed no personal relationship with the Lord, as is shown by the very formula they attempted to use: 'In the name of Jesus, *whom Paul preaches . . .*' (19:13). Their attitude was that of modern theosophy or of some forms of Buddhism, according to which Jesus is one of the so-called 'white-brotherhood', or a buddha who has escaped the necessity of reincarnation and is available, along with many other such beings, to help men and women if only they know and apply the right technique for inducing him to do so.

This is neither true Christian doctrine nor is it true faith. At best it is gross superstition, at worst, demonism. The particular ver-sion of it at Ephesus was exposed for what it was: it did but open

---

*Paul's expression in 1 Timothy 5:21 is a charge delivered in the presence of God, Christ Jesus and the elect angels; it is not an adjuration by their conjoint powers.

the men concerned to the counter-attack of a spirit-world that is all too real. And still today, those who claim to be able to harness the powers of the spirit world are themselves in fact not its masters but its victims.

The sequel

When the incident became known, says Luke, fear came upon all, and the name of the Lord Jesus was magnified (19:17). Indeed Luke's own studied use of 'the Lord Jesus' throughout this movement (19:5, 13, 17) contrasts markedly with the way Sceva's seven sons and the evil spirit itself refer simply to 'Jesus' (19:13, 15),* and surely sets us a pattern of due reverence.

The effect on those who were already believers was particularly healthy. The fear of spiritism sometimes dies hard in converts from paganism, reinforced as it is by the practice of their families and by social pressures. But liberated by this demonstration of the authority of the Lord Jesus, and shocked into seeing the true nature of spiritism, they came and confessed that they had been secretly continuing some of these evil practices. Many also brought their books on occult arts and made a public and very expensive bonfire of them.

'So the word of the Lord spread mightily and prevailed'; and though this comment is one of Luke's formal summaries that marks the end of this section and the beginning of the next (19:20), it is not otiose. The bulwark against superstition is faith; and true faith comes through the Word of God, its reading and its preaching (Rom. 10:17). It was with the detailed and authoritative statements of the Word of God, understood with the mind, believed in the heart and applied to the life, that the Lord Jesus himself met the temptations of the devil in the desert (Luke 4:4, 8, 12). Weaken or destroy faith in the Word of God, and what you get is not always unbelief, pure and simple, but the opening of the floodgates to the invasion of Christianity by the hoary superstitions and occult practices of both ancient and modern paganism, as for instance in the New Age Movement. All Christians need to be on their guard. The desire for instant spiritual experience can make both individuals and congregations impatient of serious Bible study and Bible-based preaching, and lead to the

---

*See 1 Corinthians 12:2–3. The endless repetition of the simple name 'Jesus' by hyper-spiritual groups, as if it were a form of incantation, is a disturbing feature.

temptation of down-playing Scripture in favour of more exciting programmes and procedures. But it is a temptation to be resisted at all costs if the real spiritual battle is to be won.

Section Six

Christianity and the Defence and Confirmation of the Gospel (19:21–28:31)

Section Six
Christianity and the Defence and Confirmation of the Gospel (19:21–28:31)

PRELIMINARY OBSERVATIONS

Another noticeable change comes over Luke's narrative in the sixth and final section of his work. The section opens with the statement that after two years and three months of sustained and remarkably profitable ministry at Ephesus, Paul developed a powerful impression in his spirit that he must go once again to Jerusalem, and after that, for the first time ever, to Rome (19:21). It was, then, with those intentions in mind that he eventually left Ephesus.

Had things gone altogether as he envisaged, he might well have found himself continuing to preach the gospel in the same way as before; and Luke's narrative might well have contained further summaries of his sermons. But it was not to be. On leaving Ephesus he went to Macedonia, encouraging the new churches. After that he spent three months in Greece, presumably doing the same. But just as he was on the point of setting sail for Syria, he discovered a plot laid against him by the local Jews; and instead of going by sea, he at first went back north overland through Macedonia. But as he pursued his journey, in every city he came to he began to run into warnings from the Holy Spirit that ahead of him lay hardships, bonds and imprisonment (20:22–24). Nothing deterred, he pressed on; but he had scarcely been two weeks in Jerusalem when the warnings began to come true. A riot broke out in the temple, with him in the middle of it. He was arrested by the Roman army; and thereafter spent the next four years as a prisoner.

Gone now were the days of freely preaching the gospel in the synagogues or in the market-places. Instead there began a succession of interrogations, judicial enquiries, appeals and trials.

337

Wearisome though they must have been, and frustrating though the intervening months and years of waiting in prison or under house-arrest must sometimes have seemed, it gave Paul many opportunities to do what he had not been required to do in quite the same way before. Hitherto he had straightforwardly preached, lectured and discussed the gospel; now he was obliged to defend it.

It needs no lengthy argument to prove Luke's wisdom in filling the remainder of his book with an account of Paul's defence. If he had chosen, Luke could doubtless have included many more examples of Paul's sermons and have told of the journeys he made, and of the churches he planted, after he was eventually released from prison. But a few more samples of his sermons would have added little to our understanding of the gospel he preached, since those sermons would not have differed in any substantial way from those whose summaries we have already been given. Nor would a description of his further journeys and church-plantings have given us significantly more information on the kind of work he did, only more about its extent.

On the other hand, we cannot read Luke's last section without realising that in the comparatively few years that Paul had been preaching the gospel and founding Christian churches throughout Asia Minor and Europe serious misunderstandings and misrepresentations, both of his gospel and of his behaviour, had been gaining widespread circulation. If these misunderstandings and misrepresentations had been allowed to take root and spread unchecked, without being publicly rebuffed and refuted, and that at the highest level, there would soon have been many places where sensible and knowledgeable people would no longer have been inclined to give the gospel so much as a hearing, let alone believe it. And what is more, many Christians themselves, especially in places like Jerusalem, confused by the prevailing but false rumours about what Paul stood for, might well have come to the conclusion that he was a dangerous maverick, if not a positive heretic. It was urgent, therefore, that Paul should take time off from his pioneer evangelism, and instead of simply preaching the gospel, defend it at the highest levels in both Jerusalem in the east and Rome in the west.

The misunderstandings and misrepresentations would not cease, of course, immediately Paul had publicly defended the gospel. There was also urgent need therefore that Luke should record his defence and give it maximum publicity in his contemporary world. And still to this present day Paul is not everywhere the best loved of the apostles nor his gospel the most readily understood and welcomed. People respond to John's expositions of the love of God; they identify with Peter, the apostle who once denied the Lord, appreciating his warm-hearted, sympathetic exhortations; and they admire James' forthright demand for right-living and practical good works. But Paul with his insistence on justification by faith through grace, and his denunciation of salvation by works, seems unattractively legalistic to some and to others the very opposite – dangerously antinomian. It was the very wisdom of God, therefore, that led Luke to devote the last section of his work to Paul's defence both of the gospel and of himself, so that we too may have any misconceptions we may have formed dispelled.

Some of the misunderstandings of Paul were simply wild. The Roman army commander who rescued him from the mob in Jerusalem thought he was the Egyptian leader of a terrorist group four thousand strong (21:37–39)! Other accusations levelled against him were at least specious. The bombastic orator hired by the Jews to conduct the prosecution's case before Felix asserted, 'We have found this man to be a troublemaker, stirring up riots among the Jews all over the world' (24:5). Well, undeniably riots had broken out over Paul and his preaching in cities like Thessalonica and Berea; but who started the riots was, as we earlier saw, another question altogether.

Other misinterpretations of Paul's doctrine and behaviour were more understandable. They arose because people had received a one-sided account of what Paul did and taught, and they had proceeded to make seemingly justified though actually false deductions from that one-sided account. As we hear Paul clear up these misinterpretations for his contemporaries, we too may well be saved from making false deductions from what we have read so far about his doctrine and practice in the earlier sections of Acts.

To take just one example. Paul would have agreed both in theory and in practice with the lesson taught to Peter in Section Three, that God had abrogated the food-laws and the laws of ritual purity that would have kept Peter from going into Gentile houses and eating with Gentiles. That old 'middle wall of partition' was broken down. Peter was not only free to eat with Gentiles, but in Christian circles he had a duty to eat with them. To refuse to eat with them, or even to refrain from eating with them, would have been an implicit denial of the gospel, as Paul on one occasion sharply reminded him (Gal. 2:11–21). But firmly as Paul believed and practised this principle, he would never have dreamed of extending it backwards from Christianity into Judaism. If and when he visited the temple at Jerusalem, he made no attempt to change its laws of ritual and ceremonial purity, nor did he disregard them. Contrary to what the Jews from Asia alleged (21:28–29), he never once attempted to bring Gentiles, not even Christian Gentiles, into the parts of the temple from which they were forbidden.

It is easy, then, to see Luke's wisdom in devoting the last section of his work to Paul's defence of the gospel. Not quite so easy to see at first sight (for many readers at least) is why he should have recorded it at such length – it forms about one third of the book – in such detail, and with what appears to be, again at first sight, a certain repetitiousness.

The massive detail can be accounted for at one level by the fact that for the greater part of this period Luke was once more a travel-companion of Paul's and an eyewitness of some of the events that took place. He was therefore in a position to have gathered a great deal of detailed information. Secondly, he obviously had an eye for a good story, a tremendous flair for vivid, detailed, accurate reporting, and a masterly ability to sketch in with a few strokes of his pen the idiosyncrasies, strengths, weaknesses, typical attitudes and reactions of the people whose stories he records. His long, detailed, technically and geographically accurate description of the shipwreck in Acts 27 is justly famous.* But so are his many delightful cameos, such as the way the army commander in his letter to the governor manages conveniently to telescope the order of events and create the impression that he discovered Paul's Roman citizenship earlier and in better circumstances than he did;† or the abrupt way in which Felix put an end to Paul's conscience-disturbing exposition of morality when he suddenly realised how it would interfere with the real purpose of his frequent visits ostensibly to learn about Paul's views (24:24–27).

We may be sure, however, that Luke had a deeper purpose than simply sketching in the circumstantial detail surrounding Paul's life during this period. Paul was set for the defence of the gospel, as he later phrased it in a letter to the church at Philippi (Phil. 1:16). But to defend the gospel adequately, he would have

---

*For a recent full discussion of its accuracy and historicity, see C. J. Hemer, *The Book of Acts in the Setting of Hellenistic History*, ed. Conrad H. Gempf (Tübingen: J. C. B. Mohr, 1989), pp. 133–52.

†cf. 23:27 with the actual facts of 21:31–39 and 22:24–29.

to do more than simply defend the gospel: he would have to defend himself, his character and behaviour. At the various public gatherings, judicial enquiries and trials, the bench and the public would of course be interested to hear his exposition of the gospel and to discover that it was not subversive political propaganda, nor the unhealthy notions of some bizarre sect. But they would also be weighing up his character and personality and sifting the reports of his past and recent behaviour, with the result that the impression they formed of the gospel itself would be inseparably bound up with, and influenced by, their assessment of Paul himself. In that sense Paul *was* the gospel.

Paul himself was of course aware of this; which is why he was not content simply to correct his accusers' version of what he had, and what he had not, done in the temple. Positively and of his own initiative he chose twice to relate at length the story of his conversion (22:1–21; 26:9–23); for the effect the gospel had had on his life and conduct, on his outlook, aspirations, goals and methods, was an integral and inescapable part of the defence of the gospel itself.

Not only Paul but Luke as well was aware of this, so that his long and detailed descriptions of Paul's attitudes, reactions and general behaviour in many and varied situations during this period would have allowed Luke's early readers – and still allow us – to watch Paul in action, to study his character and personality, to compare him with the other leading figures in the unfolding story, and so to draw their own conclusions about Paul.

What kind of a man was Paul, then? Luke's detailed narrative allows us to perceive the studied courtesy and propriety with which he behaved both towards the pagan temple at Ephesus and its objects of veneration (19:37), and towards the sanctity of the Jewish temple at Jerusalem (21:26; 24:12–13, 18); his attitude to money (20:33–35) compared with that of the businessmen at Ephesus (19:24–27) and with that of governor Felix (24:26); his moral and physical courage (20:19–20, 23–24, 27; 21:10–13; 21:31–32 with 21:39–22:21; 27:20–26, 30–35), and his balanced attitude to suffering – he was prepared to endure anything, death included, in his loyalty to the Lord Jesus and to the gospel if and when it was necessary (20:24; 21:13), and to do so without any desire for revenge (28:19); but he was not unhealthily keen to suffer unnecessarily (22:24–29; 25:10–11). In Luke's narrative we catch sight of a man who is concerned for high theology and doctrinal purity (20:30), but equally insistent on the social responsibility of the church (20:35), and a man who bears more

341

than his share of the down-to-earth practicalities of life (20:33–34; 27:30–36; 28:3). Luke faithfully records Festus' loud-spoken opinion that Paul was a crazed academic (26:24); but at the same time Luke's vividly detailed reporting allows us to make up our own minds as to where the real fanaticism lay (19:34; 23:12–13); in what sense, if at all, Paul was sectarian (24:14; 26:4–7); whether or not he was bigoted against his own nation, Israel (24:17; 28:17 –20), when he, unlike so many of them, held the superior status of Roman citizenship (22:27–28); and the way he responded to corruption when he came across it, whether in religion (23:1–3, 14–17) or in the civil administration (24:26; 25:3, 9–11).

One can, then, see some at least of the reason why Luke has filled the last section of Acts with so much detail. But what shall we say about the apparent repetitiousness? There are two riots connected with temples, one at Ephesus (19:23–41), one at Jerusalem (21:27–22:22). Two long journeys, one from Ephesus to Jerusalem (20:1–21:16), the other from Caesarea to Rome (27:1–28:16). Two enquiries, one before the Sanhedrin (22:30–23:10) and one before Festus and King Agrippa (25:23–26:32). Two formal trials, one before Felix (24:1–23) and the other before Festus (25:6–12). Two planned attempts to ambush and assassinate Paul, one on his way from the castle to the Sanhedrin in Jerusalem (23:12–21) and the other on the road from Caesarea to Jerusalem (25:2–3). Twice Paul relates his conversion (22:3–21 and 26:4–18); and twice we hear of important letters, one written by the army commander Lysias to the governor Felix (23:25–30) and one which Festus had to write to the Emperor, but did not know what to put in it, as he explained at length to King Agrippa (25:13–27).

The first thing to be said about these apparent doublets is that they recall the other set of apparent doublets which we encountered in Section One.* Upon closer inspection the apparent doublets in Section One proved not to be mere literary doublets, but accounts of real, similar but independent events. So it is here in Section Six. The apparent doublets are not the result of artistic fiction. The events they describe actually happened; and when

---

*See pp. 20–23. There are other noticeable similarities between Section Six and Section One: the arrest of Peter and John in the temple, and the arrest of Paul in the temple; the imprisonments of Peter and John (and subsequently of all the apostles), and the imprisonment of Paul; the appearance of Peter and the apostles on two occasions before the high priest and the Sanhedrin, and Paul's appearance before the high priest and the Sanhedrin; and the explicit mention of the Sadducees (4:1–6; 5:17 and 23:1–10).

we examine them closely the members of each apparent doublet, though similar, are in important respects different, and can often be shown to present different and complementary aspects of their common themes.

Paul did after all have to take two long journeys, the first to get from Ephesus to Jerusalem and the second more than two years later from Caesarea to Rome; but the conditions on the second journey were remarkably different from those on the first. There were two riots each concerning a temple; but the temple on the first occasion was a pagan temple, and it raised different questions from those at the heart of the second riot in the Jewish temple at Jerusalem.

There were two formal enquiries, both of them attempts on the part of Roman officials to get to the bottom of the Jews' allegations against Paul. But the two enquiries were held before two very different bodies. The Roman army commander, despairing of getting any sense out of the mob that was shouting for Paul's blood, brought Paul before the Sanhedrin in an attempt to find out what the real trouble was. Festus, not being able to discover the real truth from the formal trial he held, brought Paul before King Agrippa and his sister Bernice. It is good therefore to have the results of these enquiries before two such different bodies; and likewise important to have the explicit statements of both the army commander and the governor Festus that as far as they could make out Paul had committed no crime.

The original charge against Paul was that he had brought Greeks into the Jerusalem temple. That of course was a capital offence. Prominent notices stood at the appropriate places in the temple warning all Gentiles on pain of death not to proceed further. It was a prohibition enforced by both Jewish and Roman law. If it had ever been proved that Paul did indeed bring Gentiles into the temple, the Romans would have unhesitatingly handed him over to the Sanhedrin to be dealt with according to the law.

But upon investigation, repeatedly made in the course of two enquiries and two trials, the charge proved unfounded and was dropped. But the intensity of the Jews' animus against Paul continued unabated; and the Roman officials decided in the end that the real cause of it all was, as Festus put it, 'certain disputes about their own religion, and in particular about a man called Jesus who had died, but who Paul kept on claiming to be alive' (25:19).

With this we come to the heart of Paul's defence of the gospel. From his very first appearance before the Sanhedrin in Jerusalem to his eventual meeting with the elders of the Jewish community in Rome, Paul insisted that the real issue at stake was not his own behaviour but the resurrection of Jesus. The real argument between Christianity and Judaism, even to this day, is not, in spite of all that is said, about who was ultimately responsible for Christ's death. The real argument between them – and indeed between Christianity and all other religions and philosophies – is about whether Jesus, who died, really rose from the dead.

Luke has seen the importance of Paul's repeated insistence on this point; and obviously he was not deterred by fear of being charged with repetitiousness from recording it four times over:

23:6 'I stand on trial because of my hope in the resurrection of the dead.'

24:15 'I have the same hope in God as these men, that there will be a resurrection of both the righteous and the wicked.'

26:6–8 'And now it is because of my hope in what God has promised our fathers that I am on trial today . . . it is because of this hope that the Jews are accusing me. Why should any of you consider it incredible that God raises the dead?'

28:20 'It is because of the hope of Israel that I am bound with this chain.'

Of course it is easy to point out that the Pharisees, who were far more numerous than the Sadducees, believed that there would one day be a resurrection of the dead. They were certainly not prosecuting Paul in the Roman courts for believing in this resurrection. They too would have held it to be Israel's hope; but at the same time they would have disputed Paul's assertion that Jesus had been raised from the dead.

That is true as far as it goes. But it misses the real heart of the matter. If Paul had been maintaining that some otherwise unheard of private man had risen from the dead, even the Sadducees could have afforded to dismiss him as the lunatic Festus declared him to be. There would have been no cause for all the heated animosity and the persecution and prosecution of Paul.

Why then all the heat and anger? Because Paul was saying that the hope of Israel was far more than that there should be a general resurrection of the dead one day. According to Paul the hope of Israel, testified to by Moses and all the prophets, was that the Messiah must suffer (i.e. die), and then as the first to rise from the dead he was destined to proclaim light both to the people (of Israel) and to the Gentiles (26:22–23).

344

Now Jesus had claimed to be that Messiah; and in order to destroy his claim the nation's leaders had, ironically, seen to it that he died. Now they must at any cost deny that he had risen again. That was the real reason, according to Paul, why they were prosecuting him with such pertinacity and vigour; but in so doing they were denying what in fact was Israel's most glorious hope, and trying to put out the light which that resurrection shed over Israel and all the nations.

Of course they disagreed with Paul over this, as Festus rightly perceived (25:19). They disagree still. But there lies the crux of the matter.

Luke's formal arrangement of the material of this section in five movements is determined at its most basic level by the major geographical divisions of Paul's journey first to Jerusalem and then to Rome (19:21). The first movement covers the journey from Ephesus to Jerusalem (19:21–21:16).

The second relates what happened to him in Jerusalem (21:17–23:11); and it concludes with a special message from the Lord to Paul, praising the conduct of his witness in Jerusalem, and indicating that he must do similarly in Rome.

The third movement (23:12–24:27) describes how and why he was taken from Jerusalem to stand trial before the Roman governor Felix in Caesarea; and also why, although Paul was patently innocent, Felix deferred his verdict and left Paul in prison two years.

The fourth movement (25:1–26:32) tells how when Festus succeeded Felix, and a trial before Festus proved inconclusive, Festus was inclined to cede to the Jews' request for Paul to be sent back to Jerusalem to have his case further investigated there. Whereupon, to avoid this, Paul appealed to Caesar.

The fifth and final movement, therefore, describes how Paul was sent direct from Caesarea to Rome, tells what happened on the way, and concludes with a brief sketch of how he spent his time there as he waited for his case to be heard (27:1–28:31).

Of course this arrangement does more than teach us geography. How much more can be seen in part by perusal of the following table of contents.

MOVEMENT 1: The Defence of Nature-Worship and the Defence of the Church of God (19:21–21:16)	MOVEMENT 2: The Gospel to be Judged by its Respect for Conscience (21:17–23:11)	MOVEMENT 3: The Gospel to be Judged by its Attitude to Morality and the Law (23:12–24:27)	MOVEMENT 4: The Gospel to be Judged by its Message for Caesar and the World (25:1–26:32)	MOVEMENT 5: Nature's Storms and the Kingly Rule of God (27:1–28:31)
EPHESUS TO JERUSALEM	JERUSALEM	CAESAREA – FELIX	CAESAREA – FESTUS	CAESAREA TO ROME
A: THE RIOT AND ITS QUELLING (19:24–35)	A: THE RIOT AND THE RESCUE (21:17–36)	A: THE PROPOSED AMBUSH AND THE ESCAPE (23:12–24)	A: THE PROPOSED AMBUSH AND THE ESCAPE (25:1–12)	A: THE STORM, SURVIVAL AND LANDING (27:1–44)
1. *The complaint*	1. *The accusations*	1. *The plot*	1. *The plot* (25:1–3)	1. *The unwise decision* (27:1–13)
'. . . this fellow Paul has convinced and led astray large numbers of people . . . He says that man-made gods are no gods at all. There is danger that . . . the temple of the great goddess Artemis will be discredited . . .' (19:26–27)	'This . . . man . . . teaches . . . everywhere against our people and our law and this place. And . . . he has brought Greeks into the temple area and defiled this holy place' (21:28)	More than forty Jews 'bound themselves with an oath not to eat or drink until they had killed Paul' (23:12)	The Jewish leaders 'urgently requested Festus . . . to have Paul transferred to Jerusalem, for they were preparing an ambush to kill him along the way' (25:3)	'The majority decided that we should sail on, hoping to reach Phoenix . . . When a gentle south wind began to blow, they thought they had obtained what they wanted' (27:12–13)
2. *The peril*	2. *The peril*	2. *The peril*	2. *The peril* (25:4–9)	2. *The peril* (27:14–20)
'Soon the whole city was in an uproar' (19:29); '. . . friends of Paul [begged] him not to venture into the theatre' (19:31); 'they all shouted . . . for about two hours: "Great is Artemis of the Ephesians"' (19:34)	'The whole city was aroused . . . Seizing Paul . . . they were trying to kill him . . .' (21:30–31)	Paul's nephew reports the plot to the commander (23:19–22). 'The Jews have agreed to ask you to bring Paul before the Sanhedrin . . . Don't give in to them . . . more than forty of them are waiting in ambush for Paul' (23:20–21)	Festus, in all innocence, but wishing to do the Jews a favour, asks if Paul would be willing to go to Jerusalem to stand trial	'When neither sun nor stars appeared . . . and the storm continued raging, we finally gave up all hope of being saved' (27:20)

3. *The relief* 'The town clerk quietened the crowd' (19:35)	3. *The escape* The Roman commander extricates Paul (21:31–33)	3. *The escape* The Roman commander extricates Paul by sending him under guard to Caesarea (23:23–24)	3. *The escape* (25:10–12) Paul extricates himself by appealing to Caesar	3. *The escape* (27:21–44) '[Paul said] "Not one of you will be lost"; [an angel said] "God has graciously given you the lives of all who sail with you"; . . . everyone reached land in safety' (27:22, 24, 44)
B. THE MOB'S FALSE IDEAS OF PAUL CORRECTED BY THE TOWN CLERK (19:35–41)	**B. THE COMMANDER'S FALSE IDEA OF PAUL CORRECTED BY PAUL'S LANGUAGE (21:37–39)**	**B. THE COMMANDER'S LETTER TO FELIX REPORTS THAT NO CRIMINAL CHARGE HAS BEEN ESTABLISHED AGAINST PAUL (23:25–35)**	**B. FESTUS' ACCOUNT OF THE SITUATION TO AGRIPPA REBUTS THE ACCUSATION LAID AGAINST PAUL BY THE PRIESTS (25:13–22)**	**B. THE FALSE IDEAS OF THE MALTESE PEOPLE ABOUT PAUL ARE CORRECTED BY THE ACTUAL EVENTS (28:1–6)**
'these men . . . have neither robbed temples nor blasphemed our goddess' (19:37)	'Do you speak Greek? . . . Aren't you the Egyptian who started a revolt and led four thousand terrorists out into the desert . . . ?' (21:37–38)	'I found that the accusation had to do with . . . their law, but there was no charge against him that deserved death or imprisonment' (23:29)	'The Jews brought charges against him and asked that he be condemned . . . [But] when his accusers got up to speak, they did not charge him with any of the crimes I had expected. Instead, they had some . . . dispute with him . . . about their own religion' (25:15, 18–19)	'"This man must be a murderer [whom] . . . Justice has not allowed . . . to live"; . . . but after . . . a long time . . . they changed their minds and said he was a god' (28:4–6)

cont'd.

C. THE JOURNEY FROM EPHESUS TO JERUSALEM (20:1–21:16)	C. THE ROMAN COMMANDER'S INVESTIGATIONS (22:1–23:11)	C. THE TRIAL BEFORE FELIX (24:1–27)	C. THE ENQUIRY BEFORE AGRIPPA (25:23–26:32)	C. THE JOURNEY FROM MALTA TO ROME (28:7–31)
1. *To Miletus: via Macedonia, Greece, Philippi, Troas, Assos, Samos, with a seven-day stay and a miracle at Troas* (20:1–16) 'The people took the young man home alive and were greatly comforted' (20:12)	1. *Paul's defence before the mob* (22:1–21) He tells the story of his life, conversion, and commission to take the gospel to the Gentiles. 'When I returned . . . and was praying in the temple . . . The Lord said to me: "Go; I will send you . . . to the Gentiles"' (22:17–21)	1. *The case for the prosecution* (24:1–9) 'We have found this man to be a troublemaker, stirring up riots . . . He is a ringleader of the Nazarene sect and he even tried to desecrate the temple' (24:5–6)	1. *Paul's defence before Agrippa* (26:1–23) He tells the story of his life, conversion, and commission to take the gospel to the Gentiles. 'That is why the Jews seized me in the temple courts and tried to kill me' (26:21)	1. *To Rome via Syracuse, Rhegium, Puteoli, the Market of Appius, with a miracle at Malta and a seven-day stay at Puteoli* (28:7–15) 'When Paul saw the brothers he thanked God and took courage' (28:15)
2. *Paul's address to the elders of the church at Ephesus* (20:17–38) 1. 'I was severely tested by the plots of the Jews' (20:19) 2. 'I go bound in the Spirit . . . prison and hardships are facing me' (20:22–23) 3. Guard the flock against sectarian leaders (20:30–31)	2. *The commander's illegal proposal to have Paul examined under torture* (22:24–29) 'Is it legal for you to flog a Roman citizen?' (22:25); 'Tell me, are you a Roman citizen?' . . . 'Yes, I am' (22:27); 'The commander . . . was alarmed when he realised that he had put Paul, a Roman citizen, in chains' (22:29)	2. *The case for the defence* (24:10–23) 1. 'My accusers did not find me arguing with anyone at the temple, or stirring up a crowd . . . anywhere . . . in the city' (24:12) 2. 'I worship . . . God . . . as a follower of the Way, which they call a sect' (24:14)	2. *Festus' outburst* (26:24–25) 'You are out of your mind, Paul'; 'I am not insane, most excellent Festus. What I am saying is true and reasonable'	2. *Paul's briefing of the leaders of the Jewish community in Rome* (28:16–22) 1. 'I have done nothing against our people . . . [yet] I was arrested in Jerusalem and handed over to the Romans' (28:20) 2. 'It is because of the hope of Israel that I am bound with this chain' (28:20)

3. *The Holy Spirit's warnings to Paul through the prophets at Tyre and Caesarea (21:1–14)* 'The Holy Spirit says, "In this way the Jews . . . will . . . hand him over to the Gentiles"' (21:11) 4. *Paul's lodgings in Jerusalem (21:15–16)* '[They] brought us to the home of Mnason where we were to stay' (21:16)	3. *The investigation before the Sanhedrin (22:30–23:10)* Paul claims to have lived with a good conscience. The high priest orders him to be struck, contrary to the law. 'God will strike you, you whitewashed wall!' (23:3) 4. *The sequel (23:11)* 'The Lord . . . said, "Take courage! As you have testified about me in Jerusalem, so you must also testify in Rome"' (23:11)	3. 'I have the same hope . . . as these men, that there will be a resurrection' (24:15) 4. 'I came to Jerusalem to bring my people gifts' (24:17) 5. 'It is concerning the resurrection of the dead that I am on trial before you today' (24:21) 3. *Felix's conversations with Paul (24:24–26)* Paul reasons about 'righteousness, self-control and the judgment to come' (24:25). Felix is afraid, but looks for an illegal bribe. 4. *Paul's imprisonment in Caesarea (24:27)* 'When two years had passed, Felix was succeeded. . . , but . . . he left Paul in prison' (24:27)	3. *Paul's final appeal to Agrippa (26:26–29)* 'King Agrippa, do you believe the prophets?'; 'Do you think that in such a short time you can persuade me to be a Christian?' (26:28) 4. *The sequel (26:30–32)* 'This man could have been set free if he had not appealed to Caesar' (26:32)	3. 'People everywhere are talking against this sect' (28:22) 3. *The Holy Spirit's warning through Isaiah the prophet to the Jewish community in Rome (28:23–28)* 'The Holy Spirit spoke the truth. . . . God's salvation has been sent to the Gentiles, and they will listen.' (28:25, 28) 4. *Paul's lodgings in Rome (28:30–31)* 'For two whole years Paul stayed . . . in his own rented house and . . . preached the kingdom of God and taught about the Lord Jesus Christ' (28:30–31)

THE MOVEMENTS

MOVEMENT 1: The Defence of Nature-Worship and the Defence of the Church of God (19:21–21:16)

The major item in the first half of Movement 1 is the story of the massive riot which the citizens of Ephesus staged in order to protect their religion against the threat, as they perceived it, of Christianity (19:23–41). Before we condemn them for this, we should observe that the major item in the second half of Movement 1 is Paul's appeal to the Christian elders at Ephesus to protect the church of God from both external and internal threats (20:17–31).

It is instinctive to defend ourselves when attacked. If people really believe the religion they profess to believe, then when they feel that all they count most sacred in life is under threat, they will understandably rise to defend it. If they did not, either their faith or their loyalty would be questionable. So it was, then, both with the worshippers of Artemis and with the worshippers of the Lord Jesus in Ephesus.

But if we cannot criticise people for defending their faith, we can ask questions about the methods they adopt in its defence. And since very often the methods of defence people adopt will be conditioned by the nature of the faith they are defending, we must ask questions in this direction also of the two instances presented to us in this movement.

Nature-worship and its defence

The goddess Artemis, to whose worship the vast temple at Ephesus was dedicated, was something of a composite figure. She was thought of both as a chaste virgin and yet at the same time as the divine mother of all. In both her capacities she was felt to be a goddess of protection. As a chaste virgin, known as 'She of the Wild', she was the protectress of all wild animals, and particularly of their young. Simultaneously, she was the patron goddess of hunters. 'This is not so contradictory as it sounds,' writes W. K. C. Guthrie:

> The huntsman never regards himself as the enemy of the creatures he hunts. The fox is supposed to enjoy the chase, the owner of estates speaks of 'preserving' game and likes to visit with heavy penalties

those who disturb it at the wrong time or in the wrong way. Their sanction is now the law, but in ancient time it was religion. Perhaps the earliest example of a game preserve is the grove of Artemis where Agamemnon slew the deer and was visited by the wrath of the divine gamekeeper.*

Artemis, however, was not thought of simply as a virgin protectress of wild animals and their young, but also as the mother of all, as her many-breasted images declare. As such she was regarded as the protectress of human young and as the helper of women in childbirth, because, though a virgin, she had somehow been through their experience herself.

In Artemis, therefore, we are in the presence of that awe and mystery which people rightly feel when they contemplate the basic instincts and processes of human and animal life; and with it the natural urge to protect these processes. But Artemis is more than that: she is this awe, this mystery, this urge turned into a religion. She is Virgin Nature and Mother Nature deified. To say, then, that she was no goddess, as Paul did, and so to undermine her worship, was to threaten the deepest levels of the human psyche. Raw instinct would rise in self-defence if not in retaliation; and that is what fuelled the flames of the riot in Ephesus. But that is not quite how it started; so let us go back and read the story from the beginning.

The cult of 'the image that fell down from the sky'

Movement 1 opens calmly enough. Paul had come to the end of two years of exceedingly fruitful ministry in Ephesus. His regular, systematic preaching had flooded the whole province of Asia with the word of God, and the recent exposure of the sons of Sceva had resulted in a great surge of respect for the name of the Lord Jesus in the city.

At this point, therefore, Paul felt that now was the time to leave and go elsewhere; and he planned to visit first Jerusalem and then Rome (19:21).

Luke does not tell us what objects he had in mind in planning these two visits, though reference to his writings suggests first that he had decided personally to accompany the collection that the Gentile churches would presently be sending to the believers

---

*W. K. C. Guthrie, *The Greeks and their Gods* (London: Methuen, 1954), p. 100, to which I am much indebted.

in Jerusalem (24:17; Rom. 15:25–29), and secondly that he wished to have fellowship with the believers in Rome on his way to further pioneering evangelism in Spain (Rom. 15:23–28). Whatever objects he may in fact have had in mind, his plan, says Luke, was made 'in the Spirit',* that is, in careful dependence on the Spirit of God to guide him in his deliberations and decision. Convinced then of the Lord's direction, he sent Timothy and Erastus ahead of him into Macedonia, while he waited a while longer himself in Asia (19:22).

And then the trouble started. The huge, magnificent temple of Artemis at Ephesus was one of the seven wonders of the world. What with the throngs of local worshippers and the thousands of visitors from all over the Middle East, it was a lucrative source of income for the silversmiths whose factories turned out silver shrines for the local and tourist trades. But now, after two years, Paul's persistent preaching and the steady flow of converts began to show up in their falling bank-balances. Alarmed at this trend, a leading silversmith, Demetrius, summoned the rest to a meeting where he pointed out that if Paul was allowed to go on making converts to his view that man-made gods are no gods at all, the results would be serious. In the first place, their trade of idol-making would come into disrepute. That, of course, was a sound observation. When people lose faith in idolatry, the making of idols, even out of silver, becomes a very tawdry occupation; and to mass-produce them for the tourist trade becomes a sickeningly cynical operation.

But of course Demetrius did not want to represent himself as being interested simply in the money that could be made out of religion. So in the second place, he pointed out that 'the temple of the great goddess Artemis will be discredited, and the goddess herself, who is worshipped throughout the province of Asia and the world, will be robbed of her divine majesty' (19:27).

That put the match to the tinder. The silversmiths were furious, and began shouting 'Great is Artemis of the Ephesians!' (19:28). The fury caught on, and before long the whole city stampeded into the theatre, dragging two of Paul's travel-companions with them. Paul wanted to go and appear before the crowd, but fellow Christians and some friendly city officials begged him not to. The double instinctive urge to protect their religion and their incomes had turned the worshippers of Artemis into a confused pack of wild animals, scenting danger, not knowing exactly what it was,

---

* 19:21; the NIV, which omits the phrase, is surely defective here.

but all tensed ready to destroy the attacker. If Paul had appeared before them in the theatre, they would have torn him limb from joint.

The local Jews, perhaps wishing to dissociate themselves in the mob's eyes from the Christians, put forward a certain Alexander to make a defence (19:33). But when the mob saw he was a Jew, they all shouted in unison for two hours on end 'Great is Artemis of the Ephesians!' (19:34).

This was nature in the raw – blind, unreasoning, instinctive. But then what was Artemis whom they worshipped, if not the deification of nature's basic instincts, common to both animal and man? And if this was what Artemis really represented, perhaps it was appropriate to defend her in this way.

The city clerk, who in Ephesus was also the chief magistrate, eventually pacified the crowd with a masterly and authoritative piece of diplomacy.

First, he asserted as an undeniable fact that Ephesus was the guardian of the temple of the great Artemis and of her image which fell down from the sky; and then that the whole world knew it to be so. Seeing then the facts were undeniable, they ought to be quiet and not to do anything rash. After all, there is no danger when undeniable facts are attacked: for the simple reason that they are undeniable. And if the whole world knows them to be such, it would be impossible for anyone to overturn them (19:35–36).

Secondly, he pointed out that the Christians had not really attacked these undeniable facts. They had neither robbed temples nor blasphemed their goddess (19:37).

Thirdly, he reminded them of the law. If Demetrius and his fellow craftsmen had a legal case against the Christians, the place to settle that was the courts (19:38). If the crowd had a political or social grievance against them, the place to bring that up was a legal city assembly (19:39).

As it was, he added, with an eye on the tough Roman administration of the province, we could all be accused of rioting, and in that case, we could not account for it because, granted the previously mentioned undeniability of the facts, there was neither need nor reason for the commotion (19:40).

One or two things in the town clerk's speech call for comment. First, the image that fell down from the sky, to which he appealed as authentication of the worship of Artemis. Scholarly opinion is that this image was a meteorite. If so, what tricks nature plays on her worshippers! The thing that drew their awed veneration and devotion was but a piece of the worn-out debris of the universe. Nature is a wonderful servant-guardian of mankind, to be treated with great respect, as the modern green movements rightly stress. But she was never meant to be a goddess; nor was our care of her meant to turn itself into a religion. Whenever human beings have turned nature into a goddess, she has invariably degraded man from being king of the earth, into a slave of natural instincts with ultimately less significance than the material world and the forces of the universe which control him.

Secondly, there was his assessment of the Christians' behaviour. Here he was on delicate ground, for undeniably Paul would have many times preached that man-made gods are no gods at all, and would have called on people to turn from their idolatry to the true God. The silversmiths' bank-balance had not fallen for no reason at all. The implications for Artemis of what Paul preached were fatal.

On the other hand, the first part of the city clerk's statement was altogether true: 'these men are not robbers of temples' (19:37). In this Paul and his friends set us a permanent example. The Christian abhorrence of idols does not justify a Christian's showing anything but courtesy and respect to pagan temples. If a person on becoming a Christian destroys his own personal idols, that is good and proper. But a Christian has no business going around treating other religions' temples and idols disrespectfully.

And the second part of the city clerk's statement was also in a sense true: 'they have not blasphemed our goddess' (19:37). Paul would have regularly preached against idolatry in general. But he would not have publicly denounced Artemis, or any other pagan deity in offensive, abusive language. Nor should we.

And finally, the clerk's reference to the law-courts and the political assembly remind us that civilised, truly human life becomes impossible where raw human-animal instinct is allowed to trample over reason, morality and the law. Religion doubtless appeals to deep-seated human emotions. But a religion that encourages its followers to disregard civilised law and hunt down those who may have offended it like animals hunt down their attackers – call it what you will, it is nothing but old pagan Artemis, dressed up in other clothes. Its own defense of itself does away with its credibility, for it destroys what distinguishes man from the animal.

The case of the young man who fell out of a third-storey window

The second part of Movement 1 consists of three major items:

1. Paul's detailed itinerary from Ephesus to Miletus (via Macedonia, Greece, Macedonia, Philippi, Troas, Assos, Mitylene and Samos), with a list of his travel-companions and an account of Eutychus' miraculous return to life on the last night of Paul's week-long stay at Troas (20:1–16).
2. Paul's address to the elders of the church at Ephesus, summoned to meet him at Miletus (20:17–38).
3. Paul's detailed itinerary from Miletus to Jerusalem (via Cos, Rhodes, Patara, Tyre, Ptolemais and Caesarea), with a note on his travel-companions (21:16) and an account of the Holy Spirit's warnings about the persecution and imprisonment that awaited him, given during his week-long stay in Tyre and then again at Caesarea (21:1–16).

Central to this part of the movement, therefore, is Paul's address to the elders from Ephesus; it is concerned with the defence of the church of God, and with the motives and the methods of that defence.

But first let us consider the case of the young man Eutychus at Troas. The last night of Paul's stay there, Paul spoke to the church at very great length, for he never expected to see them again. The church meeting was being held in a third-storey room, and Eutychus was sitting in a window seat. What with the heat of the oil-lamps and of all the bodies crammed into the room, it got hotter and hotter. Eutychus was tired. The sermon droned on. Nature took her course. Eutychus dropped off to sleep – and fell out of the window three storeys down to the ground. He was picked up dead, says Luke (20:9); but Paul went down, embraced him, and announced 'His life is in him' (20:10). He then went back upstairs, broke bread, and continued talking until daylight. And when Paul departed they brought the young man alive and were greatly comforted.

Was it a miracle? Some say yes; for if Luke, as a doctor, reports that the boy was picked up dead, he must have been dead. His return to life was then miraculous. Others are not so sure. They point to Paul's comment which they understand to mean 'His life is *still* in him.' They think that the young man was knocked unconscious, that his breathing stopped just as Luke and Paul got to him, but that Paul's embrace got his breathing going again. It would be difficult to decide between the two interpretations, for in those far off days cessation of breathing would probably have been taken as a sign of death, and the resumption of his breathing therefore as a miracle anyway.

Whatever the truth of the matter, the story as it stands, intentionally or otherwise, picks up vibrations from the previous story which then reverberate through the stories that follow. The worshippers of Artemis had an 'image that fell down from the sky', a bit of an old meteorite; and they had built an enormous temple and a very profitable tourist trade round it. We can imagine what they might well have done with a young man who fell to his death and then came back to life again! They would have had the tourists queuing up to see 'the wonder miracle man' at a drachma a time. Demetrius and the local chamber of commerce would have been delighted.

The remarkable feature of Luke's miracle story, on the other hand, is its total lack of hype and its sense of proportion: the miracle is treated simply as a brief, temporary interruption in the main business of the church. The believers had met to break bread, that is, to observe the Lord's Supper (20:7). Paul had preached for hours; when Eutychus fell, Paul went down and restored him to life, and then immediately came back up and proceeded with the Lord's Supper, broke the bread, and preached on until daylight (20:11).

Secondly, the story is further put into true proportion by all that follows in the rest of the movement. There we shall find Paul, who had so recently performed this miracle, and many other extraordinary miracles as well (19:11–12), facing repeated warnings of impending persecution and imprisonment. Nothing daunted, he persists in his course, quite expecting, and perfectly prepared, to die for the sake of the Lord and of the gospel (20:23–24; 21:12–13). His fellow believers are broken-hearted when they hear it. But he makes no attempt to comfort them or buttress his own courage with triumphalist assertions that God will do miracles to save him from dying, or, should he die, to restore him to life. He knows that the cost of his ministry will sooner or later be death. He is prepared to pay it, and steels himself to face it (21:13).

The defence of the church of God

Paul's address to the Ephesian elders is remarkable for this, that his exhortation to defend the church of God occupies scarcely more than four verses; but the model he offers of how that defence should be conducted occupies at least thirteen. The model he offers is of course himself and his behaviour towards the church during the years he was with them. As we scan the model, the contrast between it and Demetrius' method of defending the religion of Artemis in the same city will be everywhere obvious.

The model covered the whole time Paul spent in Ephesus, right from the first moment he arrived until he left. That period has already been described in 19:1–20; and if that were the only account of it, we might well have formed the impression that it was two years and three months of the rigorous public preaching of a forceful man, performing extraordinary miracles and achieving triumphant success. What a different side of things the present address paints in. Here is what the work of serving the Lord was really like, and here is the real man who actually did it: marked by humility, often reduced to tears as he faced the plots of the Jews against him (20:19, 31), and constantly beset with trials.

But see his moral courage and generosity: 'I have not hesitated to preach anything that would be helpful to you', he declares in verse 20; and again in verse 27, 'For I have not hesitated to proclaim to you the whole will of God.' There is more than a hint of daunting labour and of fear overcome in the twice repeated verb 'I have not hesitated'. To preach daily for two years, as Paul did in Tyrannus' lecture hall, would by itself have been a big enough task for many a man. But verse 20 reveals what we would not have guessed from chapter 19, that Paul supplemented that public teaching with constant private instruction given to individuals and families in their homes. The labour was herculean; but if anything was profitable for you, says Paul, I did not shrink from imparting it. And he took no fee or salary for it either (20:33–34). Indeed, any time he had over from his public teaching and private instruction had to be spent largely on working at his trade in order to earn the money to pay his own expenses and those of his team.

And then his attention was given to all without discrimination. 'I have declared to both Jews and Greeks that they must turn to God in repentance and have faith in our Lord Jesus' (20:21). Just here it was that fear could have come in. Few people mind being told they must repent if all that repentance means is being sorry for some misdeed or other. But Paul believed in the necessity of a much more radical repentance than that. To 'repent towards God' as he himself had done (Phil. 3:1–9) meant coming to realise and confess that the very best religious, moral and spiritual standards we can attain to leave us ruinously short of God's requirements, utterly lost and bankrupt, and needing to accept as a gift of undeserved grace, on the same term as the worst sinner, the salvation that only God can supply. Try telling that to a proud Pharisee like Paul was before his conversion, and see if at times you do not get an indignantly hostile response to your 'morally pessimistic' message. Try on top of that to point out either to Jew or Greek that salvation can be had only through faith in the Lord Jesus Christ, and see if you are not sometimes met with the charge of narrow-minded bigotry. It would be so much easier to preach a general message on the love of God, or on the rights of the poor, or on something all agreed about. But there is a 'scandal' involved in preaching the true message of the gospel, as Paul himself had proved when he was in Corinth (1 Cor. 1:18–2:5). 'But I did not shrink back from declaring it to you,' says Paul to the Ephesians. Brave and faithful man! – if we remember that he probably suffered the same fears in Ephesus as he confesses he felt when preaching at Corinth, and persevered in spite of it.

And now he is leaving them, and of course he wants to exhort them to take over from him the task of feeding and protecting God's flock. But before he actually gets to voicing the exhortation, he has something else to point out about his own behaviour: the constraining power and the sense of values that impelled him in all his work.

'And now,' he says, 'compelled by the Spirit,* I am going to Jerusalem, not knowing what will happen to me there. I only know that in every city the Holy Spirit warns me that prison and hardship are facing me' (20:22–23).

Why then is he going? Paul takes no credit for the compulsion that impels him: for that has been produced in him by the gracious urgings and persuadings of the Holy Spirit. At the same time he is not driven onwards in blind ignorance of the outcome. The same Spirit who constrains him onwards warns him explicitly of the sufferings ahead.

Why then go on? It is, Paul explains, a sense of comparative values. He has been given a course to run and a task to fulfil by the Lord Jesus. That by itself, no matter what the course or the task might be, was in his eyes the supreme honour anyone could be given; and to complete the course and finish the task to the

---

*The NIV is surely right here in understanding the reference to be to the Holy Spirit.

satisfaction of the Lord Jesus, the supreme joy that ever a man could know!

But then consider the task. It was to testify to and proclaim the gospel of God's grace (20:24). The majestic magnificence of that grace was a perpetual dynamo of motivation and energy for Paul. It took no more of God's grace, of course, to save him than to save us. The difference is, if there is a difference, that he never forgot the wonder and splendour of it (Eph. 3:7–8; 1 Tim. 1:12–14). It changed his set of values. Life ceased to have any worth to him independent of living and working for Christ. If to complete the task Christ had given him he must surrender life itself, it was a nothing: he would gladly let it go.

Then there was another value that urged Paul to his task: the value of people. And now of course we are not thinking in terms of people's bank-balances, or profitability forecasts for industry. Demetrius' trinket-factory has long been left behind. We are thinking of what the old preachers used to call the value of a soul. What will it mean for a human being, originally made in the image of God, to perish, to be in torment (Luke 16:23), to suffer eternal punishing (Matt. 25:46), as the Saviour phrased it? To allow fellow human beings to die physically by doing nothing to save them when they could be saved, would be criminal. What then must be said of preachers who refrain from preaching the gospel by which alone people can be saved? Or even refrain from warning people that they need to be saved from the coming wrath? We know what God said about it to Ezekiel: 'When I say to the wicked, "O wicked man, you will surely die," and you do not speak out to dissuade him from his ways, that wicked man will die for his sin, and I will hold you accountable for his blood' (Ezek. 33:8). It was against this background of the awesome value of a human being that Paul wanted to point out that he had done all he could for their salvation: 'Now I know that none of you among whom I have gone about preaching the kingdom will ever see me again. Therefore I declare to you today that I am innocent of the blood of all men. For I have not hesitated to proclaim to you the whole will of God' (20:25–26).

'Have not hesitated to': here comes the phrase again, and it sets us thinking of the pressures and temptations that beset preachers, teachers and elders to content themselves with proclaiming part of God's will and counsel, but not necessarily all of it. It is no new temptation. Isaiah, all those centuries ago, knew what it was to have to face people who were unwilling to listen to the Lord's instruction; who said to the prophets 'Give us no more visions of what is right! Tell us pleasant things, prophesy illusions. Leave this way, get off this path, and stop confronting us with the Holy One of Israel!' (Isa. 30:10–11). But what will the Chief Shepherd say to under-shepherds who have neglected to warn the sheep of the most deadly enemy of all? Who have only pointed out how green the grass is, but have never warned the sheep of the existence of wolves? Who have even comforted the sheep with the thought that the Prowling and Roaring Lion himself is a mere myth?

And now at last Paul has finished citing his own example and begins his exhortation, though the exhortation will not last long and he will soon be back to citing his own example. Exhortation is always more easily swallowed when sandwiched between liberal slices of the exhorter's personal example.

'Take heed to, watch over, guard both yourselves and all the flock of which the Holy Spirit has made you overseers' (20:28). Unceasing vigilance is the essential requirement in shepherds. And first vigilance over themselves. A shepherd who grows careless over his own spiritual life, moral behaviour, study of Scripture, progress in the knowledge of God, thereby unfits himself for shepherding others

'Shepherd the church of God, which he bought with the blood of his Own' (20:28).* With this we touch the mainspring of all true defence and shepherding of the church: the cost at which God bought it. That cost was the blood of his own, that is, of his own dear, loved, cherished Son. The story still has power to stagger imagination. For here is no image of a god that fell down from the sky, but God of very God, coming deliberately down; Father and Son in holy concert paying the price that only God could measure, to obtain the repentance, faith and love of the likes of us. How cheap the silver of Demetrius' shrines compared with this! 'For . . . it was not with perishable things such as silver or gold that you were redeemed . . . but with the precious blood of Christ' (1 Pet. 1:18–19). This was not Artemis protecting the young of animal and man and avenging the rape of nature with her lethal arrows. This was not nature doing what was natural and tearing the enemy to pieces to save her own life. Here was nature's Creator, knowingly, deliberately, of his own free will, laying down his own life for us his sinful creatures (John 10:15–17). This was not nature, magnificent but fallen. This was thrice holy divine Grace.

---

* cf. the phrase in Colossians 1:13, 'the Son of his love' (i.e. his beloved Son).

The archetypal Shepherd has set the pattern for the defence of the sheep (John 10:7–13): all true defence of the gospel and of the church must follow his example. How could one ever be so false to the Shepherd as to attempt to protect the gospel or the church by either mob-rule or the use of the sword upon its enemies?

But guarded the church must be, to the last drop of our blood; and that against two principal dangers, one from without and one from within. Savage wolves, Paul warns, will come in among you and will not spare the flock (20:29). He does not stay to describe what kinds of wolf he means. But chief perhaps among the candidates for this role are such men as Jude later referred to as 'having secretly slipped in among you. They are godless men, who change the grace of our God into a licence for immorality and deny Jesus Christ our only Sovereign and Lord' (Jude 4). Peter adds his angle on the topic: 'They will secretly introduce destructive heresies, even denying the sovereign Lord who bought them' (2 Pet. 2:1). There is nothing more destructive of the church, or bewildering to the sheep, than when men who profess to be shepherds teach the sheep that the Chief Shepherd was not God incarnate, was not born of a virgin, was in fact mistaken in some of his teaching (particularly about the second coming), did not die as an atonement for sin, and did not bodily rise from the dead. Such men are not true shepherds. They are not even true sheep. They are wolves from the outside, of whom the Shepherd himself warned us: 'Watch out for false prophets. They come to you in sheep's clothing, but inwardly they are ferocious wolves' (Matt. 7:15).

The other type of person shepherds must be on guard against come from the inside, perhaps from among the overseers themselves. Their mark is first that they distort the truth, concoct odd, twisted, bizarre doctrines; which, of course, is a bad enough thing in itself. But worse than what they do is their motive for doing it: their aim, though they might not admit it, is to draw away the disciples* after themselves (20:30). Under the guise of leading the sheep, they want to dominate them. They seem to forget that the sheep do not belong to them but to the One who bought them: it is God's flock, not theirs. They are the Diotrepheses of the church (3 John); prepared to gossip maliciously about other servants of God in order to boost their own tyranny over the flock.

'So be on the watch,' says Paul – and with that he is back to

---

* NIV's 'disciples', instead of 'the disciples', is inaccurate.

citing his own practice as an example of how it should be done. 'Remember that for three years I never stopped warning each of you night and day with tears' (20:31).

But now he is leaving them and can no longer shepherd them himself, what resource will they have? A double resource. God and the word of his grace (20:32). God first of course; the living God, not a mere set of rules and regulations. But then not God alone, but the word that reveals and expounds his grace. Temperament may incline us to put the weight on one rather than on the other, or even on one to the virtual exclusion of the other. But both God and his word are necessary, and between them they are sufficient, to build up both shepherds and sheep, and to give each the inheritance among all those who are sanctified (20:32).

On that spiritual high note we might have thought Paul would have concluded. But the shepherds or elders of a truly Christian church have more to do than look after the spiritual state of the church. So once more Paul cites his own practice as a model for the Ephesian elders to follow: he had not gone about his spiritual work with one eye on the money or clothing he might hope to make out of it. 'These hands of mine', he said as he held them out for inspection, 'have supplied my own needs and the needs of my companions' (20:34). Nor was Paul boasting or presenting himself as some special hero. He worked at a secular job deliberately, in order to set an example to elders in the church as to what their duty is. 'In everything I did, I showed you that by this kind of hard work we must help the weak' (20:35). Teachers and elders can so easily become mere theorists, simply telling other people what to do. But what use is theory if not backed up by practical example? It is not an addition to a teacher's normal responsibility, it is an integral part of his ministry – a 'must' according to Paul – that he works hard so as to have enough cash to pay his own way and to help the weak (20:33–35).

Of course it is true that in other places Paul lays it down that an evangelist has a right to live from his preaching, that apostles like Peter, and even certain elders, have a God-given right to be supported by the church (1 Cor. 9:1–14; 1 Tim. 5:17–18). Clearly neither these scriptures nor Paul's remarks to the elders of Ephesus are meant to be rigid unvarying absolutes. That is to be done which is best for the Lord's work in each situation. But even so, we have missed the point if we simply insist on our rights. Paul often forwent his, so as to enjoy the superior blessedness of being able to give financial and material, as well as spiritual, help to others. It is certainly the more blessed, the happier way; we have the authority of the Lord Jesus for that. Yes, and elders have a duty, says Paul, to remember his words on that score (20:35).

Verses 36–38 depict a very moving scene, to be felt rather than expounded. What friends Paul had made himself in Ephesus! He would never see them again on earth; but one day they would welcome him into the eternal tabernacles (Luke 16:9).

Completing the course

The remainder of Movement 1 is largely filled with the geo-graphical details of Paul's resumed journey to Jerusalem (21:1–10). The two items of special interest are the two messages from the Holy Spirit relayed to Paul, one in Tyre (21:4) and the other in Caesarea (21:11). At Tyre the disciples told Paul through the Spirit not to set foot in Jerusalem; and at Caesarea a prophet named Agabus took Paul's belt, tied his own hands and feet with it, and said, 'The Holy Spirit says, "In this way the Jews of Jerusalem will bind the owner of this belt and will hand him over to the Gentiles."' But Paul persisted in going.

Some have therefore concluded that here Paul, over-confident in an excess of zeal, foolishly refused to listen to the Spirit's voice and disobeyed him, with the result that he lost his freedom when he might have retained it and so have witnessed for the Lord more effectively.

Before we consent to that extreme view, we ought to reflect a little. It was not Paul's normal habit knowingly and deliberately to disobey what he believed was a categorical prohibition of the Holy Spirit. Are we then obliged to think that on these two occasions he recognised the message conveyed to him as an absolute prohibition and, all out of character, disobeyed it? That might seem an unlikely story.

Perhaps he thought that the disciples at Tyre and Agabus the prophet had mistaken the voice of the Spirit. But if so, Luke does not mention it.

Let's think again. When Paul first decided on leaving Ephesus he 'planned in the Spirit' to go eventually to Jerusalem. That much Luke does tell us (19:21; cf. 20:22), just as clearly as he later tells us that the disciples at Tyre urged Paul through the Spirit not to go to Jerusalem (21:4). We have no right to assume that one was more mistaken than the other.

On the other hand, Agabus was not the first to warn Paul that the Jews at Jerusalem would bind him and then hand him over to the Gentiles. In every city he had stayed in on his way to Miletus the Holy Spirit had told him the same thing (20:23). But far from reading it as a prohibition against his going, he read it as the constraint, the compulsion of the Holy Spirit to persist in going. The Lord Jesus had set his course; the Holy Spirit was constraining him to complete it (20:22–24).

The people at Tyre, and even more so at Caesarea, were that much nearer to Jerusalem. So when they heard that Paul was making for Jerusalem they could vividly anticipate what would happen to him there. Even so, Agabus merely warned him of what he would suffer. He did not forbid him to go. It was the other believers who on hearing Agabus' prophecy pleaded with him not to; and Paul chided them for trying to break the resolve, formed in him by the Holy Spirit as he believed, to face bonds and if necessary death at Jerusalem for the Lord's sake (21:12–13). Paul, the man who shed tears in plenty over people's spiritual problems (20:19, 31), had no time for tears that would provoke self-pity in him and break his will to complete the task the Lord had given him.

We are left then with the one instance, that at Tyre, of a seeming prohibition from the Spirit against going to Jerusalem. There is no necessity to read it as either a mistake or a contradiction. When a man's wife tells him she plans to buy him the very latest Japanese hi-fi system for his birthday, he may well reply, 'No, you shouldn't do that; you should spend the money on a new coat for yourself.' But if, come his birthday, she presents him with the hi-fi, he does not rebuke her for disobedience; he admires her for her completely voluntary sacrifice of her needs to his pleasure. So surely there comes a point when God himself takes steps to allow our sacrifice and devotion to be voluntary.*
The Holy Spirit, who had been constraining Paul to go to Jerusalem and face the sufferings he warned him of for the sake of the Lord's name, finally left it to Paul's free choice: he did not have to go if he did not want to. Many of us would have gladly read the message at Tyre as an absolute prohibition and have grasped at the reprieve it offered. Paul read it otherwise. But then we perhaps find it easier to interpret something as the Lord's guidance when it saves us from suffering, and question the Lord's guidance when it would lead us into trouble. It is the measure of Paul's devotion to Christ that he did not think it was necessarily a prohibition to go to Jerusalem. Indeed, he thought

---

*The Nazirite vow is one example (Num. 6); 1 Corinthians 7:26–35 is another.

that the defence of the gospel was a task that might very reasonably be expected to cost a man his life.

MOVEMENT 2: The Gospel to be Judged by its Respect for Conscience (21:17–23:11)

Movement 1 opened with a riot in defence of the temple of Artemis at Ephesus; Movement 2 opens with a riot in defence of the temple of the Lord at Jerusalem. It is depressing that people should use the same method to protect the Lord's house as pagans used to protect their religion. Nevertheless, the seriousness of the charge that sparked off the riot against Paul is undeniable: 'This . . . man . . . has brought Greeks into the temple area and defiled this holy place' (21:28). Large notices in Greek and Hebrew posted at the entrances warned all Gentiles not to proceed into the inner court on pain of death. The Jews had the right, sanctioned by the Roman government, to execute even a Roman citizen if he disobeyed the prohibition. Gentiles might object that the prohibition was narrow-minded or even racist. But that would be beside the point: no one obliged them to attend the temple at all if they did not want to; and if they did, ample provision was made to accommodate them in the outer court of the Gentiles.

But Paul was not a Gentile. He had been brought up in the beliefs that lay behind this strict exclusion of Gentiles from the inner court. They were none less than this: that almighty God deigned to presence himself in the inner shrine of the temple, which was thereby constituted holy in the highest degree. Only Israel's highest priest had sanctity enough to enter that most holy shrine, and that only once a year. Outside the most holy shrine was a place of a slightly less degree of holiness. Even so, only the consecrated priests of Israel, and not the general Jewish public, could enter it. Surrounding the temple building itself was the inner court; but this too, though again possessing a lower degree of sanctity, was still holy. No Gentile might enter it; only Israelites, and even they, only after due purification.

There were several reasons for this. First and foremost, Israel believed that they were a holy nation in a sense that no other nation was. They had been called by God and appointed to be 'a kingdom of priests and a holy nation' (Exod. 19:6). Priests to function on behalf of all the nations of the world, but therefore with a holiness of position and office and nearness to God that no other nation possessed. Consistent with their priestly status, they were required throughout their daily life to observe special rules of sanctity, such as circumcision, ablutions, and food-laws; and they were strictly forbidden all participation in idolatry – even the eating of food once it had been offered to idols – and all indulgence in sexual perversions that were commonplace among the Gentiles.

Paul had been brought up in this faith, to reverence the temple and the special role Israel bore in connection with it. Now, according to his accusers, he was 'teaching all men everywhere against our people and our law and this place [i.e. the temple]' (21:28). Too bad that he now taught counter to what the Old Testament had laid down. Too bad that everywhere he went he must attack his own Jewish people who had nurtured him in the one true faith. But why could he not at least keep away from the temple? Why must he come and trample its sanctities underfoot by bringing Gentiles into the inner court and by entering it himself while in a state of ceremonial uncleanness?

The charges were untrue, of course; but for the moment let us give his accusers the benefit of any doubt there may be that they sincerely believed that Paul had done what they charged him with. When they dragged him out of the inner court and slammed the doors shut (21:30), they were fighting to protect the holiness of almighty God himself from desecration.

Modern criticisms of Paul's behaviour in the temple

But the Jews from Asia who roused the mob against Paul (21:27–29) have not been the only ones to criticise him over this incident. Many admirers of Paul's exposition of justification by faith through Christ's sacrifice of atonement have also been seriously disturbed by his behaviour in the temple. 'What was he doing in the temple in the first place?' they say. 'Did he not believe in his heart of hearts what Stephen had long since declared, that Christ had made the temple, its priesthood, sacrifices and purifications obsolete? The man who had taught his converts everywhere to celebrate the Lord's Supper, who had so recently taken part in that supper at Troas and solemnly remembered that forgiveness comes only through the sacrifice of Christ at Calvary – what was that man doing purifying himself according to the ceremonial rites of the temple and joining in the offering of animal sacrifices on its altar?'

Their understanding of how this (to them) calamitous thing

happened tends to be as follows. The Christians in Jerusalem, not a hundred-per-cent clear themselves about the relation of the gospel to Judaism, and pusillanimously concerned not to offend Jewish opinion, suggested to Paul a way of publicly placating their nation's objections to Christianity. There were four Christian men who had undertaken a Nazirite vow, and who were now at the point of fulfilling it. It was suggested therefore that Paul should take these men to the temple, join in the necessary rituals of purification, and pay the expenses of the sacrifices appropriate to the ending of the vow.

Paul, they hold, misguidedly fell in with the suggestion, and so, most unfortunately and most uncharacteristically for him, compromised the gospel. But like all compromises it did not work: for it failed to impress the very people it was meant to impress, and ended in disaster. As a result he was obliged for the next four years to preach the gospel as best he could in chains, when, if he had not compromised, he could have continued to preach it, as before, in freedom.

Actually both these criticisms of Paul have got their basic facts wrong. The first in supposing that Paul had brought Greeks into the temple: he had in fact been very careful to do no such thing. If he had introduced Greeks into the inner court, why did not the crowd arrest them as well as Paul? The Jews from Asia who first raised the hue and cry were never able to substantiate their charge in any of the subsequent enquiries or trials. Indeed their failure even to turn up in court (24:18–19) was an admission of their inability.

But the other criticism has got its basic facts wrong too, in this regard at least: it supposes that Paul and the elders of the church at Jerusalem were attempting to placate and pacify the Jews at large, the people who eventually raised the riot and the Sanhedrin who subsequently tried to make capital out of the whole affair in their attempt to get Paul executed. Neither Paul nor the elders were attempting to do any such thing. The elders were quite explicit about the particular group of people they were trying to help: not the unbelieving Jews, but the believers. 'You see, brother, how many thousands of Jews *have believed*' (21:20). It was not they who created the riot, arrested Paul and tried to kill him! They were presumably much helped by what he did, and their consciences, being still weak as they were, were saved from being further scandalised. Moreover, when they saw the unreasoning and implacable treatment of Paul by the Jews at large and his exclusion from the temple, it may well have strengthened

367

their consciences to move forward to the eventual abandonment of the temple and its rites.

What had happened, according to the elders, was this. These thousands of believing, Christian Jews had been informed that Paul taught all the Jews who lived among the Gentiles to turn away from Moses, telling them not to circumcise their children or live according to the Jewish customs (21:21). This information had enough truth in it to make it seem plausible; but, as we know from past chapters in Acts (see pp. 241–43) and from Paul's epistles, it was in fact incorrect. Paul had not demanded any such wholesale abandonment of Mosaic customs by Christian Jews.

What he had taught, and never did try to disguise, whether he was in remotest Paphlagonia or in Jerusalem city itself, was that circumcision was not necessary for salvation, neither did it contribute anything to salvation. And if circumcision didn't, neither did ritual ablutions, holy water, animal sacrifices, offerings to the temple treasury, incense, and ceremonies performed by the priests or by their high priest. On this fundamental doctrine of salvation, moreover, not only Paul, but Peter and James and all the other apostles and elders in Jerusalem stood foursquare. We remember Peter's famous affirmation, made some years earlier (15:11) in Jerusalem itself: 'We believe that it is by the grace of the Lord Jesus [and not by circumcision or any other ceremony laid down by the Mosaic law] that we [Jews] are saved, in exactly the same way as they [the Gentiles].' We likewise remember his solemn denunciation of any who would teach either Gentiles or even Jews that circumcision or any other ritual prescribed by the law of Moses was necessary for, or contributed to, a person's salvation: 'Now then, why do you try to test God by putting on the necks of the disciples a yoke that neither we nor our fathers have been able to bear?' (15:10).

Clear as they were, however, on the relation of circumcision to salvation, neither Paul nor any of the other apostles and elders taught that all Jewish believers must there and then cease circumcising their children. In the Old Testament God had commanded all Israelites to have their children circumcised. Many Jewish Christians, therefore, still felt conscience-bound to continue with this rite, not in order to gain or to retain salvation, but simply to please the Lord. They did not expect Gentile believers to circumcise their children: nowhere in the Old Testament had God commanded Gentiles to be circumcised – unless they wanted to become Jews; and the Jewish Christians were clear enough that Gentiles did not have to become Jews in order to be saved, or to live as Jews afterwards.* But many of them – thousands of them, in fact, according to what the elders told Paul – did hold that Jewish believers were still under obligation to observe the rites laid down for Israelites in the Old Testament. They were 'zealous for the law' (21:20). It was for them a matter of conscience, based on the word of God as they understood it; just as the observance of Sunday as a sabbath is still a matter of conscience for thousands – perhaps millions – of even Gentile believers, who would never dream of saying that sabbath-keeping was necessary for salvation.

Now nowhere in Acts or in the epistles do we find Paul riding roughshod over this type of conscience. Quite the opposite. Among Jews he was prepared to live as a Jew (1 Cor. 9:20). Among Gentiles he personally was likewise prepared to live as a Gentile (1 Cor. 9:21). But that did not mean that he demanded that all Christian Jews should live as Gentiles. If conscience told them they must continue to live as Jews, he honoured their conscience. Indeed, when the young Jewish Christian, Timothy, as we remember (16:1–3; see pp. 241–43), joined his team, he had him circumcised. Paul adopted this flexible strategy deliberately, in order to make it easier for people, whether Jew or Gentile, to listen to the gospel, receive it and get saved (1 Cor. 9:19). And he had another reason, too; but before we consider that, we must attend to other serious objections.

The first runs like this. It was all very well for Paul to allow Christian Jews (or even to encourage some of them like Timothy) to continue the practice of circumcision as long as they understood clearly that circumcision contributed nothing to their salvation. But in Jerusalem Paul went further than that, unacceptably further. At the suggestion of the elders, who should have known better, he purified himself according to the rites and ceremonies of the law (21:24, 26; 24:18), and so denied by implication the sufficiency of the once for all sanctification provided by Christ (Heb. 10:10, 22). Furthermore, in being prepared to pay for, and associate himself with, the burnt offerings, sin offerings and peace offerings prescribed by the law for the fulfilment of the Nazirite vow (Num. 6:13–21), he once more denied by implication the sufficiency of the sacrifice of Christ. And finally, he did not, admittedly, bring Gentile Christians into the inner court of

---

*Though they did ask the Gentile Christians to respect the conscience of their Jewish fellow believers and, where appropriate, to accommodate it. See 21:25; 15:28–29 and the discussion of these verses on pp. 237–39.

the temple, and so he escaped the charge levelled against him by the Asian Jews – but only at the cost of incurring another: he thus consented to the maintenance of that 'middle wall of partition' between Jews and Gentiles which even he (later) preached had been broken down in Christ (Eph. 2:14).

These are very serious charges. They imply that the very Paul whom God set to defend and confirm the gospel, fluffed and compromised the gospel instead of defending it. But the charges cannot be true; for when the first series of attacks and defence had ended in Paul's appearance before the Sanhedrin, then the next night the Lord himself commended Paul for the way he had conducted the defence of the gospel in Jerusalem: 'the Lord stood near Paul and said, "Take courage! As you have testified about me in Jerusalem, so you must also testify in Rome"' (23:11).* The Lord could not have spoken thus if Paul had in fact compromised the gospel in Jerusalem.

So let us ask a question: Why was it all right for Paul to consent to Jewish Christians continuing the rite of circumcision, but all wrong for him to take part with them in the rituals of the temple? Because, so it will be said, the sacrifices in the temple were prefigurements, types and shadows of the sacrifice of Christ; and to continue with the types and shadows when the reality had come was to deny by implication the sufficiency of the reality.

But the rite of circumcision was also a prefigurement, a type and a shadow! None knew it better than Paul, as we see from his remarks in Colossians 2:11: 'In him you were also circumcised, in the putting off of the sinful nature, not with a circumcision done by the hands of men but with the circumcision done by Christ.' Paul is clearly not referring in this verse to the Christian rite of water-baptism, for, unarguably, that is most definitely 'done by the hands of men'. He is speaking of that profound, inner, moral and spiritual operation that is performed in the depths of a person's heart when that person repents and trusts the Saviour. But though Paul understood and taught quite clearly that physical circumcision was thus a type, he saw no difficulty in allowing Jewish believers to continue its physical practice if their conscience demanded it of them – provided only, as always, they understood and agreed that physical circumcision did not pro-

---

*Liberal critics have a very different way of exonerating Paul. They deny the historicity of this whole episode in Luke's narrative: Paul never did what Luke says he did in the temple. Their proposed cure is not only worse than the complaint, it is unnecessary. The alleged complaint is false.

duce, contribute to or maintain that profound saving operation which only the 'circumcision done by Christ' could effect (Gal. 6:15).

And if that was so with the type of circumcision, it would have been true with all the other types connected with the temple. All Jewish Christians in Jerusalem constantly celebrated the Lord's Supper, which loudly proclaimed that forgiveness comes through the sacrifice and death of the Lord Jesus, and only through that sacrifice. No Jewish believer, elder or apostle, and certainly not Paul, felt that the sacrifice of Christ had to be supplemented by the continuance of animal sacrifices in the temple in order to secure or retain forgiveness of sins. But for the time being some of them felt they should continue the use of these types and symbols.

There was no contradiction of the gospel, therefore, in what Paul did when he joined with the four Jewish Christians in the sacrifices prescribed for the completion of their Nazirite vows. We may of course wonder why people should feel conscience-bound to continue the use of types and shadows when they now enjoyed the reality. Certainly we would raise our eyebrows if we found a pilot of a modern jumbo-jet continuing to play in his spare time with the model aeroplane he played with as a boy. But his play would become dangerous only if he himself began to think, and then to teach other people, that this model aeroplane was really able to fly them across the Atlantic.

Here too lies the answer to the charge that in attending the services in the temple Jewish Christians were maintaining the 'middle wall of partition' between Jews and Gentiles which Christ has torn down. In the fellowship of the Christian churches that wall was gone, and in social fellowship too. If, indeed, sometimes some Jewish Christians wavered inconsistently on this score, Paul would rebuke them severely, as in the case of Peter at Antioch (Gal. 2:11–21). But the practice of the Christian churches could not be carried back into the Jewish temple. The Christian Jews were not free, even had they been inclined, to knock down the wall that separated the inner temple court from the court of the Gentiles, to abolish the animal sacrifices, tear down the veil, and meet as a Christian church, together with their Gentile fellow believers, in the holy of holies! The Christian Jews, to start with, were not in charge of the temple. Responsibility for that lay with the high priest and his colleagues, and they, it need hardly be said, were not Christians. And in the second place, while the temple lasted, all its arrangements had to conform to the strict instructions laid down in the Old Testament. You could not change part of it according to Christian principles but retain the rest – that is the mistake Christendom later fell into. You had to retain the whole or abandon the whole; there was no middle path.

Then – and here comes the biggest objection of all to what Paul did – ought not all Christian Jews long since to have abandoned the temple and all connected with it? Not to have done so was plainly and directly contrary to the straightforward teaching of the epistle to the Hebrews.

Now there can be no doubt that the epistle to the Hebrews does call on all Jewish believers to abandon the temple and all its rites and services, and teaches that to continue them would be to compromise the gospel of the Lord Jesus Christ. But it is no undermining of the teaching of that epistle to point out that it was not yet written when Paul joined with the four men to fulfil their vow in the temple.* Nor is it a mere excuse for their conduct. The passage of time between the crucifixion of our Lord and the destruction of the temple (as prophesied by our Lord) in AD 70 is crucial to the matter we are discussing. Yes, most certainly, the death, resurrection and ascension of the Lord Jesus would make – had indeed already made – the temple, its priesthood and its sacrifices obsolete. Stephen in his day had already begun to perceive that; and Paul, who as Saul of Tarsus had consented to his death, surely knew it as well. But God did not demand on the day of Pentecost, or even at the death of Stephen, that all Christian Jews must forthwith and immediately forsake the temple and its services, never to return. He would eventually do so. When the epistle to the Hebrews was written he did. And when he allowed the Romans to destroy the temple in AD 70 he forced not only Christian Jews, but all other Jews as well, to leave it. But between Pentecost and AD 64 God himself deliberately allowed an interval during which the transition from Judaism to Christianity should be gradual, progressive and not immediately enforced *in toto*.

Why, then, did God do this? The answer to this question will lead us to two basic principles in God's dealings with people. Both of them lie at the heart of the defence of the gospel in this second movement of Section Six, and both are of permanent validity.

*Some have thought it was written during Paul's stay in Caesarea. A more likely date is AD 64.

Time for repentance – and the establishment of guilt

Israel's crucifixion of the Messiah, the Son of God, her throwing of the owner's Son out of his own vineyard, was an immeasurable enormity. It would, as Christ personally warned the nation, inevitably result in the destruction of the temple (Luke 13:31–35; 19:45–20:20; 21:5–6, 20–24). But between the announcement of this coming destruction and its actual execution, God's mercy gave the nation an interval of forty years as a time for repentance. And not merely to the nation at large, but more particularly to the citizens of Jerusalem, and above all to the authorities responsible for the temple, the Sadducean high priest, chief priests and elders.

It was, after all, the high priest, the chief priests and the Sadducean lay aristocracy that had been chiefly responsible for engineering the death of the Lord Jesus. Certainly they were aided and abetted by a good many leading Pharisees, and in the end they were able to manipulate the crowd to shout for his crucifixion. But the Sadducean chief priests were the ringleaders. They were responsible for the temple. It was their abuses that had profaned the temple; it was their undying hatred that the Lord Jesus had provoked by cleansing the temple. It was their temple that he had prophesied would be destroyed. Even they, perhaps they above all, were given time for repentance.

The very first disciples of Christ had not, of course, joined with the nation in shouting for the crucifixion. But when it came to those who had, God was prepared to take the view that they had acted in ignorance, rulers as well as people (3:17). There was therefore mercy for them if they would repent. Thousands of the people, as we have just heard the Christian elders tell Paul, had repented and accepted Jesus as Messiah (21:20). But the majority of the Jerusalemites, and the Sadducean aristocratic rulers in particular, had remained unrepentant.

Nevertheless, Christ himself had said that before the city and temple were destroyed God would send the rulers witnesses, especially in the form of the Christians whom they persecuted, whether brought before their council or prosecuted in the Gentile courts (Luke 21:12–15). And so God did. First came Peter and the other apostles, preaching the resurrection of Christ. The Sadducean high priest and aristocracy tried to suppress them, and would have executed them had it not been for the intervention of the Pharisee Gamaliel (5:34–40).

Then came Stephen, openly stating that Christ had made the temple and its rituals obsolete, and that one day the temple would be destroyed. But neither he nor the Christians in Jerusalem treated the temple with anything but respect. They never tried to break its rules or disregard its sanctities. They did not even ignore it like the Qumran sect did, but used it still. But the high priest and his council had Stephen executed nonetheless.

Finally God sent Paul, and sent him right into the temple. The high-priestly circle had reason to know all about him. Pharisee though he was, he had originally co-operated with an earlier high priest in trying to suppress the Christians. Of course he had subsequently been converted; and they would have heard of his evangelism in the synagogues of the Dispersion, and of his founding of Christian churches, separate from the synagogues and composed of Gentiles as well as Jews on equal terms. That doubtless did not please them, nor the non-Christian Jerusalemites. They were all too glad to believe the allegations of the Asian Jews. But they were false: Paul had acted with impeccable correctness towards the temple, honouring to the letter all its Old Testament regulations. And the high priest, the chief priests and the Sadducean aristocracy knew they had no real charge against him on that score, as Luke makes abundantly clear in the following narrative. They had no excuse, therefore, for their continuing rejection of Christ and persecution of the gospel.

But the affair brought Paul face to face once more with the high priest and his colleagues. Once in the Sanhedrin (23:1–10), once in Felix's court (24:1–23), and once again in Festus' (25:1–12), three times in all Paul witnessed to them what was the real issue at stake (as distinct from the trumped up charges they brought against him): the resurrection of Jesus whom they had murdered. Deliberately unrepentant, they determined by hook or by crook to get the Romans to execute him, just as they had persuaded them to execute Jesus.

But now the time allotted for repentance was running out; the temple's lease on life was expiring. When the Jerusalem mob in their riotous effort to defend their temple seized God's final witness, Paul, dragged him out of the inner court, slammed its gates shut behind him and tried to beat him to death (21:30–31), they were passing the point of no return. And when the skulduggery of the high priest and his colleagues (23:12–15; 25:2–3) finally forced Paul to appeal to Caesar, they were but sealing their doom as a priestly order, and that of their temple with them.

No wonder then that in AD 64 (earlier according to some) God had the epistle to the Hebrews written and put into circulation, calling on Christian Jews everywhere to abandon the temple system of worship, which had now become the centre and expression of impenitent determined rejection of the Lord Jesus. Six years later the temple was destroyed, and the Sadducean priestly class faded away; but not before their guilt had been established beyond excuse.

The gospel and the integrity of the individual's conscience

But there was another reason why God did not demand that immediately after Pentecost, or immediately after Stephen's death, all Christian Jews must abandon all the Mosaic rites, rituals and ceremonies. And the reason was God's respect for the human conscience.

Christian Jews were caught in a sea-change of unprecedented proportions. Ceremonial, ritual and food-laws for which many of them would have laid down their lives before they would break them, because they believed those laws were inspired by God – these laws were in process of being abrogated. God himself would not hurry the process unduly, but give people's consciences time to adjust to the new order.

It is not that conscience is allowed to be the final arbiter of what is true, of what is God's will. That role belongs solely to God's objective revelation in and through his word. Conscience must learn, and be prepared, to adjust itself by that word, and not arrogate to itself an authority it does not possess. My little wrist watch is not the final arbiter of Greenwich Mean Time!

On the other hand, God does not play ducks and drakes with human conscience, nor treat it in a tyrannical or arbitrary way. He respects the mechanisms by which its adjustments are rightly made, and he gives them time to work. Having educated the Israelite conscience over many centuries throughout the Old Testament to insist on the strictest observation of the Mosaic rituals, he was not going to demand it to change and abandon them overnight. He would give their conscience time to perceive that the God who originally gave those Old Testament laws was himself abrogating them. Then it would be faith on their part, and not disobedience or carelessness, to abandon them.*

*We should not abuse this principle by using it as an excuse to continue with practices that never did have any biblical authority, Old or New Testament, and are in fact contrary to explicit scriptures.

Weaker consciences would make slower progress than those which were stronger and able to adjust more quickly. Meanwhile God concentrated on getting them all, weak or strong, not to overbear each other's consciences, but to develop the habit of thinking these things through individually in the light of each individual's direct responsibility to the risen Lord Jesus (Rom. 14:1–23). And that habit, once formed, would need continually to be applied to a thousand and one other issues long after God settled the particular issues related to the Mosaic ritual first by the epistle to the Hebrews and then by the destruction of the temple.

Finally, there was another important element in the suggestion that the elders put to Paul, though neither Luke nor the elders call particular attention to it. The four men had made their solemn vow to God before Paul arrived. Faced then with the question whether they should fulfil their vow or not, there is no doubt what Paul was duty bound to answer. The gospel certainly preaches that salvation is by grace. But unless the fulfiment of a vow would in itself be positively sinful, the gospel will insist that solemn vows to God must be fulfilled. Otherwise the gospel would stand convicted of straight antinomianism. It is wrong for a believer to marry a non-believer (1 Cor. 7:39). But if such a marriage has already been entered into, and pledged with solemn vows before God, it would be a travesty of the gospel of salvation by grace to say that it permitted, let alone demanded, the Christian partner to break those vows.

Paul's defence before the Jerusalem mob

The Roman authorities were naturally nervous about religious riots in Jerusalem; they could be the match that set the whole country alight. When therefore the army commander learned there was trouble in the city he took a squad of soldiers, charged down the steps of the Antonia castle into the temple, rescued Paul from the hands of the mob, and demanded to know what all the trouble was about. Such was the confusion, however, that he could get no coherent answer. So he ordered his men to take Paul up into the castle; which they did, jostled on every side by the surging crowd baying for Paul's blood like a pack of hounds.

At the top of the castle steps Paul asked the commander's permission to address the mob. He spoke in Greek and that fact upset the explanation of the affair that had been forming in the commander's mind. Some years previously an Egyptian self-styled prophet had led a band of people out to the Mount of

Olives, promising them that God would do another Jericho and have the walls of Jerusalem fall flat so that they could then rush in and slaughter the Roman garrison. It had not happened, of course. The Roman authorities put down the rising, killing some and arresting others; while the old artful dodger himself escaped. The commander, whose recollection of the incident was somewhat confused, had jumped to the conclusion that Paul must be this Egyptian who had dared to return, much to the disgust of the crowd he had misled.

Disabused of this idea, the commander allowed Paul to speak to the crowd; perhaps he would discover from Paul's speech what the riot was all about.

But why, we may ask, did Paul think it worthwhile even trying to address the mob? He was beaten black and blue, a sorry dishevelled lump. For the time being he was now safe in Roman hands. What further good could he expect to do by addressing the crowd that stood at the bottom of the stairs demanding his blood?

The answer is, he loved them. He had done what he had done in the temple in order to help the believing Jews; for he loved them. Now he stood facing the seething mass of the unbelieving Jews; and he loved them as well. They were his own dear people. They had been whipped into fury by the allegation that he taught all men everywhere against them (21:28). But it was slanderously untrue. He taught Gentile Christians to love not only Christian Jews, but Jews in general (see Rom 11:17–32). Moreover, he understood them. As they stood there in their wild rage they thought that they were protecting the honour and holiness of God. Had the commander not intervened, they would have beaten Paul to death: but they would have done it while imagining they were offering service to God. It would be a kindness to them to disabuse them of this idea. What was in their hearts was pure murder, fed by national pride, injured self-interest, ignorance and sheer unregenerate sinfulness. Far from serving God, they would have murdered God-incarnate could they have got their hands on him. What they imagined was zeal for God was but an expression of raw, unredeemed human nature. How easily and how often does religion deceive people into thinking that they are defending God, when all the while it is Artemis who inspires them, and her defence-methods they adopt.

Paul understood it all very well. He had once felt exactly as the crowd felt now. He had felt that he was being loyal to his nation by persecuting, arresting, imprisoning, punishing and executing

377

Christian Jews. He had done all that was possible to oppose the name of Jesus of Nazareth, and had done it in all good conscience, convinced that he was serving, and protecting, the honour of God. But all the while it was not God's honour, but his own Pharisaic religious pride that he was protecting, and protecting with the rage, spite, venom and cruelty of an unregenerate man. Conversion to Christ had opened his eyes to see reality, what the God he supposed he served was really like, and what the true nature of his own supposedly religious zeal was. Conversion to Christ had not only changed his beliefs, it had converted his methods of defending them. It is an ugly sight when conversion to Christ does one without the other.

Paul, then, understood what motivated the crowd, and he loved them, even though they would freely have murdered him. They desperately needed to have their eyes opened, to be disabused of their imagined zeal for God which, if persisted in, would damn their souls. He would speak to them. Useless to protest to Paul that it was hopeless to try and convert them. The same thing would once have been said about him; and yet he had been converted. True evangelist that he was, he decided to tell them the story of his own conversion.

He had an advantage over them: they were biblically uneducated, he had been trained under that famous biblical scholar, Gamaliel, here in the highest centre of biblical studies, Jerusalem itself (22:3). They were 'zealous for God', but nothing like he had been. Their riot was a merely spontaneous eruption of emotion; his persecution was deliberate, systematic, officially authorised by the then current high priest, thorough and relentless. What could any one of them in the crowd teach him about zeal for God? Or about protecting Israel's privileges or the sanctity of the temple?

If now he had received a vision from heaven itself, and in its irresistible light had caught sight of reality, that the Jesus of Nazareth he was persecuting was in fact the risen and glorified Messiah, how could that be regarded as disloyalty to the nation on his part? Had not Moses and Isaiah and others of the prophets received similar visions of God? Why must he be dismissed out of hand as a heretic for having one?

But perhaps he had mistaken the vision, or else misinterpreted it?

No, he hadn't. The vision had been interpreted to him by one of the local Jewish community in Damascus, a devout observer of the law and highly respected by all the Jews living there. He was no heretic. Yet here were his very words authenticated by God himself, in that he was empowered by God to remove the physical blindness induced in Paul by the supernatural brilliance of the vision: 'The God of our fathers has chosen you to know his will and to see the Righteous One and to hear words from his mouth. You will be his witness to all men of what you have seen and heard' (22:14).

Here was no heresy either, denying the one true God that Israel had learned of from the patriarchs: it was the God of these very patriarchs who had chosen Paul for his special mission. He was telling Paul, and Paul was now divinely commissioned to tell everyone else, that Jesus of Nazareth was the Righteous One. He was not the impostor the nation had judged him to be. He was in fact right, and they had been wrong. He had not only been a just man, he was *the* Just One, the Messiah of God.

That was strong medicine for the crowd, and it is perhaps a wonder that they did not interrupt at that point. But then Paul, by relating all this as part of his conversion story, had made it clear that he was not claiming to be superior to the crowd, that they were guilty and he was innocent. He shared their guilt. Indeed, he had been more guilty, more rabid than they, in persecuting Jesus of Nazareth. He had admitted his guilt and found pardon: they could too.

But – and here he began to tread on very sensitive ground – why had he not stayed in Jerusalem and continued zealously to guard Israel's privileges and temple, instead of going off to the Gentiles and there diluting Israel's rights?

Because, on his return from Damascus to Jerusalem, he was in the temple when once more the Lord appeared to him in a trance and told him to get out of Jerusalem quickly because the Jerusalemites would not receive his testimony of Jesus (22:17–18).

That prophecy, if nothing else, had been proved true: the crowd themselves were proof of it. But it was really putting the knife in, to say that the Lord had had such a poor view of the Jerusalemites.

But Paul, sticking up for the people as always, had protested to the Lord that they were not as bad as all that. They were reasonable people. They knew how he had zealously persecuted the Christians. They knew how he had stood with the crowd and encouraged them when they executed Stephen. Surely they would be reasonable and listen to him as one who had always fought for them, and would not blindly dismiss him out of hand.

379

But the Lord simply repeated his order: 'Go; I will send you far away to the Gentiles' (22:21).

The crowd had been listening quietly so far; but they now exploded, and the point at which the abscess burst showed the real cause of the inflammation. It was humiliating enough to be told that the Jesus they had rejected was the Messiah; but the thought that because of their rejection God had taken Israel's Messiah and offered him to the Gentiles, and that the Gentiles were accepting him, was insufferable. They were like mummy's blue-eyed boy, who has been given a beautiful toy. But for some reason he rejects it, and refuses to play with it. Then mummy goes and offers it to another infant, who is delighted to have it. At which the blue-eyed boy is convulsed with rage. The Jerusalemites' zeal for God was not true zeal for protecting God's interests and holiness: it was zeal for protecting their own selfish privileges. It was what made them imagine they saw Gentiles invading their holy temple court when in fact there were no Gentiles in sight.

Paul recognised this as well. Their anti-Gentile jealousy had just tried to murder him. But hope rose in his heart. All was not lost. One day God would use this very jealousy to bring the nation to repentance, to follow the Gentiles in accepting their true Lord, Jesus, as God's Messiah (Rom. 11:11–16).

The commander's proposal to examine Paul

Paul's address to the crowd had probably not helped the commander much, for Paul had spoken in Aramaic (22:2). But he was determined to get to the bottom of the matter. He was responsible for the defence of law and order in that notoriously difficult city where religion and politics were a highly volatile mixture and the vapour from one hot-head could suddenly ignite spontaneously and engulf the whole city in a conflagration. And he was also answerable to some very tough, and sometimes unreasonable, masters. He meant to see justice done; but in defending law and order, you could not afford to be squeamish. The law gave him the right to examine suspect trouble-makers under torture; and he decided to use his right. He ordered Paul to be stretched and bound ready for a flogging (22:24).

Unbeknown to him – though he should have enquired first – Paul was a Roman citizen; and it was seriously illegal to string Paul up like that and flog him. Paul got word to him, and he immediately desisted. He was surprised, however, to find that such an unlikely looking character as Paul must by this time have appeared was in fact a Roman citizen. 'It cost me a large sum of money', he confessed, 'to obtain Roman citizenship.' 'But I was actually born a citizen,' Paul replied (22:28).

So now another cat was out of its bag: the sum of money the commander had paid for Roman citizenship was in fact a bribe and illegal; though, of course, thousands of people paid such bribes and a lot of people in the higher ranks made a lot of money receiving them. But then, in what country could you count on all the defenders of law and order to be above corruption themselves? And when he eventually wrote his report to the governor, Felix, he managed to cook the books a little and cover up the fact that he had bound a Roman citizen ready for examination under torture. And Paul, we may be sure, never reported him.

The commander has Paul examined before the Sanhedrin

Next day, still determined to get to the bottom of the trouble, so that the city could be pacified, the commander ordered the Sanhedrin to meet, and brought Paul before them. Paul began proceedings by looking straight at the members of the council and declaring 'I have fulfilled my duty to God in all good conscience to this day' (23:1). It was not meant as an arrogant boast, nor intended to taunt the bench. He knew that his behaviour since his conversion had enraged them all; in their eyes he was a dangerous turn-coat and apostate. He was offering them a sincere explanation: incredible though it might sound to them, he had always acted out of a genuine conscience that what he did was what God would have him do. Did they not, as responsible members of the nation's highest religious court, all of them seek to live on the same principle? Was there not at least this minimum of common ground between him and them? Much as they disagreed with what he did and taught, surely they could grant that he acted out of a sincere conscience before God. What debate, what discussion, what fair investigation was possible, if one side was not prepared to assume, at least to begin with, that the other side was motivated by a sincere, if mistaken, conscience? If it was the court's foregone conclusion that he was a deliberate religious fraud, there was an end to all discussion. And the same is still true today. It would be false to pretend that differences over the fundamentals of the faith are matters of indifference over which we can all agree to differ and yet remain united. But we must surely begin by supposing that those who stand on the other side, whatever it is, act, as far as they know, out of a sincere conscience.

But at Paul's opening remark the president of the court ordered those standing near him to strike him on the mouth; and drew an immediate retort from Paul: 'God will strike you, you whitewashed wall! You sit there to judge me according to the law, yet you yourself violate the law by commanding that I be struck!' (23:3).

Armchair critics have accused Paul of unChristlike behaviour in reacting this way. But Christ himself protested (even if with more restraint) when another high priest's official with similar injustice struck him in the face (John 18:22–23). It was plainly outrageous that the high priest should openly flout the law in the very court where he was responsible for defending and enforcing it. Religious corruption is the worst corruption of all: it is rightly rebuked in the most trenchant terms.

But at that point the men standing near Paul protested to him: 'You dare to insult God's high priest?' (23:4). And immediately Paul apologised for having unwittingly broken the law, which he then quoted, 'Do not speak evil about the ruler of your people' (Exod. 22:28). How it was that Paul had not recognised that it was the high priest who had given the order to strike him on the mouth has never been explained to everyone's satisfaction, though various explanations can be given. But the whole incident furnished uncontrived evidence that here was a man who meant what he said when he claimed to have lived with a good conscience before God. This particular high priest, perhaps more than Paul with his long absence from the city knew, was a complete rotter, so history tells us, quite prepared to rob the lower priesthood of their dues and resort to assassination when it furthered his cause. On this occasion too he had blatantly broken the law; yet Paul apologised to his office if not to him. Paul knew his biblical law; his conscience would never rest if he broke it, however unintentionally and under whatever provocation, and then did not apologise.

But the high priest had shown his hand. What kind of a hearing, what kind of justice could Paul expect from such a court? The accusations with which the Jews from Asia had incited the riot were false; and in any case they were not the real cause of the Sanhedrin's animosity against him. Paul had known the Sanhedrin well in his earlier days, particularly when he had co-operated with an earlier high priest in persecuting the Christians. He knew also, of course, why earlier still they had tried to suppress the apostles, and would have executed them all unless his teacher Gamaliel had urged wiser counsels on them. Of course they were livid against him since his conversion; and the real cause was nothing other than his preaching of the resurrection of Jesus.

But where in a court packed with Sadducees would he ever get a fair hearing for the evidence for the resurrection of Jesus? Sadducees, as Luke explains (23:8), did not accept even the possibility of resurrection – anyone's resurrection, let alone the resurrection of Jesus. They did not believe in angels, or even in the survival of the human spirit after death. The most powerful members of the council, therefore, were fundamentally prejudiced, and their prejudice would predetermine the verdict; for the Pharisees present, who did believe in the possibility of resurrection, and might be open to a reasoned presentation of the evidence for the resurrection of Jesus, would be voted down. If the Roman commander was ever going to be able to form a fair assessment of this court's findings – and Paul's life might hang on that – it was vital that the basic prejudice of half or more of the court should be exposed.

And Paul exposed it. He cried out in court: 'Brothers, I am a Pharisee, a son of Pharisees. It is in connection with the hope of the resurrection of the dead that I am here on trial' (23:6). That split the court in two; and the expert biblical scholars among the Pharisees, determining not to be put down by the Sadducees, began to argue furiously on Paul's side that he had done no wrong, that he had a right to his basic view, even allowing the possibility that in his vision on the Damascus road he might have received a genuine revelation through some angel or spirit (23:9).

In the end the uproar became so violent that the commander feared for Paul's safety. He ordered the troops in and had Paul taken back to barracks. But Paul's tactics had achieved the laudable end of letting the commander see for himself the truth of the matter, and what the real trouble was. His report to the governor eventually read: 'I wanted to know why they were accusing him, so I brought him to their Sanhedrin. I found that the accusation had to do with questions about their law, but there was no charge against him that deserved death or imprisonment' (23:28–29).

The true verdict

Again, many armchair critics have condemned Paul for his tactics, as though they were somehow underhanded and deliberately obscured the real issue, which was not whether there was to be a general resurrection of all men, but whether the particular man Jesus had risen from the dead. Presumably, they would have been quite happy for the high priest to have rendered a negative, even a damning verdict against Paul and thus against the gospel, without the commander's ever being aware of how unfairly prejudiced half the court was. And where would have been the justice in that?

But Paul, at least, need not worry. That night the Lord delivered the only verdict that counts. Announcing his pleasure at the way Paul had witnessed for him in Jerusalem, he informed him that he would do the same in Rome (23:11).

MOVEMENT 3: The Gospel to be Judged by its Attitude to Morality and the Law (23:12–24:27)

The assassins' conspiracy

The army commander was soon to discover, if he did not know it before, that religion does not always feel itself obliged to follow strict morality in the way that ordinary mortals are supposed to do. When it wishes to defend itself or destroy an enemy, it can persuade itself that the defence of truth justifies dispensing with morality altogether. So it was that the day after the meeting of the Sanhedrin, more than forty Jews decided to defend God's honour and the sanctity of the temple by binding themselves with a solemn religious oath before God not to eat anything until they had deceived the Roman commander, broken the law and committed murder (23:12–13)! Of course they did not phrase it to themselves like that; for religion can find terms that make crime seem holy and noble. But crime it was that they were proposing in God's name; and their scheme involved the willing co-operation of the high priest and elders, who were to ask the commander to bring Paul before the Sanhedrin again on the pretext that they wanted more information on his case, so that the assassins could way-lay and kill him on his road to the court. And this high priest and these elders were the very men who would later stand in Felix's Roman court and prosecute Paul on a capital charge of having broken the law!

Somehow news of the conspiracy leaked out to one of Paul's relatives, who told it to Paul, and (on Paul's advice) to the commander (23:16–18). He, sensible man, decided that the whole thing was getting him out of his depth. He was responsible for protecting the life of a Roman citizen until true justice was done. If the highest Jewish court in the land was prepared to stoop to such skulduggery to destroy Paul, then it was time to refer the whole matter to the provincial governor before the situation got completely out of hand. And that was how Paul found himself dispatched under military protection to Caesarea, to stand trial before Felix, accompanied by the explanatory letter from the commander, which we have earlier noted, explaining the details of the case so far. Felix ascertained that Paul's city of origin placed him under his jurisdiction (23:34), and then made preparations for a formal trial.

The trial before Felix

Felix's court, mercifully enough for Paul, was not the Sanhedrin. That court, the highest Jewish legal body, based its laws on the Old Testament as interpreted by as best a consensus as could be arrived at by a body composed of both Sadducees and Pharisees. Woe betide anybody in that court who differed from the Sadducees and Pharisees in the interpretation of the Old Testament! What Felix presided over was a Roman court of civil law, where a man's religous beliefs were irrelevant unless they conflicted with the laws of the state.

Moreover, the session of the Sanhedrin before which the commander had produced Paul was an investigation, not a formal trial. It had been presided over by the high priest, who was himself Paul's chief opponent. No other independent prosecutors or witnesses are mentioned as having been present. Its purpose was to let the commander discover what the Sanhedrin had against Paul. But the session in Felix's court was a formal trial. Felix was the (supposedly) impartial judge, before whom the prosecution had to produce definite charges relevant to this civil court; and the people who made the accusations embodied in the charges had to be personally present in the court so that the defendant might know and see who it was that accused him.

In court the prosecution consisted of the high priest and certain elders, some of whom must have been Pharisees, judging by Paul's later reference to them (24:15). The prosecution was represented by an orator, Tertullus, the ancient equivalent of a barrister. He opened his case with the usual (but in this instance somewhat exaggerated) compliments to the judge (24:2–3), and then laid four charges against Paul:

1. He was a 'pest' (24:5). 'Pest' (or 'troublemaker') was a vague but powerful smear word, one you would use when you wanted to insinuate that the defendant had engaged in activity treasonable to the Caesar, but you could not specify exactly what the treasonable activity was. Since it was an unsupported assertion and contained no specific item, Paul, when it came to his defence, ignored it.
2. He had 'stirred up riots among the Jews all over the world' (24:5).
3. He was 'a ringleader of the Nazarene sect' (24:5).
4. He had attempted 'to desecrate the temple; so we seized [i.e. arrested] him' (24:6).

The last charge calls for some preliminary comment. The original accusation levelled by the Asian Jews was that Paul had actually introduced Greeks into the inner court (21:28). If that accusation was true, then Paul had not merely attempted to desecrate the temple: he *had* desecrated it. But now in Felix's court the prosecution have dropped that charge, and replaced it with one of 'attempted desecration'. And the force of their next remark, 'so we seized [i.e. arrested] him', seems to be that they arrested him before he succeeded in the attempt. What form the intended desecration would have taken, had it been carried out, is not specified.

The statement 'we arrested him' likewise calls for comment. What actually happened was that the mob seized Paul, dragged him out of the inner court and began beating him to death, and the Roman army commander arrived and rescued him from this 'arrest' (21:30–33). Were the high priest and the elders through their lawyer now claiming responsibility and credit for this arrest?

Unfortunately the Greek text at this point is uncertain. In the great majority of manuscripts the lawyer simply adds 'By examining him [i.e. Paul] yourself you will be able to learn the truth about all these charges we are bringing against him' (24:8). The majority of scholars, therefore, hold this to be what Luke originally wrote.

It is worth mentioning, however, that the Western text of Acts has an addition here which turns the end of their fourth charge into a complaint against the interference of the Roman commander:

> . . . and we arrested him and wanted to judge him according to our law. But the commander, Lysias, came and with the use of much force snatched him from our hands and ordered his accusers to come before

you. By examining him [i.e. Lysias] yourself you will be able to learn the truth about all these charges we are bringing against Paul.*

This addition, then, represents the prosecution as claiming the right to judge a desecrator of the temple in their own court, the Sanhedrin – which was true; as claiming that that was what they were intending to do until the commander arrived – which was not true (if Lysias had not rescued Paul, Paul never would have been tried in any court: mob law would have killed him); as claiming that the Roman commander had no right to interfere – which again was not true (he certainly had a right to interfere to defend a citizen – and especially a Roman citizen – and to make sure that there was a prima facie case against him before handing him over to the Sanhedrin – not to the mob – for an ordered trial); and finally as claiming that the commander had used excessive force in taking Paul from them – interesting, in light of the fact that they were in process of beating Paul to death.

Whether the Western Text's addition is original or not, we should notice two things. First, Felix eventually announced that he would defer his verdict until Lysias came to Caesarea (24:22). Secondly, and more importantly, if the prosecution did in fact complain to Felix about Lysias' interference, it was no concern of Paul's: he had simply to answer the charges levelled against him.

Paul's defence before Felix

Paul's opening remarks necessarily complimented the judge – that was standard form – but they were also germane to Paul's case. Felix, as Paul pointed out (24:10–11), was an old hand: he had been governor of Judea for many years, and knew all about the internal politics of Jerusalem, the ways of both Sadducees and Pharisees, and a good deal also about Jewish religion, since his wife was a Jewess (24:24). Moreover, he was already well acquainted with Christianity and what it stood for (24:22). There would be no need to answer before him the prosecution's vague aspersion that Christianity was treasonable.

Paul proceeded at once, therefore, to the first substantial charge (no. 2 on our list above). It was that he had stirred up riots

---

*This addition was taken over here by the AV, but has been dropped even by Z. C. Hodges and A. L. Farstad, *The Greek New Testament According to the Majority Text* (Nashville: T. Nelson, 1982), p. 459. See also the discussion in Bruce M. Metzger, *A Textual Commentary on the Greek New Testament*, corrected edition (London/New York: United Bible Societies, 1975), p. 490.

among the Jews all over the world (24:5). Now it was certainly true that riots had occurred in many places as a result of Paul's preaching in the synagogues, Thessalonica and Berea being but two examples. But, as we saw earlier, there need have been no riots. All could have been calm and orderly, as it was at first in Berea. It was hot-heads who disliked Paul's teaching who took to the streets and started rioting, and followed Paul round from one city to another deliberately stirring up trouble.

Paul, however, did not choose to argue those cases all over again. The events had happened outside Felix's jurisdiction and could not be tried in his court. And what is more, Gallio, the Roman governor in Corinth, had already pronounced in Paul's favour. What Paul did, therefore, was to answer this charge of 'fomenting riots among the Jews' as it applied to his behaviour since he had been within Felix's jurisdiction. There had been no riot there until he got to Jerusalem; and the facts about his behaviour in the city were these:

> You can easily verify that no more than twelve days ago I went up to Jerusalem to worship. My accusers did not find me arguing with anyone at the temple, or stirring up a crowd in the synagogues or anywhere else in the city. And they cannot prove to you the charges they are now making against me. (24:11–13)

Actually, Paul would have been within his legal rights if he had held theological arguments with people at the temple, in the synagogues or in the streets. But he had deliberately refrained from doing so. It was reasonable for him to present his views in a synagogue in, say Antioch or Corinth, where he might expect to be listened to by the majority in a civilised manner, even if some hot-heads eventually turned violent. But in Jerusalem he was a marked man; and the Jews from Asia were watching his every move, waiting to stir up trouble. Preaching would have been not only useless, but counter-productive. For him to have attempted public debate anywhere with anybody would have immediately provoked a fanatical response and public disorder. He had had the common sense not to do it. He had not preached, lectured, debated or discussed anywhere in public. The riot in the temple was none of his making.

The next charge was that he was the ringleader of the Nazarene sect (24:5). Now the word translated 'sect' is an ambiguous term; its emotional connotation depends on who is using it of whom. In 5:17 it is used to describe the Sadducees; but there the translators tend to render it 'party'. The Sadducees were blue-blooded aristocrats, and the high priest and chief priests, as we have many times observed, were Sadducees, and were the leading group in the Sanhedrin. It would sound very odd to call them a 'sect' in the modern English sense of the term. On the other hand, small religious groups that separated themselves from the main body of Judaism, as the Christians then did, tended to be looked upon as sects in our modern sense; and as today, the label carried a bad meaning in itself and also tended to imply the added meaning 'heretical sect'. In this sense of the term, it is often sufficient to damn any group to call it a sect; and the prosecution certainly wanted to damn Paul by alleging that he was the ringleader of a very nasty little sect indeed.

Paul's response was to admit the charge! Not that he owned to being its ringleader, but he was certainly one of its members and leaders. 'However, I admit that I worship the God of our fathers as a follower of the Way, which they call a sect' (24:14). But then he proceeded to define this so-called sect's beliefs. It was 'the God of our fathers' that he worshipped – no strange, outlandish, foreign deity. Moreover, he 'believed everything that agrees with the Law and that is written in the Prophets' (24:14). What could be more orthodox? Of course that left open the question of the right interpretation of Scripture. Yet it is a curious fact that many small groups have a tendency to believe in all that is in Scripture in a way that those who dub them 'sects' sometimes do not. But can it rightly be called 'sectarian' to believe in the whole of Scripture?

Moreover, said Paul, 'I have the same hope in God as these men,' doubtless pointing out the Pharisees among the prosecutors, 'that there will be a resurrection of both the righteous and the wicked' (24:15). And who could be thought of as more orthodox than the Pharisees? Doubtless they could be described as one party, and the Sadducees as another, because they disagreed sharply over many things, and in particular about this matter of the resurrection; but nobody ever thought of damning the Pharisees as a sect.

But ugliness, like beauty, is in the eye of the beholder; and it mattered little to Paul whether unfriendly people called the Christians a sect or not. What mattered at this moment was the relevance of the charge to the civil court. What Felix would want to know was: What effect did the beliefs of this sect have on its members' attitude to the state and to its laws? And this was the point that Paul now concentrated on. Central to his faith was this belief that there would be a resurrection of both the righteous and the wicked; and it was no mere theory, but exercised its control over everything he said and did: 'So in this belief I train myself constantly to maintain a clear conscience before God and men' (24:16).

Observe the last two words. Standing before the Sanhedrin, Paul had declared that he had behaved in all good conscience towards God (23:1). But that was in a religious court. Now he stood on trial before the Roman governor in a civil court, and in declaring the scope of his conscience, his use of the words 'before God *and men*' was not mere rhetoric. The God before whom he must stand at the resurrection had, so he believed and taught, established the governing authorities, which at the present moment meant the Roman government. To rebel against them, therefore, was to rebel against God, for they were God's servants, agents of justice to bring punishment on the wrongdoer. Therefore all Christians must submit to the authorities, not only because of possible punishment, but also *because of conscience* (Rom. 13:1–2, 4–5). To break the law of the land, unless that law was contrary to the law of God himself, was to sin against God. Christians, believing sincerely as they did in the resurrection of both the righteous and the wicked, could not deliberately flout the Roman law of the land; rather, they would aim to obey it punctiliously, and so commend the gospel to the governing authorities.

The high priest and his Sadducean elders did not believe in a resurrection of the just and the wicked. What kept them behaving as they should was of course for them to decide. But a good dosage of the Christians' (and the Pharisees') belief in such a resurrection could not have done them any harm. It might even have kept them from conspiring with a bunch of assassins to flout the Roman law, ambush a small detachment of Roman soldiers and murder Paul, all in the cause of defending the sanctity of God's temple! Of course Paul did not make any such observation in front of Felix. But perhaps he had no need: Felix had read the letter from Lysias (see 23:30). But if we in our day would be in a position to defend the gospel before the civil authorities as Paul did, it is evident that we must hold the same view of those authorities as Paul did, and likewise train ourselves to obey them meticulously, for conscience's sake, for the gospel's sake, for God's sake.

The last charge they brought against Paul was that he had attempted to desecrate the temple (24:6).

The part of the original charge that claimed he had brought Greeks into the temple had been quietly dropped: no Greek had been either found in the inner court or arrested. So was the part that alleged he taught people everywhere against the Jews. So also was the part that accused him of teaching against the law and the temple (21:28). The prosecution had been wise to drop them, for according to Roman law accusers must be present in court to make their accusations; and the Asian Jews who had originally incited the crowd to riot by making these allegations when they found Paul in the temple were now conveniently not in court (24:18–19). As for the remaining charge, that he had attempted to desecrate the temple in ways unspecified: the facts were that on that occasion he was bringing gifts for the poor in his nation, and presenting offerings. He was in a state of ceremonial purity; there was no crowd with him, and he was not involved in disturbing anybody (24:17–18).

In the absence of the Jews from Asia, the only accusation the high priest and the elders could bring against him must arise out of the findings of the enquiry they conducted in the Sanhedrin in the presence of Lysias. And what findings could they report – except the fact that he had shouted out 'It is concerning the resurrection of the dead that I am on trial before you today' (24:21)? And what crime or felony was that? All the Pharisees in the Sanhedrin (and everywhere else) believed in the resurrection. Would the high priest and his colleagues have the Romans execute all the Pharisees as well?

Having heard both sides of the case, Felix adjourned the proceedings. He was, says Luke, 'well acquainted with the Way' (24:22), and must have seen that the case against Paul was not only unproved but preposterous. Then why did he not acquit Paul there and then? He gave as his reason that he must wait for Lysias to come to Caesarea so that he could question him in person before arriving at his verdict (24:22).

Meanwhile he reserved Paul in custody, though he allowed him considerable freedom and favours. But either Lysias never came down to Caesarea, or if he did, Felix forgot to consult him. For two years later, when Felix left office, Paul was still in custody. We shall now see why.

The sequel

Felix's third wife, Drusilla, was a Jewish princess. She had been the wife of the king of Emesa; and the rumour how she came to be Felix's wife would enliven the gossip column of any society magazine. Some days after the trial, he and his wife 'sent for Paul and listened to him as he spoke about faith in Christ Jesus' (24:24). It is often the case that people of their rank, who move in their particular set, behind the scenes find a certain fascination in those who have a deep personal and obviously genuine faith in Christ, as distinct from some prominent official religious leaders they have to meet with in the course of public life, like the Jewish high priest for whom religion meant little more than power, wealth and (often sordid) politics. And Christianity might well have appealed to Felix and Drusilla as a new religion with an unusual, novel appeal.

But Paul was a shrewd judge of character. What he told them of Christ, Luke leaves unrecorded. But apparently the conversation homed in on the topic of 'righteousness, self-control and the judgment to come' (24:25). What use presenting to them Jesus as Saviour, unless they first faced the serious moral and spiritual implications of the way they had lived and were living?

Presently the conversation got to Felix's conscience, and he began to feel afraid. And that fear suddenly induced another fear, as he realised where conscience might lead if it really was allowed to get working. So he took a grip on himself and broke off the conversation, though subsequently he often held further meetings with Paul. But he never let them go to the dangerous lengths the first one had; for he had rather different reasons for developing an interest in Paul and cultivating his friendship. Paul at the trial had mentioned that he had come to Jerusalem with a large amount of money which he had collected from the Christian churches all round the world for the Jewish poor in Jerusalem (24:17). And Felix would have known about it from the grapevine anyway. Perhaps the money had already been disbursed. Who knows? But in any case, if Paul was in a hurry to get out of prison, and wanted to persuade Felix to clear up the case and let him out, Paul could surely lay his hands on a suitable amount of persuasion to do the job. After all, why take on the high office of defending justice and the law, if you can't at times be open to reasonable persuasion?

But the gospel Paul defended in public with talk of the resurrection, of the judgement, of justice, of obedience for conscience's sake to the law of the land, did not permit him to flout the law in private and bribe his way out of prison, not even if the very defender of the Roman law was prepared to be a party to it. Felix never got his bribe.

And then Felix was recalled to Rome, and another consideration weighed on his mind. His recent handling of Jewish affairs had got him into severe disfavour with the Jews. If now he further angered the Sanhedrin by letting Paul out of prison, ugly complaints might follow him all the way to Rome. Felix therefore thought it wise to give the Jews a parting sweetener: he left Paul in prison (24:27). After all, the continued imprisonment of an innocent man was a small price to pay for keeping the defender of justice himself out of trouble, wasn't it?

MOVEMENT 4: The Gospel to be Judged by its Message for Caesar and the World (25:1–26:32)

The trial before Festus

Upon entering office, the new governor of the province, Festus, made it his business to contact the leading citizens of Judea as soon as he could. Three days after arriving in Caesarea he went up to Jerusalem (25:1).

When they met, the chief priests and the aristocracy raised the matter of Paul, and requested that he should be brought up to Jerusalem and the case settled. New to the province, Festus of course would not have known that they still had a bunch of assassins organised to ambush and kill Paul on the road if ever he was brought up to Jerusalem (25:3). In his innocence, and standing like a new boy on proper protocol, Festus insisted that Paul's accusers should come down to the governor's headquarters and prosecute Paul there (25:5).

So eventually another Roman trial was held in Caesarea, this time with Festus as judge. The trial doubtless followed the same general lines as the first one, and Luke does not trouble to record it so fully as the first. But one significant new detail emerges. Among the many serious but unproven charges which the prosecution brought against Paul (25:7), there must this time have been one or two more that specifically accused him of action or teaching treasonable to Caesar; for Paul in his defence specifically rebutted the charge of treason: 'I have done nothing wrong against the law of the Jews or against the temple *or against Caesar*' (25:8).

We can only imagine what the particular terms of the charge were; but in all likelihood they followed the same line as the Jews at Thessalonica had urged: that in preaching the kingdom of God, and the Lord Jesus as King, Paul was in fact advocating a form of political messianism, and was engaged in fomenting civil unrest designed eventually to lead to a popular uprising against Roman imperialism. It was, as we saw earlier, a specious charge, always worth trying, and apt to impress nervous Roman governors who were all too aware how easily religion among the Jews could be used by political activists to incite rebellion. There had been such messianic uprisings before; there would be again.

At the same time it was a difficult charge for a Roman governor, especially a new one, to deal with. Festus felt, as we know from his subsequent remarks to Agrippa (25:18–19) and from his statement at the enquiry (25:25), that Paul was completely innocent of any treasonable behaviour, as he was of the other material charges brought against him; and that would have put the prosecution in bad light in Festus' judgement. On the other hand, the prosecution was composed of the president and leading aristocratic members of the highest Jewish legal court in the land. A new governor could not afford to get into their bad books so early on in his term of office. If he did, they could make serious difficulty for him. If they as the most responsible members of the Jewish community let it be known in Rome that against their advice Festus had released from prison a man whom they knew to be a political agitator against the Caesar, he could have found himself in very hot water. An earlier high priest had blackmailed Pontius Pilate in this way, to persuade him to crucify Jesus Christ against his better judgement (John 19:12). That kind of thing could be done again.

Before delivering his verdict, therefore, Festus decided to make a gesture of good-will towards the Jews. He enquired if Paul would be willing to go up to Jerusalem and stand trial before him there on these same charges (25:9). But Paul could at once perceive how, quite apart from the risk of assassination, going up to Jerusalem again for trial could easily injure both him and the gospel. If the prosecution had contented themselves with the charges of disrespect for the Jews' law and with attempted desecration of the temple, then perhaps Jerusalem, scene of the alleged crimes, was the appropriate place to hold the trial. But now the prosecution had added the explicit charge of treason against Caesar; and unlike the other charges, this one referred not merely to his activity in Jerusalem, but to what he had done all round the Roman Empire. It concerned not merely alleged acts of visiting the temple in a state of ceremonial impurity or of bringing Gentiles into the temple: it concerned what he taught, the very heart indeed of the gospel. He did not preach political messian-

369 Wokam Road.

Dear Margaret + Stuart.

Thank you both for a lovely evening

Really enjoyed.

love Jean x

ism; it was a travesty of the truth to accuse him of doing so. But he did preach that Jesus was King Messiah.

The place for a charge of treason to be heard, therefore, was a Roman court held under the authority of the Caesar. Paul was already standing on trial before such a court in the headquarters of the Roman provincial administration. It made no sense to move the proceedings to Jerusalem. Paul could see that Festus had already grasped the fact that he was innocent of the charges relating to the Jewish law, temple and people (25:10). But to take him to be tried in Jerusalem on a charge of treason against Caesar would be dangerously prejudicial to Paul's case. For there Festus would come under enormous pressure from the high priests, chief priests and the rest of the Sadducean aristocracy. It was these Jews, not any Roman official, consul, praetor, army commander or magistrate, that had formulated this charge of treason; and they had done it not because they really believed it, nor because they were genuinely concerned for the Caesar's interests, but because it could be a very effective way of suppressing not only Paul but the message he preached, that Jesus of Nazareth was risen from the dead. If numbers of high-placed Jews – leading responsible members of the highest Jewish court (and not just some Jewish rabble, as in Thessalonica) – accused a Jew of political messianism, it could sound very convincing to a new governor who did not yet know the men he was dealing with.

Now Paul had the right as a Roman citizen to appeal to Caesar; and if he did so, that would have the effect of taking the matter out of the local provincial court altogether. It might be a risky thing to do. Justice in Nero's court was not always of virgin purity; but at least Nero could not be pressurised in the same way as a recently arrived provincial governor could be in Jerusalem. Paul was not trying to escape the death penalty if he deserved it (or if Nero decided he deserved it, which was not quite the same thing). But he refused to have the Roman provincial court virtually hand him over to the prejudices and pressures of the high priest and the aristocracy at Jerusalem, and then on that basis to publish a verdict that damned both Paul and the gospel in the name of Roman justice. Let Roman justice be Roman justice, not Sadducean prejudice masquerading under that name (25:10–11). And besides, even if Paul were acquitted by Festus in Jerusalem, that would not be the end of the matter: the Jews would bring the same charges against him in other provinces, as they had done in Thessalonica in the province of Macedonia.

Whereas, if he could obtain a favourable verdict in Rome, that would settle the matter throughout the empire.

So Paul appealed to Caesar; and not the least consideration that moved him to do so would have been the fact that the Lord himself had two years earlier informed him that he was to witness for him in Rome just as he had done in Jerusalem (23:11).

Festus consulted his advisers, and decided to allow the appeal (25:12).

Festus consults King Agrippa II

Paul's appeal to Caesar placed Festus in a difficulty. He had actually seen through the prosecution's case, and had realised that it was at least at bottom concerned with, and motivated by, a dispute over Jewish religious beliefs (25:18–19). The charge of treason was bogus. But that very realisation put him in a quandary. When Paul was eventually sent for trial in Rome, Festus would have to write a report on his case for Nero. And what could he put in it? What was the case that the emperor was meant to try (25:26–27)?

Fortunately for Festus, round about that time King Agrippa II and his wife Bernice came to Caesarea on a courtesy visit, and Festus was able to consult Agrippa on the topic. But the very fact that Festus had this quandary, and that Luke saw fit to record in detail Festus' statement of it to Agrippa (25:13–22), is for us highly significant. If Festus had had the slightest lingering suspicion that Paul may have been involved in teaching political subversion, he would have had no qualms whatever over what to put in his report to Nero. Not to have mentioned his least suspicion in that direction could have been interpreted in Rome as itself treasonable negligence or even complicity. But if he had to write that the man in his opinion was not guilty of treason, then why was he sending Paul to Rome at all? He couldn't call on Nero to settle a theological dispute between Jews, could he?

Now Agrippa II had a reputation of being an expert in all matters relating to Jewish religion and customs (26:3); and when Festus put the situation before him, he expressed a wish to hear Paul himself (25:22). And so a public hearing was arranged for the next day.

The enquiry before King Agrippa II and Bernice

Festus' instruction of the court

Festus' formal instruction of the court made a number of important points:

1. *The case so far.* The Jewish community at large had sued for the death penalty on Paul (25:24) on a number of charges.
2. *Festus' findings so far.* Although it had not been possible to proceed to a formal verdict at the trial (because Paul had stopped proceedings by appealing to Caesar), Festus now publicly announced that he personally had found all the charges unproved: Paul had done nothing worthy of death (25:25).
3. *The appeal to Caesar.* Paul had exercised his right to appeal to Caesar, and Festus had allowed the appeal (25:25).
4. *The nature of the present proceedings.* It was not a continuation of the trial: *that* had been brought to an end by Paul's appeal. It was not a new trial: *that* would take place before Caesar. It was an enquiry (25:26). It could not pronounce an official verdict: *that* must be left to Caesar.
5. *The purpose of the enquiry.* In allowing Paul's appeal to Caesar, Festus had put himself under obligation to instruct Caesar as to the case Caesar was being asked to try. The enquiry was being held to elicit from Paul what he actually believed, taught, preached and practised, so that, the information being sent to Caesar, Caesar might decide whether it constituted in part or whole a threat to the state, or treason against himself.

Important as it was for all present to understand exactly what the purpose of the enquiry was, it was doubly so for Paul. He had no longer to deal with the trumped up charges of attempted desecration of the temple; he had no longer to argue for the freedom of the individual's conscience within Judaism as he had done in the enquiry before the Sanhedrin; he had no longer to argue, as he had done in the trial before Felix, that he had not broken particular laws either of the temple or of the state, and that the basic beliefs of Christianity obliged all Christians to abide by such individual laws. He had now to do nothing less than to expound the heart and essence of the Christian gospel and to show that the gospel itself was not a form of treason against the Caesar or the government. And as he expounded the gospel before this court, he had to be aware that he was not merely informing King Agrippa and Governor Felix on what Christianity really stood for, enormously important though that was. He was in a sense already addressing the Caesar; for what he now said would form the basis of Festus' letter to the emperor. Through Paul the gospel was now to declare its message for the benefit of Caesar and of the world.

Paul's defence of the gospel

It was politic of Paul – and required form – to begin his defence of the gospel by complimenting King Agrippa, the most eminent person in the court, at whose request the hearing had been arranged (25:22). But Paul's compliments (26:2–3) were heartfelt, and that for two reasons. First, the charge that the gospel Paul preached was treasonable had been levelled against him not by the Romans but by the Jews. Secondly, he was going to argue that the gospel he preached, about which the Caesar must judge, was in fact nothing other than Israel's traditional hope; understood, of course, and interpreted as he and the other Christians understood and interpreted it, but nonetheless basically and essentially Israel's hope. It was, therefore, a comfort and encouragement to Paul to be able to expound Christianity's understanding of that hope to an eminent expert on Jewish traditions and affairs (26:3) who nevertheless was not prejudiced by the minority view and vested interests of the ruling Sadducees in Jerusalem.

Consistent with his intention to represent himself as the maintainer of Israel's traditional hope, Paul began by giving his spiritual curriculum vitae. His credentials were impeccable. Born, bred and brought up in the heart of his nation, both in Tarsus and in Jerusalem, he had from his youth been a member of the strictest of the major religious parties, namely the Pharisees (26:4–5). That was common knowledge among the Jews. And no one had ever thought hitherto of suggesting that the doctrines of the Pharisees were treasonable!

As a youth he had adopted the nation's traditional hope as he had learned it from the Pharisees; and yet, perversely enough, it was for adhering to and promulgating that hope that the Jews had put him on trial:

> And now it is because of my hope in what God has promised our fathers that I am on trial today. This is the promise our twelve tribes*
> are hoping to see fulfilled as they earnestly serve God day and night.
> O King, it is because of this hope that the Jews are accusing me.
> (26:6–7)

---

*This is of course conventional language: but the phrase 'twelve tribes' deliberately emphasises the fact that the hope was held by all sections of the nation.

What, then, was that hope? Undeniably it was Israel's messianic hope. No one who knew anything about the Old Testament prophets, or contemporary Jewish thought and the aspirations of Israel, would or could deny it. Different sections in Israel might interpret it differently; but there could be no denying that basically the hope was for the coming of the Messiah, for the establishment of the messianic age, when evil would be put down, Satan's influence and activities eliminated, universal justice secured, and universal peace enjoyed. It was not only ironic but tragic that the Jews would accuse Paul to the Roman emperor of holding and propagating Israel's hope. This was the hope that distinguished Israel from all the other nations and religions. Other nations and religions had ethical codes and moral philosophies. Only Israel had this message of hope. It was the hope that all the world unconsciously yearned for. It would be tragic if Israel were now to deny it.

True Christianity clings to that hope still, for the simple reason that, as we are about to hear Paul state, it is the heart of the Christian gospel. We empty the very gospel of its heart and soul if we represent Christianity simply as a moral code, enhanced by a few religious ceremonies, teaching people to behave as decently as they can in view of the fact that one day in the dark shadows beyond death there might possibly be a judgement. True Christianity still holds and preaches the age-long hope of the coming of God's Messiah, now bodily risen from the dead, to put down evil, to judge and administer the world in righteousness, to establish his reign of universal justice and peace.

Of course, we can understand why some of Paul's contemporaries in Judaism wanted to play down Israel's messianic hope, or to deny it altogether. There was a persistent and suicidal tendency in some quarters to interpret the hope in political terms, to think of the Messiah as a powerful military leader in the Maccabean mode, who would arm and lead Israel in battle to smash the Romans' grip on the country and to expel the hated imperialists. But it was outrageous to daub the Christians with this brush. It was their central tenet that the Old Testament preached a Messiah whose deliberate policy it was to suffer non-resistingly and to die at the hands both of the Romans and of his own nation; who when he returned to establish his messianic reign, would not be competing as one military or political power against another, but would come in the glory of God with the angels of God to establish God's own universal government.

The Sadducean priests had special reasons of their own, we

know, for rejecting even this (Christian) interpretation of Israel's hope, for wanting Paul executed and the Christian gospel suppressed. There was first of all the basic consideration that their predecessors in office had executed the Jesus whom Paul claimed to be the Messiah. But secondly, they had come to an understanding with the Romans. They were the ruling class in Israel and exercised all the political power that Israel was allowed to exercise. They held the high-priesthood and the chief-priesthoods; and they derived massive wealth from the temple's revenues from world-wide Jewry. They had no intention of giving up without a struggle and of allowing Paul to preach a gospel that would eventually undercut their authority. They were very happy with things as they were. Who wanted a messianic kingdom?

But within a few years their temple was gone, and their religio-political office; and they themselves gradually sank into obscurity. They had little or nothing to offer to continuing Judaism; and nothing at all to the world at large. And still today the only thing that Israel has to offer the world is not her ethics, noble as they are, still less her politics, but her messianic hope.

But now, openly and explicitly, Paul must raise with Agrippa the question of the resurrection of the Lord Jesus. It was not only the key and heart of the Christian interpretation of Israel's messianic hope; it was that element in it which showed beyond all doubt that the Christian gospel was not a political message nor treasonable to the Roman emperor.

Yet Paul realised clearly enough the instinctive reaction that mention of the resurrection of the Lord Jesus would provoke in Agrippa's mind: incredulity. It is, and always was, so: people of the ancient world found it no easier to believe in the bodily resurrection of the Lord Jesus than people of the modern world do. But the instinctive reaction of incredulity needs to be faced for what it is: simply an instinctive reaction. Days were when the vast majority of people thought the world was flat. And in those days, when the idea was advanced that the earth was round, people (and very thoughtful people at that) rejected it instinctively. It would imply, they said, that down on the other side of the world there would be people walking upside down, their feet so to speak opposite our feet on the ground and their heads hanging down into space. Instinct ridiculed the idea. But in the end facts prevailed over instinct.

'Why is it judged incredible among you', said Paul to Agrippa, 'that God should raise dead people?' (26:8).

He deliberately used the plural 'dead people'. The Pharisees, who were the leading religious party in the nation, already believed that there would be a resurrection of the just. They believed, of course, in the coming messianic age. Scripture taught it. But they saw clearly that unless there were a resurrection, all the generations of the godly except the last one were bound to miss participation in the joys and blessings of that age, in spite of the fact that they had waited, hoped, longed and prayed for its coming, and had, many of them, laid down their lives in loyalty to God in times of persecution. What hope was there in that? But then Old Testament scripture explicitly taught that the messianic age would be preceded and inaugurated by a resurrection of the dead (e.g. Dan. 12:2).

But if so, how could it any longer be thought incredible, at least by those who accepted Scripture (26:27), that God should raise the Messiah himself from the dead? Or indeed that he had already raised him, as the firstfruits, the first specimen, so to speak, to give substance and assurance to the hope of t⊦ ming glorious resurrection of all the redeemed (26:23)?

Well, that would depend in the first place ⁀he Messiah was due to die, and did in fact dⁱ really prescribe such a programme for ' they did. That was the Christian claim, argue (26:22–23). It was open to Agrippa

But Paul would not argue that first. Wha doing so, if he could not provide Agrippa w Lord Jesus had in fact already risen from the evidence would he cite?

He decided to tell Agrippa the story of his conv⊾ had told it to the frenzied mob at the foot of the Jerusalem two years ago (22:2–21). How different the now, and how different the audience. It would call f⌐ ₊ntly different slant and emphasis in telling the story. But it ⌐ould be the same story. Paul's conversion through his direct meeting with the risen Lord on the Damascus road was and still is a powerful part of the historical evidence for the resurrection of Christ (1 Cor. 15:4–11). But the nature of this particular piece of evidence was doubly relevant to the hearing before Agrippa. At stake and under question was the character of the Christian gospel. Was it, or was it not, treasonable to the emperor? And then, way and beyond that, was it a reasonable gospel, holding out a credible hope for the world? In that context, then, the character of the Christian messianic hope, based and centred as it was on the resurrection of the Lord Jesus, could rightly be judged and assessed by the effect it had had on Paul, the change it had made on his outlook and behaviour and the effect it was likely to have all round the Roman Empire on those who believed his preaching.

'Actually,' said Paul, looking straight at King Agrippa, 'I was convinced that I ought to do all that was possible to oppose the name of Jesus of Nazareth' (26:9).

Addressing the mob in Jerusalem, seething with their imagined (though murderous) zeal for God, Paul had let them know that he understood exactly how they felt: he too had once been filled by that same kind of zeal to protect God's honour and the sanctity of the temple. Indeed, it had taken him much further than them: he had systematically persecuted the Christians. Now he was addressing a noble, sophisticated, experienced, fair-minded, thoughtful, rational, responsible monarch. He knew exactly the incredulity Agrippa was now feeling at the mention of the resurrection of Jesus; and he wanted him to know that he too had once experienced the very same incredulity. And a much stronger dose of it than Agrippa was experiencing.

He had persecuted the Christians with a ruthless persistence and rigour, not because he had not heard their story that Jesus had risen from the dead, but because he had. He had held that their story was not only physically impossible, but, in light of what Jesus had done and claimed before his death, morally and spiritually incredible as well. The fact that these Christians were saintly in their character and behaviour (26:10) did not inhibit his punishment of them. The story of Jesus' resurrection which they were spreading was worse than incredible: it was a religiously, theologically and politically mischievous lie, carrying blasphemous implications for the character and nature of the one true God. He had tried to force them to blaspheme the name of Jesus to save their souls from the blasphemy of believing and preaching his resurrection (26:11).

Sheer madness, you say. Yes, it was madness; Paul admits it.* But it was a madness – let Agrippa and the court be reminded of it – that the high priests and the chief priests had approved of, and authorised, as being wise, shrewd, practical policy to maintain good order in the state and the dignity of orthodox religion and the true spiritual authority of the Sanhedrin (26:10).

---

*26:11, 'being exceedingly mad against them'; NIV, 'In my obsession against them'.

What then had changed Paul? He met the risen Jesus, or rather the risen Jesus came in person and confronted him. It was not an argument, or a set of arguments, that converted him, but the facts, or rather the supreme fact himself, against which it was futile to try and kick any more (26:14).

In all the accounts of his experience, and above all in this one, the overwhelming impression made on him was of light; light in every sense of the term: supernatural though physical, yet metaphorical, moral, intellectual, emotional and spiritual.

The madness was gone for ever. From that moment on – though himself suffering persecution so severe that apart from the promised divine rescuings (26:17) it would have long since destroyed him – he never again persecuted anyone, nor retaliated when persecuted himself.

Simultaneously, his commission from the chief priests was replaced by an altogether different commission from the risen Lord which not only illuminated his mind but dramatically widened his vision: in place of his obsessive, narrow concern for Israel's rights and privileges, it gave him a love and a message big enough for Israel and the whole Gentile world (26:17).

This, then, was the message and this its aim (26:18) – let Agrippa judge what, if anything, about it was treasonable:

1. 'To open people's eyes to turn them from darkness to light' – which meets a universally acknowledged need. We crave for light on our psychological and social problems; on our moral and spiritual questions; on life itself in fact, whether it has any ultimate meaning; on our world, whether justice and fair-play are a rather-less-than-adult illusion, whether progress in the end will mock us, and whether the only logical attitude is a rational pessimism in light of the fact that our world will one day be destroyed.

2. 'To turn people from the power of Satan to God.' It is clear that the problem of evil is far more than an individual problem. Nor is it simply what emerges when a lot of individuals come together in associations, groups or nations. None of us invented our innate tendency to do wrong. There is a more than human malign power at work in our world. That is not to excuse human sin, or to deny human responsibility. But it would be a heartless and grotesquely ill-proportioned diagnosis that attributed to men and women all by themselves total responsibility for the infatuate blindness and perversity that fill our world with injustice and cruelty and soak it with blood and tears. But if Satan exists and is active, God still has power to save from Satan, and to effect a deliverance that man is helpless to achieve by his own independent effort.

3. 'So that they may receive forgiveness of sins.' Real guilt, not false

403

psychological guilt, remains at the root of human unease; and unless it finds true forgiveness, honourably purchased by the sacrifice of Christ, it destroys peace of mind, corrodes all other values, and haunts the future. We need forgiveness more than we need our daily bread.

4. 'And an inheritance among those who are sanctified through faith in [Christ].' What, after all, is the only truly satisfying attainment in life, but an eternal inheritance, shared by the truly holy, the possession and enjoyment of which starts now in this life, and will last eternally? It is possible through faith in Christ.

'So then, King Agrippa, I was not disobedient to the vision from heaven' (26:19). Paul was not trumpeting his piety; he was explaining his behaviour, the motivation that drove him on his long preaching journeys, and the authority that lay behind his summons to all people everywhere to repent, to turn to God, and to prove their repentance by their deeds (26:20).

How could even Nero regard the preaching of such a message as treasonable? And yet, when all came to all, it was for the preaching of this message, said Paul, that the Jews seized him in the temple courts and tried to kill him (26:21). Only God's own help had preserved him and maintained him as a witness to the gospel of Christ (26:22).

And what, after all, was there so unorthodox, so inherently blasphemous about the message he preached, to draw the murderous hostility of the Jews against him? It was not a message that he had concocted out of his own head, or even dreamed up in a vision. He was saying nothing but what the prophets and Moses – all of them impeccably orthodox! – had said was destined to happen: that the Messiah would have to suffer, and as the first to rise from the dead was destined to proclaim light to his own people and to the Gentiles (26:22–23; cf. Isa. 53 and 61).*

Festus' interruption

At this point in the proceedings Festus announced in a voice that boomed all round the court: 'You are mad, Paul; your massive learning is driving you insane' (26:24).

Strange that! You could enjoy the gladiator shows in Rome, like

---

*It is an interesting insight into Paul's missionary life that the syntax of Luke's sentence here preserves the phrases that Paul would often have advertised as titles for his lectures and debates: 'Must the Messiah suffer?' 'Was the Messiah destined to be the first to rise from the dead?' 'Was the Messiah to bring light to his people and to the Gentiles?'

the rich and noble did, as well as the masses, and watch with amusement while men hacked each other to death – and not be charged with lunacy. You could in more recent times be so fanatical in pursuit of communist theory as deliberately to eliminate millions of human beings – and still not be called mad. But start a vigorous campaign to clean up the morals of the Roman Empire, to call on people to repent and seek the living God, to preach a message of forgiveness, peace and hope – and it will seem to Festus, and a good many more, insanity. Insanity is obviously a very discriminating epidemic.

But then Festus had not witnessed the transformation of the distraught spirit-medium at Philippi into a self-controlled human being. And he wasn't to know that one sentence from Paul's recent letter to the Christians in Rome (let alone the whole of that letter) – 'Therefore, since we have been justified through faith, we have peace with God through our Lord Jesus Christ' (Rom. 5:1) – was to bring peace of mind, freedom of spirit, mental and spiritual stability to uncountable millions throughout successive centuries down to the present time. And then again, he did not know anything about the Hebrew prophets, and Paul's address had taken him completely out of his depth. His accusation of insanity rose out of his own profound ignorance, as such accusations have a way of doing.

But Agrippa did know about the prophets (26:27), and knew, so Paul felt sure, all about the Lord Jesus, his crucifixion and the Christian claim that he was risen from the dead. These things had not been done in a corner (26:26). The question was – and Paul had now almost forgotten that he was the subject of an enquiry: the evangelist in him had been watching the king's face. Here was a man who needed to find peace with God through faith in Christ. He knew what the prophets said, he was an expert in Israel's traditional faith. He could see how Jesus matched the prophecies. The question was: Did he believe them?

'King Agrippa,' said Paul, brushing Festus' silly comment aside, and concentrating the king's attention on his need not to content himself with his expert but dilettantish knowledge of Jewish affairs, but to take the prophets seriously and personally to believe them. 'King Agrippa,' he said, 'do you believe the prophets? I know you do' (26:27).

The king perceived Paul's aim. But this was a public court; and he turned the heart-thrust of Paul's question with a whimsical, but gracious, 'Do you think that in such a short time you can persuade me to be a Christian?' (26:28).

405

And Paul replied, 'Short time or long – I pray God that not only you but all who are listening to me today may become what I am, except for these chains' (26:29).

Europe's – the world's – greatest evangelist, and God's own ambassador, had told his heart out, in the name of Jesus Christ, God's Saviour of men, for Agrippa, for Bernice, for Festus, for Nero Caesar, for all the world to hear. And the court fell silent.

Then their majesties arose and Festus conducted them out of court.

The conclusion

All three concluded it was obvious that the man was not doing anything worthy of death or imprisonment (26:31). Furthermore, as Agrippa remarked to Festus, Paul could have been set free if he had not appealed to Caesar (26:32).

MOVEMENT 5: Nature's Storms and the Kingly Rule of God (27:1–28:31)

The storm

And now in the last movement of Section Six we are back with nature. Not with Mother Nature, life-sustaining and protecting, which the Ephesians worshipped under the name of Artemis; but impersonal nature, with her gigantic forces, heartlessly regardless of human life, mindlessly cruel, amorally destructive, and always potentially lethal. The nature that makes human beings look pathetically puny; against which man must struggle, pitting brain and brawn in an unequal contest, just in order to survive.

Movement 5 is dominated by the long, detailed and vivid account of the storm which came within a hair's-breadth of sinking the ship that was conveying Paul to Italy to stand before Nero. Seeing Paul's voyage to Rome was of such prime spiritual importance, the occurrence of that near-fatal storm raises large questions. Arriving in Rome, Paul continued to preach regularly on his usual topic of the kingdom, the kingly rule, of God (28:23, 31). But what, may we ask, is the relationship between the kingly rule of God and nature's storms the like of which nearly drowned Paul, silenced his preaching, and ended all his pioneer evangelism?

The length, detail and technical and geographical accuracy of

406

the account are doubtless owed to the fact that Luke was a fellow passenger with Paul and observed everything at first hand.* But we can be sure that Luke has not included all this detail in order to represent Paul as some kind of superman, dominating and subduing nature by a spectacular series of miracles. From the moment they boarded the doomed ship to the cold wild morning it broke up on the shore of Malta there was no miracle. No divine power calmed the sea, as some years previously Galilee's tempest had subsided in recognition of her Master's voice. No angelic powers conveyed the ship unscathed into port. All the passengers and crew were saved, but only after two weeks and more of agonised suffering and a final inglorious, hair-raising scramble from the wreck through the surf to the shore.

And there lies a big question: If Paul was God's own appointed apostle and ambassador, sent to represent the gospel of God's own Son to the highest authority on earth; and if God is the God who created and controls nature, who 'rules over the surging sea, and when its waves mount up, stills them' (Ps. 89:9), then why did not God's kingly rule order the Mediterranean to give his ambassador a smoother passage, instead of torturing him for a fortnight and then throwing him up like a half-drowned rat on the beach?

The importance of nature as she is

Whatever the answer should be to our questions, it is evident from the story before us, and from the record of Christian missionary work over the course of two thousand years, that God never intended to change the way nature works in order to facilitate the spread of the gospel. Miracles, of course, there have been, and doubtless still are. But by definition they are the exception. The norm is that nature goes on working as before. Lightning and hail, snow and clouds and stormy winds that ever since creation had done the Creator's bidding in the great cosmic processes of our world and universe (Ps. 148:8), were not withdrawn, re-trained or tamed in order to guarantee safe passage for all Christian missionaries. Nature was left as she was, and as she will be until the restoration of all things. The storms were allowed

*See the famous study by J. Smith, *The Voyage and Shipwreck of St Paul* (London, [4]1848); F. F. Bruce, *The Book of the Acts*, New International Commentary on the New Testament (Grand Rapids, MI: Wm B. Eerdmans, [2]1988), pp. 474–99; and C. J. Hemer, *The Book of Acts in the Setting of Hellenistic History*, ed. Conrad H. Gempf (Tübingen: J. C. B. Mohr; 1989), pp. 132–58.

to continue; the missionaries had to learn, like anyone else, to avoid them or to ride them; and there was never any guarantee that no bona fide missionary would ever be drowned.

Let's indulge ourselves for a moment, with Luke's permission, and think of the important benefits conferred on mankind by nature as she is. The very need to struggle against her in order to survive has served to develop some of mankind's staggeringly wonderful powers, of courage, daring, ingenuity and understanding. Very early on mankind discovered that nature could be harnessed and used. The same wind that blew your house down could be taken advantage of: it could be induced to drive the sails of a windmill and grind your corn. The waves, tides, currents and winds that barred your passage could be transformed by the invention of a sailing ship into the means of transporting you where you wanted to go. The law of gravity that confines us to earth can be used to fling a space-probe from earth-orbit out towards the next planet we want to investigate.

Moreover, often enough new, daring advances in the harnessing of nature to mankind's service have themselves in the end become commonplace necessities for man's survival. The fleet of big (for those times) grain-ships that plied the sea-lanes from Alexandria in Egypt to Rome – on one of which Paul was sailing when it nearly foundered – had become an indispensable necessity to the social economics of Rome. Without the supplies brought by those ships, the massive population in the capital could not have been fed. Similarly our modern sophisticated world could hardly continue to function without air-travel, radio, radar, television and so forth. And what is more, the Christians' task of spreading the gospel has been enormously facilitated by these advances, particularly so in this last half-century. The pietistic notion that all such progress is unnatural, not to say ungodly, is self-evidently mistaken.

To this extent, then, both for man's own development and for the evangelisation of the world, we could not wish for nature to be other than she is. Of course she is lethally dangerous: electricity will kill you in an instant if you make a mistake with it. It knows no forgiveness. It will cook your dinner, or incinerate you, with indifference. It is impersonal, mindless, compassionless, like all the rest of nature's forces. They are all vastly more powerful than man, and must be treated with respect. Nor has God ever changed (nor will he normally change) the way these powers work as a special favour to Christians or missionaries. The Christian who jumps off the pinnacle of the temple will find that God has not eliminated the law of gravity. Unrealistic foolhardiness is not faith.

But nature has never been tamed, let alone subdued. The struggle between man and nature remains unequal. The very best of modern sophisticated ships still break their backs in ferocious tempests; airliners still crash in fog. We do well, therefore, realistically to face the terms on which God's servants go out to evangelise the world. It would be foolish to deny God's ability or willingness to intervene miraculously to preserve his servants when he so pleases; it would be faithlessness to discount the guardian ministry of angels (Heb. 1:14); it would be ingratitude to shut one's eyes to the thousand and one divine providences that we become aware of, or to doubt the thousands more we do not see. That said, we are wise to face squarely the actual guarantees that we are given. We are nowhere promised that no missionary will ever be drowned at sea. We have no guarantee that no evangelist will ever be lost in an air crash. We are not told that God's love will save us from ever experiencing tribulation, anguish, famine, peril or death. Our guarantee is rather that none of nature's lethal powers (nor Satan's, nor man's either) will ever be able to separate us from the love of God, not height nor depth, not death nor life, nor any other created power (Rom. 8:38–39). So wrote Paul a year or two before he set foot on the grain-ship that nearly foundered in the Mediterranean.

Lessons from the story of the storm

Four times, according to Luke, Paul intervened in the course of the voyage with a significant observation; and we should consider each in turn.

First, a warning against taking undue risks. Of course, in facing nature one cannot escape taking risks. The ancient farmer who sowed his seed in the spring had to risk the possibility that bad weather conditions might rot the seed in the ground, and destroy all prospect of a harvest and food for next year. Columbus would never have discovered the New World nor David Livingstone Central Africa if they neither of them had been prepared to take enormous risks.

Faith thrives on taking risks for God's sake; but there comes a point where the risk is unjustified, and taking it is not faith but presumption. Paul was prepared to die for the sake of the gospel, but not needlessly. He was no expert sailor, but it was accepted wisdom based on years of experience in the nautical world that the season for sailing was already passed for that year. To put to sea from Fair Havens so late in the year was to take an enormous and foolish risk (27:9–11). The purpose of putting to sea again was to reach a more commodious harbour in which it would be more comfortable and convenient to spend the winter. But to risk shipwreck, with loss of the cargo and above all of the 276 lives on board, simply in order to gain a slightly better harbour than the one they already had, was to Paul's way of thinking foolish; and he spoke his mind. But the captain and the owner of the vessel wanted to take the risk. Expertise and professional pride can often breed over-confidence; and the centurion in charge took their advice rather than Paul's.

All the same, it is instructive to notice Paul's attitude. His faith was not of the kind that would argue: 'Yes, take what risks you like. I'm God's special ambassador. God would not allow me to suffer any disaster. If necessary, he will do a miracle and keep the seas calm until we get to the next harbour.' It wasn't that he did not believe in miracles, or in God's willingness to do them where absolutely necessary. But they had no compelling need to go on to the next harbour; and to take unnecessary risks and then count on God to do miracles in nature to obviate disaster is not faith but presumption. At this point, therefore, Paul appears in Luke's record not as some super-spiritual hero, but as a man whose humble but real faith knew its proper limits.

Hope beyond nature

Very soon they ran into appalling trouble. Everything that expert seamanship knew to do, was done (27:17–19), but all in vain. Nature mocked their impotence, took away their bearings (27:20), used their experience to terrify them with (27:17). The more expert they were, the more they knew that the next mountainous wave could send them straight to the bottom. All hope of survival was gone.

It is situations like this, when mindless nature mocks all man's accumulated knowledge and expertise, frustrates all his endeavours, laughs at his progress and tosses him and his inventions aside like broken straws before the gale – it is such situations that raise life's haunting question. Is human life nothing more than an ultimately insignificant part of nature's closed system, helplessly caught up in her endless, pointless cycles of deceptive calm and mindlessly destructive storm? Or is there a purpose for man beyond and above nature's cycles? Are nature and her seasons both the stage and the whole drama that is being played out on it? Or is nature only one temporary stage on which we humans play our part of the drama that is given us to play, before we move on to bring the drama to its glorious and triumphant conclusion on a different stage elsewhere?

Thank God for the answer that came loud and confident through the howling gale and the driving rain, when all other hope was gone:

> You were foolish to undertake this voyage against common sense and my advice. But, courage! Last night an angel of the God to whom I belong and whom I serve stood beside me and said 'Do not be afraid, Paul. You must stand trial before Caesar; and God has graciously given you the lives of all who sail with you.' So keep up your courage, men, for I have faith in God that it will happen just as he told me. (27:23–25)

Unarguably, Paul's was a special case; but only a particular instance of the general truth that undergirds all God's people. There is a God before, above and beyond nature; and every believer can describe him equally with Paul as 'the God whose I am, the God to whom I belong'. We are his property – his, to him, invaluable property – purchased, as Paul reminded the church elders at Ephesus, with the blood of his own dear Son (20:28). Not all the forces of nature combined shall rob God of this his priceless possession. And every believer can add with Paul, 'the God . . . whom I serve'. Be the service large or small, public or private, the mindless forces of created nature shall never frustrate the Creator's purpose in assigning us that service. God's weather cannot hinder God's work.

Within his general commission Paul had been given a special and specific task to do at that time: to witness for Christ and the gospel before Caesar in Rome. He had been told of it before (23:11); now the angel was sent to remind him of it, and to assure him that because this was God's purpose not only he, but all those who were necessary to get him to land, would be saved, nature and all her powers notwithstanding (27:24–25).

It was not always given to Paul to know with such certainty and assurance that he would not die before some particular task was finished.* Still less is it necessarily given to us. But of this we can be sure, that as far as God is concerned, mere mindless nature will

---

*Witness the uncertainties that crept into his thinking even in Philippians 1:18–30, and particularly in the previous chapters of this section – 20:23–24; 21:13 – where he thought he might possibly be killed in Jerusalem.

411

never be allowed to overwhelm us until God has attained the goal he had in mind when he gave us our tasks.

The power of faith over panic and reckless selfishness

It is to be noted that the angel's promise that Paul and all the other passengers would be saved, was not fulfilled through any (apparent) miracle.* It still required all the experts' navigational skills and experience to get the ship to land. Even knowing how to run the ship the last few hundred yards through the breakers and to beach her as far up the shore as they could, would take every ounce of skill they could muster. When the ship had gone as near the land as they dared take her in the dark, and they anchored her by the stern so as to be able to run for the shore at first light, the sailors apparently panicked. Putting their own safety before that of the passengers', they surreptitiously tried to lower the ship's dinghy and effect their own escape.

But Paul saw what they were intending to do, pointed it out to the centurion, and insisted that the sailors remain in the ship (27:30–32). Paul had been promised that everybody would be saved; but not apart from human means, skill and effort. His faith did not excuse selfish panic and rely on miracle. Faith vigilantly concentrated on the practical necessities, pounced on and subdued reckless selfishness and panic, and gave backbone to the centurion's command of the situation. And that paid good dividends when the soldiers proposed that all the prisoners should be slaughtered, Paul included, to prevent their escape (27:42). If the prisoners had escaped, the soldiers would have subsequently been executed. It must have taken a lot of authority to stop them killing the prisoners. But the centurion did it for Paul's sake (27:43).

The power of faith over fear and despair

For two weeks passengers and crew had scarcely eaten anything. Which is no wonder: below deck everything was probably in chaos if not awash. And anyway, in their fear and misery people would have had no stomach for food, even those who were not hopelessly sea-sick. But once more Paul's faith took a grip of the practical situation. He got up and addressed all 275 of his fellow passengers. Reminding them of God's promise that they would

---

*Such as the miracle of John 6:21.

412

all get safely to land, he urged them to eat something (27:34). No angelic chair-lift would miraculously waft them to the shore. They would need every calorie of energy for their last battle with the crashing waves and undertow. So he set them an example. Openly demonstrating the secret of his calm and confidence, he took bread, gave thanks to God before them all while the gale still raged, ate, and encouraged them all to do the same (27:35–36).

Observe, then, the role of faith in this whole affair. It was not that Paul simply believed that because God had a work for him to do in Rome, God would bring him and all the others safely through in spite of the storm. It was Paul's faith in response to God's promise that he would survive to see his task of witnessing completed that enabled him to take control of the psychological situation, and to see to it that all the necessary practical steps were taken to keep the ship afloat and bring her, as best as might be, to the shore.

Ultimately it takes a faith and a purpose that are anchored beyond nature to give one the strength and courage to persist with life and life's endeavours in the face of nature's storms when it appears on other grounds that all hope is gone. Indeed, why would God himself continue with nature any longer if he had not magnificent and eternal purposes beyond all her ragings? For this reason it is that even when (and if) we lose our last struggle with nature, and she overwhelms us in death, we shall be more than conquerors through him who loved us (Rom. 8:37).

Pagan misinterpretations of nature

The survivors were soon surrounded by the local islanders who took pity on them and built a fire for them (28:2). Paul, practical as ever, gathered a pile of brushwood, but as he put it on the fire, a viper, driven out by the heat, fastened itself on his hand. At once the islanders were ready with their interpretation of this event: 'This man must be a murderer; for though he escaped from the sea, Justice has not allowed him to live' (28:4).

They fell into a cluster of mistakes that superstitious, not to say religious, people can still fall into even today. They supposed that all the natural disasters that befall human beings befall them because of their sins; and that therefore if a human being suffers some natural disaster it is safe to conclude that he or she must have secretly committed some heinous sin, even if there is no other evidence for it.

But to start with, nature and her impersonal workings are not the Judge of mankind. Her processes in themselves are amoral. A sore throat is not evidence that the patient must have been telling lies.* Sometimes God does use natural disasters to express his disapproval, and the effect is clear for all to see. The effect of the conflagration that destroyed Sodom and Gomorrah put an end to their physically and socially poisonous behaviour. But they had a reputation for it even before the disaster fell; it was not a some-thing that had to be deduced from the fact that the disaster happened.

But not all natural disasters are necessarily expressions of God's judgement. A black official limousine could be conveying a drug-baron to prison pending trial. That was the purpose of Sodom's overthrow (2 Pet. 2:4–9; Jude 6–7). But a black official limousine could also be conveying a national hero to take tea with the Queen. Many a natural disaster has ushered saintly believers into the presence of the Lord.

If we are going to take any general lesson from natural disas-ters, 'acts of God', and atrocities, it had better be the lesson taught by Christ himself: don't suppose that the people who suffer them must necessarily have been especially, and secretly, sinful while those who escape them are not. All people are sinful. Let natural disasters serve rather as reminders that all need to repent (Luke 13:1–5).

Paul shook the viper off into the fire; and when he suffered no harm the islanders jumped to the opposite conclusion, that he must be a god (28:5–6). Let's suppose it was a straightforward miracle; yet their mistake reminds us that it is possible to mis-interpret even miracles. Miracles are not proofs of foregone conclusions; they are evidence that needs to be carefully inter-preted. The great Man of Sin himself will perform stupendously impressive manipulations of nature; but they will not prove that his claims to be God are true (2 Thess. 2:3–4, 9–12). And the Maltese warn us that it is possible to interpret a genuine miracle as support for a theologically false presupposition.

Malta to Rome

The centurion stayed in Malta no longer than he was forced to. At the very earliest possible moment of the new sailing season he

---

* On the other hand, nature's workings must be respected; abuse electricity and you may well electrocute yourself, and destroy a house-full of people. Abuse the ozone layer and you could destroy the planet.

414

embarked with his prisoners on the next leg of their journey to Rome (28:11).

But even so the enforced waiting period was three months; and during that time God graciously empowered Paul to do miracles of healing that not only benefited the islanders, but repaid them for their kindness and for their out-of-pocket expenses in entertaining such unexpected and uninvited visitors. And when Paul and his friends eventually left, they provisioned them for the journey (28:10).*

During the course of the journey to Rome, Paul was allowed to stay with the Christians at Puteoli for seven days (28:13–14), and may well have thus been able to participate with them in the Lord's Supper as he did with the believers at Troas, and probably again at Tyre, during the course of his earlier journey from Ephesus to Jerusalem (20:6–7; 21:4).

Then came the last lap of the journey. We cannot know the feelings that arose in Paul's heart as he finally approached the great city where he must discharge his onerous responsibility and actually face the risk of appearing before the monster Nero himself. But we may guess them. When he saw the welcoming party of Christians who came out as far as the Forum of Appius to meet him, 'he thanked God', says Luke, then adds 'and took courage' (28:15, av). The great Paul, whose single-handed faith and strength of character had instilled courage in the crew and passengers of the foundering ship, himself found new courage in an oppressive moment from the brotherly company of unnamed fellow Christians (28:15).

Paul's briefing of the leaders of the Jewish community in Rome

At Miletus Paul had invited the elders of the church in Ephesus to come and meet him (20:17–38). Recognising their responsibility to guard and guide that church he had warned them of false prophets from the outside and false teachers from within who would damage the church. Soon after he arrived in Rome he invited the leaders of the Jewish community to come and meet him (28:17). He recognised and respected their responsibility to

---

*The illness from which Publius' father was suffering seems to have been Malta fever, caused by a microbe in goats' milk. It would not necessarily need a miracle to cure it nowadays. But then a parent who will tie a two year old's shoelaces for him will not necessarily do the same for a boy of sixteen.

guard and guide their congregations in the city synagogues. They might have received a report on him from the high priest and Sanhedrin in Jerusalem; and in any event, to find a learned and famous Jewish-rabbi-turned-Christian in the city and due to present his case, whatever that was, before Caesar, could not but have filled them with concern. Under Claudius, as a result of disputes between Christians and Jews in the city, all Jews had been temporarily banned from Rome (18:2). Then what possible trouble for the Jewish community would this Christian rabbi instigate?

Paul wanted to put their minds at rest by telling them the facts as he saw them. The chief fact was this: he wanted to assure them that in appealing to Caesar his purpose never had been, nor was it now, to accuse or to bring any charge against the Jewish people (28:19). Indeed, he would never have thought of appealing to Caesar unless the Jews of Judea had forced him to it. They had falsely accused him of wrongs against the nation and against the traditional customs which he had not committed; and it was as a result of their actions that he had come into the hands of the Romans. The Romans, with their sense of justice and fair-play, had wanted to release him as innocent of the charges (28:18). That could have been the end of the matter. But the Judean Jews would not accept their verdict, and so had obliged him to appeal to Caesar to save his very life.

Nevertheless, he had no intention of accusing the Jews of anything before Caesar. He would appear before the emperor as a representative and champion of 'the hope of Israel' (28:20), would plead that that hope was not treasonable or subversive of the government, and so would obtain, if possible, Caesar's favourable assessment of Israel's hope.

There spoke a Christian, if ever there was one. The Jews in Judea had tried to murder him themselves. Failing that, they had tried to get the Romans to execute him. But to Paul they were still 'my own people' as he called them (28:19). He loved them loyally still; and just as he had exhorted the Christian elders to protect the church, so would he do his utmost to protect his people Israel himself.

Actually the elders of the Jewish communities in Rome had not received (as yet) any report on Paul from Jerusalem (28:21). All they knew was that this Christian 'sect' was badly spoken of in all Jewish communities; and they welcomed an opportunity to come and hear its beliefs expounded. So Paul set them a date and time (28:22–23).

The Holy Spirit's final warning to Judaism

On the day appointed they turned up in large numbers, and Paul talked to them at great length on the topic of the kingdom of God, expounding 'from the Law of Moses and from the Prophets' scriptures that were relevant to the claims of Jesus to be Israel's Messiah. Some were impressed almost to the point of believing; others repudiated the teaching altogether. The company eventually left arguing among themselves (28:23–25).

But before they departed Paul pronounced a very solemn warning couched not in his own words, but in the words of the Holy Spirit through Isaiah to ancient Israel. In dark days of Israel's past God had given Isaiah a vision of the King (Isa. 6:5), the only king that could ever save them from individual sin and national disaster. God had commissioned Isaiah to go and tell Israel this vision of their King; but in the very moment of his commissioning him, God had warned Isaiah that his preaching would do them little good. For where fallen and sinful nature has led people in their pride and sinful self-sufficiency unrepentantly to suppress their consciences, barricade their minds, shut their ears and close their eyes, there comes a point where the preaching even of the gospel has the effect of aggravating the condition rather than healing it (28:25–27; cf. Isa. 6:9–10).

Even so, there was one piece of evidence left that even to people in their condition was and would ever remain unavoidable and undeniable. First, please observe, said Paul, this salvation from God was sent to the Gentiles: 'was sent' in the sense that in God's purpose and plan it was designed that it should be sent to the Gentiles (28:28). Beyond all possible denial or contradiction Isaiah's repeated and explicit announcements had declared that God would raise up his Messiah as a rallying standard, a light, a salvation for the Gentiles (Isa. 42:6; 49:6). Secondly, when God raised up his Messiah for the Gentiles, the prophet had said that the Gentiles would in fact listen to him. Already, as Paul sat talking to his fellow Jews in Rome, hundreds of Gentiles round the Roman Empire had listened and responded. Thousands more would.

The centuries have proved it true. Listening to Jesus Christ, uncountable millions of Gentiles have come to faith in the God of Israel. Some 'natural branches' were broken off because of unbelief. But myriads of Gentiles, all against nature, have been 'grafted in'. One day the natural branches too will be grafted back into their own olive tree (Rom. 11:17–24).

With that Luke closes his history. It was never meant to be a complete record of the rise and progress of Christianity. But it was meant to be a representative account of what Christianity was and what it, or rather the risen Lord, began and continued to do. The full record of what he would achieve could naturally not be written. But at the point where Luke laid down his pen, Paul – though in chains – and the gospel of God's kingly rule were irrepressibly surging ahead without let or hindrance in spite of human opposition or nature's storms (28:31).

Appendices

Appendix 1
Is Christianity Essentially
Anti-Semitic?

Some will feel that stressing the differences between Christianity and Judaism as we have done throughout this book is sadly out of tune with a great deal of modern thinking on the relationship between the two great faiths. Centuries of harping on the crucifixion of the Son of God by the Jews, they argue, is what has fomented the infamous anti-Semitism which has so disgraced the annals of Christendom, and which has culminated in our own day in Hitler's gas-chambers. After the Holocaust, they suggest, it would be obscene for Christians to try to convert Jews. Rather, it should be admitted that Judaism is as equally valid an approach to God as is Christianity. Nothing at least should be said by Christians about Judaism that could not be said with decency standing in Auschwitz and Dachau.

Since, then, I am responsible for this book, perhaps I may be allowed to speak in the first person and explain the spirit in which it is written.

First, it would seem to me unjust to accuse the whole nation of ancient Israel of being responsible for the death of Jesus. We cannot, of course, undo the deeds of history. The leaders of the nation *were* involved in engineering his crucifixion by the Romans; and the crowds in Jerusalem who up until the last moment were favourable to Jesus, allowed themselves, as fickle crowds will, to be swayed to shout for his death. But thousands and thousands of Jews, living in the Dispersion at the time, only heard about the crucifixion months or even years after it had happened. They cannot be said to have been responsible for the deed. Moreover, God had it announced through his apostles that in his estimation even the priestly leaders and the Jerusalem crowd did what they did in ignorance

(3:17); and on that score mercy was offered to them upon repentance.

Secondly, I believe, as all true Christians believe, that when Jesus died, he died for, and because of, my sins. The Jewish leaders and the crowd were in their hostility unwitting agents in carrying out God's purpose that his Son should die for the sin of the world (2:23; 3:17–18). I am humbly grateful to be able to say in consequence: 'Jesus bore my sins in his body on the tree' (1 Pet. 2:24); 'I have redemption through his blood, even the forgiveness of sins' (Eph. 1:7); and then to know that forgiveness and salvation on these terms are offered to all, Jew and Gentile, without discrimination (Rom. 3:22–24). I would not think of charging any Jew with the death of Jesus Christ except in the sense that my sins too, as well as his, were the cause of Messiah's death. But at the same time I believe that there is no other ground of forgiveness and acceptance with God for any man or woman on the face of the earth than the death of Jesus. I must, therefore, and I do, hold that for a Jew to reject Christ's sacrifice and salvation carries the same solemn and eternal consequence as for a Gentile.

Thirdly, I hold with all my heart to God's emphatic assertion that he 'has not rejected his people whom he foreknew' (i.e. the physical nation of Israel; Rom. 11:1–2). One day 'all Israel' (i.e. the literal nation of Israel as a whole) will be saved (Rom. 11:26). God's gifts and his call are irrevocable (Rom. 11:29). The nation whom he once called and appointed to a special role in the world will yet again be given an honoured role to play for God. They will not have it by right; nor do they enjoy it at the moment. It waits upon the nation's repentance and reconciliation with God's Son, their Messiah; but it shall happen. Along with Professor C. E. B. Cranfield, and multitudes of other Christians, I deplore 'the ugly and unscriptural notion that God has cast off His people Israel and simply replaced it by the Christian Church';* and I regret the fact that large sections of Christendom over many centuries and right up to the present have fallen into the very arrogance against which Paul warns us Gentile Christians, of imagining that there is no future for Israel as such (Rom. 11:18, 20, 25).

But it seems to me that if we would truly repent of Christendom's disgraceful treatment of Judaism in the past, we must ask serious questions about what first led to it.

My former colleague, Professor E. Mary Smallwood, in an

---

*C. E. B. Cranfield, *A Critical and Exegetical Commentary on The Epistle to the Romans*, vol. 2 (Edinburgh: T. & T. Clark, 1979), pp. 448.

inaugural lecture entitled very aptly but very sadly 'From Pagan Protection to Christian Oppression', explains it as follows. After pointing out that all Rome's pagan rulers from Julius Caesar onwards had passed, or maintained, special legislation for the protection of Jews, she goes on to say:

> Constantine's conversion to Christianity in 312 inevitably meant a change in the official Roman attitude towards Judaism. Church and state changed from bitter enemies to allies almost overnight. Unlike pagan Rome, the Church had a theological quarrel with Judaism, and it was now in a position of political power. The daughter of Judaism had been at odds with her parent all her life, but hitherto her only weapon had been the verbal sword of the sermon and the treatise. Now she had in her hands if she chose to use it, the weapon of legislation.*

And later:

> What had begun under Constantine as an attempt to protect Christianity from Judaism while at the same time safeguarding the Jews' own religious rights had developed by the time of Justinian into the start of serious oppression of Judaism by the government in the name of Christianity.†

The trouble started, then, when the church joined up with the state. Of course, in Old Testament times when Israel was a theocracy and her kings were 'the anointed of the Lord', Israel's religious authorities were commanded by God to use the civil power to chastise, and if need be to eliminate, idolaters and apostates (Deut. 13:12–18; 17:2–7). And even as late as New Testament times, when the Jews of Jerusalem had lost control of the civil power, they were delighted, Luke tells us (12:1–3), when one of the Herods used his civil power to persecute the infant church.

But Christianity was supposed to be different from Judaism. Christians followed a King whose kingdom was not of this world, and who forbade his disciples the use of the sword either in the propagation or the defence of the gospel (John 18:36–37; Matt. 26:52; 2 Cor. 10:4). No one was ever to be forced into becoming a Christian under threat of civil punishment, or to be discriminated against or persecuted by the civil power for not being a Christian.

---

*E. Mary Smallwood, *From Pagan Protection to Christian Oppression* (The Queen's University of Belfast, 1979), p. 7.
†ibid., p. 24.

It was an utter disaster, therefore, when Christendom lapsed into becoming a sacral state like ancient Israel had been, imagined that it was the intended continuator of earthly Israel, and got it into its head that it had a right, and even a God-given duty, as Israel had, to use the civil power to oppress and eliminate heretics, apostates and unbelievers. From this lapse into Judaism came political discrimination in the name of Christianity, crusades against infidels, inquisitions and massacres of heretics, rivers of blood and of tears in the name of Jesus.

If our study of Luke's emphasis in Acts on the intended difference between Christianity and Judaism helps to save us from ever lapsing into that mistake again, our study will not have been in vain.*

---

*For further reading: Menachem Benhayim, *Jews, Gentiles and the New Testament Scriptures: A study of the charges of alleged anti-Semitism in the New Testament* (Jerusalem: Yanetz, 1985).

Appendix 2
If Acts Is a Carefully Structured Literary Work, Can It Still Be Regarded As Historically Reliable?

Why not? This exposition, at any rate, has been based on the firm conviction that it can. True enough, we have not set out to demonstrate the historicity of Acts. Others have done that in great detail, and none more fully than the late C. J. Hemer in his work, much referred to in this volume, *The Book of Acts in the Setting of Hellenistic History*, ed. Conrad H. Gempf (Tübingen: J. C. M. Mohr, 1989) which contains ample references to the findings of other scholars who have worked, and still are working, in this field, along with detailed discussion of arguments raised in support of the contrary view. The present exposition, therefore, has not thought it necessary to repeat all the massively detailed arguments that others have advanced for the historicity of Acts. It has assumed that historicity, and on that basis it has proceeded to the next necessary stage in the understanding of the book: a study of the material which Luke has selected for inclusion in his history; of the way he has put together the items he has selected; of the thought-flow which his arrangement of the narrative creates; and of what that can tell us about the book's major themes.

But if Luke has in fact, as we have suggested, divided his narrative into six formal sections, and has so selected and arranged the material in each section that it presents one or more major themes, does not that procedure automatically forfeit all claim to rigorous historicity?

Of course not! Why ever should it? I have before me, as I write, a historical work by Professor A. J. P. Taylor entitled *The Struggle for Mastery in Europe 1848–1918* (Oxford: Clarendon Press, 1954, repr. 1969). The work is divided into twenty-three separate sections; only the work itself does not call them sections, as I have called Luke's divisions: it calls them chapters. No one, I think, would call Prof. Taylor's work unreliable history simply because he has divided his account of seventy-one years' events into sections!

But there is worse. Although his account of the events of this period follows a chronological sequence, the individual chapters are very unequal in the span of time they cover: some cover three, four or five years, some only one. At first sight, then, the divisioning looks very arbitrary. Worse still, this unequal carving up of chronology into arbitrary sections has apparently been contrived so that the contents selected to fill each section shall present a common theme. Chapter 1, for instance, covers only one year (1848), and is said by the title Prof. Taylor has given it to present the theme 'The Diplomacy of Revolution'. Chapter 2 covers the events of two years (1849–50), so that it can present the theme 'The Diplomacy of Reaction' (and these two successive titles look dangerously like the beginning of a symmetry!). And Chapter 17 covers four years (1899–1902), so that it can exhibit the theme 'The Era of "World Policy"'.

Now not all modern historians may accept Prof. Taylor's interpretations of the events he selects and describes; I am not a historian enough to know. But who in his right mind would suggest that Prof. Taylor's work has forfeited all claim to being reliable history because he has not included every single event that happened in Europe from 1848 to 1918; and because he has divided the events he has selected into sections or groups, because, as he sees it, the events within a group share a leading theme? And if Prof. Taylor has not forfeited all claim to be writing reliable history, why should Luke be thought to have done so, by dividing his history into sections, and then selecting the contents of each section so that they shall present a common theme or themes? If anything – may Prof. Taylor forgive me for saying so – Luke might be thought to be the more reliable of the two, since he has added the barest minimum of interpretative comment beyond his record of the facts. He has not even invented titles for his sections. And for the necessarily interpretative element involved in the compilation of Acts, he had the authority of the Holy Spirit who inspired him.

Yes, but Luke has not simply divided his work into sections, and not simply filled each section with carefully chosen material bearing on one or more major themes. He has laid out the material in each section in symmetrical form – or at least according to the foregoing exposition he has. And that, someone may argue, must mean that his work is not historically accurate, because you cannot force real history into the strait-jacket of a literary symmetry without distorting it.

Well no, you cannot, if by 'real history' you mean an account of everything that everybody said, did and experienced, plus everything that happened during the course of a certain period of time. But nobody, to my knowledge, ever attempted to write a history of that kind; only God could do it anyway.

But suppose some historian decided to write a short monograph on the Second World War, and constructed his monograph in five parts thus:

1. The causes leading up to the declaration of war.
2. The period of Axis superiority.
3. The turning of the tide.
4. The period of Allied superiority.
5. The cease-fire and the immediate aftermath of the war.

The form of his monograph would be symmetrical. But that would not mean that the historian had imposed an arbitrary symmetrical structure on the events of the war. His structure would simply reflect a pattern that inhered in the course of the events themselves. Nor would he have had to distort the facts of history by undue selectivity in order to make the chosen events reveal this pattern.

And so it is with Luke. The two major journeys which stand one in the first and one in the last movement of Section Six, for example, form part of an obvious symmetry. But Luke did not invent either or both of the journeys in order to make a symmetrical structure. Paul could not have got from Ephesus to Jerusalem without a long journey, nor from Caesarea to Rome without another.*

Admittedly, Luke has been very selective in what he has recorded (see p. 11). But then he nowhere claims that he has written an exhaustive account of the rise and spread of Christianity; and we cannot criticise him for not doing what he never set out to do. Our trouble here is that many assume before they begin to read Acts that Luke must have been intending to write an exhaustive history of the spread of Christianity, and they judge his work accordingly. Whereas, what we should do is to come to Acts with an open mind, and let what Luke has actually written, his selection of material and the proportions he has given it, build

*See also the discussion of the apparent doublets in Section One, pp. 20–22.

427

up in our minds a picture of what he was aiming to do and what he has in fact done.

Or take the way that the first and last movements of Section Five balance each other: both speak in detail of the Holy Spirit, the first about his guidance, the last about his reception. Both give a detailed account of a demon-possessed person, the first of Paul's exorcism of the demon in question, the last of the attempted exorcism of the evil spirit by certain itinerant Jewish exorcists. Here we may, so to speak, catch Luke at his work of constructing a symmetry. Just before the incident of the itinerant Jews, he tells us that through Paul's ministry at Ephesus, many evil spirits came out of their victims (19:12). But he gives no detailed description of these exorcisms by Paul. What point would there be in doing so? He has already given a detailed description of Paul's successful exorcism of an evil spirit in the first movement (at 16:16–18) and of the results it led to. In the last movement Luke chooses to give a detailed description of the Jewish exorcists' unsuccessful attempt to exorcise an evil spirit and the results that followed. The common theme, and yet the glaring difference, give significant point to the resultant symmetry.

There's no denying, then, that in the process of forming the symmetry Luke has been very selective in what he has chosen for detailed description, and what he has decided to mention only in summary form. But there is no need to deny it, for it does not call in question the historicity of the incidents he has described in detail. Luke has maintained a basically chronological sequence (just like Prof. Taylor did: remember?); but then, admittedly, he has, like a jeweller constructing a necklace out of stones of different colours and sizes, selected events along the course of that chronological sequence that form meaningful symmetries. But how does that in itself form a ground on which to question the historicity of his narrative?

Suppose he had adopted a different method. Suppose, instead of following a basically chronological sequence, he had chosen to present his history in thematic form. He could then have had a chapter which began with the announcement: 'In this chapter I propose to group together a representative selection of incidents showing the apostolic attitude towards spiritism and exorcism, contrasted with paganism's attitude to spiritism and its methods of attempted exorcism.' Such a chapter could then have included Paul's successful exorcism of the evil spirit from the medium at Philippi, and the unsuccessful attempt of the itinerant Jews at Ephesus to exorcise a demon. Nobody then, I fancy, would have complained that the two incidents concerned must be unhistorical because Luke selected them out of a mass of others to stand in this chapter. But why should the other narrative method, which Luke has in fact followed, cast doubt on the historicity of these two incidents, while this method does not?

Some people, admittedly, have what they feel is a justified prejudice against seeing structures, and particularly symmetrical structures, in a narrative like Acts: it unduly restricts their freedom of interpretation. To take one example. Why must we, they ask, be compelled to read the first six verses of chapter 6, with their reference to Stephen, as the last item of a carefully constructed symmetry, chapters 1:1–6:7 (which is what this exposition of Acts has suggested)? Why can't we read 6:1–6 as the beginning of Stephen's ministry, which is then continued at length in 6:8ff? The answer is that there is no reason on earth why you should not read 6:1–6 as the beginning of Stephen's ministry if you want to. An author's division of the stream of events into well-defined sections does not cancel out the fact that those events are an integral part of the ongoing historical continuum. 6:1–6 is the record of a historical event. The fact that Luke himself may have presented it as the last item in Section One does not remove from the record that feature which all genuinely historical events have, namely that the reader is free to make any deduction he wishes (that can legitimately be made from it) beyond the prime purpose the author may have had in recording it.

To find at last, after many unsuccessful attempts, a hotel with a room free, at the end of a gruelling eighteen-hour drive on a foreign motorway, may well be so significant for the traveller concerned that he will record it in his diary as the last event of that exhausting day. His diary entry for the next day may not mention that he set out from that same hotel in the morning, since that fact did not seem to the traveller himself so significant as his finding of the hotel the night before. But there would be no reason at all why some reader of the diary might not rightly deduce that the traveller did in fact set out from that hotel in the morning, and see interesting significance in that fact for the subsequent journey as described in the diary.*

___

* For further discussion of the relation between Luke's literary methods and the historicity of Acts, see I. Howard Marshall, 'The Present State of Lucan Studies', *Themelios* 14.2 (1989), pp. 52–7; *Luke: Historian and Theologian* (Exeter: Paternoster Press, 1970); C. J. Hemer, 'Acts and Historicity', chapter 1 of his *The Book of Acts in the Setting of Hellenistic History*, ed. Conrad H. Gempf (Tübingen: J. C. B. Mohr, 1989); and my own *According to Luke* (Leicester: IVP, 1987), pp. 357–62.

And this brings us to another feature in Luke's narrative. In the foregoing exposition I have concentrated on the major structures of the book, that is on its six formal sections and on the symmetrical structuring of the material within the sections. I have done so because it is structure of this kind that controls and exhibits the thought-flow of the ongoing narrative; and because first and last we have to read Acts detail by detail, verse after verse, as an ongoing story. Of patterns of other kinds I have said very little. But of course such patterns do exist. It is perhaps inevitable in any lengthy work that certain patterns of thought or event will recur, and a close comparative study of them can be very fruitful and instructive.

There are, for instance, in the course of Acts three escape-from-prison stories:

Section One   An angel miraculously releases the twelve apostles from prison (5:17–32).

Section Three   An angel miraculously releases Peter from prison (12:5–10).

Section Five   An earthquake opens the doors of the prison in which Paul and Silas are being kept, and undoes their chains (16:25–28).*

As a diagnostic tool for discerning the message of the book as a whole, the study of a string of events like this can be invaluable. It makes possible a differential diagnosis that examines first the similarities shared by all three incidents; then, more importantly, the significant differences; and finally the way in which the peculiar features of each otherwise similar episode fit into the context of the section in which the episode occurs.

Patterns of this kind, however, are not necessarily part of the basic structure of the book – though of course they are not in conflict with it. Structure and pattern are two different things, as can be seen from the fact that elements belonging to one and the same pattern do not necessarily or regularly chime in with the basic structures of the book. Take, for instance, what is the most famous example of patterning in Acts, from which all kinds of deductions have been made: the studied balance that Luke apparently maintains between Peter and Paul's activities.

If one divides the book structurally into two halves (chs 1–12 and chs 13–28) with three sections in the first half and three in the second, it would be generally true to say that Peter predominates

*I owe this observation, along with many other helpful insights, to Dr R. S. Matthews.

in the first half and Paul in the second. But there are exceptions. Peter scarce appears in Section Two. Stephen, Philip and Saul (Paul) are all prominent; but Peter personally gets only eleven verses (8:14–24; and less if one counts only the verses in which he is explicitly mentioned). On the other hand in Section Four Peter and James are necessarily more prominent in the Jerusalem Conference than Paul (15:6–29).

Again, it is interesting and instructive to observe that Peter heals a lame man (3:1–10), rebukes a false prophet (8:18–24), raises the dead (9:37–41), is released from prison (12:5–10); Paul likewise heals a lame man (14:8–10), rebukes a false prophet (13:8–12), raises the dead (20:8–12), is released from prison (16:25–28). But if one plots the positions at which similarities of this kind occur, we find as follows:

Peter heals a lame man (ch. 3)	Section 1	Paul heals a lame man (ch. 14)	Section 4
Peter defends himself before the Sanhedrin (chs 4 and 5)	Section 1	Paul defends himself before the Sanhedrin (ch. 23)	Section 6
Peter rebukes a false prophet (ch. 8)	Section 2	Paul rebukes a false prophet (ch. 13)	Section 4
Peter raises the dead (ch. 9)	Section 3	Paul raises the dead (ch. 20)	Section 6
Peter is released from prison (chs 5 and 12)	Sections 1 and 3	Paul is released from prison (ch. 16)	Section 5

From all this it would appear that structure and the symmetrical arrangement of the material within each section are not the same thing as these wide-ranging patterns. Both are important and deeply significant; they are not mutually exclusive but complementary; and they will enrich us most if we do not confuse them, but allow each its special function within the totality of Luke's richly variegated tapestry.

But now at the end of this long study let us reward ourselves by contemplating one simple but striking set of correspondences between the first and second halves of Acts which may serve to sum up for us the message that lies at the very heart of the book. First this:

Section One
The Lord Jesus, King David's Son, destined to sit on David's throne (2:29–35)

'You will not allow your Holy One to see corruption . . . He was not abandoned to the grave, nor did his body undergo corruption.' (2:27, 31)

Section Four
The Lord Jesus, King David's Son, raised up as a Saviour (13:22–26)

'As to the fact that he [God] has raised him from the dead, now no longer to return to corruption, he has said as follows: "I will give you the holy and sure blessings promised through David . . ." For in another place he says "You will not let your Holy One see corruption . . ." He whom God raised up saw no corruption.' (13:34–37)

The similarities of thought, phrase and quotation proclaim the Lord Jesus, then, as the King who never underwent corruption and is now enthroned in glory. One difference is significantly apt. Section One describes the Lord Jesus as God's Holy One (Heb. *hasîd*; Gk. *hosios*): it concentrates our attention on Christ's loyalty to the Father (see pp. 62–63). Section Four, by contrast, picks out the Father's loyal response to Christ, by citing his promise 'I will give you the holy [Heb. *hasdê*; Gk. *hosia*] and sure blessings of David'. Then this:

Section Two
'However, the Most High does not live in houses made by men. As the prophet says: "Heaven is my throne, and the earth is my footstool. What kind of house will you make for me?" says the Lord . . . "Has not my hand made all these things?"' (7:48–50)

Section Five
'The God who made the world and everything in it is the Lord of heaven and earth and does not live in temples built by hands.' (17:24)

In Section Two it is Stephen addressing the Jews, in Section Five Paul addressing Gentiles; but whether through Stephen or Paul, whether to Jews or Gentiles, the message is the same. But the relevance of all this to the theme that we are following at the moment emerges as the two speakers come to the end of their addresses.

Here is Stephen to his audience: 'But Stephen . . . looked up to heaven and saw the glory of God and Jesus standing at the right hand of God. "Look," he said, "I see heaven open and the Son of

432

Man standing at the right hand of God."'' He saw the Lord Jesus as his Counsel for Defence, as his Vindicator in the Supreme Court; and as the Jews stoned him to death he appealed to him in confidence, 'Lord Jesus, receive my spirit'; and in compassion for his enemies, 'Lord, do not hold this sin against them' (7:55–56, 59–60).

Paul in his climax speaks of the risen Lord as Judge: 'God . . . now commands all people everywhere to repent. For he has set a day when he will judge the world with justice by the man he has appointed. He has given proof of this to all men by raising him from the dead' (17:30–31).

Then this:

Section Three	Section Six
Peter is imprisoned by King Herod Agrippa I, but with the help of an angel escapes. (12:1–10)	Paul, in chains, makes his defence before King Herod Agrippa II and is declared not guilty. (26:1–32)

More significant than this straightforward historical comparison are the sequels to these two events which form the end not only of their respective sections but also of each half of the book. At the end of Section Three we are told that King Herod Agrippa I sat on his throne, dressed in his royal robes, and in foolish pride allowed the people to address him as a god. Immediately an angel struck him down: he was eaten by worms and died (12:21–23). So, then, the first half of Acts opens by introducing the King who saw no corruption, now raised to the right hand of God, to sit upon the very throne of God, demonstrated to be both Lord and Christ. And it closes with a mere mortal sinful king who, apeing divine honours, came to corruption of the most hideous and humiliating kind.

At the end of Section Six we are told that Paul addressed the leaders of the Jewish community in Rome on the topic of the kingly rule of God, and tried to convince them about Jesus from the Law of Moses and the Prophets. But many would not believe. Paul therefore quoted the solemn warning given by God through Isaiah, that Israel's unbelief would finally blind their eyes, close their hearts, and make salvation impossible. So it is that the second half of Acts opens by presenting once more the King who saw no corruption, destined never to die again, raised up by God as Israel's Saviour. And it ends with God's words to Isaiah given him on the occasion when Isaiah saw the King high and exalted upon his throne, whose glory filled the temple – the King whose glory so many in Israel would, alas, never see (Isa. 6:1–10; Acts 28:23–28).

Index